Prentice-Hall
HANDBOOK *for* WRITERS
Second Edition

GLENN LEGGETT
UNIVERSITY OF WASHINGTON

C. DAVID MEAD
MICHIGAN STATE COLLEGE

WILLIAM CHARVAT
OHIO STATE UNIVERSITY

New York
PRENTICE-HALL, INC.
1954

PRINTED IN THE UNITED STATES OF AMERICA

Preface

THIS HANDBOOK is designed to serve both as a guide and as a reference work. As a summary of grammatical usage and elementary rhetoric, it will provide a knowledge of the essentials of clear writing. The *Introduction* sketches the growth of English to its present character and discusses standards of Good English. *Grammar* (Sections 1-7) outlines basic material—parts of speech, case, agreement, principal parts, and so forth. *Manuscript Mechanics* (Sections 8-11) describes the conventions of manuscript form, the writing of numbers, abbreviations, and word division (syllabication). *Larger Elements* (Sections 12-13) discusses the planning and organization of the complete paper and the structure of paragraphs. *Effective Sentences* (Sections 14-27) describes the problems of sentence structure, from the elementary of "subordination" to the more subtle one of "variety." *Logic* (Section 28) discusses briefly how illogical thinking interferes with clear and honest communication.

Information on dictionaries and ways of improving vocabulary appears in the first two sections (29-30) under *Words;* a special test to measure vocabulary range is also provided. The last sections (31-34) under *Words* discuss the three principles of word choice—"exactness," "directness," and "appropriateness"—and include a glossary which lists troublesome words. Sections 35-47 offer solutions to the persistent problems of spelling and punctuation. Section 48, *The Library Paper,* will be helpful in research work. As a special aid it includes two facsimile research papers, the second of which can be used as a model. Section 49 discusses the requirements of conventional business letters and social correspondence. Section 50 is an *Index to Grammatical Terms;* Section 51 provides a discussion of the principles of summarizing, or *précis* writing. Throughout the book the emphasis is on the practical problem of what you need to know and consider when you write. The introductions to the main divisions are designed to explain some of the basic assumptions underlying the standards of writing—to show why most of the "rules" of writing are necessary.

It is as a reference work, however, that this book will be most useful. It was designed primarily to help you correct and revise your own writing more quickly and accurately. It classifies the standards and conventions of writing and provides reference to them in three ways: (1) through the index; (2) through the table of contents; and, most quickly of all, (3) through the charts on the endpapers of the book. Each major rule is given a number, and each subrule is designated by the number of the major rule and an alphabetical letter (5a, 16b, 22c, 37x, etc.). Instructors may wish to use these numbers to mark errors on papers, so that the proper usage can be found in the handbook and the paper revised accordingly.

For an illustration of this procedure, consider the two copies of the specimen paper on the next pages. *Specimen A* shows the paper after it has been marked by the instructor with handbook numbers. *Specimen B* shows the theme after it has been revised.

SPECIMEN A

(marked, but not corrected)

THE IDEAL EDUCATION *12b*

More than ever before, a good education is required if one is going to seek the fortunes of opportunity. The past few years college enrollments have been increasing steadily because people are realizing the importance of higher education *20a* The best jobs are held by people who have an advanced education, therefore the value of education cannot be *37x* stressed too much

19a In choosing a college to enter, the differences of colleges must be considered. For instance, a student considering Normal State must realise *35a* that this university has many thousands of students When a student comes to State, he feels as though he is coming to live in a new town *43x* Right away he finds that he is on his "own." He feels that high school was more like kindergarten. The college with a small enrollment is more compact, *28b* which helps the new student considerably at first. He *15c* always receives more personnel attention from the faculty than he *35d* would at a college as large as Normal St. *10a*

26b Now that we have seen the big differences between large and small universities, you probably see that there are advantageous aspects to *32a* both or they would not be in existence At Normal State the student *55d* sacrifices personnel attention for the better equipment he has to work with. At a small college the situation is reversed. Irregardless, the *32c* fact remains that the student coming from high school is facing a new situation and needs guidance in many cases. *32a*

(See also Sections 13 and 28.)

(marked and corrected)

A SMALL COLLEGE OR A LARGE UNIVERSITY?

THE IDEAL EDUCATION *(12 b)*

More than ever before, a good education is required if one is going
to seek the fortunes of opportunity. ~~In~~ The past few years college enroll- *(20a)*
ments have been increasing steadily because people are realizing the
importance of higher education. *Because* The best jobs are held by people who
have an advanced education, ~~therefore~~ the value of education cannot be *(37x)*
stressed too much.

(19a) In choosing a college to enter, *one must consider their* ~~the~~ differences, ~~of colleges must be
considered~~ For instance, a student considering Normal State must realise *(35a)*
that this university has many thousands of students. When a student
comes to State, he feels as though he is coming to live in a new town.
(43x) Right away he finds that he is on his own. He feels that high school
was more like kindergarten. *a circumstance* The college with a small enrollment is
more compact, (which helps the new student considerably at first.) He *(15c)*
(28b) *usually* ~~always~~ receives more ~~personnel~~ *personal* attention from the faculty than he *State.*
(35d) would at a college as large as Normal ~~St.~~ *(10a)*

Now that (we) have seen the big differences between large and small *advantages*
(26b) universities, ~~you~~ *we* probably see that there are ~~advantageous aspects~~ to *(32a)*
both or they would not be in existence. At Normal State the student
personal
(35d) sacrifices ~~personnel~~ attention for the better equipment he has to work *Regardless,*
with. At a small college the situation is reversed. ~~Irregardless~~ the *(32c)*
fact remains that the student coming from high school is facing a new
may
situation and needs guidance ~~in many cases.~~ *(32a)*

(See also Sections 13 and 28.)

Acknowledgments

FOR SUGGESTING ways to improve the original edition of the *Handbook for Writers,* we are grateful to many persons, but especially to Jerome Judson of The Ohio State University; to Donald Lee, formerly of the University of Pittsburgh; to James O'Brien of State Teachers College, Bellingham, Washington; to Hans Gottschalk and his colleagues at State Teachers College, Eau Claire, Wisconsin; to Albert Kitzhaber of the University of Kansas; to Professor T. A. Barnhart of State Teachers College, St. Cloud, Minnesota; to Professor Charles Roberts of the University of Illinois.

Special thanks are extended to the Freshman English Staff of the University of Washington for help in the exercises on punctuation.

In addition, we are grateful to Mr. Norman Jay Abramson, a student at the University of Washington, and to Mr. John Power, a student at The Ohio State University, for giving us permission to reprint their library papers as Specimens B and C in Section 48.

We wish also to thank the following for their permission to reproduce copyrighted material in the revised *Handbook:*

George Allen and Unwin, Ltd.: the selection from "The ABC of Relativity," in *Selected Papers,* by Bertrand Russell, used by special permission of George Allen and Unwin, Ltd.

The American Historical Association: the selection from "History," by Carl Becker, reprinted from *The American Historical Review of January,* 1932, and used by special permission of the American Historical Association.

Appleton-Century-Crofts, Inc.: the selection from *English Words and Their Background,* by G. H. McKnight, copyright 1923 by Appleton-Century, Inc., and used by special permission of Appleton-Century-Crofts, Inc.

The Bobbs-Merrill Company, Inc.: the selections from *Lake Erie,* by Harlan Hatcher, copyright 1945, and used by special permission of

Acknowledgments

The Bobbs-Merrill Company, Inc.; the selection from *The Life of Andrew Jackson,* by Marquis James, copyright 1938, and used by special permission of The Bobbs-Merrill Company, Inc.

Brandt and Brandt: the selection from "a man who had fallen among thieves," by e e cummings, copyright 1926 by Horace Liveright, published by Harcourt, Brace and Company, Inc., and used by special permission of Brandt and Brandt.

Columbia University Press: the selections from *Five Travel Scripts,* edited by H. W. Troyer, copyright 1933 (Facsimile Text Society), and used by special permission of the Columbia University Press.

Crown Publishers: the selection from *The Columnists,* by Charles Fisher, copyright 1944 by Howell, Soskin, and used by special permission of Crown Publishers.

Dodd, Mead and Company: the selection from *A Miscellany of Men,* by Gilbert Chesterton, copyright 1912, and used by special permission of Dodd, Mead and Company.

Doubleday and Company, Inc.: the selection from *Winston Churchill: An Informal Study of Greatness,* by Robert Lewis Taylor, copyright 1952, and used by special permission of Doubleday and Company, Inc.; the facsimile entry from the Thorndike-Barnhart *Comprehensive Desk Dictionary,* used by special permission of Doubleday and Company, Inc.

E. P. Dutton and Company, Inc.: the selection from *Science Is a Sacred Cow,* by Anthony Standen, copyright 1952, and used by special permission of E. P. Dutton and Company, Inc.

Mrs. Charles M. Flandrau: the selection from *Viva Mexico!,* by Charles M. Flandrau, copyright 1937, published by D. Appleton-Century Co., Inc., and used with Mrs. Flandrau's special permission.

Funk and Wagnalls Company: the selection from the *New College Standard Dictionary,* copyright 1947, and used by special permission of Funk and Wagnalls Company.

Harcourt, Brace and Company, Inc.: the selection from *Seventeenth Century Prose,* edited by R. P. T. Coffin and Alexander Witherspoon, copyright 1929, and used by special permission of Harcourt, Brace and Company, Inc.; the selection from *Collected Poems,* by T. S. Eliot, copyright 1930, 1934, 1936, and used by special permission of Harcourt, Brace and Company, Inc.; the selection from *Main Street,* by Sinclair Lewis, copyright 1920, and used by special permission of Harcourt, Brace and Company, Inc.; the selection from *The Conduct of Life,* by Lewis Mumford, copyright 1951, and used by special permission of Harcourt, Brace and Company, Inc.; the selection from "The Old Order," in *The Leaning Tower and Other Stories,* by Katherine Ann Porter, copyright 1944, and used by special permission of Harcourt, Brace and Company, Inc.

Harper & Brothers: the selections from the *American College Dictionary,* copyright 1947, 1948, 1949, 1950, by Random House, Inc., text edition copyright 1948 by Harper & Brothers and used by special permission of Harper & Brothers; the selection from *The Mind in the Making,* by James Harvey Robinson, copyright 1921, and used by special permission of Harper & Brothers; the selection from Mark Twain's *Europe and Elsewhere,* used by special permission of Harper & Brothers; the selection from Mark Twain's *Life on the Mississippi,* used by special permission of Harper & Brothers; the selections from *One Man's Meat,* by E. B. White, copyright 1950, and used by special permission of Harper & Brothers.

Henry Holt and Company, Inc.: the selections from *Anglo-Saxon Reader,* Fourth Edition, edited by James G. Bright, and used by special permission of Henry Holt and Company, Inc.

Houghton-Mifflin Company: the selection from *The Big Money,* in *U.S.A.,* by John Dos Passos, copyright 1930, 1932, 1933, 1934, 1935, 1936, 1937, and used by permission of Houghton-Mifflin Company; the selection from *The Making of the Modern Mind,* Revised Edition, by J. H. Randall, copyright 1940, and used by special permission of Houghton-Mifflin Company.

Alfred A. Knopf, Inc.: the selection from *God, Graves, and Scholars,* by C. W. Ceram, copyright 1952, and used by special permission of Alfred A. Knopf, Inc.; the selection from *In Defense of Women,* by H. L. Mencken, copyright 1918, revised 1922, and used by special permission of Alfred A. Knopf, Inc.; the selection from "The Human Mind," in *Prejudices 6th Series,* by H. L. Mencken, copyright 1929, and used by special permission of Alfred A. Knopf, Inc.; the selection from "Bryan," in *Selected Prejudices,* by H. L. Mencken, copyright 1927, and used by special permission of Alfred A. Knopf, Inc.

J. B. Lippincott Company: the selection from *Sheridan of Drury Lane,* by Alice Glasgow, copyright 1940 by Frederick A. Stokes Company, and used by permission of the present holders of the copyright, J. B. Lippincott Company.

Little, Brown and Company: the selection from *Man Against Myth,* by Barrows Dunham, copyright 1947, and used by special permission of Little, Brown and Company.

Acknowledgments

Arthur D. Little, Inc.: the selection from *The Turbo-Encabulator*, by J. H. Quick, first published in the *Students' Quarterly Journal*, the Institution of Electrical Engineers, London, England, 1944, and used by special permission of Arthur D. Little, Inc.

The Macmillan Company: the selection from *Life on Other Worlds*, by H. Spencer Jones, copyright 1940, and used by special permission of The Macmillan Company; the selection from *The Aims of Education*, by A. N. Whitehead, copyright 1929, and used by special permission of The Macmillan Company; the selection from *Science and the Modern World*, by A. N. Whitehead, copyright 1925, and used by special permission of The Macmillan Company.

G. and C. Merriam Company: the selection from *Webster's New International Dictionary*, Second Edition, copyright 1934, 1939, and used by special arrangement with G. and C. Merriam Company; the selections from *Webster's New Collegiate Dictionary*, copyright 1949, and used by special arrangement with G. and C. Merriam Company.

The New American Library of World Literature, Inc.: the selection from *Russia: Its Past and Present*, by Bernard Pares, copyright 1943, 1949, by The New American Library of World Literature, Inc., and used by special permission.

Oxford University Press, Inc.: the selection from *The Sea Around Us*, by Rachel Carson, copyright 1951, and used by special permission of the Oxford University Press, Inc.; the selections from *Growth of the American Republic*, by S. E. Morison and H. S. Commager, copyright 1930, 1937, 1942, and used by special permission of the Oxford University Press, Inc.

Prentice-Hall, Inc.: the selection from *Ideas and Men*, by Crane Brinton, copyright 1950, and used by special permission of Prentice-Hall, Inc.; the selection from *The Development of Modern English*, Second Edition, by Stuart Robertson and Frederic G. Cassidy, copyright 1953, and used by special permission of Prentice-Hall, Inc.; the selection from *Foundations of Speech*, by C. M. Wise *et al.*, copyright 1941, and used by special permission of Prentice-Hall, Inc.

Random House, Inc.: the selection from *Track of the Cat*, by Walter Van Tilburg Clark, and used by special permission of Random House, Inc.; the selection from "Delta Autumn," reprinted from *Go Down Moses*, by William Faulkner, copyright 1942, and used by special permission of Random House, Inc.; the selection from *Sanctuary*, by William Faulkner, copyright 1931, and used by special permission of Random House, Inc.; the selections from *Keep It Crisp*, copyright 1943, 1944, 1945, 1946, and used by special permission of Random House, Inc.; the selection from *The Harder They Fall*, by Budd Schulberg, copyright 1947, and used by special permission of Random House, Inc.

Rinehart and Company: the selection from *Three Keys to Language*, by Robert M. Estrich and Hans Sperber, copyright 1952, and used by special permission of Rinehart and Company; the selection from *Colonial American Writing*, by Roy H. Pearce, copyright 1950, and used by special permission of Rinehart and Company.

Charles Scribner's Sons: the selection from *Farewell to Arms*, by Ernest Hemingway, copyright 1929, and used by special permission of Charles Scribner's Sons; the selection from "Big Two-Hearted River: II," reprinted from *In Our Time*, by Ernest Hemingway, and used by special permission of Charles Scribner's Sons; the selection from *Look Homeward, Angel*, by Thomas Wolfe, and used by special permission of Charles Scribner's Sons.

William Sloane Associates, Inc.: the selection from *The Desert Year*, by Joseph Wood Krutch, copyright 1952, and used by special permission of William Sloane Associates, Inc.; the selections from *All the Ship's at Sea*, by W. J. Lederer, copyright 1950, and used by special permission of William Sloane Associates, Inc.; the selection from *Back Home*, by Bill Mauldin, copyright 1947, and used by special permission of William Sloane Associates, Inc.; the selection from *Road to Survival*, by William Vogt, copyright 1949, and used by special permission of William Sloane Associates, Inc.

Simon and Schuster, Inc.: the selection from *Van Loon's Geography*, by Hendrik Willem Van Loon, copyright 1932, and used by special permission of Simon and Schuster, Inc.

Mr. James Thurber: the selections from "There's an Owl in My Room" and "Something to Say," from *The Middle-Aged Man on the Flying Trapeze*, published by Harper & Brothers, and used by special permission of Mr. Thurber.

The Viking Press, Inc.: the selection from *Biography of the Earth*, by George Gamow, copyright 1941, and used by special permission of The Viking Press, Inc.; the selection from *Sons and Lovers*, by D. H. Lawrence, used by special permission of Mrs. Frieda Lawrence, William Heinemann, Ltd., and The Viking Press, Inc.

The John C. Winston Company: the selection from *The Winston Dictionary*, copyright 1942, and used by special arrangement with The John C. Winston Company.

The World Publishing Company: the selection from Webster's *New World Dictionary*, and used by special permission of The World Publishing Company.

The University of Michigan Press: the selection (with revisions) "Radio: Best Source of News," from *Preparation for College English*, edited by Clarence D. Thorpe, copyright 1945, and used by special permission of the University of Michigan Press.

Contents

	PAGE
INTRODUCTION	1

The origin and growth of English, 1. The standards of modern English, 4.

Sections 1-7: GRAMMAR (GR) 13

1. SENTENCE SENSE (SS) 16

a. Recognizing sentences, 16. b. Recognizing parts of speech, 18. c. Recognizing phrases, 22. d. Recognizing clauses, 24.

2. CONFUSED STRUCTURE (STR) 28

a. Sentence fragment, 29. b. Comma splice or comma fault, 31. c. Run-together or fused sentence, 32.

3. ADJECTIVES AND ADVERBS (AD) 35

a. Modifying nouns and pronouns, 36. b. Modifying verbs, 36. c. Comparative and superlative, 37.

4. CASE (CA) 40

a. Subjects, 41. b. Complements after *is, are,* etc., 42. c. Complements after *to be,* 42. d. s-possessive, 43. e. With gerunds, 43. f. With *which, whose,* 44. g. Objects of verbs, verbals, prepositions, 44.

5. AGREEMENT (AGR) 47

a. Subject and verb, 47. b. Pronoun and antecedent, 51. c. Demonstrative and its noun, 53.

6. TENSE AND MOOD (T) 55

Conjugation of *choose,* 56. a. Tense in subordinate clauses, 60. b. Tense with infinitives, 60. c. Tense in statements generally true, 60. d. Principal parts, 61. e. Subjunctive in formal idioms, 65. f. Subjunctive in conditions contrary to fact, 65. g. Subjunctive in *that* clauses, 65.

Contents

PAGE

7. DIAGRAMING 69

    a. Subject and verb, 69. b. Complements, 70. c. Modifiers, 71. d. Verbals, 72. e. Phrases, 74. f. Clauses, 76. g. Independent elements, 78.

Sections 8-11: MANUSCRIPT MECHANICS (MS) . 81

8. THE MANUSCRIPT (MS) 81

    a. Materials, 81. b. Legibility, 82. c. Arrangement, 82. d. Proof-reading, 83. e. Correction, 83.

9. NUMBERS (NOS) 85

    a. Generally spelled out, 85. b. Dates, 85. c. Street numbers, decimals, etc., 85. d. In parentheses, 85. e. Beginning sentences, 85.

10. ABBREVIATIONS (AB) 87

    a. When appropriate, 87. b. States, months, days, etc., 88. c. Street, avenue, etc., 88.

11. SYLLABICATION (SYL) 90

    a. One-syllable words, 90. b. Single letters, 90. c. Compound words, 90.

Sections 12-13: LARGER ELEMENTS 93

12. THE WHOLE COMPOSITION (PLAN) 93

    a. Selecting the subject, 94. b. Limiting the subject, 96. c. Preliminary outline, 98. d. Thesis statement, 99. e. Completed outline, 100. f. Beginning the paper, 105. g. First draft, 107. h. Second draft, 108. i. Final revisions, 109.

13. EFFECTIVE PARAGRAPHING (¶) 114

    a. Topic sentence, 117. b. Singleness of purpose, 123. c. Logical order, 127. d. Connection, 130. e. Adequate development, 136. f. Ways of developing, 140. Paragraphs for study, 154.

Sections 14-27: EFFECTIVE SENTENCES (EF) . . 165

14. SUBORDINATION (SUB) 168

    a. False and unrelated co-ordination, 168. b. "Upside-down" subordination, 171. c. "Primer" sentences, 172. d. Excessive subordination and overloading, 174. e. Connectives, 176.

15. REFERENCE OF PRONOUNS (REF) 179

a. Ambiguous reference, 179.   b. Remote reference, 180.   c. Vague *this, that, which*, 181.   d. Illogical reference, 182.   e. Indefinite *they, you, it*, 183.

16. PARALLELISM (//) 185

a. Co-ordinate elements, 185.   b. Faulty *and who, and which*, 186. c. Correlatives, 187.

17. COMPARISONS (COMP) 188

a. Illogical *than any*, 188.   b. Illogical *of any*, 188.   c. Items incapable of comparison, 188.   d. Incomplete comparisons, 188. e. Omitted term, 189.   f. Omitted basis of comparison, 189.

18. MISPLACED PARTS (MIS PTS) 190

a. *almost, only*, etc., 190.   b. Modifying phrase, 191.   c. Modifying clause, 192.   d. "Squinting" modifiers, 193.   e. Split infinitives, 193.   f. Subject, verb awkwardly separated, 194.

19. DANGLING CONSTRUCTIONS (DGL) 196

a. Participles, 196.   b. Gerunds, 197.   c. Infinitives, 198.   d. Elliptical clauses, 199.

20. OMISSIONS AND INCOMPLETE CONSTRUCTIONS (OM) 201

a. Careless omissions, 201.   b. Incomplete constructions, 202.

21. MIXED CONSTRUCTIONS (MIX) 204

22. GENERAL AWKWARDNESS AND OBSCURITY (AWK, OBSC) 207

a. Awkward phrasing, 207.   b. Obscure, illogical meaning, 209.

23. TRANSITIONS (TRANS) 211

a. Inexact, 211.   b. Omitted, 212.

24. EMPHASIS (EMP) 214

a. Position of words, 214.   b. Periodic structure, 215.   c. Logical order, 217.   d. Repetition, 218.

25. WEAK PASSIVE (WP) 220

26. POINT OF VIEW (PV) 222

a. Shift in subject, voice, 222.   b. Shift in person, number, 223. c. Shift in tense, mood, 224.

Contents

PAGE

27. VARIETY (VAR) 225
a. Short simple sentences, 225. b. Long compound sentences, 226. c. Monotonous pattern, 228.

28. LOGIC (LOG) 235
a. Definition, 236. b. Generalization, 239. c. Fairness, 241. d. Sound reasoning, 243.

Sections 29-34: WORDS (WDS) 249

29. THE DICTIONARY 249
Unabridged dictionaries, 249. Desk dictionaries, 251. Uses of the dictionary, 253. Special dictionaries, 259.

30. VOCABULARY 261
Active and passive vocabulary, 261. Measuring vocabulary (with test), 262. Increasing vocabulary, 272.

31. EXACTNESS (EX) 278
a. Words nearly synonymous, 279. b. Words of similar sound, 280. c. Invented words, 281. d. Improprieties, 282. e. Grammatical change, 283. f. "Elegant variation," 284. g. Idiomatic use, 285. h. Specific word, 289.

32. DIRECTNESS (DIR) 292
a. Deadwood, 293. b. Approximate words, 294. c. Needless repetition, 295. d. Awkward repetition, 296. e. Needless complexity, 298.

33. APPROPRIATENESS (APPR) 302
a. Slang, 302. b. Substandard English, 304. c. Triteness, 305. d. Jargon, 307. e. Fine writing, 308. f. Mixed metaphors, 309.

34. GLOSSARY OF USAGE (GLOS) 314

35. SPELLING (SP) 337
a. Preferred spelling, 339. b. Careless misspellings, 340. c. Faulty pronunciation, 341. d. Similar words confused, 342. e. Spelling rules (singular, plural, compounds), 343.

Sections 36-47: PUNCTUATION (P) 355

36. END PUNCTUATION (END P) 359
a. Assertions, 359. b. Abbreviations, 359. c. Ellipsis, 360. x. Period fault, 360. d. Direct question, 360. e. Use of (?), 361. y. Question fault, 361. f. Emphatic statements, 361. z. Exclamation fault, 362.

Contents

PAGE

37. SEPARATING MAIN CLAUSES 367

a. With co-ordinating conjunctions, 367. b. Without co-ordinating conjunctions, 368. c. With conjunctive adverbs, 368. d. When second clause amplifies, 369. x. Comma fault, 369.

38. SEPARATING SUBORDINATE ELEMENTS . . . 373

a. Introductory clauses and phrases, 373. b. Clauses, phrases following main clause, 374. c. Nonrestrictive elements, 374. d. Prevention of misreading or awkwardness, 376. e. Separation of quoted and unquoted material, 376.

39. SETTING OFF PARENTHETICAL ELEMENTS . . 379

a. Appositives, 379. b. Mild interrupters, 380. c. Abrupt interrupters, 380. d. Nonrestrictive or parenthetical elements, 381.

40. SEPARATING ITEMS IN A SERIES 384

a. Co-ordinate series, 384. b. Dates, addresses, etc., 385. c. Semicolons used in a series, 386.

41. SUPERFLUOUS COMMAS 388

a. Between single adjective and noun, 388. b. Between subject and verb, 388. c. Between verb and complement, 388. d. Between two co-ordinates, 389. e. After introductory words, 389. f. With restrictives, 389. g. With indirect quotations, 389.

42. DIRECTING ATTENTION TO FINAL APPOSITIVES . 392

a. Short final appositives, 392. b. Long, formal appositives, 392.

43. PUNCTUATING QUOTED MATERIAL 396

a. Double quotes, 396. b. Single quotes, 396. c. Quoting paragraphs, 397. d. Titles, 398. e. Words used in special senses, 398. x. Faulty use of quotes, 398. f. Brackets: editorial use, 399. g. comma and period with quotes, 399. h. Colon and semicolon with quotes, 399. i. Dash, question mark, and exclamation point with quotes, 400. j. Punctuation of *he said*, etc., 400. k. Quotations at beginning of sentence, 401. l. Quotations which are divided, 401.

44. ITALICS 403

a. Titles, 404. b. Ships, aircraft, etc., 404. c. Letters, words used as words, 404. d. Foreign words and phrases, 404. e. Special stress, 405. x. Unnecessary italics, 405.

45. CAPITALS 407

a. First word in sentence, 407. b. *I* and *O,* 408. c. Proper nouns, 408. x. Unnecessary capitals, 410.

46. APOSTROPHE 413

a. Possession, 413. b. Omission, 414. c. Plurals of letters, numbers, 414. x. Faulty use, 415.

xix

Contents

PAGE

47. HYPHEN 416

    a. Compound words, 416. b. Two words as single adjective, 416.
    c. Awkward union of letters, 417. d. Compound numbers, 417.
    e. Prefixes and suffixes, 417.

Sections 48-51: SPECIAL AIDS 425

48. THE LIBRARY PAPER 425

    The use of a library, 425. Finding a subject, 439. Bibliography,
    441. Bibliography cards, 442. Preliminary organization, 444.
    Note-taking, 444. Footnotes, 446. Specimen library papers, 452.

49. BUSINESS AND SOCIAL CORRESPONDENCE . . 489

    Business letters, 491. Personal letters, 494. Social notes, 496.

50. INDEX OF GRAMMATICAL TERMS 499

51. WRITING SUMMARIES 513

    SUPPLEMENTARY EXERCISES 519

    GENERAL INDEX 531

Prentice-Hall

HANDBOOK *for* WRITERS

Second Edition

BLOT OUT, CORRECT, INSERT, REFINE,
ENLARGE, DIMINISH, INTERLINE;
BE MINDFUL, WHEN INVENTION FAILS,
TO SCRATCH YOUR HEAD, AND BITE YOUR NAILS.

—JONATHAN SWIFT

. . . ALL WRITING IS AN EXERCISE IN
DRAWING UP AN ARMISTICE BETWEEN A MAN'S
PRIVATE FANCIES AND THE REAL WORLD OUTSIDE . . .

—ALISTAIR COOKE, *A Generation on Trial*

Introduction

ALL LIFE THEREFORE COMES BACK TO THE QUESTION OF
OUR SPEECH, THE MEDIUM THROUGH WHICH WE COM-
MUNICATE WITH EACH OTHER; FOR ALL LIFE COMES
BACK TO THE QUESTION OF OUR RELATIONS WITH ONE
ANOTHER.

—HENRY JAMES, *The Question of Our Speech*

(1) The Origin and Growth of English

ENGLISH IS BASICALLY a Teutonic language, being founded upon the
speech of the Germanic tribes (Angles, Saxons, and Jutes) who invaded the British Isles in the fifth century A.D. The surviving
specimens of this language—now called "Old English" or Anglo-
Saxon—hardly seem like English at all.

> Hēr Æðelstān cyning, eorla drihten,
> *Here Athelstan the king, the earls' leader,*
>
> beorna beāhgifa, and his brōðor ēac,
> *the heroes' ring-giver, and his brother also,*
>
> Eadmund aeðeling, ealdor langne tīr
> *Edmund the prince, life-long glory*
>
> geslōgan aet saecce, sweorda ecgum,
> *won at war, by the edges of swords,*
>
> ymbe Brunanburh:
> *at Brunanburh:*
>
> —*Battle of Brunanburh*, A.D. 937

In the centuries following the coming of the Germanic tribes to
the British Isles, their language was subjected to a variety of influences. Its structure was loosened by the effects of a Danish and

1

then a French invasion of the British Isles. To its vocabulary were added thousands of Latin, French, and Scandinavian words. Spelling and pronunciation changed; word meanings were modified or extended. There was a gradual change in syntax, in sentence structure. Like Latin, Old English was a highly inflected language, with an involved system of declensions and conjugations. In the process of change, this system was greatly simplified. The order of words in a sentence, not the endings attached to words, came to be with few exceptions the determining factor in grammatical function and therefore in meaning. Some of the great language changes that occurred in the six hundred years after the Battle of Brunanburh are illustrated in the following passages:

Ðis gēar cōm Henrī Kīng tō þis lānd. Þā cōm Henrī abbot and wreide
In this year came Henry the king to this land. Then came Henry
þē muneces of Burch tō þē kīng forþī ðat hē wolde underþēden ðat
the abbot and denounced the monks of Burch to the king for that
mynstre tō Clunīe, swā ðat tē kīng was wēl nēh bepaht and sende
he would subjugate the monastery to Cluny, so that the king was
efter þē muneces.
well nigh deceived and sent after the monks.
—*Peterborough Chronicle,* 1132

A knyght there was, and that a worthy man,
That from the tyme that he first bigan
To ryden out, he loved chivalrye,
Trouthe and honour, fredom and courteisye.
—CHAUCER, *Canterbury Tales, Prologue,*
ca. 1385

Hit befel in the dayes of Uther Pendragon, when he was kynge of all Englond, and so regned, that there was a myghty duke in Cornewaill that helde warre ageynst hym long tyme, and the duke was called the duke of Tyntagil.
—SIR THOMAS MALORY, *Morte d'Arthur, ca.* 1470

A Proude Man contemneth the companye of hys olde friendes, and disdayneth the sight of hys former famyliars, and turneth hys face from his wonted acquayntaunce.
—HENRY KERTON, *The Mirror of Man's Lyfe;* 1576

To us, of course, the specimens given above illustrate a steady and inevitable progress toward modern English. But to Englishmen living through the process of change the development represented not growth but chaos. It appeared to them that the English language would not hold still long enough to have any value as an instrument of communication. Some of them, like Sir Thomas More and Sir Francis Bacon, felt it the better part of discretion to write their most pretentious works in Latin, a safe and completely stable language. Fortunately their attitude was not shared by all Englishmen, and we can be thankful that people like Geoffrey Chaucer and Sir Thomas Malory wrote in their native language and staked their future reputations on the chance their language would survive. In so doing, they gave English part of the prestige it needed, and this fact, coupled with the development of English printing and the growth of a national spirit in England, helped to dignify and standardize the language. By the end of the sixteenth century, English was a truly national language, a condition signalized by the great English translation of the Bible in 1611.

Since that time English has never ceased to grow and change and adapt itself to the character of the people who write and speak it, but these processes have slowed down considerably. The widespread use of printing has tended to stabilize the language. The specimen below, written some 250 years ago, has its amusing oddities of spelling and capitalization, but in all important respects it is almost "modern" English. And the selection from Oliver Goldsmith, written almost two centuries ago, is different from modern prose only in its old-fashioned tone and its over-use of the comma.

> The Country, by its Climate, is always troubled with an *Ague* and *Fever;* As soon as ever the Cold fit's over, tis attended with a Hot: and the *Natives* themselves, whose Bodies are Habituated to the suddain changes, from one Extream to another, cannot but confess, They *Freez* in Winter and Fry in Summer.
> —[NED WARD], *A Trip to New England,* 1699

> I was ever of the opinion, that the honest man who married and brought up a large family, did more service than he who continued single and only talked of population. From this motive, I had scarce taken orders a year, before I began to think seriously of matrimony, and chose my wife, as she did her wedding gown, not for a fine

glossy surface, but such qualities as would wear well. To do her justice, she was a good-natured, notable woman; and as for breeding, there were few country ladies who could show more. She could read any English book without much spelling; but for pickling, preserving, and cookery, none could excel her. She prided herself also upon being an excellent contriver in housekeeping; though I could never find that we grew richer with all her contrivances.

—OLIVER GOLDSMITH, *The Vicar of Wakefield,* 1766

LIST OF BOOKS FOR STUDY AND REFERENCE

The following books discuss in detail the backgrounds of English:

Baugh, Albert C., *A History of the English Language.* New York: Appleton-Century-Crofts, 1935.

Bryant, Margaret M., *Modern English and Its Heritage.* New York: Macmillan Company, 1948.

Jesperson, Otto, *Growth and Structure of the English Language.* London: Basil Blackwell, 1935.

McKnight, George H., *Modern English in the Making.* New York: Appleton-Century-Crofts, 1928.

Robertson, Stuart, and Frederic G. Cassidy, *The Development of Modern English,* 2nd edition. New York: Prentice-Hall, Inc., 1954.

(2) The "Standards" of Modern English

Our discussion of the growth of English pointed out the importance of English printing and the emergence of a national English character; any talk of the "standards" of modern English must emphasize, at least in the beginning, the efforts of eighteenth century grammarians to standardize and "refine" English. To their credit it can be said that they helped to stabilize the language by making dictionaries that tended to fix spellings and meanings, and rhetorics that established some useful standards of syntax—*i.e.,* sentence structure. But today we look upon their efforts with mixed feelings. Many of them tried to refine English by forcing upon it the pattern and terminology of Latin grammar, and in general to impose arbitrary rules on English which often conflicted with actual usage and common sense. Their general attitude is represented (perhaps a

4

little unfairly) by the following statement from an eighteenth century grammarian:

> The Particle *a* should never be prefixed to the Word *few: a* always denotes a singular number, and *few* is of the plural.
> —*Observations Upon the English Language,* 1770

This particular bit of advice was futile, but a good many rules which were inspired by a similarly unrealistic notion of language behavior were rewarded with widespread acceptance. The result is that even today a great many users of English feel that the language obeys (or at least *ought to*) a kind of abstract logic instead of doing what it obviously does and must do—follow the actual usage of people who write and speak it. The arbitrary condemnation of split infinitives, of prepositions at the end of sentences, of "It's me," and so on, all grow out of the eighteenth century attitude toward English, an attitude that has passed into the subconsciousness of the English and American people and makes realistic discussion of the "standards" of modern English difficult.

Perhaps the clearest way to illustrate what we mean by "standards" is to ask you to play an imaginary but not a necessarily improbable rôle. Remove from the typewriter the letter you have just written to your best friend. Now write another to a man you have never seen who can give you a job you are anxious to get. Compare the two letters. In the first, you spoke of the "swell job" you are "after." In the second, the job becomes a "position." In the first, you were sure you "had the stuff to make a go of it." In the second, you "assure" the man that you have had "excellent training" which will "enable you to succeed." In the first, you hoped "to get together" with your friend over "Xmas for a whing ding or two." In the second, you "suggest" that the "Christmas holidays might provide an opportunity for an interview."

As you compare the two still further you will probably assume that in the second letter you were writing "good"—or at least your best—English. In the first you are merely saying "what comes natural." Whether or not the second was "good" and the first was relatively "bad" is arguable. Probably many of our most distinguished creative writers and our modern linguists would say that the English in your first letter was better. But that is beside the

5

point because in neither letter were you addressing a creative writer or a linguist. You were communicating in one with a friend, and in the other with a prospective employer. And you were unconsciously, in each case, adjusting yourself to an audience and a situation.

This adjustment of English usage to different audiences and situations results in what John S. Kenyon, a famous dictionary editor, calls "cultural levels and functional varieties of English." By "cultural levels" we mean (1) *standard* and (2) *substandard* English, the first as descriptive of the writing and speaking of cultivated people, the second as descriptive of the writing and speaking of the uncultivated. In other words, the division between *standard* and *substandard* (which is by no means definite) depends roughly on the cultural status (or ambitions) of people using the language.*

We can illustrate the two levels as follows:

STANDARD   Society never advances. It recedes as fast on one side as it gains on the other. It undergoes continual changes; it is barbarous, it is civilized, it is christianized, it is rich, it is scientific; but this change is not amelioration. For everything that is given something is taken. Society acquires new arts and loses old instincts. What a contrast between the well-clad, reading, writing, thinking American, with a watch, a pencil and a bill of exchange in his pocket, and the naked New Zealander, whose property is a club, a spear, a mat, and an undivided twentieth of a shed to sleep under! But compare the health of the two men and you shall see that the white man has lost his aboriginal strength. If the traveller tell us truly, strike the savage with a broad-axe and in a day or two the flesh shall unite and heal as if you struck the blow into soft pitch, and the same blow shall send the white to his grave.

—R. W. EMERSON, "Self-Reliance," 1844

SUBSTANDARD   So I said to him, I said, you was dead wrong thinking you'd get away with that dough. We had you spotted

* The words "acceptable" and "unacceptable" are often equated with *standard* and *substandard,* respectively. The equation is frequently accurate, but before assuming that *substandard* English is always unacceptable, we ought to ask "unacceptable to whom?"

from the beginning, smart boy. And we was sure
when we seen you put that roll in your pocket. So
I starts to move in on him, easy-like, and all at oncet,
he grabs in his pocket and comes out with a gun.
Don't nobody move, he yells, and starts for the door.
But he trips over his own big feet and goes down,
hard. Right then I lets him have it with five quick
shots. He was the deadest double-crosser you ever
seen.

By "functional varieties of English," on the other hand, we refer
to the different uses or functions of language to which most people
instinctively adapt their own English, just as you changed yours
when you changed your audience from a classmate to a prospective
employer. The chief functional divisions are *informal* and *formal*.
In the broadest terms *informal* describes the English of conversation, of private correspondence, and of ordinary, everyday writing
and speaking. *Formal* describes the English of platform or "pulpit"
speech, most legal and scientific writing, and academic and literary
prose. Until a generation or two ago most school teachers and text-
books in English recommended the cultivation of formal usage.
Formal came to be implicitly equated with *standard,* and *informal*
English, though obviously then as now the real workaday language,
was suspected of being not quite proper. At its best, this state of
affairs was unrealistic; at its worst, it led some people to assume that
only a pretentious sounding English was "good English." Nowadays
we recognize that both *informal* and *formal* usage are *standard*
English and that neither is necessarily "more correct" than the
other. Everything depends on their suitability to audience and situation; appropriateness is now the only real measure of "good" English.

In the examples below, note the oratorical structure of the *formal*
selection, its Latinized vocabulary (*exposition, application, mortification*), its serious eloquence. Then note the easy structure, the
relaxed and personal tone, the everyday vocabulary of the *informal*
selection. But if you catch yourself thinking that one is better than
the other, remember that the purpose, subject-matter, and audience (as well as the temperaments) of the authors are quite different, and that these differences account for the differences in style.

7

FORMAL   Dean Donne in the pulpit of old Paul's, holding his audience spellbound still as he reversed his glass of sands after an hour of exposition and application of texts by the light of the church fathers, of mortification for edification, of exhortation that brought tears to the eyes of himself and his hearers, and of analogies born of the study, but sounding of wings,—there was a man who should have had wisdom, surely. For if experience can bring it, this was the man.

    —R. P. T. COFFIN *and* A. M. WITHERSPOON, "John Donne," in *Seventeenth Century Prose*

INFORMAL   Of all the common farm operations none is more ticklish than tending a brooder stove. All brooder stoves are whimsical, and some of them are holy terrors. Mine burns coal, and has only a fair record. With its check draft that opens and closes, this stove occupies my dreams from midnight, when I go to bed, until five o'clock, when I get up, pull a shirt and a pair of pants on over my pajamas, and stagger out into the dawn to read the thermometer under the hover and see that my 254 little innocents are properly disposed in a neat circle round their big iron mama.

    —E. B. WHITE, *One Man's Meat*

One more commonly occurring yet confusing label, *colloquial*, remains to be discussed. *Colloquial* is sometimes erroneously used to designate a *substandard* level of usage, and so unfortunately has come to carry overtones of disreputability. Technically, the word means "spoken" and therefore may refer to any spoken English, whether "culturally" *standard* or *substandard*, or "functionally" *formal* or *informal*. Many students of language, however, use the word to refer to a kind of writing which has the easy and unpretentious vocabulary, the loose constructions and the contractions of everyday spoken English. Charles Fries, one of the editors of the *American College Dictionary*, defines *colloquial* as those words and constructions

    . . . whose range of use is primarily that of the polite conversation of cultivated people, of their familiar letters and informal speeches, as distinct from those words and constructions which are common

8

also in formal writing. The usage of our better magazines and of public addresses generally has, during the past generation, moved away from the formal and literary toward the colloquial.

In this sense *colloquial* is hardly distinguishable from *informal*.

The existence of "levels" and "varieties" of English means, among other things, that there is no absolute standard of correctness. But it does not mean that we can do without standards at all, or that what is good enough for familiar conversation is appropriate for all kinds of communication. It is true that if people wrote as naturally as they talk, a great deal of affectation would disappear from their writing. But it is also true that conversational English depends for much of its force upon the physical presence of the speaker. Personality, gesture, and intonation all contribute to the success of spoken communication.* Written English, on the other hand, whether *formal* or *informal*, requires a structure that makes it clear without the physical presence of the writer. It must communicate through the clarity of its diction and the orderliness of its sentence structure, a fact which presupposes that the writer has met certain standards.

A handbook somewhat arbitrarily classifies standards of "Good English" into rules or conventions. These cannot always be defended on logical grounds. Rather they reflect the practices—some old, some new—of English and American writers. Most of these conventions are quite flexible. Punctuation and sentence structure have a general standard of correctness, but within this standard many variations are possible. Matters of diction and paragraphing are less standardized. The truth is that the rules of writing are generalizations of typical or "normal" practice. Skillful writers interpret them very loosely and sometimes ignore those that seem too restrictive. For beginning writers, however, the rules offer a discipline and a security. Observing them will not make a writer great, by any means, but it will make his writing clear and orderly, and these are qualities of basic importance in all good writing.

* Let anyone who doubts this assertion test it by arranging for a tape- or wire-recording of an ordinary argument or discussion—without informing the speakers. The transcript will probably seem absurd and only partly intelligible.

LIST OF BOOKS FOR REFERENCE AND FURTHER STUDY

Aiken, Janet R., *Commonsense Grammar*. New York: Thomas Y. Crowell Co., 1936.

Berry, Lester V., and Melvin Van den Bark, *The American Thesaurus of Slang*. New York: Thomas Y. Crowell Co., 1952.

Bryant, Margaret M., *A Functional English Grammar*. New York: D. C. Heath and Co., 1935.

Curme, George O., *Parts of Speech and Accidence*. Boston: D. C. Heath and Co., 1935.

———, *Syntax*. Boston: D. C. Heath and Co., 1931.

Estrich, Robert M., and Hans Sperber, *Three Keys to Language*. New York: Rinehart and Co., 1952.

Fowler, Henry W., *A Dictionary of Modern English Usage*. New York: Oxford University Press, 1926.

Fowler, Henry W. and F. G., *The King's English*. London: Oxford University Press, 1931.

Fries, Charles C., *American English Grammar*. New York: Appleton-Century-Crofts, 1940.

———, *The Structure of the English Sentence*. New York: Harcourt-Brace and Co., 1952.

Goldberg, Isaac, *The Wonder of Words*. New York: Appleton-Century-Crofts, 1938.

Gray, Louis H., *Foundations of Language*. New York: Macmillan Company, 1939.

Horwill, H. W., *Modern American Usage*. New York: Oxford University Press, 1935.

Greenough, J. B. and George L. Kittredge, *Words and Their Ways in English Speech*. New York: Macmillan Company, 1923.

Jesperson, Otto, *Essentials of English Grammar*. New York: D. C. Heath and Co., 1933.

Kennedy, Arthur G., *Current English*. Boston: Ginn and Co., 1935.

10

Marckwardt, Albert H., and Fred G. Walcott, *Facts about Current English Usage*. New York: Appleton-Century-Crofts, 1938.

McKnight, George H., *English Words and Their Background*. New York: Appleton-Century-Crofts, 1923.

Mencken, H. L., *The American Language*. New York: Alfred Knopf, Inc., 1936. Supplement One, 1945. Supplement Two, 1948.

Myers, L. M., *American English*. New York: Prentice-Hall, Inc., 1952.

Partridge, Eric and John W. Clark, *British and American English Since 1900*. London: Andrew Dakers Limited, 1951.

Partridge, Eric, *A Dictionary of Slang and Unconventional English,* 3rd edition. New York: Macmillan Company, 1950.

Pence, R. W., *A Grammar of Present Day English*. New York: Macmillan Company, 1947.

Perrin, Porter G., *An Index to English,* rev. edition, Chicago: Scott-Foresman and Co., 1950.

Pooley, Robert C., *Teaching English Usage*. New York: Appleton-Century-Crofts, 1946.

Pyles, Thomas, *Words and Ways of American English*. New York: Random House, 1952.

Roberts, Paul, *Understanding Grammar*. New York: Henry Holt and Co., 1954.

Schlauch, Margaret, *The Gift of Tongues*. New York: Modern Age Books, Inc., 1942.

Shipley, Joseph, *A Dictionary of Word Origins*. New York: Philosophical Library, Inc., 1945.

Summey, George, *American Punctuation*. New York: Ronald Press, 1949.

University of Chicago, *A Manual of Style,* 11th edition. Chicago: University of Chicago Press, 1949.

11

Grammar = GR

GOOD GRAMMAR IS NOT MERELY GRAMMAR WHICH IS
FREE FROM UNCONVENTIONALITIES, OR EVEN FROM THE
IMMORALITIES. IT IS THE TRIUMPH OF THE COMMUNI-
CATION PROCESS, THE USE OF WORDS WHICH CREATE IN
THE READER'S MIND THE THING AS THE WRITER CON-
CEIVED IT; IT IS A CREATIVE ACT. . . .
—JANET AIKEN, *Commonsense Grammar*

English grammar is perhaps not one of your favorite subjects, and the authors of your handbook are not working under the illusion that they can magically change your opinion. But they do think some preliminary remarks about what grammar is and what it does will make the rest of this section more interesting than it might otherwise be.

Of what use is a knowledge of English grammar? Just this: it tells us what classes of words there are (nouns, pronouns, prepositions, etc.), how they are related to one another (subject-predicate, pronoun-antecedent, etc.), and how they all go together to make up a sentence. In one sense, then, English grammar describes the way words work together to make our language. In another and more usual sense, however, English grammar gives advice and prescribes 'rules" about the ways words *should* (or *should not*) go together to make "correct" English—and it is undoubtedly this prescriptive function that may make a study of grammar somewhat distasteful.

But the real difficulty in learning grammar lies not in our resistance to it but in the nature of English itself. English is an "unprotected" language: it has been subjected to more influences, and more inconsistently so, than any other major language. As we

13

pointed out in the previous section, on the Anglo-Saxon base of modern English is a superstructure of Latin, Danish, French, and other languages. To use linguistic terms, English is chiefly "analytical" and yet partly "inflected." It is chiefly analytical in the sense that the position of words in a sentence, not their endings or changes in form, almost always determines their relationship to one another and hence the meaning of the sentence. It is inflected in that it has declensions (nominative, possessive, and objective forms for pronouns, for example) and conjugations (present, past, and perfect forms for most verbs).

This complication seems all very natural when we look at the history of English and the forces that have influenced it, but it is frankly a nuisance when we are looking for comforting and dependable grammatical rules to guide us. The categorical rule that the personal pronoun which follows forms of *to be* must always be in the nominative case (*It is I, It is they,* etc.) is contradicted by the fact that the position of the pronoun in the sentence has become more important in deciding its form than traditional theory, and so *It is me, It is them,* and so on, are now standard English. The attraction of the normal English sentence pattern—subject-verb-object—is too compelling; putting the nominative after the verb does not seem quite natural to most people. At the same time most people feel awkward in starting a sentence with an objective form (*Whom* do you wish to see?); the nominative *who* seems more natural, and so the sentence is often spoken or written "*Who* do you wish to see?" and to say that the sentence is "incorrect" would be somewhat unrealistic.

These examples will give an idea of the major tug-of-war going on between traditional theories of grammar, which by and large emphasize the inflected character of English, on the one hand, and actual usage, with its feeling for word-order, on the other. Though it is certain that actual usage is winning, the victory is by no means complete at the moment. For every student of language who points to the facts of actual usage there are many people who ignore or minimize these facts and cling to the traditional theories they learned in their childhood.

The major advantage of a knowledge of grammar is that it gives us a terminology which enables us to talk about and criticize the

14

language we speak and write. It gives us a method of analysis with which we can repair our own English. Take, for example, the sentence "While enjoying our hamburgers and coffee, the halfback broke away for his third touchdown." Only bad grammar makes this miracle possible, but a knowledge of grammatical principles helps turn nonsense into sense. Grammar tells us that the words "While enjoying our hamburgers and coffee" have nothing to modify except the subject of the sentence, "the halfback," which they cannot modify without producing a ludicrous picture of a halfback racing for the goal line while munching sandwiches and juggling several cups of coffee. Therefore the sentence should have a subject to which the introductory group of words can logically apply. Such a subject might be "we": "While enjoying our hamburgers and coffee, we saw the halfback break away for his third touchdown." As long as we realize that grammatical analysis of this kind is not an end in itself but a way of identifying and correcting errors, we find it more a useful servant than a disagreeable taskmaster.

1. SENTENCE SENSE = SS

1a. Recognizing sentences

> A sentence is a grammatically independent group of
> words which serves as a unit of expression. It nor-
> mally contains a subject and a predicate.

A sentence is grammatically independent and complete. It may
contain words which cannot be fully understood without reference
to the preceding or succeeding sentences, but it is grammatically
self-sufficient even when lifted out of context and made to stand
alone. By way of illustration, consider the following passage:

(1) Old Dinger's ghost was said to live in the surrounding hills.
(2) It had been seen several times from the tavern window.

Both of these sentences are complete, grammatically independent
assertions. The full meaning of sentence (2) depends on the identification of the subject "it" with its antecedent "Old Dinger's ghost"
in sentence (1). But sentence (2) is structurally independent because the pronoun "it" is a recognizable grammatical substitute for
"Dinger's ghost." *

The main ingredients of a typical English sentence are the subject
and the predicate. The subject is a noun, a pronoun, or a word or
word-group functioning as a noun. The predicate consists of a verb
and its complements and modifiers. The verb asserts something
about the subject. In the following sentences the subjects are in
italic type, the verbs in small capitals.

NOUN AS SUBJECT	*Sheep* GRAZE. *Telephones* RING
PRONOUN AS SUBJECT	*She* IS DANCING. *They* DISAP-PEARED.

* The independence of a grammatically complete sentence is signalized by
means of "end punctuation." See Section 36.

WORD GROUP (PHRASE) AS SUBJECT   *Over the fence* IS out.
WORD GROUP (CLAUSE) AS SUBJECT   *That he failed* IS certain.

Recognition of subject and verb is the starting point in sentence analysis. Normal English word order places the subject before the verb, although in the inverted sentence the subject comes after the verb (Happy AM *I*). In some commands (GO home. SHUT the door.) the subject *You* is not expressed but is understood. In questions, where the subject may separate the parts of the verb (HAS *he* GONE?), the subject may be identified by recasting the sentence in the form of a declarative statement (*He* HAS GONE).

EXERCISE 1. Indicate the subjects and verbs in the following sentences:

(1) The wind blows violently.
(2) His problems are nearly solved.
(3) Are you feeling well today?
(4) Tomorrow will be Thursday.
(5) Father has been washing his car.
(6) Many are the problems of a husband.
(7) Where will 1 find the dishpan?
(8) Leave your pistols at the door.
(9) He shouldered his pack and trudged into the forest.
(10) I think he arrived this morning.
(11) Reflected in the mirror was a lovely woman's face.
(12) Of all the errors a beginning golfer makes, swinging without watching the ball is probably the most common.
(13) Whatever hit me on the head bounced into the lake.
(14) To write an epic poem was Dryden's lifelong ambition.
(15) That 1 was driving at a reasonable speed is my only defense.
(16) Throwing my shoe at the window, I finally attracted her attention.
(17) However, throwing my shoe at the window put my arm out of shape for the next day's game.
(18) Grasping at trees and bushes, clawing the earth, pulling great boulders loose with bleeding hands, the wounded man slid down the hill and out of sight, his screams echoing distantly off the canyon walls.

17

(19) Because Milton considered a man who did not act according to "right reason" a slave to his passions, he felt that such a man had no right to participate in government.

(20) One gadget that will certainly make life easier for the common man, that will assure the leadership of this country in world affairs and will secure the lasting respect of all posterity, is the newly patented electric toothpaste squeezer.

1b. Recognizing parts of speech.

In modern English we usually recognize eight parts of speech: noun, pronoun, adjective, verb, adverb, preposition, conjunction, and interjection. There are three bases for classifying a word as a particular part of speech: (1) its grammatical function, such as subject or modifier; (2) its grammatical form, such as the *'s* of a possessive noun; (3) its type of meaning, such as the name of a person or statement of an action.

In the sentence "Lee's army marched," *Lee's* is classified as an adjective because of its function (modifier of the noun *army*), its form (noun made into an adjective by addition of the possessive ending *-'s*) and its type of meaning (a descriptive or limiting word). *Army* is a noun because of its function (subject of the sentence) and its type of meaning (name of a thing). *Marched* is recognizable as a verb because of its function (asserting something about the subject *army*), its form (past tense made with the common ending *ed*) and its type of meaning (statement of an action).

Many words function in more than one way. For example, the word *place* may be used as noun, adjective, or verb:

NOUN   The seashore is a restful *place.*

ADJECTIVE   She bought *place* mats for the table.

VERB   *Place* the book on the desk.

(1) *Nouns*

A noun names a person, place, or thing (*Carl, Detroit, studio committee, fountain pen, truth*). Nouns normally change their form to make the plural (*boy, boys; man, men;* but *sheep, sheep; deer, deer*). The addition of *'* or *'s* shows the possessive (*Bess' purse, cow's horns*).

18

(2) *Pronouns*

A pronoun is a word used as a substitute for a noun. The meaning of a pronoun is usually completed, or made clear, by reference to a noun that is the antecedent of the pronoun. In the sentence "Clara Barton is the woman who founded the American Red Cross," the pronoun *who* refers to its antecedent, *woman.* Occasionally the antecedent is not expressed at all but is implied by the context in which the pronoun stands. In the proverb "He who hesitates is lost," the pronoun *He* refers to any person who hesitates to take action. Indefinite pronouns such as *anybody* or *somebody* are self-sufficient and have no antecedents.

The personal pronouns *I, we, he, she, they,* and the relative or interrogative pronoun *who,* have distinctive forms for the nominative, possessive, and objective cases; *you* and *it* are the same in the nominative and objective cases but have a distinctive form for the possessive. The grammatical problems which arise from the use of these various forms are discussed in "Case," Section 4.

(3) *Adjectives*

An adjective modifies a noun or pronoun. For example: *brown* dog, *Victorian* dignity, *your* coat, *paper* hat, *this* house, *one* football, *the* mountain, *damaging* fire. Predicate adjectives are used to complete the meaning of a verb and to modify the subject. Usually predicate adjectives follow the verbs *be, seem, become, appear,* and the verbs pertaining to the five senses, *look, smell, taste, sound, feel.* (She is *sad.* He looks *happy.*)

Adjectives have no definite forms to show number and case (except pronoun adjectives such as *my, ours*). The special forms by which adjectives show comparison are discussed in "Adjectives and Adverbs," Section 3.

(4) *Verbs and Verbals*

A verb expresses action or state of being. The main function of a verb is to assert something about its subject. Linking verbs (*be, seem, become,* etc.) and verbs pertaining to the senses (*see, smell, taste,* etc.) often serve as connectives between the subject and a predicate noun or a predicate adjective. (He *became* an athlete. The cake *tastes* good.)

A verb may consist of from one to four words, depending on its inflectional form. (The pet duck *eats* too much. It *should have been eaten* long ago.) When a verb is combined with *not* (*cannot*) or with a contraction of *not* (*mustn't*), the *not* or its contraction is regarded as an adverb rather than a part of the verb.

Infinitives, participles, and gerunds, which are derived from verbs, are called *verbals*. Verbs make an assertion. Verbals do not; they are used as nouns and modifiers.

INFINITIVE
> *To see* is *to believe*. (Both infinitives are used as nouns.)
> It was time *to leave*. (Infinitive is used as an adjective.)
> I was ready *to go*. (Infinitive is used as an adverb.)

PARTICIPLE (adjective derived from a verb)
> *Screaming*, I jumped out of bed. (present participle)
> *Delighted*, we accepted his invitation. (past participle)

GERUND (noun derived from a verb)
> *Swimming* is healthful exercise.
> His wife enjoyed *nagging* him.

(5) *Adverbs*

An adverb modifies a verb, an adjective, or another adverb.

MODIFIER OF A VERB	He stayed *outside*.
MODIFIER OF AN ADJECTIVE	She was *very* sad.
MODIFIER OF AN ADVERB	I walked *quite* slowly.

Adverbs, like adjectives, have special forms to show comparison; these are discussed in "Adjectives and Adverbs," Section 3.

(6) *Prepositions*

A preposition relates a noun or pronoun to some other word in the sentence.

> He was young *in* spirit. (*Spirit* is related to the adjective *young*.)
> See the shower *of* sparks. (*Sparks* is related to the noun *shower*.)
> I apologized *to* her. (*Her* is related to the verb *apologized*.)

English has gradually lost its system of case endings for nouns; noun functions once shown by their endings are now shown by the use of prepositions and their objects. The object of the preposition is in the objective case (*between you and him; to John and me*). Even the last remaining use of the inflected noun, the possessive, is often replaced by a preposition and its object (*day's end, end of the day*). Some of the more common English prepositions are *at, between, by, for, from, in, of, on, through, to, with*.

(7) *Conjunctions*

A conjunction is a word used to join words, phrases, or clauses. Conjunctions show the relation between the sentence elements which they connect.

Co-ordinating conjunctions (*and, but, or, nor, for*) join words, phrases, or clauses of equal grammatical rank. (*See* 1d, "Recognizing Clauses.")*

WORDS JOINED   We ate ham *and* eggs.
PHRASES JOINED   Look in the closet *or* under the bed.
CLAUSES JOINED   We wanted to go, *but* we were too busy.

Subordinating conjunctions (*because, if, since, when, where,* etc.) join subordinate clauses with main clauses. (*See* 1d, "Recognizing Clauses.")

We left the party early *because* we were tired.
If the roads are icy, we shall have to drive carefully.

(8) *Interjections*

An interjection is an exclamatory word expressing emotion and having no grammatical relation to other words in the sentence. Mild exclamations are usually followed by commas. *Oh, is that you? Well, well, how are you?* If the emotion is strong, an exclamation point may follow the interjection. *Ouch! You are hurting me. Oh, I hate you!*

EXERCISE 2. Indicate the part of speech of each word in the following sentences:

* For a discussion of the punctuation of clauses separated by a co-ordinating conjunction, see Section 37a.

(1) We entered the diner, and Higgins served us coffee and rolls.

(2) After the others left we had a private talk.

(3) From the distance came the wail of a steamboat.

(4) Stop! You have trespassed on my property.

(5) Washing dishes is a waste of time.

(6) He soon recovered from his very severe injuries.

(7) The snow-covered Michigan forests are very impressive in winter.

(8) The boys clambered up the hill to the lighthouse.

(9) The woodsman was angry because somebody had robbed his traps.

(10) Galileo disclaimed his support of the theories of Copernicus under the torture of the Inquisitors.

(11) Descartes said that there was only one vacuum in the universe, the one in Pascal's head.

(12) In reading tales of knights of old you should keep in mind that the medieval doctrine of courtly love is silly and immoral by most modern standards.

(13) Some people still believe that men and women have an unequal number of ribs.

(14) Having slept through the lecture, he felt himself well qualified to criticize it in detail.

(15) "Pshaw!" said old Granny Hoskins, "you don't have to help me get off the horse."

(16) Spot the frogs with your flashlight; then shoot before they jump.

(17) We watched the phosphorescent water boiling under the stern.

(18) Whenever a pocket of air shook the bomber the tailgunner shouted over the intercom, threatening the pilot with court martial and announcing repeatedly that he was going home.

(19) That cave is unsafe; even the bats have left it.

(20) Saw off this fence post even with the top of the gate.

1c. Recognizing phrases.

A phrase is a group of related words lacking a subject and predicate and used as a single part of speech. Typical phrases are a preposition and its object (I fell *on the sidewalk*), or a verbal and its object (I wanted *to see the parade*).

Prepositional phrases are classified, according to their function, as adjective, adverb, and noun phrases. An adjective phrase modifies a noun or pronoun. (He is a man *of action*.) An adverb phrase modifies a verb, adjective, or adverb. (The train arrived *on time*. We were ready *at the station*.) A noun phrase is used as a noun. (*Before breakfast* is the best time for calisthenics.)

Verbal phrases are classified as participial, gerund, or infinitive phrases. A participial phrase functions as an adjective, modifying a noun or pronoun. (The man *sitting on the porch* is my father. The dog *found in the street* was homeless.) Such phrases are formed with the present participle of a verb (*seeing, calling*) or the past participle (*seen, called*). A gerund phrase is used as a noun. (*Collecting stamps* is my hobby.) As both gerunds and present participles end in *-ing*, they can be distinguished only by their separate functions as nouns or adjectives. An infinitive phrase is used as an adjective, adverb, or noun. (It is time *to go to bed*. We were impatient *to start the game*. I wanted *to buy a house*.)

EXERCISE 3. In the following sentences identify the prepositional and verbal phrases and explain their functions:

(1) The girl with brown eyes is my sister.

(2) For two years I worked in Chicago.

(3) The library located on the campus needs repair.

(4) Keeping a budget requires great patience.

(5) I am glad to see you.

(6) He entered the room through the door on the right.

(7) Paying one's bills is sometimes difficult.

(8) John wanted to become an engineer.

(9) Playing handball is pleasant exercise.

(10) The boy flying the kite was envied by the other children.

(11) Twisting to face me, she chewed her already swollen lower lip.

(12) Suddenly morning burst, spilling onto the lake, trickling like glowing lava through the forest.

(13) Crumpled on the davenport were his tuxedo and his aging topcoat.

(14) Having managed to work loose from the wreck, he vaulted the fence and ducked behind a tree, stopping only then to find out who was shooting.

23

(15) To insure quiet in his room while he was studying for the final examinations Roger dropped the radio down the laundry chute.

(16) To prevent such drastic action in the future was the purpose of the housemother's rule forbidding use of the laundry chute by anyone but the maid.

(17) Passing the examination was more important to Roger than using the laundry chute.

(18) Smith wanted to hold the foreman to his promise.

(19) He was unable, however, to force him to put vinegar in the plant superintendent's thermos bottle.

(20) Reports of flying saucers grew more frequent in the summer.

1d. Recognizing clauses.

A clause is a word group containing a subject and predicate. Usually a clause is related to the rest of the sentence by means of a conjunction. There are two kinds of clauses: (1) subordinate or dependent clauses, and (2) main or independent clauses.

(1) Subordinate clauses are frequently introduced by a subordinating conjunction (*as, since, because,* etc.) or by a relative pronoun (*who, which, that*). Functioning as an adjective, adverb, or noun, a subordinate clause expresses an idea which is less important than the idea expressed in the main clause. The exact relationship between the two ideas is indicated by the writer's choice of a connective to join the subordinate and the main clause.

(*a*) An adjective clause modifies a noun or pronoun.

This is the airship *that broke the speed record.* (The clause modifies the noun *airship.*)

Anybody *who is tired* may leave. (The clause modifies the pronoun *anybody.*)

Canada is the nation *we made the treaty with.* (The clause modifies the noun *nation.*)

(*b*) An adverb clause modifies a verb, adjective, or adverb.

The child cried *when the dentist appeared.* (The clause modifies the verb *cried.*)

I am sorry *he is sick.* (The clause modifies the adjective *sorry.*)

He thinks more quickly *than you do.* (The clause modifies the adverb *quickly.*)

24

(*c*) A noun clause has the function of a noun. It can be subject, predicate nominative, object of a verb, or object of a preposition.

> *What John wants* is a better job. (The clause is the subject of the verb *is*.)
> This is *where we came in.* (The clause is a predicate nominative.)
> Uncle Joe said *that he was lonely.* (The clause is the object of the verb *said*.)
> In spite of *what I had said* she smiled. (The clause is object of the prepositional phrase *in spite of*.)

EXERCISE 4. Indicate the subordinate clauses in the following sentences and tell whether they are adjective, adverb, or noun clauses:

  (1) He was a man who never found happiness.
  (2) When the fire started, I grabbed a bucket.
  (3) The apples that make the best pies are the sour ones.
  (4) What you want is hard to obtain.
  (5) If wishes were horses, beggars would ride.
  (6) I read the books which he recommended.
  (7) Hawkeye knew that he was being watched.
  (8) I was alarmed by what she said.
  (9) He enrolled in college because he wanted to be a lawyer.
 (10) What annoyed me was the clerk's indifference.
 (11) You are the man I am looking for.
 (12) We went swimming on a day when the sun was bright.
 (13) While she was gossiping, the supper burned on the stove.
 (14) His suggestion was that we pool our cash.
 (15) We left before the concert was finished.

(2) A main clause has both subject and verb and is not introduced by a subordinating word. A main clause makes an independent statement and thus is never used as a modifier, for it is never dependent on other parts of the sentence.

The number of main or subordinate clauses in a sentence determines its classification: *simple, compound, complex,* or *compound-complex.*

25

A *simple sentence* has a single main clause.

The wind blew.

A *compound sentence* has two or more main clauses.

The wind blew and the leaves fell.

A *complex sentence* has one main clause and one or more subordinate clauses.

When the wind blew, the leaves fell.

A *compound-complex sentence* contains two or more main clauses and one or more subordinate clauses.

When the sky darkened, the wind blew and the leaves fell.

EXERCISE 5. In the following sentences point out the main and subordinate clauses. Indicate the function of each subordinate clause as an adjective, adverb, or noun clause.

(1) After the meeting ended I hurried back to my attic apartment.

(2) The tramp told us that he was homeless.

(3) He has two sons who are excellent horsemen.

(4) You may go whenever you wish.

(5) Do you remember the night when we first met?

(6) The judge wondered why the jury had deliberated so long.

(7) Golf is a sport which requires co-ordination.

(8) It was his opinion that taxes were too high.

(9) Although I am a heavy sleeper, I awoke with a start when the lightning flashed.

(10) A sentence that has a main clause and one or more subordinate clauses is called a complex sentence.

(11) A clause is subordinate if it functions as a single part of speech.

(12) When I marry I want a wife who can cook.

(13) If you will give me your telephone number, I will call you tomorrow.

(14) The price that he wanted for the house was too high.

(15) A man of action forced into a state of thought is unhappy until he can get out of it.

(16) The day I leave this place will be the happiest of my life.

(17) It is said that Dryden arrived in London dressed in simple drugget.

(18) She cried because I left and she pouted when I came home.

(19) Some mothers let their children do whatever they please.

(20) As he came in the door he said he could whip any man in the room.

2. CONFUSED STRUCTURE: FRAGMENT, RUN-TOGETHER SENTENCE, THE COMMA SPLICE = STR

Fragmentary, "spliced" and run-together (or fused) sentences should be avoided except when a special effect is desired.

Certainly not all "good English" consists of sentences as they are defined in Section 1. However, a violation of the normal pattern of the sentence always has a special effect, and the good writer learns to control his violations so that the special effect is the one he desires. Some beginning writers interrupt a unified thought with a period simply because a group of words looks about as long as they think a sentence ought to be. Or they hook one sentence to another with a comma (or even without one!) because they fail to recognize how or why the units in their writing should be separated. We have no trouble detecting which of the following passages is merely clumsy and out of control and which is deliberately irregular.

A lifeguard must be able to swim a variety of strokes, he sometimes uses the breaststroke. But when supporting a tired but rational swimmer he uses the sidestroke and the backstroke to carry a swimmer who is unconscious or too frightened to cooperate, moreover when he approaches a drowning person he uses a modified form of the crawl. In which he keeps his eyes above the water level.

His motor idling, he cut off the lights and waited. One minute. Two minutes. Three minutes. He bounced his foot on the clutch, he toyed with the holster at his side, he waited. A whine of tires going too fast, a sudden streak of headlights, and he was into gear and onto the highway. Another screaming chase. Another hostile meeting. Another traffic ticket.

28

2a. Sentence fragment = FRAG

Although the usual sentence contains a subject and a verb, some types of sentences omit the subject or verb. These sentences are more common in spoken English than in formal writing. Conversational language contains questions, answers, and exclamations which, for reasons of emphasis or economy, do not follow the usual sentence pattern. "Really?" "Yes." "How absurd!" Familiar expressions such as "The sooner, the better," or transitional phrases such as "So much for this point. Now for my second argument" are used even in formal English. Although these sentences are technically fragmentary, they are justifiable in a suitable context.

Writers occasionally omit the verb in descriptive passages, particularly if the details of the description consist of a series of sense impressions. The following passage is meaningful in spite of the omission of verbs; indeed the omission aids the writer's purpose, which is to give the effect of sense impressions.

> Howland & Gould's Grocery. In the display window, black, overripe bananas and lettuce on which a cat was sleeping. Shelves lined with red crêpe paper which was now faded and torn and concentrically spotted.
>
> —SINCLAIR LEWIS, *Main Street*

Similarly, the verb is sometimes omitted in passages which portray a person's thoughts. In this case, the omission is understood and the verb can be readily supplied by the reader.

> He looked at the old photograph and was suddenly unhappy. The old gang all split up now. Smitty in L.A., Frank in Berlin, Joe on a two-year stretch in Alaska. Weather observer. Good joke, that one. Heard Joe say once he'd never live north of Miami. Serves him right. Never second-guess destiny.

Most other types of sentences lacking the normal subject-verb sequence are ineffective in writing.* A phrase or subordinate clause is usually closely related in meaning to an independent clause. Thus when the phrase or subordinate clause is carelessly punctuated as a

---

* Contrary to a popular notion, complete sentences may begin with a coordinating conjunction (*and, but,* etc.). Such sentences, when used sparingly, are effective ways of emphasizing transitional statements.

sentence, the reader senses its inadequacy as a statement. Observe the following example:

> He leaped through the window with a crash. Because there was no other way of escaping the fire.

Here the *because*-clause depends directly and grammatically on the preceding main clause. Punctuating subordinate elements in this way, as though they were complete sentences, results more often from a writer's failure to recognize what a complete sentence is than from his deliberate choice of unconventional punctuation. The failure is often called "the period fault," and whether deliberate or not is likely to be ineffective. In the example above, the relationship between the two clauses is clarified and strengthened when they are combined in a single sentence:

> He leaped through the window with a crash, because there was no other way of escaping the fire.

Another means of revising the weak use of the subordinate clause as a sentence is to turn the subordinate clause into a main clause.

> He leaped through the window with a crash; there was no other way of escaping the fire.

Or again:

> He leaped through the window with a crash. There was no other way of escaping the fire.

With so many methods available for showing the appropriate relationship between a phrase or subordinate clause and other sentence elements, a writer can easily avoid ineffective sentence fragments.

EXERCISE 6. In the following sentences eliminate any ineffective fragments (1) by joining the fragment with the main clause, or (2) by giving the fragment a normal subject-verb sequence:

(1) I was frightened. Probably because I had never before seen a gun battle in the street.
(2) She used to dislike me. Though I never knew why.
(3) The pilot feared that his plane had insufficient fuel. The nearest landing field being nearly a hundred miles away.

(4) Prospectors invaded the newly discovered gold field. Some in wagons, some on horseback, and a few in heavily laden canoes.

(5) The twins are almost identical. The only difference being a small mole on Judy's cheek.

(6) We had a wonderful vacation. Chiefly because the fishing was good.

(7) She was constantly making suggestions to her husband. Such as how much soap he should use in the dishwater.

(8) No rain for a month. The streams were beginning to dry up.

(9) She talked almost incessantly. But intelligently nevertheless.

(10) There shouldn't be any secrets. At least between you and me.

(11) Where the corn stands in the sunlight, where the folks eat clabber and blackberries, where the stores charge things to your first name. That's where I want to spend my life.

(12) My mother gained twenty pounds and her health improved generally. After she had her tonsils removed.

(13) Because I know that my mother will be angry and insist that I never see you again, if we get home after midnight. I think we should go home.

(14) In spite of the fact that Hobbes was able to explain rationally almost every phenomenon of the supernatural. He was afraid of the dark.

(15) You will serve a specified period in the army. Whether you want to or not.

(16) Weaving baskets is an educational and useful hobby. For young or old.

(17) Usually trees grow along both banks of a stream, but when they grow only along one bank. The stream very likely flows along a fault line.

(18) He struck out three times during the game. Every time he was up.

(19) He left without a word of goodbye. And we never heard from him again.

(20) A red sunset is not only a beautiful sight. But also is usually a sign of good weather the following day.

2b. Comma splice = CS or CF

The use of a comma between two main clauses *not* joined by a co-ordinating conjunction results in the comma fault, or comma splice.* The comma splice can be corrected in one of the following ways:

(1) By connecting the main clauses with a co-ordinating conjunction.

(2) By replacing the comma with a semicolon.

(3) By making a separate sentence of each main clause.

(4) By changing one of the main clauses to a subordinate clause.

COMMA SPLICE	The witness was unwilling to testify, he was afraid of the accused man.
REVISED (1)	The witness was unwilling to testify, for he was afraid of the accused man.
REVISED (2)	The witness was unwilling to testify; he was afraid of the accused man.
REVISED (3)	The witness was unwilling to testify. He was afraid of the accused man.
REVISED (4)	Because he was afraid of the accused man, the witness was unwilling to testify.

The last correction—(4)—is the most specific. It shows the relationship between the two clauses clearly and precisely. Though the other revisions eliminate the comma splice, they have much of the loose quality of the original. The truth is that merely to eliminate a comma splice by change of punctuation alone is seldom sufficient. The sentence itself may have to be reworked. More often than not, this means subordinating one of the clauses, as was done in revision (4). (See also "Subordination," Section 14.)

2c. Run-together or fused sentence = FS

Run-together or fused sentences occur when main clauses are joined without a co-ordinating conjunction or any mark of punctuation. They can be corrected in the same way as the comma splice.

FUSED	Balboa gazed upon the broad Pacific his heart was filled with awe.
REVISED (1)	Balboa gazed upon the broad Pacific, and his heart was filled with awe.

* The common co-ordinating conjunctions are *and, but, for, or, nor.* In informal English *yet* is sometimes used to mean *but.* Informal English often uses *so* as a co-ordinating conjunction.

REVISED (2)   Balboa gazed upon the broad Pacific; his heart was filled with awe.

REVISED (3)   Balboa gazed upon the broad Pacific. His heart was filled with awe.

REVISED (4)   When Balboa gazed upon the broad Pacific, his heart was filled with awe.

EXERCISE 7. Eliminate comma splices and run-together sentences in the following and give your reasons for the changes you make:

(1) Its tires screaming, the automobile crashed headlong into the bridge culvert then all was quiet.

(2) The automobile crashed headlong into the bridge culvert, none of the occupants was injured severely.

(3) The automobile was not in good condition it had been wrecked twice and its brakes were completely ineffective.

(4) The automobile crashed headlong into the culvert its occupants were all killed.

(5) The automobile crashed headlong into the culvert however its occupants were not severely injured.

(6) Below us the train rounded a mountain curve, we thought it looked like a mechanical snake.

(7) After the blood transfusion the patient was conscious for a short while, the doctor left the hospital for a meal.

(8) We used to behave just as wildly I can remember riding my sled in the street without regard for the traffic.

(9) Trapped in the center of the court, Charley pivoted and passed the basketball through his legs from the stands he looked like a football center.

(10) This is the reason I stopped reading books, they invariably made me think too much.

(11) The hero deserted the army when he realized that the war had no significance for him only one human being meant anything, the nurse he was in love with.

(12) I would lie for hours watching the goldfish playing checkers was my only other amusement.

(13) My brother must be color-blind, he calls everything from purple to black navy blue.

(14) Every day the rooster would fly into the pigpen, he delighted in tormenting the lazy creatures.

(15) The Puritans were the source of many of our democratic ideals, however the government of Cromwell was in many ways an absolute dictatorship.

(16) Twain knew that Howells was shocked, nevertheless he sent the editor copies of all his coarse productions.

(17) In the kitchen are three chairs on the porch are four more.

(18) Santa Anna was surprised by the Texan forces at San Jacinto, afterwards he was captured while trying to escape dressed as a common soldier.

(19) The rock formations of the Arbuckle Mountains in Oklahoma are gnarled and polished as a geologist told us, these are some of the oldest mountains in the world.

(20) No one can say that Walpole had no principles, one of them was that every man had his price.

3. ADJECTIVES AND ADVERBS = AD

The functions of adjectives and adverbs should be clearly distinguished.

The writer who understands the functions of adjectives and adverbs is not likely to confuse them. The misuse of these modifiers can usually be traced to carelessness, such as allowing an adjective to modify a verb, or to unfamiliarity with the forms of certain adjectives and adverbs.

Although most adverbs end in -*ly* (*slowly, quickly*), this ending is not a dependable means of identifying an adverb. Some adjectives also end in -*ly* (*manly, holy*),* while other adjectives have the same form as adverbs (*late, well*). Certain adverbs have two forms (*quick, quickly, slow, slowly*), though in general the form ending in -*ly* is preferable in formal usage. In informal English the shorter forms are widely used, particularly in commands such as "Drive slow" or "Go fast."

The only sound way of distinguishing between adjectives and adverbs is by distinguishing between their functions. Does the word in question modify a noun or pronoun? If so, it is an adjective. Does it modify an adjective, verb, or adverb? If so, it is an adverb. Sometimes adjectives are wrongly allowed to modify verbs, as in the following sentences.

> He writes *careless*. (The adverb *carelessly* is needed to modify the verb *writes*.)
> She talks modest. (*Modestly*, the adverb, is needed.)

Adjectives are sometimes misused to modify other adjectives and adverbs:

* Many of the ways in which adjectives are formed from nouns are discussed in Section 30, "Vocabulary."

35

He was *terrible* wounded. (The adverb *terribly* is needed to modify the adjective *wounded.*)

She works *considerable* harder than he does. (*Considerably*, the adverbial form, is needed.)

The misuse of adjectives is of course more common in conversation than in formal or informal writing. Indeed, the careless use of the adjective *real* as an emphatic *very* to modify adjectives and adverbs is often heard in the familiar speech of educated people.

FORMAL   You will hear from me *very* soon.

COLLOQUIAL*   You will hear from me *real* soon.

3a. The verbs BE, BECOME, APPEAR, SEEM, **and the verbs pertaining to the senses** (LOOK, SMELL, TASTE, SOUND, FEEL) **are called linking verbs and are followed by an adjective if the modifier refers to the subject rather than to the verb.**

In sentences such as the following, the verb joins the subject and a predicate adjective which modifies the subject.

Jane looks *pretty* tonight. (*Pretty* modifies *Jane.*)

The butter smells *sour*. (*Sour* modifies *butter.*)

He appears *jubilant*. (*Jubilant* modifies *He.*)

A common misuse of the predicate adjective is illustrated by the tendency to use the adverb *badly*, instead of the adjective *bad*, after the verb *feel*. This construction is common, not because of the speaker's carelessness, but because of his zeal to be correct. He feels a "grammatical necessity" to use an adverb after a verb, whatever the verb might be.

FORMAL   He feels bad (*ill*).

COLLOQUIAL He feels *badly*.

FORMAL   He felt *bad* about it.

COLLOQUIAL He felt *badly* about it.

3b. An adverb rather than an adjective is used if the modifier describes the manner of the action of the verb.

He looked *suspiciously* at me. (The adverb *suspiciously* modifies the verb *looked*. Contrast *He looks suspicious to me.*)

* We use the term *colloquial* to signify the qualities of familiar spoken English.

The thief felt *carefully* under the pillow. (The adverb *carefully* modifies the verb *felt.*)

In these examples the verbs *look* and *feel* express action, and must be modified by adverbs. But in constructions such as "He *looks* tired" or "He *feels* well," the verbs serve less as words of action than as links between the subject and a predicate adjective. The choice of adjective or adverb thus depends upon the function and meaning of the verb. In other words, the choice depends upon whether or not the verb is being *used* as a *linking* verb. Does the writer want a modifier for the *subject* or for the *verb?*

In some sentences either an adjective or an adverb may be used, with little difference in meaning.

ADJECTIVE   The sun shines *bright.* I bolted the gate *tight.*

ADVERB   The sun shines *brightly.* I bolted the gate *tightly.*

3c. The comparative and superlative forms of adjectives and adverbs should be accurately distinguished.

Adjectives and adverbs show degrees of quality or quantity by means of their positive, comparative, and superlative forms. The positive form (*slow, quickly*) expresses no comparison at all. The comparative, formed by adding *-er* or by prefixing *more* to the positive form (*slower, more quickly*), is used to express a greater degree or to make a comparison. The superlative, formed by adding *-est* or by putting *most* before the positive form (*slowest, most quickly*), is used to indicate the greatest degree of a quality or quantity among three or more persons or things. Some common adjectives and adverbs retain old irregular forms (*good, better, best; badly, worse, worst*).

More and *most* can be used with almost any adjective or adverb and are always used with modifiers of three or more syllables (*more beautiful, most regretfully*). Most adjectives, and a few adverbs, of one syllable form the comparative and superlative with *-er* and *-est.* Adjectives of two syllables often have variant forms (*fancier, more fancy; laziest, most lazy*). Where there is such a choice, writers usually select the form that sounds better, or better fits the rhythm of the particular expression.

Some adjectives and adverbs, such as *unique, empty, dead, per-*

fect, entirely, are absolute in their meaning and thus cannot logically be compared. There are no degrees of *uniqueness, deadness,* or *perfection.* In the ambiguous area between substandard and informal usage, however, such words are often compared.*

FORMAL	His diving form is *more nearly perfect* than mine.
COLLOQUIAL	His diving form is *more perfect* than mine.
FORMAL	The new stadium is *more nearly circular* than the old one.
COLLOQUIAL	The new stadium is *more circular* than the old one.

In formal usage, the comparative and superlative forms of the adjective are clearly distinguished. The comparative is used to refer to one of two objects; the superlative, in constructions referring to three or more objects.

COMPARATIVE	His horse is the *faster* of the two.
SUPERLATIVE	His horse is the *fastest* in the county.
COMPARATIVE	Ruth is the *more* attractive but the *less* good-natured of the twins.
SUPERLATIVE	Ruth is the *most* attractive but the *least* good natured of his three daughters.

EXERCISE 8. In the following sentences indicate any errors in the use of adjectives and adverbs in accordance with formal usage:

(1) He should take his profession more serious.

(2) The poor fellow sure did feel bad.

(3) Owls can see good at night.

(4) Little Joe is the biggest of the two dogs.

(5) I have been real lucky.

(6) Since Sarah's illness, she looks considerable older.

(7) This is the emptiest reservoir I have ever seen.

(8) We drove slow through the heavy traffic.

(9) The music had a most unique melody.

(10) I get along perfect with my wife.

(11) Don't feel badly; occasionally we all make mistakes.

(12) A good pitcher throws the ball fast and hard over the plate.

* See the specimen under "Substandard," Section 33b.

(13) They told us that to do good on our jobs we had to do good throughout the community.

(14) The book, one of the most unique I ever read, probed relentlessly for the motives of the characters and described them candidly.

(15) Curtseying, Martha looked prettily at the crowd, seeming more and more confidently as the cheers and applause increased.

(16) The clipper ships sailed majestic over the seven seas.

(17) She remained constantly to her husband while he was overseas.

(18) The more perfect the negative, the better the print will be.

(19) Herbert was a sickly child, and therefore seldom played outside except when the weather was real perfect.

(20) Our car jerked as the tire blew out and then swerved down the highway, wobbling and dangerously.

(21) The hunter aimed careful at the flying ducks.

(22) Scarface divided the loot more equal than the boys expected.

(23) We are going camping most any day now.

(24) Junior's head is rounder than Sister's.

(25) I was never more fully insulted in my life.

Case is a means of showing the function of nouns and pronouns in the sentence.

In the sentence "He gave me a week's vacation," the nominative case form *He* indicates the use of the pronoun as subject; the objective case form *me* shows that the pronoun is an object; the possessive case form *week's* indicates that the noun is a possessive.

In some languages, such as German, adjectives as well as nouns and pronouns are fully declined, with endings for the nominative, possessive, dative, and objective cases. In Anglo-Saxon times the English language too was highly inflected. Nouns were used mainly in four different cases, so that case endings were extremely important in showing the function of the word and its meaning in the sentence. Modern English, however, retains only a few remnants of this complicated system of inflection. Adjectives, once declined in five cases, have no case endings at all. With the loss of case inflections, English has had to rely increasingly on word order to show the relation of a particular word to other parts of the sentence. For example, the object of a verb or preposition normally follows the verb or preposition and thus is easily identified. In the following sentences the position of the nouns determines their function.

Jack threw Bill the ball.
Bill threw Jack the ball.

Modern English nouns have only two case forms, the possessive (*student's*), and a common form (*student*) which serves all other functions. The few problems of case which exist in English are concerned mainly with the personal pronouns (*I, you, he, she, it*) and the relative or interrogative pronoun (*who*), which are inflected in three cases—nominative, possessive, and objective.

40

PERSONAL PRONOUNS

	Nominative	*Possessive*	*Objective*
SINGULAR			
FIRST PERSON	I	my, mine	me
SECOND PERSON	you	your, yours	you
THIRD PERSON	he, she, it	his, her, hers, its	him, her, it
PLURAL			
FIRST PERSON	we	our, ours	us
SECOND PERSON	you	your, yours	you
THIRD PERSON	they	their, theirs	them

RELATIVE OR INTERROGATIVE PRONOUNS

SINGULAR	who	whose	whom
PLURAL	who	whose	whom

NOMINATIVE CASE

4a. The subject of a verb is in the nominative case.

We are happy.

He is tired.

There are several types of sentences in which the subject is not easily recognized and is sometimes confused with the object.

(1) *In formal English the nominative case of the pronoun is used after the conjunctions* AS *and* THAN *if the pronoun is the subject of an elliptical clause.*

In informal English there seems a growing tendency to use *as* and *than* as prepositions.

FORMAL	He is taller than *I* (am). (*I* is the subject of the verb *am*, which must be supplied by the reader.)
INFORMAL	He is taller than *me*.
FORMAL	She is not as rich as *they* (are).
INFORMAL	She is not as rich as *them*.

41

(2) *The pronoun* who *used as subject of a verb is not affected by parenthetical expressions such as* I think *or* he says *intervening between the pronoun and its verb.*

He is a man *who* I think deserves praise. (*Who* is the subject of *deserves.*)

We invited only the people *who* he said were his friends. (*Who* is the subject of *were.*)

(3) *The nominative case is used when the pronoun is the subject of a clause which in its entirety functions as the object of a verb or preposition.*

I shall welcome *whoever* wants to attend. (*Whoever* is the subject of *wants.* The object of *welcome* is the entire clause *whoever wants to attend.*)

A reward is offered to *whoever* catches the escaped lion. (The entire clause is the object of the preposition *to.*)

4b. In formal English the nominative case of the personal pronoun is used after forms of the verb BE **such as** IS, ARE, WERE, HAVE BEEN.

The use of the objective case of the personal pronoun after these forms of *be,* however, has gained widespread acceptance. "It's me" is freely used by good speakers, and the prejudice against *us, him,* and *them* after *be* seems to be yielding to the strong tendency to use the objective form of the pronoun after a verb, regardless of what the verb may be.

FORMAL   It was *I.* I thought it was *he.* It was not *we.*
INFORMAL   It is *me.* I thought it was *him.* It was not *us.*

4c. In formal usage, when the infinitive TO BE **has no expressed subject, a pronoun following the infinitive is in the nominative case.**

Informal English commonly uses the objective case of the pronoun in this construction.

FORMAL   I would not want to be *he.* (The infinitive *to be* has no expressed subject.)
INFORMAL   I would not want to be *him.*

42

POSSESSIVE CASE

4d. The s-possessive (boy's, Paul's) is generally used with nouns denoting animate objects, but the possessive of nouns denoting inanimate objects is usually formed with an OF-phrase.

ANIMATE a man's hat; the ladies' coats; Jack's wife.

INANIMATE the floor of the house; the power of the machine; the point of the joke.

The s-possessive is commonly used in expressions which indicate time (*moment's notice, year's labor*) and in many familiar phrases (*heaven's sake, heart's content*). In some expressions the choice of possessive forms depends upon sound or rhythm, the s-possessive being more terse than the longer, more sonorous *of*-phrase (*morning's beauty, beauty of the morning*).

4e. In formal English a noun or pronoun preceding a gerund is usually in the possessive case.

In informal English, however, the objective rather than the possessive case is often found before a gerund.

FORMAL What was the excuse for *his* being late?

INFORMAL What was the excuse for *him* being late?

FORMAL He complained of *Roy's* keeping the money.

INFORMAL He complained of *Roy* keeping the money.

Even in formal English the objective case is frequently used with plural nouns.

The police prohibited *children* playing in the street.

The choice of case sometimes depends on the meaning which the writer intends.

Fancy *his* playing the violin. (The act of playing the violin is emphasized.)

Fancy *him* playing the violin. (The emphasis is on *him*. *Playing* is here used as a participle modifying *him*.)

And note the difference in the meaning of the following sentences:

I hate that *woman* riding a bicycle.

I hate that *woman's* riding a bicycle.

We must confess here, however, that the illustrations above are a little abstract. A person wishing to state his dislike for a *woman's riding a bicycle* would probably say *I hate the way that woman rides a bicycle.*

4f. WHICH **is generally used to refer to impersonal antecedents; but when the phrase** OF WHICH **would result in awkwardness,** WHOSE **may be substituted.**

We saw a house *whose* roof was falling in. (*Compare:* We saw a house the roof of which was falling in.)

This is the car *whose* steering wheel broke off when the driver was going seventy miles an hour. (*Compare:* This is the car the steering wheel of which broke off when the driver was going seventy miles an hour.)

OBJECTIVE CASE

4g. The object of a verb, verbal, or preposition is in the objective case.

OBJECT OF A VERB. I saw *him*. *Whom* did you see?

OBJECT OF A VERBAL. Visiting *them* was enjoyable. (*Them* is the object of the gerund *visiting*.) *Whom* does he want to marry? (*Whom* is the object of the infinitive *to marry*.)

OBJECT OF A PREPOSITION. Two of *us* policemen were wounded. With *whom* were you dancing?

Formal English usage observes the distinction between *who* and *whom*, as well as the grammatically correct case of pronouns following the conjunction *and*. In informal usage, the nominative form *who* is commonly found before the verb or preposition of which it is the object.

FORMAL   *Whom* are you discussing? (*Whom* is the object of *are discussing*.)

INFORMAL   *Who* are you discussing?

FORMAL   *Whom* are you looking for? (*Whom* is the object of the preposition *for*.)

INFORMAL   *Who* are you looking for?

The following sentences illustrate the use of the pronoun after the conjunction *and*.

> He found Tom and *me* at home. (Not "Tom and *I*." *Me* is an object of the verb *found*.)
>
> He must choose between you and *me*. (Not "between you and *I*." *Me* is an object of the preposition *between*.)
>
> She had dinner with *him* and *me*. (*Him* and *me* are objects of the preposition *with*.)

(1) *After the conjunctions* THAN *and* AS *a pronoun is in the objective case if it is used as the object of an elliptical clause* (see Section 50 for definition of *elliptical*).

> She needs him more than [she needs] *me*.
>
> I called him as well as [I called] *her*.

(2) *When the infinitive* TO BE *has an expressed subject, a pronoun following the infinitive is in the objective case.*

> He took him to be *me*.

EXERCISE 9. In the following sentences correct the errors in case in accordance with formal usage. Give the reasons for your corrections.

(1) The newspaper told about him finding the treasure.

(2) Jane was the kind of secretary who we wanted in the office.

(3) I knew it was her.

(4) Who do you think you are fooling?

(5) He has lived in Cleveland longer than me.

(6) I found Harry and she in the park.

(7) The barn's roof needs repairing.

(8) There was no reason for me staying any longer.

(9) He divided the money between Dick and I.

(10) I am the one who the committee selected.

(11) It was him who we wanted for questioning.

(12) We will consider whomever applies for the position.

(13) Let's you and I get married, Mabel.

(14) Whom do you think is the best candidate?

(15) Is it me you are looking for?

45

(16) The truant officer found Don as well as I.

(17) Whom shall I say called?

(18) I will box with whoever they choose as my opponent.

(19) She left without him saying goodbye to her.

(20) It wasn't them I was looking for.

(21) He asked Jay and I to help with the harvest.

(22) I wonder whom is being questioned by the detectives.

(23) Mrs. Kay was upset by Sue going to the dance.

(24) She blamed you as well as I.

(25) Lightning Boy is a horse of the speed of which I am well aware.

5. AGREEMENT = AGR

Agreement is a means of showing the exact grammatical relationship between a subject and verb, or a pronoun and its antecedent, or a demonstrative adjective and the word it modifies.

Since modern English nouns and verbs have few inflections, or special endings, agreement is usually not a difficult matter. However, there are some grammatical patterns, such as the agreement in number of a subject and verb, or a pronoun and its antecedent, which the writer must watch carefully.

AGREEMENT OF SUBJECT AND VERB

a. A verb agrees in number with its subject.

Sometimes a lack of agreement between subject and verb is merely the result of carelessness in composition or revision. But more often, writers use a singular subject with a plural verb or a plural subject with a singular verb, not because they misunderstand the general rule, but because they are uncertain of the number of the subject. This problem in agreement is most likely to arise when other words intervene between the subject and verb.

(1) *A noun or a parenthetical expression intervening between the subject and verb does not affect the number of the verb.*

> The first two *chapters* of the book *were* exciting. (The verb agrees with the subject, *chapters,* not with the nearest noun, *book.*)
> The *size* of the bears *startles* the spectators.

When a singular subject is followed by such expressions as *with, together with, accompanied by, as well as,* a singular verb should be used. The erroneous use of a plural verb is partly the result of a

47

conflict between form and meaning: the grammatical form of the subject is singular, but the added parenthetical expression suggests a plural meaning, as if the sentence had a compound subject. The following sentences illustrate this problem in agreement.

> FAULTY   The *coach,* as well as the players, *were* happy over the victory.
>
> REVISED   The *coach,* as well as the players, *was* happy over the victory.
>
> FAULTY   The horse *thief,* with his two accomplices, *have been hanged.*
>
> REVISED   The horse *thief,* with his two accomplices, *has been hanged.*

One way of testing such constructions is to bring the subject and verb together ("coach were"; "horse thief have"). Then the difficulty may be avoided by reconstructing the sentence.

> Both the coach and the players were happy over the victory.
>
> The horse thief and his two accomplices have been hanged.

(2) *Singular pronouns take singular verbs. The common singular pronouns are* each, everyone, everybody, anyone, anybody, anything, one, no one, nobody, someone, somebody.

> *Everyone is* ready to go.
>
> *Somebody is* calling from the attic.

Actually, the convention that a singular pronoun must take a singular verb is seldom violated, even by poor writers. No one says "Everyone are present," or, "Nobody win all the time." What does cause some difficulty is remembering to make a pronoun agree with a singular pronoun antecedent such as *anyone, everyone, nobody.* Formal usage prefers "Everyone took off his coat." But violations are common, and "Everyone took off their coats" is acceptable in informal usage. (See 5b [1].)

None, either, neither, any may be followed by either a singular or a plural verb, the choice depending on whether a singular or plural meaning is intended.

> SINGULAR   *None* but a fool *squanders* his time.
>
> PLURAL   *None* but fools *squander* their time.

48

(3) *Two or more subjects joined by* and *take a plural verb.*

A dog and a cat *are* seldom friends.

A singular verb is used when the two parts of a compound subject refer to the same person or thing.

My friend and benefactor *was* there to help me.

(4) *Two or more singular subjects joined by* or *or* nor *take a singular verb. If the subjects differ in number or person the verb agrees with the nearer one.*

Either the dean or his assistant *was* to have handled the matter.
Neither the farmer nor the chickens *were* aware of the swooping hawk.
Either you or he *has* to be here.

(5) *When the verb precedes the subject of the sentence, particular care is necessary to identify the subject and make it agree with the verb:*

There *are* only a chair and a table left to auction.
In the balcony there *are* many seats.

In informal English the verb is often singular when it is followed by a compound subject.

FORMAL   As a result, there *are* confusion, trouble, and uncertainty.

INFORMAL   As a result, there *is* confusion, trouble, and uncertainty.

(6) *Collective nouns take singular verbs when the group is considered as a unit, plural verbs when individual members of the group are considered separately.* (For definition of *collective*, see Section 50.)

The committee *is* meeting today.
The committee *are* unable to agree on a plan of action.

(7) *A verb agrees with its subject, not with a predicate noun.*

The best part of the program *is* the vocal duets.
Men *are* a necessity in her life.

(8) *A relative pronoun takes a singular verb when the antecedent
is singular, but a plural verb when the antecedent is plural.*

He is the only one of the councilmen who *is opposed* to the plan.
   (The antecedent of *who* is *one,* not *councilmen.*)
He is one of the best baseball players that *have come* from Texas.
   (The antecedent of the relative pronoun *that* is *players,* not *one.*)

Expressions like "one of the best baseball players that" commonly
take a singular verb in informal usage. Although the antecedent of
that is the plural noun *players,* the writer or speaker is influenced,
in his choice of a verb, by the fact that *one* is singular.

FORMAL   He is one of those people who *are* afraid to act.
INFORMAL   He is one of those people who *is* afraid to act.

EXERCISE 10. In the following sentences correct any errors in
agreement in accordance with formal usage. Then indicate those
sentences which would be acceptable in informal English.
 (1) The poor widow with her five children live in a small flat.
 (2) Either Johnny or his sister have the measles.
 (3) His only interest are his studies.
 (4) There is several ways of skinning a cat.
 (5) Each of the contestants claim the prize.
 (6) Fatima is one of the largest elephants that has ever been captured.
 (7) Does the victor and the vanquished share in the spoils?
 (8) This is the only one of all his plays that were successful on
      Broadway.
 (9) The coach and not the players suffer most in defeat.
(10) Ten miles are a long distance to walk.
(11) He is one of those fellows who is always whistling at the girls.
(12) A fool and his money is soon parted.
(13) The first two quarters of the game was evenly fought.
(14) Either the candidate or his advisers was wrong about public
      sentiment before the election.
(15) Is there any leaks in the roof?
(16) Twelve dollars are too much money for these shoes.

50

(17) Neither the loyalist nor the rebel leader were certain of popular support.

(18) Among my favorite plays are *Romeo and Juliet.*

(19) There is many good reasons for studying foreign languages.

(20) The Great Plague and not the Dutch Wars were the tragedy of England in 1665.

(21) The final two sets of the tennis match was bitterly fought.

(22) He is one of those candidates who is reluctant to take a stand on specific issues.

(23) Tabby, as well as her kittens, are suspicious of strange dogs.

(24) *Gulliver's Travels* are read by young and old.

(25) Her only company are three Siamese cats.

AGREEMENT OF PRONOUN AND ANTECEDENT

5b. A singular pronoun refers to a singular antecedent; a plural pronoun refers to a plural antecedent.

SINGULAR   The small *boy* put *his* penny in the collection box.

PLURAL   The *cows* lost *their* way in the storm.

Ambiguity in the use of pronouns is one of the commonest of all offenses against clarity. When the reference is exact, the meaning of the pronoun is clear. Skilled writers make sure that the form of the pronoun is appropriate to the antecedent. The following general rules are guides to be used in testing the reference of pronouns in formal writing:

(1) *In formal writing it is customary to use a singular pronoun to refer to antecedents such as* person, man, woman, one, any, anyone, anybody, someone, somebody, each, every, everyone, everybody, either, neither.

In informal English *any, every,* and their compounds, and *each, someone, somebody, either, neither* are often used with a plural pronoun, especially when a plural meaning is suggested.

FORMAL   *Everybody* held *his* breath.

INFORMAL   *Everybody* held *their* breath.

FORMAL   He asked *each* of us to bring *his* own lunch.

INFORMAL   He asked *each* of us to bring *our* own lunch.

(2) *A collective noun used as an antecedent takes a singular pronoun when the group is considered as a unit, but a plural pronoun when individual members of the group are considered separately.*

The *militia* increased *its* watchfulness.
The *band* raised *their* instruments at the conductor's signal.

(3) *Two or more singular antecedents joined by or or nor are referred to by a singular pronoun; if one of two such antecedents is singular and the other plural, the pronoun usually agrees with the nearer.*

Neither Jack nor Jim has finished *his* work.
Neither the father nor his sons were ready for *their* dinner.

EXERCISE 11. In the following sentences make every pronoun agree with its antecedent in accordance with formal English usage. Indicate any sentence that would be acceptable in familiar speech or informal writing.

(1) Somebody lost their temper in the argument.
(2) Nearly everybody has some worthless souvenirs which they would not willingly part with.
(3) Each of the Scouts took their turn at keeping up the campfire.
(4) Any customer may obtain a refund if they are dissatisfied with the hair restorer.
(5) The committee submitted their report.
(6) A person usually objects if they think their political beliefs are being attacked.
(7) Neither Bill nor Dick have brought their lunch.
(8) The longer a man lives, the wiser they become.
(9) Each of the witnesses gave their account of the accident.
(10) Neither of the recruits failed in their physical examinations.
(11) Anyone can attend the meeting if they don't heckle the speaker.
(12) Everybody is requested to bring their own food to the picnic.
(13) The school board disagreed in its opinions of the superintendent's policies.
(14) He can take almost any raw rookie and develop them into an expert player.

(15) Neither the farmer nor the hired man has finished their chores.

(16) A person should be willing to defend their principles.

(17) The student council fined two of their own members for being absent from meetings.

(18) If a physician or a lawyer would come to this town, they would make a good living.

(19) The Brown family is loyal to every one of their members.

(20) Every country is jealous of their rights.

AGREEMENT OF THE DEMONSTRATIVE ADJECTIVE AND ITS NOUN

5c. A demonstrative adjective (THIS, THAT, THESE, THOSE) **agrees in number with the noun it modifies.**

The demonstrative adjectives cause little difficulty except when combined with the singular nouns *kind* and *sort*. Since *kind* and *sort* are closely related to the noun which follows them, there is a strong tendency to make the demonstrative adjective agree in number with that noun. When a plural noun follows the demonstrative with *kind* or *sort*, such constructions as *these kind* or *those sort* are likely to occur, but standard usage requires exact agreement in number between the adjective and its noun.

STANDARD   *This kind* of strawberry tastes sweet.

SUBSTANDARD   *These kind* of strawberries taste sweet.

STANDARD   *This sort* of watch is expensive.

SUBSTANDARD   *These sort* of watches are expensive.

EXERCISE 12. In the following sentences correct every error of agreement in accordance with formal usage:

(1) The influence of journalism is evident in the writing of many American literary artists.

(2) The finance committee do not approve the club's policy of low annual dues.

(3) Cora is one of those kind of people who sacrifice their happiness for money.

(4) Miriam is the only one of the children who are opposed to selling the family home.

(5) On my car there is a windshield washer and fog lights.

(6) The courage of the rebellious peasants move their enemies to admiration.

(7) If one enters politics they must expect partisan criticism.

(8) Everybody likes to flatter themselves that their thoughts are original.

(9) The solution of the city's traffic problems are certain to require long study.

(10) Either the cook or the dinner guest have taken the silver spoons.

(11) Radios is a necessity in the modern home.

(12) Neither the pianist nor the vocalist were capable of moving the emotions of the audience.

(13) Poverty is one of the major forces that encourage crime.

(14) In maturity one forgets the romantic world of their childhood imagination.

(15) A chorus of jeers and cheers were heard from the theater gallery.

(16) The king with his small band of devoted followers have escaped the vengeful mob.

(17) The patrol encountered heavy fire and lost two of their men.

(18) These sort of planes can exceed the speed of sound.

(19) Either lime or commercial fertilizer are useful for fall treatment of lawns.

(20) He is one of the finest orators that has come from the South.

6. TENSE AND MOOD = T

Tense is a grammatical property indicating the time of the action expressed by the verb; *mood* is the manner in which the action of the verb is conceived.

TENSE

PRESENT TENSE (*expressing present or habitual action*). He *is talking* to the gun club now. He *talks* to the gun club at least once every year.

PAST TENSE (*expressing past action distinct from the present*). He *talked* to the gun club yesterday.

FUTURE TENSE (*expressing action yet to come*). He *will talk* to the gun club tomorrow.

PRESENT PERFECT TENSE (*expressing past action extending to the present*). He *has talked* to the gun club every day.

PAST PERFECT TENSE (*expressing a past action completed before some other past action*). This morning I saw the speaker who *had talked* to the gun club last month.

FUTURE PERFECT TENSE (*expressing action which will be completed before some future time*). He *will have talked* to the gun club before next Thursday.

English has few verb endings. Except for the present tense (he *talks*) and the past tense (he *talked*), most English verbs show distinctions of time by means of verb phrases formed with auxiliary or helping verbs (he *is talking*, he *has been talking*, he *has talked*, etc.). All six tenses are formed from the three principal parts of the verbs: the present infinitive (*to talk*), the past (*talked*), and the past participle (*talked*). In most English verbs the past and past participial forms are indicated by the addition of -*ed*: *smoked, hammered, played, worked*. Such "regular" verbs are sometimes called "weak" verbs. Other English verbs indicate their past and past participial forms by more individualistic changes, frequently a vowel change within the word: *grow, grew, grown; swim, swam, swum.* Such irregularly formed verbs are sometimes called "strong" verbs.

A few verbs have only one form for all three principal parts (*burst, cost, split*). These verbs frequently indicate time by an auxiliary verb (I *did split* the wood) or by a modifying word or phrase (I *split* the wood *yesterday*).

In the following conjugation of the verb *to choose,* it will be observed that in the active voice the present and future tenses are based on the present infinitive (*to choose*), and the perfect tenses on the past participle (*chosen*).

INDICATIVE MOOD, ACTIVE VOICE

Present Tense

I choose	we choose
you choose	you choose
he, she, it chooses	they choose

Past Tense

I chose	we chose
you chose	you chose
he, she, it chose	they chose

Future Tense

I shall * choose	we shall choose
you will choose	you will choose
he, she, it will choose	they will choose

Present Perfect Tense

I have chosen	we have chosen
you have chosen	you have chosen
he, she, it has chosen	they have chosen

* In spite of the efforts of many teachers to perpetuate it, the distinction between *shall* and *will* is largely ignored by Americans. There is undoubtedly some loss in precision, but in general the situation need not be lamented. In all *future* tenses *will* may be substituted for *shall* in the first person singular and plural.

Past Perfect Tense

I had chosen   we had chosen
you had chosen   you had chosen
he, she, it had chosen   they had chosen

Future Perfect Tense

I shall have chosen   we shall have chosen
you will have chosen   you will have chosen
he, she, it will have chosen   they will have chosen

INDICATIVE MOOD, PASSIVE VOICE

Present Tense

I am chosen   we are chosen
you are chosen   you are chosen
he, she, it is chosen   they are chosen

Past Tense

I was chosen   we were chosen
you were chosen   you were chosen
he, she, it was chosen   they were chosen

Future Tense

I shall be chosen   we shall be chosen
you will be chosen   you will be chosen
he, she, it will be chosen   they will be chosen

Present Perfect Tense

I have been chosen   we have been chosen
you have been chosen   you have been chosen
he, she, it has been chosen   they have been chosen

Past Perfect Tense

I had been chosen   we had been chosen
you had been chosen   you had been chosen
he, she, it had been chosen   they had been chosen

Future Perfect Tense

I shall have been chosen   we shall have been chosen
you will have been chosen   you will have been chosen
he, she, it will have been chosen   they will have been chosen

SUBJUNCTIVE MOOD, ACTIVE VOICE

Present Tense

if I choose	if we choose
if you choose	if you choose
if he, she, it choose	if they choose

Past Tense

if I chose, etc.	if we chose, etc.

Present Perfect Tense

if I have chosen, etc.	if we have chosen, etc.

Past Perfect Tense

if I had chosen, etc.	if we had chosen, etc.

SUBJUNCTIVE MOOD, PASSIVE VOICE

Present Tense

if I be chosen	if we be chosen
if you be chosen	if you be chosen
if he, she, it be chosen	if they be chosen

Past Tense

if I were chosen, etc.	if we were chosen, etc.

Present Perfect Tense

if I have been chosen, etc.	if we have been chosen, etc.

Past Perfect Tense

if I had been chosen, etc.	if we have been chosen, etc.

IMPERATIVE MOOD

Present Tense

ACTIVE VOICE	PASSIVE VOICE
choose	be chosen

INFINITIVES

Present Tense

to choose	to be chosen

58

Present Perfect Tense

to have chosen   to have been chosen

PARTICIPLES

Present Tense

ACTIVE VOICE   PASSIVE VOICE
choosing   being chosen

Past Tense

chosen*   been chosen

Present Perfect Tense

having chosen   having been chosen

GERUNDS

Present Tense

choosing   being chosen

Present Perfect Tense

having chosen   having been chosen

PROGRESSIVE FORMS, INDICATIVE MOOD

Present Tense

I am choosing, etc.   I am being chosen, etc.

Past Tense

I was choosing, etc.   I was being chosen, etc.

PROGRESSIVE FORMS, SUBJUNCTIVE MOOD

Present Tense

if I be choosing, etc.

* The active form of the past tense is frequently substituted, as a measure of economy, for the longer passive. In the sentence *Chosen as prom queen, Margaret was very proud,* the sense of the passive (*Having been chosen*) is not violated.

Past Tense

if I were choosing, etc.

EMPHATIC FORMS

Present Tense

I do choose, etc.

Past Tense

I did choose, etc.

6a. **The tense of a verb in a subordinate clause should relate logically to that of a verb in the main clause.**

ILLOGICAL   As the day *ends,* a few stars *appeared* in the sky.

LOGICAL   As the day *ends,* a few stars *appear* in the sky.

LOGICAL   As the day *ended,* a few stars *appeared* in the sky.

ILLOGICAL   If he *tried,* he could *have avoided* the accident.

LOGICAL   If he *had tried,* he *could have avoided* the accident.

ILLOGICAL   If he *had eaten,* he *had felt* better.

LOGICAL   If he *had eaten,* he *would have felt* better.

LOGICAL   If he *had eaten,* he *would feel* better.

6b. **A present infinitive is regularly used after a verb in a perfect tense. A perfect infinitive may sometimes be used after a verb not in a perfect tense.**

ILLOGICAL   I would have liked *to have gone.*

LOGICAL   I would have liked *to go.* (At the time indicated by the verb, I desired *to go,* not *to have gone.*)

LOGICAL   I would like *to have gone.*

ILLOGICAL   I hoped *to have visited* you.

LOGICAL   I had hoped *to visit* you.

6c. **The present tense is ordinarily used in statements that are generally true or have no reference to time.**

Brevity *is* the soul of wit.

Corn *grows* rapidly in warm, humid weather.

BUT

"Men *were* deceivers ever."

60

6d. The principal parts of verbs similar in meaning or spelling should be carefully distinguished.

The writer who is in doubt about the principal parts of a particular verb should consult the dictionary, which gives the present infinitive (*begin*), the past tense (*began*), and the past participle (*begun*) of irregular verbs. Only the present infinitive is given for regular verbs, which form the past tense and past participle by adding -*d* or -*ed* (*live, lived, lived*).

Especially troublesome are the verbs *lie, lay* and *sit, set,* the correct use of which has become a social necessity among educated people. The principal parts of *lie* (meaning *to recline*) are *lie, lay, lain;* the principal parts of *lay* (meaning *to place*) are *lay, laid, laid.* Much of the trouble, of course, results from confusing the past tense of *lie* (*i.e., lay*) with the present tense of *lay.* And quite frequently, the nonexistent form *layed* is made up to serve as the past tense of *lay.*

LIE

Correct	(present)	*Lie* down for a while and you will feel better.
Correct	(past)	The cat *lay* in the shade and watched the dog carefully.
Correct	(present participle)	His keys *were lying* on the table where he dropped them.
Correct	(past participle)	After he *had lain* down for a while, he felt better.

LAY

Correct	(present)	*Lay* the book on the table and come here.
Correct	(past)	He *laid* the book on the table and walked out the door.
Correct	(present participle)	*Laying* the book on the table, he walked out the door.
Correct	(past participle)	*Having laid* the book on the table, he walked out the door.

The principal parts of *sit* (meaning *to occupy a seat*) are *sit, sat, sat;* the principal parts of *set* (meaning *to put in place*) are *set, set, set.*

SIT

Correct	(present)	*Sit* down and keep quiet.
Correct	(past)	The little girl *sat* in the corner for half an hour.
Correct	(present participle)	*Sitting* down quickly, he failed to see the tack in the chair.
Correct	(past participle)	*Having sat* in the corner for an hour, the child was subdued and reasonable.

SET

Correct	(present)	*Set* the basket on the table and get out.
Correct	(past)	Yesterday he *set* the grocery cartons on the kitchen table; today he left them on the porch.
Correct	(present participle)	*Setting* his spectacles on the table, he challenged John to wrestle.
Correct	(past participle)	*Having set* the basket of turnips on the porch, Terry went to play the piano.

The principal parts of some difficult verbs are listed below. Learn to use these verbs correctly; add to the list any verbs that you have used incorrectly in your writing.

PRESENT INFINITIVE	PAST TENSE	PAST PARTICIPLE
begin	began	begun
bid (*offer*)	bid	bid
bid (*command*)	bade	bidden
bite	bit	bit, bitten
blow	blew	blown
break	broke	broken
bring	brought	brought
burst	burst	burst
catch	caught	caught
choose	chose	chosen
come	came	come
dive	dived, dove	dived
do	did	done

PRESENT INFINITIVE	PAST TENSE	PAST PARTICIPLE
drag	dragged	dragged
draw	drew	drawn
drink	drank	drunk
drive	drove	driven
eat	ate	eaten
fall	fell	fallen
fly	flew	flown
forget	forgot	forgot, forgotten
freeze	froze	frozen
get	got	got, gotten
give	gave	given
go	went	gone
grow	grew	grown
hang (*suspend*)	hung	hung
hang (*execute*)	hanged	hanged
know	knew	known
lead	led	led
lend	lent	lent
lie (*speak falsely*)	lied	lied
lose	lost	lost
pay	paid	paid
prove	proved	proved, proven
raise	raised	raised
ride	rode	ridden
ring	rang, rung	rung
rise	rose	risen
run	ran	run
see	saw	seen
shake	shook	shaken
shrink	shrank	shrunk
sing	sang, sung	sung
sink	sank, sunk	sunk
speak	spoke	spoken
spring	sprang	sprung
steal	stole	stolen
swim	swam	swum
swing	swung	swung
take	took	taken
tear	tore	torn
throw	threw	thrown

PRESENT INFINITIVE	PAST TENSE	PAST PARTICIPLE
wear	wore	worn
weave	wove	woven
wring	wrung	wrung
write	wrote	written

Beginning writers must be especially careful not to substitute substandard verb parts for standard, as *he seen* for the correct *he saw* or he *had eat* for the correct he *had eaten*. Such substitution is looked upon as an illiteracy.

EXERCISE 13. Correct the verb forms in the following sentences:

(1) The housing project was began in the early spring.

(2) Before the sun had rose over the hills, Cactus Pete had rode all the way to Cactus Gap.

(3) The new dress shrunk when it was washed.

(4) He sprung from his seat; a spider had bit him.

(5) The defendant denied that he had stole the horse.

(6) Mabel run to the gate and welcomed her sister.

(7) Snow laid on the barn roof all winter.

(8) On her first trip across the lake, the *Morning Mist* has broke the speed record.

(9) The Harrisons use to live in Vermont.

(10) I remember the day she bid me farewell.

(11) I should have liked to have seen the flying saucer.

(12) Soon after the fire started, dozens of rats come rushing out of the barn.

(13) I hoped to have bought a new car in Detroit.

(14) Gertrude Ederle, who swum the English Channel, become one of the great female athletes of her time.

(15) She has wore that same old hat for three years.

MOOD

The term *mood* is used to describe three forms of the verb and their distinctive changes in meaning and manner of action. The three moods are the *indicative,* expressing a statement of fact; the *imperative,* expressing a command or entreaty; and the *subjunctive,* expressing doubt, condition, wish, or probability. The distinctions in meaning between the indicative and subjunctive moods are often slight, the choice of mood depending on the speaker's feelings toward the statement he is making. The subjunctive expresses shades of feeling and meaning which are not expressed by the more direct indicative.

Use of the subjunctive is confined chiefly to formal English. In constructions where formal English prefers the subjunctive, informal English often uses the indicative. The few distinctive forms of the subjunctive retained in modern English include the present tense, except for the second person singular and plural, of the verb *to be* (If I be, If he be); the past tense singular, except for the second person, of *to be* (If I were, If he were); and the third person singular of all verbs (I desire that he *give* a report).

6e. The subjunctive mood is retained in some formal idioms.

> *Suffice it to say* that I am disappointed. (*Suffices* would be the indicative verb form.)
>
> I shall help him *if need be*. (*Is* would be the indicative verb form.)

Such idioms have survived from earlier times, when the subjunctive was more common in English.

6f. In formal English the subjunctive is used in conditions contrary to fact, in expressions of doubt, and in regrets or wishes.

FORMAL	If I *were* tired, I would go home.
INFORMAL	If I *was* tired, I would go home.
FORMAL	The elm tree looks as if it *were* dying.
INFORMAL	The elm tree looks as if it *was* dying.
FORMAL	If this man *be* guilty, society will condemn him.
INFORMAL	If this man *is* guilty, society will condemn him.
FORMAL	I wish that I *were* taller.
INFORMAL	I wish that I *was* taller.

6g. The subjunctive is used in THAT clauses for formal demands, resolutions, or motions.

I demand that he *resign* his position.

Resolved, that Mr. Smith *investigate* our financial condition.

I move that the meeting *be* adjourned.

EXERCISE 14. In the following sentences make any necessary changes in accordance with formal English usage. Indicate those sentences which would be acceptable in informal English.

(1) The track was carefully drug in preparation for the horse races.

(2) Bill's books were laying on the table.

(3) Our guide lead us into a dense forest.

(4) He could have made the team if he would have practiced regularly.

(5) If I was a farmer I would raise dairy cattle.

(6) I would have liked to have gone to the movies.

(7) The swimmer dove into the pool.

(8) When the play ended, the audience applaud enthusiastically.

(9) He wishes that she was a rich widow.

(10) They haven't spoke to each other for years.

(11) If you are tired, come in and set a while.

(12) The boys seen a flying squirrel.

(13) He looks as if he was unhappy.

(14) The thirsty children drunk a whole gallon of water.

(15) The clown was so funny that we nearly bursted with laughter.

(16) After striking the rocks the freighter sunk almost immediately.

(17) At the first sound I raised from my pillow.

(18) The birds sung all day in the apple tree.

(19) Early in life he seen the folly of his ways.

(20) Never before had the bishop spoke to such a multitude.

GRAMMAR REVIEW EXERCISE. Correct the grammatical errors in the following sentences according to formal usage:

(1) The challenger seen at once that the champion was a harder puncher than him.

(2) The Turkish battalion were real eager to fight the Chinese invaders of Korea.

(3) The second and third movements of Mozart's symphony was beautifully played.

(4) Now that September is here I wish that summer was only beginning.

(5) It was them and not us who forgot the dinner engagement.

(6) The lieutenant ordered Willis and I to report for guard duty.

(7) Everybody withheld their applause until the end of the announcement.

(8) He was sure delighted to learn that the damaged car would still run good.

(9) There is only one engine and two freight cars left on the branch line.

(10) The residents forbade foreigners living in the new subdivision.

(11) There is seldom a good reason for you being absent from class.

(12) The northern states will be grateful to whomever discovers a way to save the deer herds from winter starvation.

(13) This information is a secret between you and I.

(14) Before the banquet began, the toastmaster asked each of us to introduce ourselves and our wives.

(15) The climax of the tragedy are the noble deaths of the hero and heroine.

(16) He did not say that it was me who he wanted to see.

(17) At the request of the governor the legislature are meeting in a special session.

(18) Most of us are annoyed by those kind of people who we know are always trying to get something for nothing.

(19) My home town is deader than it use to be.

(20) Fred is one of the few Americans who has been awarded the European scholarship.

(21) In a good phonograph assembly there is a wide-range amplifier and a large speaker.

(22) After the play ended, the cast appears for curtain calls.

(23) Sheriff Hayes felt badly because he was compelled to arrest a neighbor whom he knew had never stole before.

(24) The sailors sprung to the ship's side, drug up the anchor, and fastened it to the cathead.

(25) The ambassador, as well as his staff, were embarrassed by the incident.

(26) Charley is one of those players who is always complaining to the umpire.

(27) That snake looks as if he was getting ready to strike.

(28) In the darkness the police took him to be I.

(29) Billy Budd was hung from the main yard, in full view of the ship's company.

(30) Either sapphire or osmium are used to make the ordinary phonograph stylus.

(31) Do you really think that you are wiser than me?

(32) The lifeguard run quick to the pool, dove into the water, and swum toward the screaming girl.

(33) My friends, there is war, pestilence, and famine in the world.

(34) When the lights went out everybody held on to their wallets.

(35) These kind of errors often appear in student themes.

(36) I would not have hesitated to have called his bluff.

(37) Neither of the hockey teams have improved their defensive play.

(38) The United Nations protested about China mistreating war prisoners.

(39) The television audience were sure pleased with the new variety program.

(40) Whom do you think suffers most in periods of currency inflation?

7. DIAGRAMING

Diagraming is a means of picturing the relationship between parts of the sentence. A conventional method of diagraming is illustrated below.

7a. Subject and verb.

The *subject and verb* are placed on a horizontal line and separated by a vertical line.

Flowers bloom.   Flowers | bloom

He has been sleeping.   He | has been sleeping

Questions are diagramed in the same manner as declarative sentences.

Are you listening?   You | are listening?

Compound subjects or predicates are placed on parallel horizontal lines.

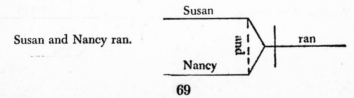

Susan and Nancy ran.

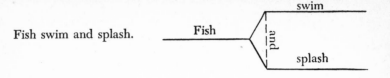

Fish swim and splash.

EXERCISE 15. Diagram the following sentences:
(1) Dogs bark.
(2) John has been swimming.
(3) Is she singing?
(4) Dogs and cats fight.
(5) Girls chatter and giggle.
(6) Are you going?
(7) Owls hoot.
(8) Has she been shopping?
(9) Airplanes climb and dive.
(10) Revenues and taxes rise.

7b. Complements.

The *direct object* is separated from the verb by a vertical line above the horizontal line.

Ellen loves children.

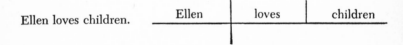

The *indirect object,* which is usually the implied object of the preposition *to,* is placed on a horizontal line under the verb.

We gave him money.

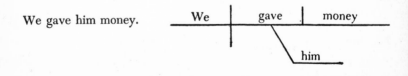

Give men liberty. (Observe the understood subject *you*.)

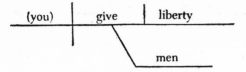

The *predicate noun,* or *predicate adjective,* is preceded by a diagonal line sloping toward the subject.

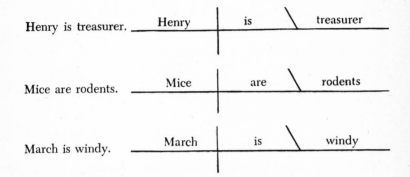

EXERCISE 16. Diagram the following sentences:

(1) Goats eat cans.
(2) We gave them food.
(3) Bring me water.
(4) George is shy.
(5) Mike is captain.
(6) Business is good.
(7) Religion offered them peace.
(8) Whales are mammals.
(9) China attacked Korea.
(10) Autumn is invigorating.

7c. Modifiers.

Adjectives (except predicate adjectives) and *adverbs* are joined by diagonal lines to the words they modify.

71

The white rooster crowed proudly.

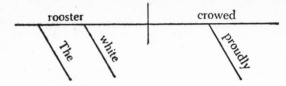

The light blue airplane disappeared very quickly.

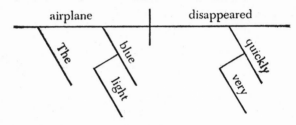

EXERCISE 17. Diagram the following sentences:

(1) The farmer bought a fine Jersey cow.
(2) The dignified professor reprimanded the student **severely**.
(3) The little girl closed the gate tightly.
(4) Our new automobile arrived yesterday.
(5) The old mare and her colt suddenly jumped the pasture fence.
(6) Many students attended the rally.
(7) A rolling stone gathers no moss.
(8) The falling leaves gradually covered the grass.
(9) The painter carefully sketched the landscape.
(10) The tenants and their guests luckily escaped the fire.

7d. Verbals.

A *participle* is placed under the word it modifies, as follows:
Laughing children are playing tag.

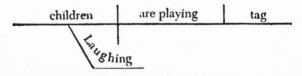

A *gerund* is placed on lines joined as follows:

72

Walking is fun.

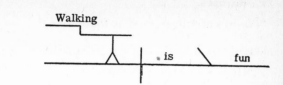

The *infinitive used as a noun* is placed above the main line of the sentence.

She wanted *to sing*.

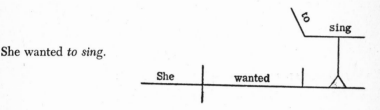

(In this sentence, *to sing* is the direct object.)

The *infinitive used as a modifier* is joined to the word it modifies.

We are ready *to go*.

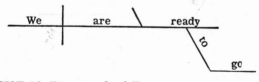

EXERCISE 18. Diagram the following sentences:

(1) Falling leaves covered the ground.

(2) Swimming is good exercise.

(3) The little child wanted to run and play.

(4) He is willing to help.

(5) Knitting requires patience.

(6) Wandering minstrels entertained the court.

(7) The witness refused to talk.

(8) Our visitors were content to stay.

(9) Harvesting is hard work.

(10) To work and succeed were his ambitions.

73

7e. Phrases.

Phrases are diagramed as follows:

PREPOSITIONAL PHRASE USED AS AN ADJECTIVE:

He is the owner *of the store.*

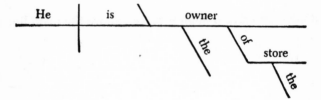

PREPOSITIONAL PHRASE USED AS AN ADVERB:

The cow jumped *over the moon.*

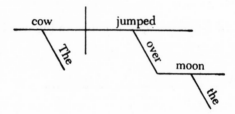

PARTICIPIAL PHRASE:

Having made his fortune, he retired.

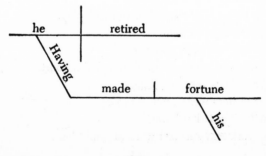

74

GERUND PHRASE:

Breaking a forest trail is strenuous work.

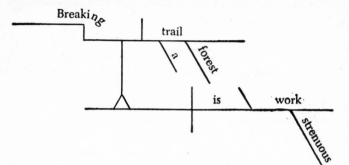

INFINITIVE PHRASE:

Kate is learning *to drive an automobile.*

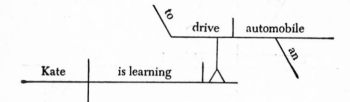

To walk under a ladder requires courage.

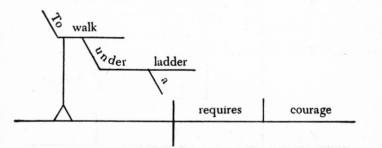

EXERCISE 19. Diagram the following sentences:

(1) Swimming the English Channel is a difficult feat.

(2) Lillian wanted to catch a large bass.

(3) He is the leader of the rebel army.

75

    (4) Dave led Marguerite out of the woods.

    (5) Having eaten a large dinner, Jim retired to the veranda.

    (6) Observing traffic rules is every motorist's responsibility.

    (7) The angry hornets stung him on the face.

    (8) Having discovered a clue, Holmes easily solved the crime.

    (9) Manasseh Cutler was the founder of the Ohio settlement.

  (10) To refinish old furniture demands much painstaking labor.

7f. Clauses.

Two or more *main clauses* in a compound sentence are diagramed separately, and the diagrams joined as follows:

The speaker finished his address; the crowd cheered wildly.

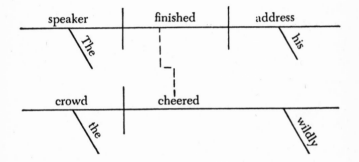

Hawkeye was pursued by Indians, but they did not catch him.

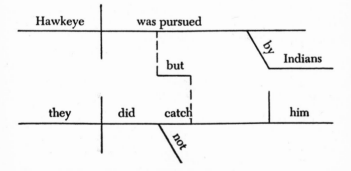

Subordinate clauses are diagramed as follows:

76

NOUN CLAUSE:

His weakness was *that he had no ambition.*

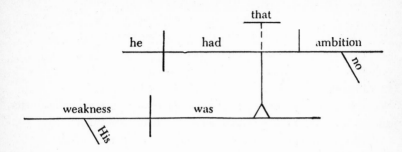

ADJECTIVE CLAUSE:

The girl *who won the contest* is a college freshman.

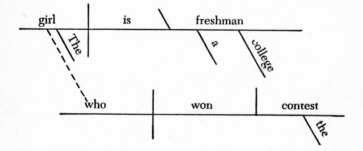

ADVERB CLAUSE:

We will meet him *when the train arrives.*

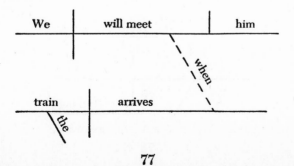

EXERCISE 20. Diagram the following sentences:

(1) Our main problem was that we had no money.

(2) They are refugees who escaped from oppression.

(3) When we arrived, the fire was blazing fiercely.

(4) This is the new tractor that my neighbor bought.

(5) The old gentleman insisted that I take the reward.

(6) The land was fertile, but floods ruined the crops.

(7) Her promise was that she would read his poems.

(8) The man who repaired the shoes could speak many languages.

(9) We were eating lunch when the telephone rang.

(10) My advice is that you consult a psychiatrist.

7g. Independent elements.

Absolute phrases, expletives, interjections, words of direct address, and other dependent elements* are diagramed separately above the rest of the sentence.

Generally speaking, he is a good student.

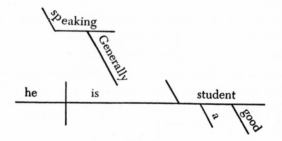

There is a proper time for everything.

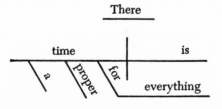

* See Section 50.

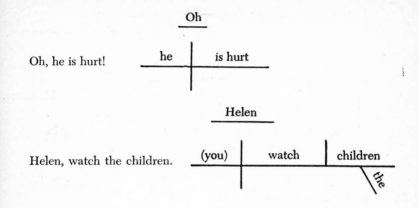

Oh, he is hurt!

Helen, watch the children.

EXERCISE 21. Diagram the following sentences:

(1) There was once a very wise old man.
(2) Listen, gentlemen, to my story.
(3) Help! I am drowning.
(4) Considering everything, you have achieved much.
(5) Well, the team has finally won a game.
(6) There is a small elephant in the garden.
(7) I know, fellow Americans, that you will give generously.
(8) Hey! Bring back my fountain pen.
(9) Your recovery, we hope, will be rapid.
(10) Oh, you are surely wrong.

EXERCISE 22. Diagram the following sentences:

(1) Having completed our chemical experiment, we studied the results.
(2) Following the old Indian trail, we found a good camping site.
(3) I know, friends, that you question my intentions.
(4) Benson is the president of the insurance company.
(5) Dying fish struggled in the polluted water.
(6) Help! My hands are slipping off the window ledge.
(7) The tattered beggar asked for a dime.

79

(8) The old chief's argument was that Manhattan really belonged to the Indians.

(9) After they leave the assembly line the new cars are thoroughly tested.

(10) I am tempted to buy a new gazetteer.

(11) We visited the house where Lincoln lived.

(12) His secret ambition was to find Captain Kidd's buried treasure.

(13) The neighbors stubbornly refused to sign his petition.

(14) After reading the telegram she collapsed in her chair.

(15) To filibuster is an old political stratagem.

(16) Who is the spokesman for the rioting prisoners?

(17) The marines were ready when the enemy forces attacked.

(18) We lit the fuse and waited for the explosion.

(19) Wendell Phillips was a famous lecturer during the Civil War years.

(20) The carpenter put a new blade on his power saw.

Manuscript Mechanics = MS

IT WAS VERY PLEASANT TO ME TO GET A LETTER FROM
YOU THE OTHER DAY. PERHAPS I SHOULD HAVE FOUND
IT PLEASANTER IF I HAD BEEN ABLE TO DECIPHER IT.
                              —THOMAS BAILEY ALDRICH

8. THE MANUSCRIPT = MS

Manuscripts should be carefully prepared, legibly written, and neatly arranged. They should be thoroughly proofread before they are submitted. After they are returned, they should be corrected according to the instructor's suggestions.

8a. Suitable materials should be used for manuscripts.

(1) *Paper.* Instructors usually require the use of standard theme paper (8½ by 11 inches). If the manuscript is handwritten, the lines on the paper should be far enough apart to allow space for corrections. Some instructors prefer that students write on every other line. If the manuscript is typewritten, regular unlined typewriter paper or the unruled side of theme paper should be used.

(2) *Pen and ink.* Manuscripts should be written on the ruled side of the paper with a good pen and with black or blue-black ink.

(3) *Typewriter.* A fresh, black ribbon should be used for typewritten manuscripts, and the type should be clean.

8b. Manuscripts should be written legibly.

(1) *Handwritten manuscripts.* Adequate spacing between words in a sentence and between lines adds to legibility. Words should be written as units, without unnecessary breaks between letters and syllables. Letters should be distinctly formed, with clear and conspicuous capitals. Neatness requires that *t*'s be crossed and that *i*'s be dotted with real dots, not with decorative circles. Artistic flourishes should be avoided, as they detract from readability and antagonize the reader. Excessively large and spreading, as well as small and cramped, script should be avoided, as should script which leans excessively to the right or left.

(2) *Typewritten manuscripts.* Lines should be double-spaced to provide room for both the writer's and the instructor's corrections. It is customary to leave one space between words and two spaces between sentences in a paragraph.

8c. Manuscripts should be physically uniform and orderly.

(1) *Margins.* Uniform one-inch margins should be kept on each page on both right and left sides. It is important not to crowd words at the right and bottom of the page.

(2) *Title.* The title should be centered about two inches from the top of the page, or on the first line. A blank line is left between the title and the first paragraph of the manuscript. The first word and all other words in the title except the articles *a, an, the,* and short prepositions or conjunctions are capitalized. Titles should not be underlined or quoted, unless the title is an actual quotation. Punctuation is not used after titles except when a question mark or exclamation point is required by the meaning of the title. The title need not be repeated after the first page.

(3) *Indenting.* The first line of a paragraph should be indented about an inch, or five spaces if the manuscript is typewritten. Quoted lines of poetry should be indented one inch from the regular margin, or centered on the page, and single-spaced when typewritten.

(4) *Paging.* All pages after the first should be numbered in the upper right-hand corner with Arabic numerals (2, 3, 4, etc.).

(5) *Endorsement.* An endorsement usually gives the name of the student, the course number, the date, and other information required by a particular instructor.

8d. Manuscripts should be carefully proofread before they are submitted.

Before a manuscript is handed in, the writer should give it a close reading. It is best to allow a cooling-off period between actual composition and proofreading. A writer usually knows his own weaknesses; if he is poor in spelling and punctuation, he should give his paper a separate reading for each kind of error. When errors are numerous, the composition should be rewritten. When rewriting is not necessary, specific changes should be made as follows:

(1) If words are to be deleted, the writer should draw a horizontal line through them. Parentheses should not be used to cancel words.

(2) If the writer wishes to begin a new paragraph with a sentence which is written as part of another paragraph, he should put the sign ¶ or *Par.* before the sentence which is to begin the new paragraph. When a paragraph division is to be removed, he should write *No* ¶ or *No Par.* in the margin.

(3) If brief additions are to be inserted in a sentence, the new material should be written above the line and the point of insertion indicated by a caret ($\wedge$) placed below the line.

Individual instructors may have additional suggestions.

8e. After a manuscript has been marked by an instructor it should be corrected by the student and resubmitted.

Correction of one's own errors is invaluable practice. The instructor designates errors by numbers or symbols which refer to specific parts of the handbook. The writer should study these sections of the handbook carefully before making his revisions.

On the following page is shown a paragraph from a composition, with the instructor's markings, before and after correction. (For a more detailed example, see Specimen Papers A and B, at the front of the book.)

The only equipment of a "bug" operator is a
small manual telegraph key connected to a panel of
sockets. In appearance the instrument resembles a
<u>miniture</u> stapler, which office workers use to fasten   *35c ord sp*
sheets of paper. Each time the handle of the "bug"
descends electrical currents contact and send an   *38a ⌃/*
impulse through the panel and out into the
atmosphere Series of impulses, or dots and dashes
in varied combinations, <u>stands</u> for letters in the   *5a agr*
International Morse Code. The receiving operator
picks up the message, perhaps half a world away,
and <u>translating</u> it into the language of his   *2a frag*
country.

MARKED BY THE INSTRUCTOR

The only equipment of a "bug" operator is a
small manual telegraph key connected to a panel of
sockets. In appearance the instrument resembles a
miniature ~~miniture~~ stapler, which office workers use to fasten   *35c ord sp*
sheets of paper. Each time the handle of the "bug"
descends electrical currents contact and send an   *38a ⌃/*
impulse through the panel and out into the
atmosphere. Series of impulses, or dots and dashes
in varied combinations, *stand* ~~stands~~ for letters in the   *5a agr*
International Morse Code. The receiving operator
picks up the message, perhaps half a world away,
and *translates* ~~translating~~ it into the language of his   *2a frag*
country.

CORRECTED BY THE WRITER

84

9. NUMBERS = NOS

9a. Numbers or amounts that can be expressed in two or three words should ordinarily be spelled out.

He spent two hundred dollars for a camera.

The boy saved $4.53.

Miriam is twenty-two years old.

On their vacation they drove 2,468 miles.

9b. Figures should ordinarily be used for dates.

The letters *st, nd, rd, th* are not necessary after days of the month.

May 4, 1913; July 2 (or *second,* if the year is not given)

The year is written out only in formal social correspondence.

9c. Figures should be used for street numbers, decimals and percentages, chapter and page numbers, and hours given with A.M. **or** P.M.

13 Milford Avenue; 57 121st Street.

The bolt is .46 inches in diameter.

The price was reduced 15 per cent.

The quotation was in chapter 4, page 119.

A train arrived from Chicago at 11:20 A.M.

9d. A number that is spelled out should not be repeated in parentheses except in legal or commercial writing, or unless extreme accuracy is required.

COMMERCIAL   The interest on the note was fifty (50) dollars.

UNNECESSARY   The boys caught three (3) fish.

REVISED   The boys caught three fish.

9e. Numbers at the beginning of a sentence should ordinarily be spelled out.

AWKWARD   17 horses were lost in the fire.

REVISED   Seventeen horses were lost in the fire.

Very often a sentence can be recast to eliminate the figure at the beginning.

AWKWARD   655 entries were received in the puzzle contest.

REVISED   In the puzzle contest 655 entries were received.

EXERCISE 1. In the following sentences make any necessary corrections in the use of numbers:

(1) Franklin died at the age of 84.

(2) She retired on January 1st, 1948.

(3) 130 families were made homeless by the flood.

(4) My profit on the investment was ten per cent.

(5) The economics class met at one P.M.

(6) My vacation lasted fourteen (14) days.

(7) The lump of gold was three and thirteen hundredths inches in circumference.

(8) He employed 300 men in his factory.

(9) The child spent $.05 for candy.

(10) Helen attended college for 2 years.

(11) Samuel Johnson was born in the year seventeen nine.

(12) 25,000 people listened to the general's address.

(13) The jangle of a telephone roused me at three A.M.

(14) Our community is sponsoring a celebration on July 4th.

(15) Big Harry was sentenced to 25 years in the penitentiary.

10. ABBREVIATIONS = AB

In general, only established, conventional abbreviations should be used.

10a. The following abbreviations are appropriate in formal and informal writing.

(1) *Titles before proper names.* Such abbreviations as *Mr., Mrs., Dr.,* are used when the surname is given: *Dr. Hart* or *Dr. J. D. Hart;* but not *the Dr.* *St.* (Saint) is used with a Christian name, as in *St. James, St. John.* Informal writing uses abbreviations such as *Hon., Rev., Prof., Sen.,* before names, but only when both the surname and given name or initials are given: *Hon. O. P. Jones;* but not *Hon. Jones.* In formal usage these titles are spelled out.

INAPPROPRIATE	He has gone to consult the Dr.
REVISED	He has gone to consult Dr. Hart (*or* the doctor).
FORMAL	The Reverend W. C. Case delivered the sermon.
INFORMAL	Rev. W. C. Case delivered the sermon.

(2) *Titles after proper names.* The following abbreviations are used only when a name is given: Jr., Sr., Esq., M.C., D.D., LL.D., Ph.D.

(3) *Abbreviations used with dates or numerals.* Some abbreviations should be used only when specific dates and numerals are given: 42 B.C., 818 A.D., 8:30 A.M., 11:15 P.M., No. 47, $5.79.

INAPPROPRIATE	What was the No. of the play the coach discussed yesterday P.M.?
REVISED	What was the number of the play the coach discussed yesterday afternoon?
APPROPRIATE	He was No. 2 on the list posted at 6:30 P.M.

(4) *Phrasal abbreviations.* Usually abbreviations such as *i.e.* (that is), *viz.* (namely), *e.g.* (for example), *etc.* (and so forth) are

avoided in formal writing. (The English equivalents are used instead of the Latin abbreviations.) Very often the overuse of *etc.* or of the phrases "and so forth" and "and the like" is indicative of lazy writing habits.

INEFFECTIVE   We swam, fished, etc.

REVISED   We swam, fished, and danced in the moonlight.

The ampersand (&) should not ordinarily be used for *and* except in names of firms (Barnes & Noble, Inc., for example). Other abbreviations used in technical and specialized writing are given in any good dictionary.

10b. In formal writing the names of countries, states, months, and days of the week should be spelled out. Personal names are never abbreviated in formal writing.

INAPPROPRIATE   Geo., a student from Eng., joined the class last Wed.

REVISED   George, a student from England, joined the class last Wednesday.

10c. In formal writing the words STREET, AVENUE, COMPANY, **and references to a** SUBJECT, VOLUME, CHAPTER, **or** PAGE **should be spelled out.**

INAPPROPRIATE   The Perry Coal Co. has an office at Third Ave. and Mott St.

REVISED   The Perry Coal Company has an office at Third Avenue and Mott Street.

INAPPROPRIATE   The phys. ed. class is reading ch. 3 of the textbook.

REVISED   The physical education class is reading the third chapter (*or* Chapter Three) of the textbook.

EXERCISE 2. In the following sentences correct all faulty abbreviations to conform to formal usage:

(1) At six o'clock post meridian the explorers reached the top of the mt.

(2) The prof. instructed the class to read ch. 2, p. 43.

(3) Thom. Kell began working for the Ace Camera Co. in Oct.

(4) After graduating from the U. of Minn. Mister Harper moved to New Eng.

(5) The Pres. & Sen. Gale discussed U. S. trade with Gr. Brit.

(6) Wm. Greer has opened a garage on Main St.

(7) The car's license No. was concealed by rust and mud.

(8) During his furlough the capt. visited relatives in Mass.

(9) Rev. John Howe's sermons reveal his wide reading in lit.

(10) The sts. are slippery because of the big snow this A.M.

(11) This book of yrs. on chem. is useless.

(12) In the part of the mts. where Roberto went to blow the bridge, Span. was the only language spoken.

(13) Geo. had several $$ left from his Feb. paycheck.

(14) The sgt. said we would have to march by Tues.

(15) At three-thirty P.M. we boarded the plane for Tex.

(16) Without a col. educ. you'll never be an elec. eng.

(17) You bring the girl; I'll bring the Rev.

(18) Prof. Wilson spent most of his time in the Brit. Museum drinking tea with the guards.

(19) Rbt. Sellars was sleeping in a hammock when he should have been studying for his exam.

(20) Judson Wm.son, however, spent at least eight hrs. a wk. studying hist. and Eng. lit.

11. SYLLABICATION = SYL

> **Awkward division of words at the end of a line should be avoided.**

When it is necessary to give only part of a word at the end of a line and continue the word on the next line, division should occur between syllables, with a hyphen indicating the break at the end of the line. For correct syllabication of a word the writer should consult a good dictionary.

bankrupt	bank-rupt	*grammar*	gram-mar
barren	bar-ren	*hindrance*	hin-drance
collar	col-lar	*pageant*	pag-eant
defraud	de-fraud	*puncture*	punc-ture
either	ei-ther	*theism*	the-ism

antonym	anto-nym	OR	an-tonym
caliber	cal-iber	OR	cali-ber
collective	collec-tive	OR	col-lective
definite	defi-nite	OR	def-inite
malignant	ma-lignant	OR	malig-nant

11a. Words of one syllable should never be divided.

WRONG   thr-ee, cl-own, yearn-ed, plough-ed

REVISED   three, clown, yearned, ploughed

11b. Words should not be divided so that a single letter is set off as a syllable.

WRONG   wear-y, e-rupt, a-way, o-val

REVISED   weary, erupt, away, oval

11c. Compound words should be divided only at the point where the hyphen already occurs.

AWKWARD   pre-Shake-spearean, well-in-formed, Pan-Amer-ican

REVISED   pre-Shakespearean, well-informed, Pan-American

EXERCISE 3. Which of the following words may be divided at the end of a line? Where would you separate the words that may be divided?

drowned	enough	walked
swimmer	twelve	automobile
learned	through	exercise
abrupt	acute	open
envelope	ex-President	pre-eminent

MANUSCRIPT REVIEW EXERCISE. Correct the errors in the following sentences:

(1) A discount is offered to consumers who pay their utilities bills within ten (10) days.

(2) Mr. Peebles misses the bus every day at exactly seven forty nine A.M.

(3) In the absence of the pres., the secy. acted as chmn. of the meeting.

(4) A new church is being erected at the corner of Elm and Pine Sts.

(5) At the picnic we played ball, pitched horseshoes, etc.

(6) 2 soap coupons or facsimiles thereof must accompany each application for a monogrammed pencil.

(7) When Bill has no chem. class, he usually sleeps late in the A.M.

(8) Mr. & Mrs. Karns are spending the winter in Fla.

(9) We visited the shops on Fifth Ave.

(10) The town hall was built more than 60 yrs. ago.

(11) The bd. of education will meet on the 1st Wed. in Nov.

(12) The salesman grudgingly granted a 5 per cent reduction in the price of the property.

(13) Semester examinations begin on Mon., June 3rd.

(14) This trailer was made by the Wells Mfg. Co. of Detroit, Mich.

(15) Princess Pearl set a track record in the race for 3 yr. old fillies.

(16) Tad caught a 30 lb. catfish in the Miss. R.

(17) Rev. Barnes agreed to deliver a lecture at the Methodist Ch.

(18) Columbus Day is celebrated on October 12th.

(19) While in Washington we visited the Lib. of Cong.

(20) At great personal sacrifice I saved six dollars and seventy five cents for Hilda's birthday present.

Larger Elements

IF YOU WISH TO BE A WRITER, WRITE.

—EPICTETUS

ANYONE WHO WISHES TO BECOME A GOOD WRITER SHOULD ENDEAVOUR, BEFORE HE ALLOWS HIMSELF TO BE TEMPTED BY THE MORE SHOWY QUALITIES, TO BE DIRECT, SIMPLE, BRIEF, VIGOROUS, AND LUCID.

—H. W. FOWLER

12. THE WHOLE COMPOSITION = PLAN

TWO CONSTANT and nagging difficulties face every writer. Can he say what he really means, and can he make that meaning clear to his readers? There are no pat solutions to this double problem, no easy rules, no short cuts. Every writer has to decide first *what* he wants to write, and second *how* he wants to write it. And then, having written it, he has to stand off and look at the results of his labor from the point of view of a reader. Does his writing have an immediate clarity? A sense of direction and purpose? If not, he has not succeeded as a writer. The fundamental test of writing is this—does it communicate clearly?

Though there can be no safe generalization about "how to write," there are some useful guiding principles:

(1) Decide definitely what you are going to write about. (See "Selecting the Subject," Section 12a, and "Limiting the Subject," Section 12b.)

(2) Make a rough but full list of ideas, assertions, facts, and

illustrations which may possibly have a bearing on your subject. (See "Making the Preliminary Outline," Section 12c.)

(3) Frame a statement that contains the gist of what you want to say about your subject. (See "Framing the Thesis Statement," Section 12d.)

(4) Sort out the items in your rough outline, putting all ideas together that belong together and eliminating those that seem irrelevant or unsupportable. (See "Making the Complete Outline," Section 12e.)

(5) Try to find a concrete instance, illustration, anecdote, or example for a good beginning. If you cannot find such a beginning or cannot use one for your particular purpose, proceed to the next step immediately. (See "Beginning the Paper," Section 12f.)

(6) Begin to write as rapidly as possible. Do not allow problems of wording and phrasing to slow you down, or you will lose momentum and direction. (See "Writing the First Draft," Section 12g.)

(7) Once the first draft is finished, go back over your paper and polish your words, sentences, and paragraphs. Check the ending of your paper to make sure that it gives the impression of finality and completeness. (See "Writing the Second Draft," Section 12h.)

(8) If possible, allow your paper to get cold for a few days before making final revisions. You will gain perspective in this way, and errors in logic and presentation will reveal themselves more clearly. (See "Making the Final Revisions," Section 12i.)

From this list, you can see that the writing process consists of two basic steps: (1) *planning,* or thinking about what you are going to say, and (2) *actual writing and rewriting.* Of these, the first is more important than most people are willing to admit; they must rid themselves of the notion that writing is something they can do without thinking long and hard about it beforehand.

SELECTING THE SUBJECT

12a. The writer should choose a subject that interests him.

In composition classes you often have the opportunity to select your own topics. Your chances for success are better if you select one which interests you and about which you have or want to have ample knowledge. You can begin by asking yourself what you know

94

how to do. Can you clean a gun, take an alarm clock apart, roll a cigarette with one hand, or make a coffee table? Such subjects—suggested by the experiences of everyday living—often make interesting papers. The advantage of such subjects as theme topics is that you know what you are talking about. More abstract subjects may be equally interesting, but because they tempt the beginner out of the sphere of what he knows into large generalizations, they must be managed more carefully. A Francis Bacon may know enough about the subject of "Prejudice" to write a short paper about it. But ordinarily an inexperienced writer is less informed about "Prejudice" as a concept than in examples of prejudice which he has actually observed (for example, "Prejudice Against Traffic Laws in My Home Town"). He will write more interestedly—and interestingly—about an example than about the concept.

The list below may be helpful, not only for the specific subjects it gives, but also for those it brings to mind.

SUGGESTED TOPICS FOR COMPOSITIONS

General	*More Specific*
1. How I Learned the Value of Thrift	1. How to Get a Pig Out of a Piggy Bank
2. The Value of Music in the Home	2. We Sing Together Since We Can't Sing Separately
3. How to Be a Baby-Sitter	3. Love Thy Neighbor's Children
4. The Problems of an Oldest Child	4. Why I Nearly Drowned My Baby Sister
5. Does College Teach Self-Reliance?	5. The House Mother Doesn't Wash Our Socks
6. The College Newspaper	6. The Dean of Men Is My Beat
7. Playing the Infield in Softball	7. Leave First Base to Lefties
8. Fishing for Trout	8. Lake Trout and the Dry Fly
9. Fun in Photography	9. Salon Shots for Christmas Cards
10. College Snobs	10. The Trojans Learned to Beware of Greeks
11. The California Gold Rush	11. What Became of Sutter's Mill?
12. Home-Built Furniture	12. A Simple Coffee Table Design
13. Care of the Corn Field	13. Tasseling Hybrid Corn

95

General	More Specific
14. Life of a Ranch Hand	14. "Work? Naw, Them's Just *Chores*"
15. High School Debating	15. The Art of Making Lies Emphatic
16. Showing Hereford Bulls	16. A Bath for Herodotus III
17. Golfing	17. Approaching the Green
18. Learning to Knit	18. My First Sweater Was a Flop
19. Churches in Local Politics	19. Methodist Ladies and the Boilertown Taverns
20. Are We Progressing Backwards?	20. Bigger and Better Traffic Accidents
21. Army and the College Student	21. I Study to Avoid the Draft
22. Vocational Guidance in High School	22. They Told Us All to Be Engineers
23. Women Think for Themselves	23. Why Should Girls Have Curfew?
24. Moms and Momma's Boys	24. Crybabies at College
25. Will Small Towns Accept Education?	25. They Call My Uncle "Professor"

EXERCISE 1. Make a list of five titles suggested by your tastes in motion pictures, as "Why Are 'Westerns' So Popular?", "Are Double Features Necessary?"

EXERCISE 2. Make a list of five titles suggested by the advantages or disadvantages of living in a large city, *e.g.* "Horses: You Can Have Them; I'll Take a Buick," "Keeping a Great Dane in a Small Apartment."

EXERCISE 3. Make a list of five titles suggested by your hobbies or your interest in sports, as "The World's Most Expensive Stamp," "The Time I Did *Not* Strike Out with the Bases Loaded."

LIMITING THE SUBJECT

12b. The subject should be so limited that it can be treated adequately in the space at the writer's disposal.

Most young writers are too ambitious; they undertake to do too much in a paper of three hundred to five hundred words. They try to discuss the general implications of the atom bomb, or the history of mass production, or the growth of scientific medicine, or the origin and development of baseball. The result at best is a series of vague and half-supported generalizations that never come to focus, to *mean* anything. Experienced writers are constantly aware of the limitations dictated by the time and space at their disposal. For a short paper they reject a subject like "Swimming" in favor of one restricted to a single aspect, such as "How to Swim the Backstroke" or "Developing Speed in Swimming." It is equally important that the title of the paper reflect the limitations that have been put on the subject. A paper discussing the cleaning of guns should not be entitled simply "Guns," and a report on the stories ot H. P. Lovecraft should not be called "Fantasy Fiction."

Another limiting factor is of course the character of the audience for which the writing is intended. The artificiality of the usual Freshman English course where the "all-knowing" (and extraordinarily adaptable) instructor is the only audience, needs constantly to be admitted. In real situations, writing is almost always aimed at a specific audience, even if it is as large a group as "general readers." The level at which a subject will be presented determines to a very great extent whether it is to be handled as simple or complex, popular or technical, general or specific. If a writer is honestly trying to communicate, he does not forget that the nature of his subject matter, his point of view, the extent of his detail and explanation, and even his terminology must take the character of his audience into consideration. All this does not mean a person has to write "up" or "down," to be pretentious or condescending; a writer has to be himself, but "being himself" means first of all that he has the wisdom to know what he's trying to say and to whom he is saying it.

No audience, of course, can be analyzed perfectly (even single members of your family or of your group of friends have their indefinable vagaries as audiences), but its general character can be safely guessed at. The practice of focusing on a particular audience helps to clarify your intention and to keep your eye on your target.

EXERCISE 4. List five topics which would be appropriate for themes of several thousand words. Select a single aspect of each of these topics which would make an appropriate title for a theme of 200-300 words.

EXERCISE 5. Choose five items in the list of GENERAL SUGGESTED SUBJECTS and write your own specific titles for them.

EXERCISE 6. Write specific titles for five of the general topics listed below:

(1) Book Clubs   (6) Going on a Hike
(2) Going to Church   (7) Designing Clothes
(3) Teachers   (8) Home-made Furniture
(4) A Scenic Wonder   (9) Detective Stories
(5) At the Racetrack   (10) Political Conventions

EXERCISE 7. Use the "open letter" device and write a one-paragraph paper on a subject you think should be of general interest (*e.g.* taxes, traffic signs, a municipal memorial, fresh air in the classroom) addressed to a very small audience, such as a school board, the city council, your parents, or your fellow students in this course.

MAKING THE PRELIMINARY OUTLINE

12c. A preliminary outline, however rough, is a necessary first step toward organization.

An outline is a brief working plan which describes the material contained in a composition. Making an outline is a way of finding out what we have to say on a subject. Suppose that we wish to write a short composition on "Trapping the Wily Muskrat." A list of ideas on the subject might include the following:

(1) Places to set the traps
(2) A dozen #1 traps
(3) Trapping the muskrat's feeding grounds
(4) Trapping the narrows of streams
(5) Need for wearing high boots
(6) Demand for pelts
(7) Financial profits of trapping
(8) Prices of pelts
(9) Protective clothing
(10) Need for a short, heavy jacket
(11) Trapper's equipment
(12) Healthful recreation of trapping

We see at once that this is a mere list of notations, without order or logical arrangement. But it is a valuable first step; it gets the writer's ideas onto a piece of paper and shows him concretely just what he has to work with.

EXERCISE 8. Make preliminary outlines for two of the theme titles you prepared for EXERCISES 1-3.

EXERCISE 9. Which of the titles listed under SUGGESTED TOPICS could you write a 200-300 word theme about without any further study or research? Make preliminary outlines of three of the subjects you choose, to see whether you know as much about them as you think you do.

EXERCISE 10. Make a preliminary outline of one subject you can write about from personal experience (for example, "Problems of an Oldest Child") and one you know about only from hearsay or guesswork, as "The Life of a Ranch Hand," and compare the results.

FRAMING THE THESIS STATEMENT *

12d. Framing a "thesis statement" helps a writer avoid irrelevancies in planning his composition.

A "thesis statement" sums up the idea and purpose of a composition in one or two sentences. It guides the writer as he begins to re-order and arrange the items in his preliminary outline; it helps him keep on the track and avoid pointless details. The preliminary outline of "Trapping the Wily Muskrat" (12c) suggests some such thesis statement as this: "Profitable trapping of muskrats requires adequate equipment and a knowledge of good trapping places." Notice that the statement catches all the ideas (*profit, equipment, places*) which are to be dealt with and gives them a meaningful order. You can now begin to revise the preliminary outline in the light of a clearly understood purpose.

EXERCISE 11. Make thesis statements for the two themes you outlined in EXERCISE 8.

EXERCISE 12. Write a thesis statement for an essay or the chapter in a textbook assigned to you as outside reading. (Do you see how

* Practice in the writing of *précis* or brief summaries of other peoples' writing is excellent training for writing clear thesis statements of your own writing. See Section 51.

valuable the making of a thesis statement can be to a reader as well as a writer?)

EXERCISE 13. Write a thesis statement of the paragraph beginning "Another marvelous but sinister invention . . ." on page 142.

MAKING THE COMPLETE OUTLINE

12e. The complete outline arranges details in logical order and provides the writer with a definite plan.

A well-constructed outline distinguishes clearly between important ideas and less important ones. It follows some understandable principle of organization—chronological, general to specific (deductive), specific to general (inductive), spatial, and so on. Related ideas are carefully brought together and not repeated in other parts of the outline.

The classification of details listed in the preliminary outline of "Trapping the Wily Muskrat" (12c) reveals two general headings, "Places to set the traps" and "Trapper's equipment." It also reveals that a third general heading, "Advantages of trapping," must be added, because the list contains no heading to include such items as "Healthful recreation of trapping" and "Financial profits of trapping." Logical arrangement of details under the three major headings gives the following outline:

TRAPPING THE WILY MUSKRAT

I. Advantages of trapping
   A. Financial profit
      1. Demands for pelts
      2. Prices for pelts
   B. Healthful recreation
II. Trapper's equipment
   A. A dozen #1 traps
   B. Protective clothing
      1. Boots
      2. Short, heavy jacket
III. Places to set the traps
   A. Muskrat feeding grounds
   B. Narrows of streams

Such an outline should help you keep your plan in mind as you write your paper (adherence to purpose). It should indicate the order in which you want to discuss each idea (logical development) and the relative importance of each (proportion of material).

Because your instructor may ask you to prepare a complete formal outline, you should know something of the formal mechanics of outlining, as well as the various types of outlining that may be required.

(1) *A consistent method should be used for numbering and indenting major headings and subheadings in the outline.* For most outlines, it is unnecessary to divide subheadings more than two degrees. A conventional system of outline notation is shown below.

```
I. . . . . . . . .
   A. . . . . . . . .
      1. . . . . . . . . . .
         a. . . . . . . . .
         b. . . . . . . . .
      2. . . . . . . . .
   B. . . . . . . . .
II. . . . . . . . .
```

(2) *The outline should use consistently the topic, the sentence, or the paragraph form.* In a *topic outline* the separate headings are expressed with a noun, or with a word or phrase used as a noun, and its modifiers. In a *sentence outline,* which has the same structure as the topic outline, the separate headings are expressed in complete sentences. The sentence outline is sometimes more informative than the topic outline, because it states ideas more fully, but the topic outline can be read more quickly. The *paragraph outline* gives a summary sentence for each paragraph in the theme. It does not divide and subdivide headings into subordinate parts.

The most common confusion to be found in outlines is the mixing of topics and sentences. All parts of the outline should be parallel in structure (see "Parallelism," Section 16), as in the following models.

THE TELEGRAPHER: KEEPER OF THE KEYS
(*Topic Outline*)

```
I. Importance of telegraphic communication
   A. International telegraphic networks
   B. Emergency means of communication
II. Telegrapher's instrument
```

    A. Manually operated key, or "bug"
       1. Appearance of the key
       2. Operation of the key
    B. Modern teleprinter
       1. Appearance of the teleprinter
       2. Operation of the teleprinter
 III. Comparative skills of telegraphers
    A. Complex skills of the "bug" operator
    B. Simple skills of the teleprinter operator

THE TELEGRAPHER: KEEPER OF THE KEYS
(Sentence Outline)

  I. Telegraphy is one of our most important means of communication.
    A. The nations of the world are bound together by telegraphic networks.
    B. The telegraph is of great value foɪ sending emergency messages.
 II. Telegraphic instruments are of two general types.
    A. The manually operated key, or "bug," is used in small or remote communication centers.
       1. The "bug" resembles a miniature stapler connected to a panel of sockets.
       2. The "bug" produces long and short electrical impulses, or dots and dashes.
    B. The modern teleprinter is used in large communication centers.
       1. The teleprinter is a complicated machine with a manually operated keyboard.
       2. The teleprinter records, or prints, messages.
III. Operators of the "bug" and the teleprinter have different skills.
    A. The "bug" operator sends, receives, and translates the International Morse Code.
    B. The teleprinter operator uses a simple keyboard like that of a typewriter.

THE TELEGRAPHER: KEEPER OF THE KEYS
(Paragraph Outline)

  1. Telegraphers are the keepers of a world-wide network of communications.

2. The small key, or "bug," sends electrical impulses through a panel of sockets and out into the atmosphere.
3. The modern teleprinter, operated by a keyboard, records messages in large communication centers.
4. The "bug" operator must employ great skill in sending and receiving messages in the International Morse Code.
5. The teleprinter operator must have only the simple skill of using a typewriter keyboard.

(3) *The outline should not contain single headings or subheadings.* A heading or subheading should have two or more topics listed under it. Thus a "I" should be followed by a "II," an "A" by a "B," a "1" by a "2," an "a" by a "b." A single subheading should be incorporated into the heading of which it was thought to be a part.

(4) *The items in the outline should be cast in parallel grammatical constructions.* (For a discussion of *parallelism,* see Section 16.) Consistency of grammatical form emphasizes the logic of the outline and gives it clarity and smoothness. Inconsistency of form, on the other hand, makes a perfectly rational ordering of items seem illogical.

NON-PARALLEL

The Game of Tennis

I. The playing court
  A. The surface materials for it
    1. Made of clay
    2. Grass
    3. The asphalt type
  B. Measuring the court
    1. For singles
    2. Doubles
  C. Net
  D. Backstops necessary

II. Equipment needed
  A. Racket
  B. The tennis balls
  C. The wearing apparel of players

PARALLEL

The Game of Tennis

I. The playing court
  A. Surface materials
    1. Clay
    2. Grass
    3. Asphalt
  B. Measurements
    1. Singles
    2. Doubles
  C. Net
  D. Backstops

II. Equipment
  A. Racket
  B. Ball
  C. Wearing apparel

NON-PARALLEL	PARALLEL
The Game of Tennis	*The Game of Tennis*
III. Rules for playing tennis	III. Playing rules
A. The game of singles	A. Singles
B. Doubles	B. Doubles
IV. Principal strokes of tennis	IV. Principal strokes
A. Serving the ball	A. Serving stroke
B. The forehand	B. Forehand stroke
1. Drive	1. Drive
2. Lobbing the ball	2. Lob
C. The backhand stroke	C. Backhand stroke
1. The drive	1. Drive
2. Lob	2. Lob

(5) *Vague headings such as "introduction," "body," and "conclusion" should be avoided.* The outline is intended to give information. If the paper has an introduction, the outline should indicate what is in it. If there is a formal conclusion, the outline should tell what conclusions the writer has drawn. An introduction or conclusion which cannot be described is usually an empty gesture which can be dispensed with.

EXERCISE 14. Write a complete outline for one of the titles given under SUGGESTED SUBJECTS, Section 12a. Write it in each of the three forms just described: (1) topic, (2) sentence, (3) paragraph.

EXERCISE 15. Write a topic outline for one of the theme titles you prepared for EXERCISES 1-3, Section 12.

EXERCISE 16. Revise the following topic outline:

THE VALUE OF PUBLIC OPINION POLLS

  I. Introduction
    A. Operation of public opinion polls
      1. Selection of an important issue
      2. Constructing a set of questions
        a. Scientific nature of this construction
      3. A cross section of the population is selected
    B. Replies are tabulated and results summarized
  II. Importance of poll's results
      1. Attitudes of public revealed to lawmakers

2. Power of present groups revealed
3. Polls are a democratic process
   A. Polls reveal extent of people's knowledge

BEGINNING THE PAPER

12f. A good beginning serves as a springboard into the subject. But writing a good beginning is difficult work—and often treacherous. Inexperienced writers tend to spend too much time on the first paragraphs of their papers; they write and rewrite until either exhaustion or boredom sets in and the rest of the paper suffers accordingly. Experienced writers often write their beginning paragraphs only after they have finished the first draft of their work. At any rate, the beginning of a short paper hardly requires special treatment.* The best way to begin is to begin directly. If the paper is on how to clean guns, it can say quite simply, "The best method of cleaning guns is . . ." Or if the paper is entitled "I Hate Cats," it can begin "Cats are a menace to mankind. They should be exterminated."

The beginning should be self-explanatory. Our readers have to have some idea of what we are talking about. The following is intelligible only if the title is read as part of the theme. The beginning itself is therefore not self-explanatory.

HOW TO CLEAN A GUN

The first thing to do is to take your gun apart. Then lay all the parts out on the floor in front of you. Next, pick up each piece and clean it in the following manner. . . .

The beginning should not ramble. At the other extreme of the "abrupt approach" is the decorative beginning that simply delays the introduction.

FATHER KNOWS BEST

You probably wonder from my title what I am going to write about. Well, it's a long story. It started way back in 1934 when I was born. My mother announced to my father that I was a boy! "We're going to send him to State University!" my father exclaimed. So here I am at State, a member of the freshman class.

---

* The advice of the philosopher Pascal is worth noting: "The last thing we find in making a book is to know what we must put first."

It was my father's idea from the first that I should come to State. He had been a student here in 1929 when he met my mother. . . .

The writer of this rambling and ineffective beginning meant well. He thought his friendly casualness would appeal to his reader; he wanted what newspapermen call a "human interest" beginning. His theory was sound, but his practice unsuccessful. He should have omitted his first paragraph completely and begun his paper with the second.

There are a number of ways to begin a paper effectively, among them the following:

(1) *By repeating the title.*

FATHER KNOWS BEST

I was not much taken with the idea that I should enter State University this year. After visiting the campus for a few days, however, I became convinced that Father knows best when it comes to matters of his alma mater. . . .

(2) *By repeating a key word in the title.*

THE SACRED HAG

For many years now the American people have felt that Science is the most sacred of man's achievements. We find this feeling expressed almost daily in our newspapers, our magazines. . . .

Caution. A title is not a part of the first paragraph, and the use of a pronoun to refer to the title should be avoided.

Not

FATHER KNOWS BEST

I decided this when my father persuaded me that State University was the place to go. . . .

But

FATHER KNOWS BEST

I decided that my father knows best after he had persuaded me that State University was the place to go. . . .

(3) *By paraphrasing the title.*

COLLEGE FOOTBALL: A GAME OR A BUSINESS?

How much longer must we pay lip service to the notion that big-time college football is a sport played for fun by amateurs? It is time. . . .

(4) *By beginning with an anecdote.*

FATHER KNOWS BEST

When Mark Twain left home at an early age, he had no great respect for his father's intelligence. When he returned a few years later, however, he was astonished at how much his father had learned in the meantime. Similarly, it was only after I had been away from home for a few years that I became aware that Father knows best. . . .

It goes almost without saying that the anecdote ought to be directly related to the subject of the paper.

EXERCISE 17. Write beginnings for three themes, the titles of which appear in the list of SUGGESTED SUBJECTS (Section 12a). Use a different technique for each beginning.

EXERCISE 18. After studying the following example, make similar plans for two of the SUGGESTED SUBJECTS.

Example: GAY BLADES: A GUIDE TO HAND SAWS AND SAWING

   I. Picture of an inexperienced person with a saw: wobbly cut, splintered wood, aching arm. He is using wrong saw and wrong technique.
  II. Quick survey of the kinds of saws and their uses.
 III. Sawing technique: marking wood, beginning cut, leaning into stroke, holding wood to avoid splintering.
 IV. Precautions while sawing.
  V. Another picture of our tenderfoot, impatient with fine points, using machine saw: straight cut, no aching muscles, and losing only unimportant fingers.

WRITING THE FIRST DRAFT

12g. Sometimes you will want to write special introductions: a concrete example, anecdote, a question, or a dramatic statement.

Sometimes you will be able to use your thesis statement (12d) as a first sentence. Then, with one eye on the outline—your working plan—you should proceed quickly, without much concern for polished phrasing. The major headings of the outline will suggest the topic sentences of paragraphs, and the subheadings will suggest the content of the supporting sentences. Problems of diction, punctuation, mechanics—yes, even spelling—should be set aside temporarily. The important thing is to pick up momentum, to cover the ground quickly and completely—in short, to get it all down.

WRITING THE SECOND DRAFT

12h. After a cooling-off period of several hours, you are ready to check, revise, and rewrite. Over-all organization should get attention first. The following questions will serve as a convenient checklist:

(1) Does the title fit the discussion?

(2) Is the material of the paper divided into distinct sections?

(3) Are these sections arranged in logical order? (Is there an orderly sequence of thought from one section to the next, and from the beginning of the paper to the end?)

(4) Is all the material relevant to the central purpose of the paper?

(5) Is the beginning direct and pertinent?

(6) Does the ending of the paper give an impression of finality and completeness? (Or does it trail off weakly with a minor detail?)

Assuming that these basic questions can be answered satisfactorily, the next step is to check the individual paragraphs, *i.e.*, the units of discussion. The topics of these units should be clear-cut and adequately developed (see Section 13). Generalizations should be supported by sufficient evidence—facts, illustrations, examples. When an opinion or assertion lacks evidence, supply it—or discard the opinion entirely.

Once organization is checked and revised, rewriting can proceed rapidly. Clumsy sentences should be recast, phraseology repaired, and diction made more exact and precise. Transitions can be supplied, or if they already exist, checked for accuracy. Punctuation and questionable spellings should also be checked. The whole paper should then be recopied or retyped in the required format. (See "The Manuscript," Section 8.)

MAKING THE FINAL REVISIONS

12i. It is good practice to set aside the manuscript for a day or two before making final revisions. By then thinking processes are less involved with the language of the paper, and you can approach the manuscript with some of the objectivity of a reader. Minor revisions —punctuation, spelling, word substitution—can be made directly (but neatly) on the manuscript. More fundamental revisions—paragraph and sentence structure—may necessitate recopying one or more pages. Usually the reaction of an unofficial reader—a roommate, a good friend, a parent, even a well-disposed stranger—is helpful. One of them can answer the basic question about the paper: does it communicate clearly? The revisions he suggests may be minor: a word here, a punctuation mark there. When the trouble is more fundamental, the paper must be rewritten. Good writers are patient folk, with infinite capacity for revision.

> EXERCISE 19. The next pages are devoted to three specimen papers, one of which has a critical commentary. After studying them carefully write critical commentaries on the final two specimen papers.

SPECIMEN PAPER 1

BEST SOURCE OF NEWS: THE RADIO

The radio is our best means of securing news. Consider the international situation, for example. We would not receive our news as rapidly as we do if it were not for the radio. All the news -- newspaper, radio, television -- is censored before we get it, but the radio provides us with as accurate reporting as is possible Moreover, radio reports, particularly those coming from "on the spot" observations, are likely to be more exciting than newspaper reports, which are usually written several hours after the event has happened. Yes, speed is the important thing today.

The radio has also saved the lives of many people. Airplanes depend on radio, not only to make their own travel safer, but also to direct the rescue of people marooned by floods, snowstorms, etc. In areas inaccessible by any other means, the airplane is essential for patrolling and observation work.

These facts establish the importance of radio in modern civilization. There is no end to the contribution of radio in making the world safer to live in.

CRITICAL   COMMENTARY

This paper is almost completely unsuccessful. Its real virtues—competent sentence structure, punctuation, spelling—all go begging because of the author's failure to establish the statement of his title. The paper illustrates what usually happens when we try to write without a preconceived plan, an outline. And, further, the paper testifies to the failure of writing which deals in unsupported generalizations.

The paper begins effectively; the first sentence repeats the title and states clearly what we assume will be the central purpose of the paper. The second sentence introduces a concrete illustration, to be offered (we suppose) in support of the first sentence. The author then speaks of the speed with which radio gets the news to us. But instead of establishing this generalization with facts and illustrations, he proceeds at once to another idea—that of the accuracy of radio reporting. His comment here is purposeless; the question of the accuracy of radio reporting cannot be dismissed simply by calling it "as accurate as possible." The author then speaks of the "on the spot" quality of radio reporting, a matter which he treats far too summarily. And the last sentence in his first paragraph appears as an afterthought. He should have omitted it, or perhaps worked it into that part of the paragraph concerned with the rapidity of radio as a means of reporting news.

The second paragraph, as the opening sentence informs us, has nothing to do with radio as a source of news. The author has departed completely from his original purpose and is now talking of the value of radio in rescue and patrolling work. Moreover, the last sentence of the second paragraph has very little to do with radio at all; it is simply a comment on the usefulness of the airplane.

The last paragraph is also unrelated to the expressed purpose of the paper. Neither sentence mentions radio as a source of news. Moreover, the first sentence of the last paragraph deserves a special condemnation. The author has not really *established* anything. He has merely written a list of unconnected and unsupported generalizations about radio. To call them "facts" is absurd. Finally, we have only to compare the statement of the last sentence with that of the first sentence of the paper to see how far the author has strayed from his original purpose.

SPECIMEN PAPER 2

THE LIGHTEST GAS

Hydrogen is a very important and well-known gas. Its preparation is very simple. There are many ways of preparing it for commercial uses. Cavendish, an Englishman, has been recognized as the discoverer of hydrogen. He was the first to get it into a pure condition and recognize it as an independent substance different from any other known inflammable gases.

Of the many ways hydrogen is prepared, the Bosch process is most common. This process consists of passing steam over hot carbon. The carbon and steam, which is made up of oxygen and hydrogen, unite and form carbon monoxide and free hydrogen. Another common method is by combining methane, a common natural gas, with steam. The methane gas is composed of carbon and hydrogen. The carbon combines with the oxygen to form carbon monoxide and in turn sets the hydrogen free.

Hydrogen has many uses. One of its uses is inflating balloons and airships. Helium is most frequently used in airships because hydrogen is inflammable and helium is almost as light. Hydrogen is also used in the manufacture of ammonia, which, in turn, has many uses, especially in the production of fertilizers.

Hydrogen has many properties like those of oxygen. It is colorless, odorless, and tasteless. It is slightly soluble in water. And it is the lightest gas or substance known to man. Hydrogen is getting more popular and important every day. An example of this is the H-bomb, the greatest bomb ever created.

SPECIMEN PAPER 3

THE IDEAL EDUCATION

More than ever before, a good education is required if one is
going to seek the fortunes of opportunity. In the past few years
college enrollments have been increasing steadily because people
are realizing the importance of higher education. Because the
best jobs are held by the persons who have an advanced education,
the value of education cannot be stressed too much.

In choosing a college to enter one must consider their differences.
For instance, a student considering Normal State must realize that
the university has many thousand students. When a student comes to
State, he feels as though he is coming into a new town. Right away
he finds that he is on his own. He feels that high school was more
like kindergarten. The college with a small enrollment is more compact,
a circumstance which helps the new student considerably at first.
Moreover, the student usually receives more personal attention from
the faculty than he would at a college as large as Normal State

Now that we have seen the big differences between the large
and small universities, we can probably see that there are advantages
to both, or they would not be in existence. At Normal State
the student sacrifices personal attention for the better equipment
he has to work with. At a small college the situation is reversed.
Regardless, the fact remains that the student coming from high school
is facing a new situation and may need guidance.

113

13. EFFECTIVE PARAGRAPHS = ¶¶

LOOK TO THE PARAGRAPH AND THE DISCOURSE WILL
LOOK TO ITSELF. . . .

—ALEXANDER BAIN

The purpose of paragraphing is not to rest the eye or "break up the page" but to reveal the order and unity of the subject matter. A sentence is a group of words expressing a single statement; a paragraph is a group of such statements which are related to each other, and which, taken together, make a single coherent part of a larger unit, the theme.

Let us examine a good paragraph to see how each sentence serves as part of a larger unit. (The sentences are numbered for easy reference.)

(1) Tourists in Old Ontario often journey out to a cemetery near Chatham on the Thames. (2) They stand by a wooden marker and read with surprise the words: "The grave of Rev. Josiah Henson, the original Uncle Tom of Uncle Tom's Cabin by Harriet Beecher Stowe." (3) The famous Negro, after years of labor for his master, escaped from his slavery, endured starvation, fought off wolves in the Indiana and Ohio wilderness, and passed with his wife and child through friendly hands across the border into Canada to become the most notable of the fugitives. (4) He aided 600 Negroes to reach Ontario; he visited Queen Victoria and fanned the flames of war to attain immortality through the pen of Harriet Beecher Stowe. (5) He died at last in peace, and his abused and honored bones lie at the foot of this painted marker.

—HARLAN HATCHER, *Lake Eri*

First, all these sentences serve a single purpose. Sentence (1) provides a physical setting. Sentence (2) identifies Henson as "Uncle Tom." Sentences (3) and (4) describe his adventures. Sentence (5), the last, serves the double purpose of concluding the nar rative and referring the reader back to the starting point—the wooden marker in the cemetery. Every sentence has to do specifically with why the grave of Josiah Henson is of interest and renown. Because all the sentences contribute directly to a single purpose, the paragraph has *unity.*

Second, the individual sentences are not only related to each other in subject matter; they are specifically tied together by logic and grammatical structure. Sentence (2) refers to (1) in two ways: it specifies a particular place in a cemetery there identified; and the pronoun *They* has its antecedent in the word *Tourists.* Sentences (3), (4), and (5) are bound together by chronology, since they describe Henson's activities in the order of time, from the years of his slavery, through his escape, to his death. The pronoun *He* in sentences (4) and (5) links these sentences with (3), which contains the antecedent *The famous Negro.* The last three sentences are also linked by a uniform verb tense—*escaped, endured, fought off, passed, aided, visited, fanned, died.* In short, the paragraph has *coherence.*

Third, the information given by the group of sentences is sufficient to realize the central aim of the paragraph they make up. Our curiosity about the significance of the wooden marker has been satisfied. Less detail would not make Henson's grave a topic worth treating in a separate paragraph; more detail would tend to make the reader forget that his original curiosity concerned a grave marker, not the detailed biography of the man buried under it. The paragraph therefore is *adequately developed.*

The elements of a good paragraph, then, are (1) *unity,* (2) *coherence,* and (3) *adequate development.* For purposes of explanation and easy reference, the following discussion treats each of these elements as separate and distinct, but the truth is that none of them is really so. As the illustration above shows, a coherent paragraph is also unified and adequately developed. In other words, in the process of supporting a topic sentence clearly and purposively, a paragraph becomes adequately developed, and its sentences become logically connected with one another. If we realize this fact, then we will understand that making a good paragraph calls for several closely related skills, none of which is sufficient in itself to do the job properly.

EXERCISE 20. Analyze the following paragraphs just as the paragraph above was analyzed:

(1)

(1) What people do not seem to realize is that the editors of the various "digests" do not simply delete a word here and there. (2) They do not cut only extraneous material. (3) Instead, they "blue pencil" paragraphs and pages. (4) We depend upon the discretion of these editors, and what seems of importance to them becomes the text we read. (5) We have no idea what has been cut. (6) What we do read may be so removed from its original context that the remainder of the article is completely distorted. (7) The reader, however, has no way of knowing of this distortion and thus reads his digest version in good faith. (8) Consequently, when he tries to discuss his mutilated concept with someone who has taken the time to read the unabridged version, he may find himself unfamiliar with a point which was the basis of the entire thesis.

—Student paragraph

(2)

(1) It was a very proper wedding. (2) The bride was elegantly dressed; the two bridesmaids were duly inferior; her father gave her away; her mother stood with salts in her hands, expecting to be agitated; her aunt tried to cry; and the service was impressively read by Dr. Grant. (3) Nothing could be objected to when it came under the discussion of the neighbourhood, except that the carriage which conveyed the bride and bridegroom and Julia from the church door to Sotherton was the same chaise which Mr. Rushworth had used for a twelvemonth before. (4) In everything else the etiquette of the day might stand the strictest investigation.

—JANE AUSTEN, *Mansfield Park*

(3)

(1) It would be difficult to underestimate a foe more dangerously than Britain did the Boers. (2) Because they were generally bucolic, canting, and untutored, they were thought to be a military joke. (3) After all, it was argued, what could these bushmen know of cavalry maneuvers? (4) It was doubted if they could even ride a straight line. (5) What they could do, though, was ride for days on end with little food or rest, cover with dazzling speed a country they knew thoroughly, and think for themselves, according to the

116

rules of common sense rather than those of antiquated army text-books. (6) The Boers had been toughened by a code of religious spartanism incomprehensible to the average Britisher. (7) They were a suspicious people, with an implacable God, and were disinclined to frivolity or friendship. (8) If immigrants settled within a day's ride of a man's farm, that neighborhood was viewed as congested, and he picked up and moved. (9) A Boer usually carried a Bible with him and read it as he did his chores, accepting the Old Testament as the Law and discarding the New as untested and disreputable. (10) In the main, a man's chores consisted in caring for huge herds and in hunting, at which he was expert. (11) Most Boers were exceptional shots and could drop an antelope or a wildebeest, in which the country abounded, at distances up to several hundred yards. (12) Agriculture was in bad repute with the Boers; for some reason they thought it sissified. (13) Also, herds were mobile while crops were uncomfortably fixative. (14) Household recreation in the Transvaal depended upon the daily singing of a collection of pretty frightening hymns that left no doubt where a person was likely to lodge if he strayed from the paths of righteousness. (15) Further spicing up life, each family annually made a giddy expedition a hundred or so miles to the nearest church for Holy Communion. (16) And now and then a number of Boers got together to war on nearby natives—the Zulus, the Hottentots, the Tembus, and the Swazis.

—ROBERT LEWIS TAYLOR, *Winston Churchill,*
An Informal Study of Greatness

UNITY IN THE PARAGRAPH = ¶UN *

13a. A unified paragraph has a clear intent: its topic is either summed up in one of its sentences or definitely implied by its subject matter.

In expository or argumentative writing the topic of the paragraph generally appears as either the leading or final sentence of the para-

* An understanding of paragraph "unity" will help make the typical "essay examination" in any course less of a hurdle for you. In your next essay examination rephrase the essay question into a topic sentence and then go about "supporting" it as you would the topic sentence of a regular paragraph. You may have to write two or three actual paragraphs before you feel the topic sentence is completely supported, but the technique (using illustrative detail, sticking to the subject, etc.) is the same you use in writing a regular paragraph.

graph. The writer of the first paragraph below, for example, states his topic first and then explains it. His method is deductive. The writer of the second paragraph, on the other hand, reveals his purpose inductively; he saves his real point for his final sentence.

TOPIC SENTENCE FIRST:

The American colonies of France and England grew up to maturity under widely different auspices. Canada, the offspring of Church and State, nursed from infancy in the lap of power, its puny strength fed with artificial stimulants, its movements guided by rule and discipline, its limbs trained to martial exercise, languished, in spite of all, from the lack of vital sap and energy. The colonies of England, outcast and neglected, but strong in native vigor and self-confiding courage, grew yet more strong with conflict and with striving, and developed the rugged proportions and unwieldy strength of a youthful giant.

—FRANCIS PARKMAN, *The Conspiracy of Pontiac*

TOPIC SENTENCE LAST:

Along the road walked an old man. He was white-headed as a mountain, bowed in the shoulders, and faded in general aspect. He wore a glazed hat, an ancient boat-cloak, and shoes; his brass buttons bearing an anchor upon their face. In his hand was a silver-headed walking-stick, which he used as a veritable third leg, perseveringly dotting the ground with its point at every few inches' interval. One would have said that he had been, in his day, a naval officer of some sort or other.

—THOMAS HARDY, *The Return of the Native*

Some paragraphs begin with a topic sentence the sense of which is repeated in the concluding sentence.

TOPIC SENTENCE FIRST AND LAST:

The material problems of the war could be solved and the material devastation repaired; the moral devastation was never wholly repaired. The North was demoralized by victory, the South by defeat. During the war violence and destruction and hatred had been called virtues; it was a long time before they were recognized again as vices. The war had been brutalizing in its effects on combatants and non-combatants alike. Ruthlessness and wastefulness, extravagance and corruption, speculation and exploitation had accompanied the conflict, and they lingered on to trouble the post-war years. Above all, the war left a heritage of misunderstanding and even of bitterness, that colored the thinking and conditioned the actions of men, North and South, for over a generation.

> —S. E. MORISON and H. S. COMMAGER, *The Growth of the American Republic*

In narrative and descriptive paragraphs, the topic is often not directly stated but is implicit in the details or in the point of view from which the details are seen by one of the characters. The implied topic of the paragraph below, for example, is "a description of the Grand Ball at Bath, England, in the late eighteenth century."

IMPLIED TOPIC SENTENCE:

The hour is just on nine. At six, with the playing of a minuet, the dancing had started; now there is the usual pause for the gentlemen to hand tea to the ladies, and for the musicians to wet their tired throats. Tonight being something of an occasion there will be supper as well, and behind screens footmen are busily laying a long table with cold ham and pheasant, biscuits, sweetmeats, jellies and wine. And now the Master of Ceremonies in plum satin and paste buckles offers his arm to the ranking lady present, Her Grace the Duchess of Marlborough, and together they swing across the room. Behind them rustle the others, Her Grace's inferiors. Countesses and ladyships, wealthy tradesmen's wives and daughters, the mothers and mistresses of bone-setters and shipbuilders and swindling gamesters, all come to Bath to taste the salubrious "Spaw" waters at the Pump Room, to take the cure, to ogle their partners at balls at the Assembly Rooms —and best of all, to be stared at themselves in return.

> —ALICE GLASGOW, *Sheridan of Drury Lane*

EXERCISE 21. What is the topic sentence, expressed or implied, in each of the following paragraphs?

(1)

(1) The columnist is the autocrat of the most prodigious breakfast table ever known. (2) He is the voice beside the cracker barrel amplified to trans-continental dimensions. (3) He is the only non-political figure of record who can clear his throat each day and say "Now, here's what I think . . ." with the assurance that millions will listen. (4) His associates—remembering, it may be, the days before his casual opinions were regarded as canonical—regard him with wonder and a faintly sour envy. (5) The editorial writers of

the papers which buy his work envy his freedom from restraint and
the loyalty he engenders. (6) The ranking novelists of the age envy
his income. (7) Even his readers, it may be conjectured, envy the
facility with which he passes daily judgment upon all the perplexities
of life. (8) And in truth, there is something enviable in the daily
and profitable projection of an unfettered personality.

—CHARLES FISHER, *The Columnists*

(2)

(1) The generation that came to maturity between the Peace of
Paris and the inauguration of President Washington had to solve
more serious and original political problems than any later generation of Americans. (2) It was then that the great beacons of American principles, such as the Declaration of Independence, the Virginia
Bill of Rights, and the Federal Constitution, were lighted; it was
then that institutions of permanent and profound import in the history of America and of liberty were crystallized. (3) The period was
not only revolutionary and destructive, but creative and constructive;
moreover the British connection was not the most important thing
that was destroyed, nor was national independence the most important thing that was created. (4) A new federal empire was erected
on the ruins of the old empire, American ideas proclaimed, and the
American character defined.

—S. E. MORISON and H. S. COMMAGER, *The Growth
of the American Republic*

(3)

(1) When Captain Rook left the ship he was relieved by Captain
John Z. Smith. (2) As a skipper, Captain Smith was just what you'd
expect a John Smith to be like: a solid character who knew his business, a plain man, quiet, and very Regulation; the kind of a guy
who raises tomatoes in his back yard and takes his family for a
drive on Sunday afternoon. (3) Captain Smith was neither an out-
standingly good nor bad officer—he stood average. (4) He had no
idiosyncrasies and the chances are that most of the men who served
with him wouldn't remember his name two years after parting company. (5) But he was a good man, cool in combat, and reasonable.

—W. J. LEDERER, *All the Ship's at Sea*

(4)

(1) Call me Ishmael. Some years ago—never mind how long precisely—having little or no money in my purse, and nothing particular to interest me on shore, I thought I would sail about a little

and see the watery part of the world. (2) It is a way I have of driving off the spleen, and regulating the circulation. (3) Whenever I find myself growing grim about the mouth; whenever it is a damp, drizzly November in my soul; whenever I find myself involuntarily pausing before coffin warehouses, and bringing up the rear of every funeral I meet; and especially whenever my hypos get such an upper hand of me, that it requires a strong moral principle to prevent me from deliberately stepping into the street, and methodically knocking people's hats off—then, I account it high time to get to sea as soon as I can. (4) This is my substitute for pistol and ball. (5) With a philosophical flourish Cato throws himself upon his sword; I quietly take to the ship. (6) There is nothing surprising in this. (7) If they but knew it, almost all men in their degree, some time or other, cherish very nearly the same feelings towards the ocean with me.

—HERMAN MELVILLE, *Moby Dick*

(5)

(1) It is the fact that a word not only "means" what its logical definition makes it mean but can call to life all sorts of associative ideas and emotions which makes language such an excellent material for poetry and, at the same time, such an imperfect and even dangerous instrument for any sort of discussion of a scientific or political nature. (2) In poetry, the word *moonlight* is a highly effective word because, apart from meaning "the light of the moon," it also calls up visions of stillness, mystery, beauty, and perhaps love. (3) That these visions are not absolutely the same for each reader of a poem to the moon is no disadvantage to the poet. (4) On the contrary, the more varied the associative values of the word, the greater the number of readers to whom it may appeal in one way or another. (5) In logical discussion, on the other hand, the peripheral elements of meaning represent a constant danger. (6) Even if we tried, we could not keep our language free from words whose emotional value is strong enough to blunt our own mental functions and those of our listeners. (7) As long as words express ideas and conditions about which we are concerned, the word can arouse exactly all the emotion of the thing of which it is the symbol. (8) If, as is often the case, the two parties in a discussion use the same words with different connotations it becomes difficult to reach an agreement. (9) Many scientific discussions have been prolonged and many political conflicts embittered by this insufficiency of language.

—ROBERT M. ESTRICH and HANS SPERBER,
Three Keys to Language

121

EXERCISE 22. Following are three topic sentences, each accompanied by a set of statements. Some of the statements are relevant to the topic, some are not. Eliminate the irrelevant ones, and organize the remaining statements as a paragraph.

(1) Given my choice I would sooner be in the Air Force than any other service branch.

     1. I am more interested in flying than in any other military occupation.

     2. Opportunities for advancement are greater in the Air Force.

     3. Wages in certain brackets of the Air Force are higher than in other branches.

     4. There are many opportunities to travel.

     5. The Navy gives one travel opportunities too.

     6. My cousin has been in the Navy for two years, and he has sailed around the whole world.

     7. I think, though, that I still like the Air Force better.

(2) The wreck on route 64 at Mt. Nixon was caused entirely by carelessness and reckless driving by the driver of the Buick.

     1. When the wreck occurred the lights were green for the cars coming off the side road.

     2. A heavy truck loaded with hay was pulling out to cross the highway.

     3. The Buick came speeding down the main road, went through the stoplight, and crashed into the truck.

   —4. You could hear the screeching of the tires and then the crashing and grinding of metal a quarter of a mile away.

   — 5. We could hear it in our house up the road.

     6. Both drivers were killed, and I will never forget how awful the accident was.

(3) We owe some of our notions of radar to scientific observation of bats.

   —1. Most people hate bats.

   — 2. Women especially are afraid of them, since they have been told that bats are likely to get into their hair.

   —3. Bats are commonly considered unattractive, ugly creatures.

   —4. They really look more like mice with wings than anything else.

5. Scientists noticed that bats rarely collided with anything in their erratic flight.

6. Keen eyesight could not be the reason for their flying the way they do, since bats are blind.

7. It was found that bats keep sending out noises inaudible to people and that they hear the echoes of those noises.

8. This principle whereby they fly safely was found to be similar to the main principle of radar.

13b. The sentences in a unified paragraph develop a single central idea. coherence

The intent of a paragraph must not only be clear; it must also be held to consistently. The intent of the following paragraph, for example, changes three times in the first three sentences; and the last sentence appears as a kind of afterthought:

Henry James' extensive travel during his early years greatly influenced his later writings. Born in New York in 1843, Henry was destined to become one of the first novelists of the world. He received a remarkable education. His parents took him abroad for a year when he was only an infant. He was educated by tutors until he was twelve, and then taken abroad for three more years by his parents. His father wanted him to absorb French and German culture. His older brother, William, received the same education.

One way of revising this paragraph is to restrict its subject matter to what seems to be its chief topic:

Henry James, the novelist, had an unusual childhood. In 1844, while still an infant, he was taken abroad by his parents for a year. Upon his return, he and his older brother, William, were given private tutoring until Henry was twelve. At that time both boys were taken abroad to spend three years absorbing French and German culture.

Sometimes an inexperienced writer violates the principle of unity by introducing a new topic or new point of view in the final sentence of his paragraph. The writer of the following paragraph, for example, is objective until he reaches his final sentence. Then, without preparing his readers, he suddenly begins to take sides in the argument.

In the years following World War II there has been much discussion on the question of lowering the minimum voting age to eighteen. Among those people who believe that the age limit should be lowered, the favorite statement is, "If a boy is old enough to die for his country, he's old enough to vote in it." Those people who want the age limit to remain at twenty-one think eighteen-year-olds will be unduly influenced by local wardheelers who will urge them to vote a "straight ticket." But the young voter who has not had a chance to become a "dyed-in-the-wool" party member will tend to weigh the merits of the individual candidate rather than those of the party itself.

Revised, the paragraph might read:

In the years following World War II there has been much discussion on the question of lowering the minimum voting age to eighteen. Among those people who believe that the age limit should be lowered, the favorite statement is, "If a boy is old enough to die for his country, he's old enough to vote in it." Those people who want the age limit to remain at twenty-one think eighteen-year-olds will be unduly influenced by the promises of dishonest politicians.

EXERCISE 23. Explain how the following paragraphs violate the principle of unity. Point out exactly where each paragraph starts to go wrong.

(1)

(1) Racial discrimination has existed in the United States for many years. (2) It began when the first white settler decided that the Indians were an inferior breed. (3) It was given impetus by the arrival of the first Negro slaves. (4) A civil war was fought largely because the spokesman of the North, Abraham Lincoln, believed that all men are created equal. (5) Slavery was abolished and the Negro set free by act of Congress.

(2)

(1) The life of Thomas A. Edison illustrates the truth of the old saying "Genius is ten percent inspiration and ninety percent perspiration." (2) Edison was born in Milan, Ohio, and was expelled from school because his teachers thought he was a moron. (3) So Edison was educated at home by his mother, who helped him build a laboratory in the basement. (4) Edison spent long hours here, sometimes working as long as sixteen hours a day.

(3)

(1) Hardy's *The Return of the Native* is one of the finest novels I have ever read. (2) I was amazed to see how Hardy makes his major and minor episodes culminate in a great climax, and how inextricably he weaves the fortunes of his chief characters with those of his lesser characters. (3) Moreover, his handling of the landscape—gloomy Egdon Heath—is masterful. (4) He makes it a genuine, motivating force in the story. (5) My favorite character, however, was Diggory Venn.

(4)

(1) Many people who use the word *Fascism* in discussing current world problems confuse it with *Communism*. (2) Both Fascism and Communism are totalitarian, but Fascism is the economic antithesis of Communism. (3) Fascism uses military force to sustain capitalism; Communism uses force to suppress capitalism. (4) Obviously, no two systems of government could be more different. (5) But there has never been a clear explanation of the two systems. (6) The popular mediums of information—newspapers, radio, and movies—refer indiscriminately at times to Communism and Fascism in the same terms.

(5)

(1) The advantages of modern transportation are many. (2) An enormous amount of time is saved by the great speeds at which vehicles of today travel. (3) Cross-country trips are much more comfortable than they were, and they can be made in days rather than months. (4) For land travel today the automobile, motorcycle, and bus have taken the place of the horse and wagon, stage coach, and mule. (5) The railroad has been developed and extended since the use of the diesel. (6) Sailing ships are now chiefly a hobby and few consider them seriously as a means of transportation.

EXERCISE 24. Below are a number of paragraphs. Each of them fails to adhere to a single idea, the idea that the writer evidently had in mind when he started; each of them introduces extraneous material. The sentences are numbered. Write down the numbers of those sentences which threaten the unity of the paragraphs.

(1)

(1) Exhibition cycling is a sport which was popular in America for a time. (2) In the twenties large crowds attended bicycle races in

New York and other large cities. (3) As many as thirty thousand fans might attend motorbike races or six-day bike races. (4) In the first of these, motorcyclists would pace bicyclists who attempted to keep their front wheels touching or very near bars attached to the ends of motorcycles. (5) The bicyclists would thus receive a "tow" which gave them extra speed. (6) This sport was quite dangerous; several bicyclists were killed or injured in motorbike races. (7) Strangely enough, the most dangerous cycling was found in the sprint races. (8) When one cyclist fell in a sprint race, as many as ten others might collide and fall.

(2)

(1) It is still too early to tell what effect television will have on publishing. (2) Some analysts of publishing have brought out statistics showing some decreases in total receipts, but blaming television alone for these decreases is not plausible. (3) Some consumption analysts conclude that book and magazine buying may fall off in a family for six months after the purchase of a television set, but that it is likely to be resumed after that time. (4) It seems that just as radio did not interfere with the sale of books and magazines, so television may not ultimately. (5) Television is undoubtedly having its effect on American home life. (6) Now the television set is often the center of the family's recreational life. (7) Instead of going out for a good time they are content to stay at home. (8) Whether what they see is always worthwhile is of course debatable.

(3)

(1) If you intend to plant a strawberry bed, there are several things that you should consider. (2) Strawberries do best in a sandy loam or sandy clay that has been enriched with humus. (3) Blueberries and blackberries are better in acid soils. (4) Strawberries should be set out in an area which receives adequate drainage. (5) Too much moisture in the soil will kill them or interfere with their growth. (6) Other kinds of plants do better in marshy soils. (7) On account of frost dangers it is better to plant strawberries on a hillside or on a relatively high level area. (8) The effects of frost are rather peculiar; in general, plants in low-lying areas are more likely to be harmed by frost than those on hills. (9) The growth of young strawberries is actually increased if one pinches off the first runners from the plants.

Phi Gamma Delta

COHERENCE IN THE PARAGRAPH = ¶COH

13c. The sentences in a coherent paragraph are arranged in a logical order.

"Logical order" refers to organizational pattern. (See also Section 13f.) The writer of the following paragraph neglected one of the simplest organizing devices—the chronological listing of events.

> The Declaration of Independence was the instrument by which the thirteen colonies declared their independence of Great Britain. It was signed originally by only the president and secretary of the Continental Congress. When the declaration was originally voted on, June 28, 1776, the delegates from Pennsylvania and South Carolina refused to approve it until it carried an amendment. The declaration was written by Thomas Jefferson, who was one of a special committee of five assigned by Congress to draw up a form of declaration. The declaration was finally approved on July 4. The signatures of the delegates were added as their states confirmed the action of Congress.

Revised, the paragraph might read:

> The Declaration of Independence was the instrument by which the thirteen colonies declared their independence of Great Britain. It was written by Thomas Jefferson, one of a special committee of five assigned by the Continental Congress to draw up a form of declaration. When the declaration was originally brought before Congress on June 28, 1776, the delegates from Pennsylvania and South Carolina refused to approve it until it carried an amendment. That amendment was then written into the declaration, which was finally approved on July 4. Originally, only the president and secretary of the Continental Congress affixed their signatures; the delegates added their signatures as their individual states confirmed the action of Congress.

The incoherence of the following paragraph, on the other hand, results from another kind of failure in organizing. The discussion does not make a clear-cut distinction between causes and consequences:

> Juvenile delinquency is a major problem in this country. The cause of this problem is World War II. Parents of youngsters grow-

ing up during these years either avoided their responsibility or were unable to maintain it. Everywhere we read about the vicious crimes committed by young people. During the war the newspapers and the movies depicted violence, cruelty, and bloodletting as heroic rather than vicious. The war inspired brutality by distorting and twisting humane values. It is no wonder that the younger generation has made a problem of itself. During the war many of them had fathers who were in the service; their mothers were working in war plants. Consequently, they were unhappy and undisciplined. Many of them are organized in gangs and proud of their devotion to a life of crime.

Revised, the paragraph might read:

Juvenile delinquency is a major problem in this country. Everywhere we read and hear about the vicious crimes committed by younger people. Many of them are organized in gangs and are proud of their devotion to a life of crime. Certainly this unfortunate situation has its roots in the years of World War II. For one thing, the war itself inspired brutality in the younger generation by distorting and twisting humane values. The newspapers and the movies depicted violence, cruelty, and bloodletting as heroic rather than vicious. For another, parents of youngsters growing up during the war either avoided their responsibilities or were unable to exercise them. Many fathers were in the service; mothers were often busy working in war plants. The result was an unhappy, undisciplined group of young people. It was no wonder they soon made a problem of themselves.

EXERCISE 25. Write a coherent paragraph which incorporates, in your own words, all the following information about Eugene Field:

(1) He was a reporter on the St. Louis *Evening Journal* at the age of 23.

(2) He died in Chicago in 1895.

(3) All his life was devoted to journalism.

(4) He was born in St. Louis in September, 1850.

(5) He collaborated with his brother, Roswell, in *Echoes from a Sabine Farm*, 1893.

(6) He wrote literary columns for the Denver *Tribune* and the Chicago *Daily News*.

(7) He wrote a great deal of journalistic verse.

EXERCISE 26. Write a coherent paragraph which incorporates all the following information about Robert La Follette. Begin your paragraph with the topic sentence "Robert La Follette truly deserved the epithet 'Fighting Bob.' "

(1) When he was twenty-five he ran for district attorney of Madison County, Wisconsin, as a Republican but against the organized Republicans. He was elected.

(2) After serving one term as district attorney he ran for Congress and was elected.

(3) While a student at the University of Wisconsin he became known as a debater, once winning an interstate contest.

(4) In 1924 he ran for president and, though defeated, received 4½ million votes.

(5) After serving three terms as Governor of Wisconsin, he was elected to the United States Senate, where he became known as a spokesman for small businessmen and farmers.

(6) After graduation from college, he worked in a law office.

(7) After serving one term as a Representative, he was elected Governor of Wisconsin, a position he used to help initiate laws of direct primary, referendum, and recall.

(8) During the years just preceding the United States entry into World War I, La Follette set himself against the proposed neutrality legislation of Woodrow Wilson, arguing vehemently that such legislation would help get the United States into war.

EXERCISE 27. The following paragraphs are marred by lack of coherence because of the arrangement of the sentences. Rearrange the sentences to form a coherent paragraph.

(1)

(1) Once upon a time, before 1920, the whole American League hoped that by some freak of fortune the weak New York Yankees might be able to win a pennant. (2) The mighty Red Sox and Athletics, often tail-enders after 1920, were riding high. (3) Things move in cycles in sports, and a weak team five years ago may be a champion now. (4) So let's not lose interest in the home team; they may be up there again soon. (5) Even the Browns, the last team to play in a World's Series, were very strong in 1922 and finally won the pennant in 1942. (6) The standings are never the same two years straight, and second-division teams of last year

often are strong contenders this year. (7) During the last thirteen years Detroit teams have ended up in all eight positions.

(2)

(1) There were various reasons for the popularity of canasta. (2) It could be played by different numbers of players. (3) Bridge, of course, required no more and no less than four. (4) Many people naturally continued to like bridge. (5) Some players found canasta more dramatic than bridge. (6) They liked the appeal of the different combinations of cards. (7) Canasta became popular about 1950. (8) Many card players liked the freedom of personal choice and independence from a partner's decisions.

(3)

(1) After World War II our leaders had various problems in framing our foreign policy. (2) Few experts could be sure of the policy of the U.S.S.R. (3) The strength and the determination of our proven allies were questionable. (4) Seemingly no one anticipated developments in Indo-China and Korea. (5) The attitudes of the defeated Germans, Italians, and Japanese were uncertain. (6) Whether the war-time cooperation with the Russians could be continued, no one knew. (7) The attitude of India and Pakistan on future developments was hard to determine.

13d. The sentences in a coherent paragraph are carefully related and connected to one another.

There are various ways of connecting the individual sentences of a paragraph: (1) by *consistency in point of view;* (2) by *repetition of grammatical structure;* (3) by *repetition of words or ideas;* (4) by *transitional words or phrases.* A writer is not restricted to any single method; he sometimes makes use of all four.

(1) *Consistent point of view.* Unnecessary shifts in person, tense, or number within a paragraph tend to diminish coherence.

UNNECESSARY SHIFT IN PERSON

A pleasant and quiet place to live is essential for a serious-minded college student. If possible, you should rent a room from a landlady with a reputation for keeping order and discipline among her renters. Moreover, a student ought to pick a roommate with the same temperament as his own. Then you can agree to and keep a schedule of study hours.

UNNECESSARY SHIFT IN TENSE

During my vacation I saw the best movie I have ever seen, *The Male Animal*, by Elliott Nugent and James Thurber. I particularly liked the character of the returning football hero. The part is played by Jack Carson; he looked like a football player—big, good-natured, proud of the noisy acclaim that follows him everywhere. The part of the English professor was played by Henry Fonda; he looks the part, too—morose, unfed, somewhat confused by all the trouble he starts.

UNNECESSARY SHIFT IN NUMBER

Of great currency at the moment is the notion that education should prepare students for "life." A college graduate no longer goes out into the world as a cultivated gentleman. Instead students feel obliged to prepare themselves for places in the business world. Consequently, we are establishing courses on how to get and keep a mate, how to budget an income, and how to win friends and influence people—that is, how to sell yourself and your product. The study of things not obviously practical to a businessman is coming to be looked upon as unnecessary.

(2) *Repetition of grammatical structure.* A writer may connect his sentences coherently by casting them in parallel grammatical form, as in the following paragraph.

Concerning the world and all that is in it man has had many strange opinions, but none more strange than those about himself. From time to time he has been thought the victim of chance or of fate, the sport of gods or of demons, the nursling of divinity or of nature, the "rubbish of an Adam" or evolution's last and fairest animal. He has spun mythical genealogies and embroidered those that were actual. He has mourned lost Edens, golden ages, states of nature; and with equal conviction he has awaited new heavens, new paradises, and new perfections. He has explored the cosmos, and he has mastered the atom. He has seemed to know everything except himself.

—BARROWS DUNHAM, *Man Against Myth*

(3) *Repetition of key words and phrases.* The connection between ideas in a paragraph may be shown by the repetition of key

words and phrases. In the following paragraph such words are indicated by italics.

> In discussing the pre-Civil War South, it *should be remembered* that the large plantation owners comprised only a small part of the *total Southern population.* By far the greater part of *that population* was made up of *small farmers,* and of course the Negro slaves themselves. Some *small farmers* had acquired substantial acreage, owned three or four slaves, and were relatively prosperous. But most of the *small farmers* were terribly poor. They rented their land and worked it themselves, sometimes side by side with the slaves of the great *landowners.* In everything but *social position* they were worse off than the Negro slaves. But *it must also be remembered* that they were as jealous of that superior *social position* as the wealthy *landowner* himself.
>
> —Student paragraph

Repeated words may increase or change in significance when the thought of the paragraph hinges upon them, as in the following examples:

> Because they [the colonists] had first of all to survive, they took life with deadly *seriousness.* And in their *seriousness* they were able to record memorably life and living as they knew it. When their writing has distinguished *style,* as it often does, it is *style* which serves a higher purpose than itself; it is *style* which expresses the very *seriousness* of the colonial enterprise. Indeed, when one studies *stylistically* the best of colonial writing, one is studying the *quality* of colonial *seriousness.* The very forms of expression—sermons, histories, diaries, poems, and the like—themselves characterize the men who write, the society to which they write, and the occasion for writing. The difference between the writing of a Mather and of a Byrd, between that of a Sewall and of a Woolman, is in the *style and form* as well as the content. One can see not only what each believes in, but the *quality* of the belief. Theirs is the *style and form* which develop when an idea or an attitude is *seriously put* into action.
>
> —ROY HARVEY PEARCE, *Colonial American Writing*

> It is true that *protestantism* spread widely among tradesmen who recognized in it a philosophy which was generally good for business. *Protestantism* was, in part, a *protest* against a large power interfering in *private rights*. Too, it made a virtue of productive labor. The

132

middle classes found in it a warrant for working hard for *private* gains, unhampered by restrictions by outside authority. But even Luther and Calvin recognized the concept of a *fair price*. They believed that it wasn't *fair* to take advantage of a *shortage* of goods, much worse to artificially create such a *shortage*. It wasn't *fair* to exploit ignorance or need. They expected tradesmen to accept only a *fair* return on their risk or on their labor. However these teachings were increasingly disregarded as the element of economic freedom in *protestantism* became more pronounced; the notion of a *fair price* limited *private rights,* and if a man said he made a *fair* profit it was likely he was referring not to its justice but to its size.

—Student paragraph

(4) *Transitional words or phrases.* Sentences may be connected coherently by the use of transitions. The following list will be helpful:

TO INDICATE ADDITION

again, also, and, and then, besides, equally important, first, finally, further, furthermore, in addition, last, lastly, likewise, moreover, next, second, secondly, third, thirdly, too

TO INDICATE CONTRAST

and yet, after all, at the same time, although true, but, for all that, however, in contrast, nevertheless, notwithstanding, on the contrary, on the other hand, still, yet, in spite of

TO INDICATE COMPARISON

likewise, in a like manner, similarly

TO INDICATE SUMMARY

in brief, in short, on the whole, to sum up, to summarize, in conclusion, to conclude

TO INDICATE SPECIAL FEATURES OR EXAMPLES

for example, for instance, indeed, incidentally, in fact, in other words, that is, specifically, in particular

TO INDICATE RESULT

accordingly, consequently, hence, therefore, thus, truly, as a result, then, in short

133

TO INDICATE THE PASSAGE OF TIME

afterwards, at length, immediately, in the meantime, meanwhile, soon, at last, after a short time, while, thereupon, thereafter, temporarily, until, presently, shortly, lately, of late, since

TO INDICATE CONCESSION

at the same time, of course, after all, naturally, I admit, although this may be true

Note the use of transitional words and phrases (indicated by italics) in the following paragraph:

> *As I have remarked,* the pilots' association was now the compactest monopoly in the world, perhaps, and seemed simply indestructible. *And yet* the days of its glory were numbered. *First,* the new railroad, stretching up through Mississippi, Tennessee, and Kentucky, to Northern railway-centers, began to divert the passenger travel from the steamboats; *next* the war came and almost entirely annihilated the steamboating industry during several years, leaving most of the pilots idle and the cost of living advancing all the time; *then* the treasurer of the St. Louis association put his hand into the till and walked off with every dollar of the ample fund; *and finally, the railroads intruding everywhere,* there was little for steamers to do, when the war was over, but carry freights; *so straightway* some genius from the Atlantic coast introduced the plan of towing a dozen steamer cargoes down to New Orleans at the tail of a vulgar little tug-boat; *and behold,* in the twinkling of an eye, *as it were,* the association and the noble science of piloting were things of the dead and pathetic past!
>
> —MARK TWAIN, *Life on the Mississippi*

Transitions are, of course, as important within the sentence as within the paragraph. (See Transitions, Section 23.)

EXERCISE 28. Make a coherent paragraph of the following statements by, first, putting them in logical order and, second, giving them a consistent point of view, linking them smoothly with whatever transitional words or phrases are necessary. Revise the wording of the statements if necessary, but use all the information given.

(1) This attitude shows a naïve faith in the competency of secretaries.

(2) Practicing engineers and scientists say they spend half their time writing letters and reports.

(3) Many of us foolishly object to taking courses in writing.

(4) College students going into business think their secretaries will do their writing for them.

(5) A student going into the technical or scientific fields may think that writing is something he seldom has to do.

(6) Young businessmen seldom have private secretaries.

(7) Our notion that only poets, novelists, and newspaper workers have to know how to write is unrealistic.

(8) Other things being equal, a man in any field who can express himself effectively is sure to succeed more rapidly than a man whose command of language is poor.

EXERCISE 29. See instructions for Exercise 28. Use the topic sentence "English is rapidly assuming the character of an 'international language.'"

(1) It is estimated that well over 500 million people use English as a native or secondary language.

(2) The inventions that make communication possible—radio, telephone, telegraph, the motion picture—are largely controlled by English-speaking peoples.

(3) English has replaced French as the language of diplomacy.

(4) Various corrupt forms of English, like Pidgin English, are widely spoken in the Pacific area.

(5) English is made up largely of words from both Teutonic and Romance languages; a good part of its vocabulary is already familiar to those who speak a European language.

(6) The 400 million who speak Chinese are separated in innumerable and mutually unintelligible dialectal groups.

EXERCISE 30. See instructions for Exercise 28.

(1) Gene Wright, a neighbor of mine, complains to me daily of the corruption and inefficiency of the city officials.

(2) The "independent" voter too often shows his independence by not voting at all.

(3) One great problem is getting the American people to exercise their voting privilege.

(4) It is estimated that less than 70 per cent of the eligible voters go to the polls on election days.

(5) Gene Wright did not vote in the last two city elections because he forgot to register.

(6) Many people refuse to vote because they say their single votes will make little difference in the outcome of the election.

(7) The organized political parties make a point of getting "straight-ticket" voters to the polls.

(8) Democracy will work only when all the people accept the responsibilities their liberties give them.

EXERCISE 31. The following paragraphs and paragraph parts are marred and made incoherent by shifts in person, tense, and number. Rewrite the paragraphs to insure consistency and coherence throughout.

(1) Every time a nation is involved in a war it must face problems about its ex-soldiers after that war. The veteran is entitled to some special considerations from society, but treating them with complete fairness is a baffling problem. Livy reports that grants to the former soldier caused some troubles in the early history of Rome. There were many disagreements between them and the early Roman senators.

(2) Preparing a surface for new paint is as important a step in the whole process as the application of paint itself. First, be sure that the surface is quite clean. You should wash any grease or grime from the woodwork. The painter may use turpentine or a detergent for this. One must be careful to clean off whatever cleanser they have used. Then sand off any rough or chipped paint.

(3) One of the books I read in high school English was Dickens' *Tale of Two Cities*. In it the author tells of some of the horrors of the French Revolution. He spent several pages telling about how the French aristocrats suffered. The climax part of the book tells how a ne'er-do-well who had failed in life sacrifices himself for another. He took his place in a prison and went stoically to the guillotine for him.

PARAGRAPH DEVELOPMENT = ¶DEV

13e. A paragraph should develop its topic sentence adequately.

A topic sentence is usually a general statement. When a writer uses one he is obligated to establish its validity. Generally speaking, a topic sentence is established in one of two ways: (1) by giving reasons which support it, or (2) by giving examples or details which clarify it.

(a) *Lack of reasons to support topic sentences*

The president should be elected for an eight-year term. In a four-year term the president cannot establish a smooth-running administration. He has to spend much of his time being a politician rather than being an executive.

Representatives should also be elected for longer terms. Under the present situation, they no more than get elected when they have to begin preparations for the next election.

(b) *Lack of examples and details to clarify topic sentences*

English is made up of many words taken from early Church Latin. These words probably came into the language shortly after the Christianization of the British Isles in the seventh century. One such word is *altar;* another is *temple.*

It was the Norman Conquest, beginning in 1066, that had the greatest effect, however, on English. According to one authority about ten thousand French words came into the English language, about three-fourths of which still remain in the language.

The length of a paragraph is determined by the nature of the subject, the type of topic sentence, the intention of the writer, and the character of the audience. In general, modern writers tend to make their paragraphs shorter than did older writers, and informal writers use shorter paragraphs than do formal writers, not because they feel any less the obligation to support their statements, but because, for the accommodation of the reader, they break up their material into smaller units. Ultimately, the length of a paragraph is a matter which each writer must determine for himself. But inexperienced writers ought to question their own judgment when their paragraphs contain less than four or more than eight sentences. On the one hand, they may be developing their topic sentences too briefly; on the other, they may be permitting excessive detail to obscure their central aim.

Some excessively long paragraphs can be revised by a rigorous pruning of detail; others by division into two or more paragraphs. Insufficiently developed paragraphs are usually the result of undirected thinking, or of a poverty of imagination, observation, or knowledge. The paragraphs below, for example, are all insufficient. Their argument is undirected, their generalizations inadequately supported by reasons, examples, and details. They cannot be improved merely by combining them. Revision would entail almost complete rewriting.

I am in favor of lowering the minimum voting age to eighteen. I think the average eighteen-year-old has more good judgment to put to use at the polls than the average middle-aged person.

Among the members of the two major parties there is too much straight-ticket voting. I think the candidate himself and not his party should be voted on. The young voter would weigh the virtues of the candidate and not his party.

It is unlikely that the young voter would be influenced by corrupt politicians. The majority of eighteen-year-olds are high school graduates and would surely have learned enough about current affairs to use good judgment.

If the question of lowering the voting age were put to a nationwide vote, I am sure it would pass.

In conclusion I say give young Americans a chance. I am sure they will make good.

EXERCISE 32. Group the following statements into two or three paragraphs. You need not rewrite the sentences, even though they obviously need revision as they stand.

Frederick Winslow Taylor was born in 1856. His mother was a cultured easterner. She took the family abroad for three years. Fred's father was a lawyer. While at Exeter Fred was a star baseball player and head of his class. Fred began work as a machinist. He liked the men he worked with. He was short, heavily built, and sharp tongued. When he became a foreman he forgot about his working pals. He thought up new ways of doing things. The idea of producing things efficiently went to his head. He divided up jobs. When he was thirty-four, he married. In six years he became chief engineer. Then he went to work for Bethlehem steel. This job did not last long. He began to play golf and entertain. He lectured on production techniques at various colleges. The reason he lost his job was that he was more interested in production than in profit. He died in 1915 of pneumonia. He was one of the first efficiency experts.

EXERCISE 33. Develop two of the following topic sentences into paragraphs by supporting them with reasons or examples:

(1) There are three great advantages to airplane travel—speed, comfort, thrills.

(2) Driving an automobile in big city traffic requires a nice co-ordination of nerve and skill.

(3) The first day at college is a nerve-shattering experience.

(4) Making homemade furniture is less difficult than it appears.

(5) Our national parks provide excellent and inexpensive camping sites.

(6) Keeping a detailed budget is more trouble than it's worth.

(7) The greatness of Abraham Lincoln was not in his efficiency as an administrator but in the nobility of his character.

(8) Most doctors look upon alcoholism as a disease, not as a mark of immorality.

(9) The modern engineer has to be a businessman as well as a technician.

(10) A good hitter is far more valuable to a baseball team than a good fielder.

EXERCISE 34. Rewrite the following passage as one or two paragraphs, combining relevant ideas and eliminating irrelevant ones:

The word *modern* has many meanings. It may mean something new-fashioned or something characteristic of present or recent times, as modern painting, modern automobiles, or modern poetry.

To be *modern* means something pleasant, hard to understand, or something my grandmother never seemed to be.

A modern painting is a very unrealistic painting of something very realistic. It is unrealistic in the sense that the painter is trying to give you his interpretation of his impression of the object rather than a picture of the object itself. This is sometimes very exciting, but often hard to understand.

To many people, particularly middle-aged and ancient adults, *modern* is a word of condemnation. These people usually speak longingly of "the good old days" and anything modern is a "contraption," a device to make young people either sinful or lazy.

But to young people in general *modern* is a word of high praise. They use it to refer to things and ideas which are up-to-date, clever, speedy.

But I have little doubt that within twenty or thirty years these young people-grown-old will be using the word just as their parents and grandparents use it now—as a word of condemnation.

139

13f. The subject matter of the paragraph and the intent of the writer determine the way in which a paragraph is developed.

Every paragraph has its own problems of structure, and every writer has his own solutions, but a satisfactory paragraph will usually be seen upon analysis to depend on a standard organizational principle or on some slight variation of it—(1) *chronological,* (2) *spatial,* or (3) *logical.* A person who understands these principles does not automatically write sound and consistently developed paragraphs, but he is at least in a position to analyze his own paragraphs and thus to detect and remedy any faulty structure in them.

(I) *Chronological order* is the method whereby happenings or processes are described in the order of time in which they took place or should take place. Jonathan Swift's opening paragraph in his *Gulliver's Travels* is a classic illustration of the chronological method which narrates what happens, as Benjamin Franklin's famous instructions for making a kite are a classic illustration of the chronological method which describes how something is done.

(1)

My father had a small estate in Nottinghamshire; I was the third of five sons. He sent me to Emanuel College in Cambridge at fourteen years old, where I resided three years, and applied myself close to my studies: but the charge of maintaining me (although I had a very scanty allowance) being too great for a narrow fortune, I was bound apprentice to Mr. James Bates, an eminent surgeon in London, with whom I continued four years; and my father now and then sending me small sums of money, I laid them out in learning navigation, and other parts of the mathematics, useful to those who intend to travel, as I always believed it would be some time or other my fortune to do. When I left Mr. Bates, I went down to my father; where, by the assistance of him and my uncle John, and some other relations, I got forty pounds, and a promise of thirty pounds a year to maintain me at Leyden: there I studied physic two years and seven months, knowing it would be useful in long voyages.

—*Gulliver's Travels,* 1726

(2)

Make a small cross of two light strips of cedar, the arms so long as to reach to the four corners of a large thin silk handkerchief

140

when extended; tie the corners of the handkerchief to the extremities
of the cross, so you have the body of a kite; which being properly
accommodated with a tail, loop, and string, will rise in the air, like
those made of paper; but this being of silk, is fitter to bear the wet
and wind of a thunder-gust without tearing. To the top of the upright stick of the cross is to be fixed a very sharp-pointed wire, rising
a foot or more above the wood. To the end of the twine, next the
hand, is to be tied a silk ribbon, and where the silk and twine join,
a key may be fastened. This kite is to be raised when a thunder-gust
appears to be coming on, and the person who holds the string must
stand within a door or window or under some cover, so that the silk
ribbon may not be wet; and care must be taken that the twine does
not touch the frame of the door or window. As soon as any of the
thunder-clouds come over the kite, the pointed wire will draw the
electric fire from them, and the kite, with all the twine, will be
electrified, and the loose filaments of the twine will stand out every
way, and be attracted by an approaching finger. And when the rain
has wet the kite and twine, so that it can conduct the electric fire
freely, you will find it stream out plentifully from the key on the
approach of your knuckle. At this key the phial may be charged;
and from electric fire thus obtained, spirits may be kindled, and all
the other electric experiments be performed, which are usually done
by the help of a rubbed glass globe or tube, and thereby the same-
ness of the electric matter with that of lightning completely demonstrated.

—Letter to Peter Collinson, 1752

(II) *Spatial order* is the method whereby things are described
in the order of their physical relationship to one another—east to
west, north to south, small to big, up to down, center to circumference, here to there, and so on. The author of the selection below,
wishing to give his readers an elementary but clear guide to a map
of the British Isles, follows an east-to-west organization:

On the east, England is bounded by the North Sea, which is really
nothing but an old depression which has gradually run full of water.
Again a single glimpse at the map will tell you more than a thousand
words. There on the right (the east) is France. Then we get something that looks like a trench across a road, the British Channel and
the North Sea. Then the great central plain of England with London
in the deepest hollow. Then the high mountains of Wales. Another
depression, the Irish Sea, the great central Irish plain, the hills of

Ireland, a few lonely rocks further toward the west, rearing their tops above the shallow sea. Finally the rock of St. Kilda (uninhabited since a year ago as it was too hard to reach) and then suddenly down we go, down, down, down, for there the real ocean begins and the last of the vast European and Asiatic continent, both submerged and semi-submerged, here comes to an end.

—HENDRIK WILLEM VAN LOON, *Van Loon's Geography*

(III) *Logical order* is the method whereby the individual sentences in the paragraph are presented as reasons or arguments in support of the topic sentence. How the sentences are related to one another depends on the nature of the topic sentence and the intent of the writer. This means that many "logical orders" are possible, but more often than not, the order follows one of these patterns:

(1) the topic sentence as a definition needing details or particulars to make it clear

(2) the topic sentence as a comparison, direct or implied, needing illustrative particulars to establish it

(3) the topic sentence as a general statement or argument needing the evidence of examples or reasons

The last, (3), often takes the form of

(4) a general statement of cause or effect needing explanation, or

(5) an explanation arrived at through the discussion and elimination of possible alternative explanations

Though all these methods are closely allied, indeed often indistinguishable, classifying them has value as training in rhetorical analysis. The classification is illustrated below by actual paragraphs.

(1) *Paragraphs developed by definition.* The purpose of such paragraphs is to describe an object or explain a term.

(*a*) Another marvelous but sinister invention of science is the lie detector. It does not literally detect lies; it detects emotional changes, such as a catch in the breath, and changes in the blood pressure and heartbeat when making the little effort required to sustain a falsehood. The subject sits, with a cuff round his arm to record blood pressure and pulse rate, a tube round his chest for rate of respiration, and electrodes on his left hand for electrodermal

142

response (or psychogalvanic reflex). He is required to answer a list of questions, beginning with innocuous ones, the nasty ones bearing on "who dunnit?" being slipped in later. The same list of questions is given three times over, and a twitch in the various records is not considered significant unless it occurs at the same place all three times. It is not easy to fool the machine, but neither is it entirely foolproof. In any case the results have to be interpreted by a specialist, and a specialist is very uncomfortable to have against you in a law court, because you cannot meet him on his own ground. Lie detectors have been admitted in court many times, when both parties agreed to their use. If either party objects, the evidence obtained from them would probably be ruled inadmissible, but the legal status is not entirely cleared up. Some of the scientists engaged in these matters (but not all) consider the lawyers a bunch of slowpokes for not rushing to accept the wonderful findings of science. Thus, for the immunity from compulsory lie detecting which we enjoy at present, we can thank lawyers rather than scientists.

—ANTHONY STANDEN, *Science Is a Sacred Cow*

(*b*) I ought first of all to explain that when I use the term history I mean knowledge of history. No doubt throughout all past time there actually occurred a series of events which, whether we know what it was or not, constitutes history in some ultimate sense. Nevertheless, much the greater part of these events we can know nothing about, not even that they occurred; many of them we can know only imperfectly; and even the few events that we think we know for sure we can never be absolutely certain of, since we can never revive them, never observe or test them directly. The event itself once occurred, but as an actual event it has disappeared; so that in dealing with it the only objective reality we can observe or test is some material trace which the event has left—usually a written document. With these traces of vanished events, these documents, we must be content since they are all we have; from them we infer what the event was, we affirm that it is a fact that the event was so and so. We do not say "Lincoln is assassinated"; we say "it is a fact that Lincoln was assassinated." The event *was*, but is no longer; it is only the affirmed fact about the event that *is*, that persists, and will persist until we discover that our affirmation is wrong or inadequate. Let us then admit that there are two histories: the actual series of events that once occurred; and the ideal series that we affirm and hold in memory. The first is absolute and unchanged—it was what it was whatever we do or say about it; the second is relative, always changing in response to the increase or refinement of knowledge. The two series correspond more or less; it is our aim to make the correspondence as exact as possible; but the actual series of events exists for us only in terms of the ideal series which we affirm and hold in memory. This is why I am forced to identify history with knowledge of history. For all practical purposes history is, for us and for the time being, what we know it to be.

—CARL BECKER, "History," from *The American Historical Review,* 1932

(2) *Paragraphs developed by comparison or contrast, direct or implied.* The purpose of such paragraphs is to discuss the similarities or differences between two or more ideas or things.

(*a*) Speech and language have contrasting advantages and disadvantages. Speech can be changed, even while being uttered, to fit the mood, audience, and occasion; language cannot be so changed, for once printed, it is unchangeable and cannot even be brought up to date without the necessity of a revised edition. Audible speech is augmented by its own possibilities of variation in pitch (intonation), force, volume, and intensity, and by the simultaneous aid of the visible facial, gestural, and postural code; language has none of these aids when read silently, and it is at the mercy of the voice and pantomime of the reader when read aloud. Speech stands or falls on its single momentary utterance—unless, perhaps, the speaker repeats what he has just said, or expounds it—and the hearer cannot stop to think upon a statement, for fear of losing the next statement; language may be read and reread, pondered upon, and discussed at any point, without danger of losing what follows on the next page.

—C. M. WISE *et al., Foundations of Speech*

(*b*) Eventually the whales, as though to divide the sea's food resources among them, became separated into three groups: the plankton-eaters, the fish-eaters, and the squid-eaters. The plankton-eating whales can exist only where there are dense masses of small shrimp or copepods to supply their enormous food requirements. This limits them, except for scattered areas, to arctic and antarctic waters and the high temperate latitudes. Fish-eating whales may find food over a somewhat wider range of ocean, but they are restricted to places where there are enormous populations of schooling fish. The blue waters of the tropics and of the open ocean basin offers little to either of these groups. But that immense, square-headed, formidable toothed whale known as the cachalot or sperm

144

whale discovered long ago what men have known for only a short time—that hundreds of fathoms below the almost untenanted surface waters of these regions there is an abundant animal life. The sperm whale has taken these deep waters for his hunting grounds; his quarry is the deep-water population of squids, including the giant squid Architeuthis, which lives pelagically at depths of 1500 feet or more. The head of the sperm whale is often marked with long stripes, which consist of a great number of circular scars made by the suckers of the squid. From this evidence we can imagine the battles that go on, in the darkness of deep water, between these two huge creatures—the sperm whale with its 70-ton bulk, the squid with a body as long as 30 feet, and writhing, grasping arms extending the total length of the animal to perhaps 50 feet.

—RACHEL L. CARSON, *The Sea Around Us*

(*c*) In his own person, man represents every aspect of the cosmos. Reduced to his lowest terms, he is a lump of carbon and a puddle of water mixed with a handful of equally common metals, minerals, and gases. But man is likewise a unit of organic life; he is a member of the animal world, and of a special order of the animal world, the vertebrates, with capacity for free movements, for selective intercourse with the environment, for specially canalized responses through a highly developed nervous system. Still further, man belongs to the family of warm-blooded animals, the mammals, whose females give milk to their young and so form a close and tender partnership, often fiercely protective, for the nurture of their off-spring; and through his own internal development, his whole life is suffused with emotions and erotic responses which have persisted, like so many other traits of domestication—the cow's milk or the hen's eggs—in exaggerated form. Starting as an animal among the animals, man has stretched and intensified certain special organic capacities in order to develop more fully what is specifically human. In a fashion that has no rivals in other species he thinks: he plays: he loves: he dreams.

—LEWIS MUMFORD, *The Conduct of Life*

(3) *Paragraphs developed by examples or details.* The purpose of such paragraphs is to support a topic sentence with particulars or reasons.

(*a*) Lack of variety has often been urged in criticism of American place-names. Certain it is that not only do the European names *Berlin, Cambridge, Belmont, Burlington,* and their kind, appear in endless repetition, but words more distinctively American lose their distinctiveness through constant iteration. Not only do *Washingtons* and *Franklins* and *Jacksons* appear in wearisome numbers, but a name such as *Brooklyn* (a modification of Dutch *Breukelen*) is worn out by adoption in 21 states outside New York. The effectiveness of *Buffalo* admirably American in quality, is spoiled by its application including compounds, in about 75 different places. Compounds with *Elk-, Bald-, Maple-, Beech-, Oak-, Red-,* and the like are open to similar objection. In many instances inventive power seems to have been entirely lacking. *Disputanta* is said to owe its name to lack of agreement on a name, and in a number of instances settlements have been named like streets by the use of numerals, as in the case of *Seven* (Tennessee), *Fourteen* (West Virginia), *Seventeen* (Ohio), *Seventy-six* (Kentucky and Maryland), *Ninety-six* (South Carolina).

—G. H. MC KNIGHT, *English Words and Their Background*

(*b*) The pyramids were built with sheer muscle-power. Holes were bored in stone in the quarries of the Mokattam Mountains, wooden sticks were driven into them, and these, swelling when soaked with water, cracked apart the rock. On sledges and rollers the resulting blocks were dragged to the site. The pyramids rose layer by layer. Candidates for a doctorate in archaeology write theses on the question of whether one construction plan was used or several. Lepsius and Petrie occupy diametrically opposed positions on this controversy, but modern archaeology inclines to support the Lepsian point of view. Apparently there were several plans of construction, drastic changes being necessitated by suddenly conceived additions. The Egyptians, forty-seven hundred years ago, worked with such precision that mistakes in the lengths and angles of the great pyramids can, as Petrie says, "be covered with one's thumb." They fitted the stone blocks so neatly that "neither needle nor hair" can, to this day, be inserted at the joints. The Arab writer, Abd al Latif, remarked on this in wonder eight hundred years ago. Critics point out that the old Egyptian master builders misjudged their stresses and strains, as for example, when they made five hollow spaces over the burial-chamber ceiling to reduce the downward pressure, when one would have sufficed. But these fault-finders forget, in our own day of electronically analyzed T-beams, that it was not so long ago that we used to build with a safety factor of five, eight, or even twelve.

—C. W. CERAM, *Gods, Graves, and Scholars*

(*c*) The motor car is, more than any other object, the expression of the nation's character and the nation's dream. In the free billowing fender, in the blinding chromium grilles, in the fluid control, in the ever-widening front seat, we see the flowering of the America that we know. It is of some interest to scholars and historians that the same autumn which saw the abandonment of the window crank and the adoption of the push button (removing the motorist's last necessity for physical exertion) saw also the registration of sixteen million young men of fighting age and symphonic styling. It is of deep interest to me that in the same week Japan joined the Axis, DeSoto moved its clutch pedal two inches to the left—and that the announcements caused equal flurries among the people.

—E. B. WHITE, *One Man's Meat*

(4) *Paragraphs developed by explanation of causes or effects.* The purpose of such paragraphs is to describe the forces that produce a situation or to describe the results produced by one.

(*a*) Lake Erie, the last of the Great Lakes to be discovered, was the first to take form. In pre-glacial ages a mighty river flowed eastward through what is now the Lake Erie basin. When the ice sheet formed and moved south, it rammed one lobe along the axis of this stream. It gouged heavily into the soft Devonian shales to the east, and it carved deep grooves in the hard, resistant Devonian limestone at Sandusky Bay to the west. These grooves are conspicuous on the islands, especially on Kelleys Island, where one exposed section of this glacial sculpture has been made into a state park. The southwestern lobe of its basin, where the white pioneers found the Black Swamp, was first uncovered when the last of the ice sheets, known as the Wisconsin, began to melt back from the corner of present Ohio, Indiana and Michigan. The sun had beat upon the advancing front of this ice sheet, melting it down and releasing from its frozen grip the billions of tons of rock and gravel which were left piled up in terminal moraines 500 feet deep in places. The water filled in between the moraine and the receding ice sheet and discharged out of the Maumee lobe down the Wabash River. And when the water was extensive enough to be called a lake, Lake Erie had begun its metamorphosis to its present shore lines.

—HARLAN HATCHER, *Lake Erie*

(*b*) The fading of ideals is sad evidence of the defeat of human endeavour. In the schools of antiquity philosophers aspired to impart

147

wisdom, in modern colleges our humbler aim is to teach subjects.
The drop from the divine wisdom, which was the goal of the ancients, to text-book knowledge of subjects, which is achieved by
the moderns, marks an educational failure, sustained through the
ages. I am not maintaining that in the practice of education the
ancients were more successful than ourselves. You have only to read
Lucian, and to note his satiric dramatizations of the pretentious
claims of philosophers, to see that in this respect the ancients can
boast over us no superiority. My point is that, at the dawn of our
European civilisation, men started with the full ideas which should
inspire education, and that gradually our ideals have sunk to square
with our practice.

—A. N. WHITEHEAD, *The Aims of Education*

(*c*) Peter the Great opened the first modern breach in the Western
wall, and the intellectual forces that flowed through that gap are
not yet in a condition of equilibrium. Clive and Hastings grafted
the riches of the Indies onto the body of the British Empire, and
we can still not foresee the results an amputation may bring. When
Admiral Perry pried open the gates of Japan less than a hundred
years ago he let loose a Pandora's horde that was checked only at
the cost of thousands of American lives and billions of American
dollars. The horde has quieted down, but since it seems to have
firmly seated itself at the American dinner table we can scarcely
hope that our troubles with it have ended. The future of the West
is inextricably joined with the people and future of Asia, and the
direction of the joint future may well depend on the intelligence
with which we develop our relationships with that sprawling continent.

—WILLIAM VOGT, *Road to Survival*

(5) *Paragraphs developed by elimination of alternatives.* The
purpose of such paragraphs is to establish the validity of their
propositions by eliminating any alternative propositions.

(*a*) If the Moon had been separated from the Earth at a time
when the latter was still completely molten, the liquid would have
immediately covered the site of the rupture, and no more trace
would have been left on the body of our planet than there is on the
surface of a well from which a bucketful of water has been taken.
But if at the time of rupture the Earth was already covered with
solid crust, the newborn satellite must have carried away a large
section of this rocky crust, leaving a clearly visible scar. A glance

at the map of the Earth's surface discloses such a scar in the deep basin of the Pacific Ocean, which now covers about one-third of the total surface of the Earth. It would, of course, be rather unwise to draw such a far-reaching conclusion merely from the vast area and roughly circular form of the Pacific, but geologists have discovered an additional fact that lends strong support to the hypothesis that the Pacific basin is really the "hole" left in the Earth's crust by the separation of its satellites. We have already mentioned that the upper crust of the Earth is a layer of granite from 50 to 100 kilometres thick resting on a much thicker layer of heavier basalt. This is true of all the continents and also of parts of the Earth's crust that are submerged beneath the waters of the Atlantic, Indian, and Arctic oceans where, however, the granite layer is considerably thinner. But the vast expanse of the Pacific is a striking exception— *not a single piece of granite has ever been found on any of the numerous islands scattered through that ocean.* There is hardly any doubt that *the floor of the Pacific is formed exclusively of basaltic rocks, as if some cosmic hand had removed the entire granite layer from all this vast area.* Besides, in contrast to the other oceans, the basin of the Pacific is surrounded by a ring of high mountain chains (Cordilleras, Kamchatka, the islands of Japan, and New Zealand) of pronounced volcanic activity, known as the "ring of fire." This indicates that this roughly circular border line is much more closely connected with the structure of the entire crust than the shore lines of other oceans. It is therefore, quite likely that the area now occupied by the Pacific is the very place where the huge bulk of matter now forming the Moon was torn away from the Earth.

—GEORGE GAMOW, *Biography of the Earth*

(*b*) It is customary to regard the course of history as a great river, with its source in some small rivulet of the distant past, taking its rise on the plains of Asia, and flowing slowly down through the ages, gathering water from new tributaries on the way, until finally in our own days it broadens majestically over the whole world. Men have even personified this flow, made of it a being that develops of its own volition, following its own laws to the achievement of some preconceived goal. They have spoken of the "dialectic of ideas," and regarded men and whole civilizations as the passive instruments employed by this great Being in the working-out of its purposes. The observer not already committed to faith in such an interpretation finds it difficult to discern any such steady sweep in the course of human events, and above all he feels that to look upon humanity as a passive tool to which things are done and with which ends are accomplished, is a falsification of the cardinal fact that it is men who have made history and not history which has made men. Men have built up civilization, men have patiently and laboriously found out every way of doing things and toilingly worked out every idea that is to-day a part of our heritage from the past—men working at every turn, to be sure, under the influences of their environment and with the materials at hand, individual men and races and not even some such being as "humanity." The complex of beliefs and ideals by which the modern world lives and with which it works is not a gift from the gods, as ancient myth had it, but an achievement of a long succession of generations.

—J. H. RANDALL, *The Making of the Modern Mind*

CONSISTENT TONE IN PARAGRAPH DEVELOPMENT

Any discussion of paragraph development would be incomplete if the matter of consistent "emotional tone" were not mentioned. In reading effective writers we are often struck by the fact that what seems to hold their sentences together is not merely their adherence to an organizational principle but also an atmosphere of wit or mellowness or serious authority which unites everything they say into a consistent whole. The matter is more easily illustrated than described.

(1)

What men, in their egoism, constantly mistake for a deficiency of intelligence in woman is merely an incapacity for mastering that mass of small intellectual tricks, that complex of petty knowledges, that collection of cerebral rubber-stamps, which constitute the chief mental equipment of the average male. A man thinks that he is more intelligent than his wife because he can add up a column of figures more accurately, or because he is able to distinguish between the ideas of rival politicians, or because he is privy to the minutiae of some sordid and degrading business or profession. But these empty talents, of course, are not really signs of intelligence; they are, in fact, merely a congeries of petty tricks and antics, and their acquirement puts little more strain on the mental powers than a chimpanzee suffers in learning how to catch a penny or scratch a match.

—H. L. MENCKEN, *In Defense of Women*

150

(2)

It is not easy to live in that continuous awareness of things which alone is true living. Even those who make a parade of their conviction that sunset, rain, and the growth of a seed are daily miracles are not usually so much impressed by them as they urge others to be. The faculty of wonder tires easily and a miracle which appears everyday is a miracle no longer, no matter how many times one tells oneself that it ought to be. Life would seem a great deal longer and a great deal fuller than it does if it were not for the fact that the human being is, by nature, a creature to whom "*O altitudo*" is much less natural than "So what!" Really to see something once or twice a week is almost inevitably to have to try—though, alas, not necessarily with success—to make oneself a poet.

—JOSEPH WOOD KRUTCH, *The Desert Year*

(3)

Outside of the three Rs—the razor, the rope, and the revolver—I know only one sure-fire method of coping with the simmering heat we may cheerfully expect in this meridian from now to Labor Day. Whenever the mercury starts inching up the column, I take to the horizontal plane with a glass graduate trimmed with ferns, place a pinch of digitalis or any good heart stimulant at my elbow, and flip open the advertising section of *Vogue*. Fifteen minutes of that paradisaical prose, those dizzying non sequiturs, and my lips are as blue as Lake Louise. If you want a mackerel iced or a sherbet frozen, just bring it up and let me read the advertising section of *Vogue* over it. I can also take care of small picnic parties up to five. The next time you're hot and breathless, remember the name, folks: Little Labrador Chilling and Dismaying Corporation.

—S. J. PERELMAN, *Keep It Crisp*

(4)

They talked about religion, and the slack way the world was going nowadays, the decay of behavior, and about the younger children, whom these children always brought at once to mind. On these topics they were firm, critical, and unbewildered. They had received educations which furnished them an assured habit of mind about all the important appearances of life, and especially about the rearing of young. They relied with perfect acquiescence on the dogma that children were conceived in sin and brought forth in iniquity. Childhood was a long state of instruction and probation for

151

adult life, which was in turn a long, severe, undeviating devotion to
duty, the largest part of which consisted in bringing up children.
The young were difficult, disobedient, and tireless in wrongdoing,
apt to turn unkind and undutiful when they grew up, in spite
of all one had done for them, or had tried to do: for small painful
doubts rose in them now and again when they looked at their
completed works. Nannie couldn't abide her new-fangled grand-
children. "Wuthless, shiftless lot, jes plain scum, Miss Sophia Jane;
I cain't undahstand it aftah all the raisin' they had."

—K. A. PORTER, "The Old Order"

(5)

At length as the craft was cast to one side, and ran ranging along
with the White Whale's flank, he seemed strangely oblivious of its
advance—as the whale sometimes will—and Ahab was fairly within
the smoky mountain mist, which, thrown off from the whale's spout,
curled round his great Monadnock hump; he was even thus close
to him; when, with body arched back, and both arms lengthwise
high-lifted to the poise, he darted his fierce iron, and his far fiercer
curse into the hated whale. As both steel and curse sank to the
socket, as if sucked into a morass, Moby Dick sideways writhed;
spasmodically rolled his nigh flank against the bow, and, without
staving a hole in it, so suddenly canted the boat over, that had it
not been for the elevated part of the gunwale to which he then
clung, Ahab would once more have been tossed into the sea. As it
was, three of the oarsmen—who foreknew not the precise instant of
the dart, and were therefore unprepared for its effects—these were
flung out; but so fell, that, in an instant two of them clutched the
gunwale again, and rising to its level on a combining wave, hurled
themselves bodily inboard again; the third man helplessly dropping
astern, but still afloat and swimming.

—HERMAN MELVILLE, *Moby Dick*

(6)

At first they had come in wagons: the guns, the bedding, the dogs,
the food, the whiskey, the keen heart-lifting anticipation of hunting;
the young men who could drive all night and all the following day
in the cold rain and pitch a camp in the rain and sleep in the wet
blankets and rise at daylight the next morning and hunt. There had
been bear then. A man shot a doe or a fawn as quickly as he did
a buck, and in the afternoons they shot wild turkey with pistols to

152

test their stalking skill and marksmanship, feeding all but the breast
to the dogs. But that time was gone now. Now they went in cars,
driving faster and faster each year because the roads were better and
they had farther and farther to drive, the territory in which game
still existed drawing yearly inward as his life was drawing inward,
until now he was the last of those who had once made the journey
in wagons without feeling it and now those who accompanied him
were the sons and even grandsons of the men who had ridden for
twenty-four hours in the rain or sleet behind the steaming mules.
They called him "Uncle Ike" now, and he no longer told anyone
how near eighty he actually was because he knew as well as they
did that he no longer had any business making such expeditions,
even by car.

—WILLIAM FAULKNER, "Delta Autumn"

EXERCISE 35. Which would seem to be the most appropriate way
of developing each of the following topic sentences into a paragraph? Why? After you have answered this question, choose one
of the topics and write a paragraph for it. Was your paragraph
developed according to your original notion?

(1) The farmer is the backbone of this country's economic pros-
    perity.
(2) Attending a big university has disadvantages as well as ad-
    vantages.
(3) A fraternity house is not an ideal place for study.
(4) The notion that women are poor automobile drivers is not
    supported by any real evidence.
(5) The most enjoyable book I ever read is . . . .
(6) Pride in his personal appearance should be one of the chief
    characteristics of a soldier.
(7) To watch a college "prom" is to see every type of human
    being.
(8) Movies are our best entertainment.
(9) The construction of a wren house is simple.
(10) The farmer uses every possible method to conserve moisture
    in the soil.
(11) The differences in education and social conditioning for boys
    and girls in our society make for an enormous waste of female
    talent.
(12) Anxiety is an active paralysis.

153

(13) A child who has learned to live and love in the movies will suffer when he enters a world in which there is odor as well as sight and sound.

(14) We are too much inclined to measure progress by the number of television sets rather than by the quality of television programs.

(15) The people you see at a patriotic rally are not very likely to be the ones that move you to love your country.

(16) Good government begins at the local level.

(17) Conservation is a farmer's best investment.

(18) Fraternities have to watch carefully the line between fellowship and snobbishness.

(19) A freshman's biggest problem is learning to sever the umbilical cord.

(20) Some people come to college wanting to learn, but refusing, at the same time, to change a single idea they came with.

EXERCISE 36. "You cannot do wrong without suffering wrong." Write two separate paragraphs each of which develops this topic sentence. In the first paragraph, demonstrate by abstract argument or theory how the statement is true or false. In the second, demonstrate the truth or falsity of the statement by giving examples.

EXERCISE 37. "My reading tastes have changed since I came to college." Write three separate paragraphs each of which develops this topic sentence. In the first paragraph, show *why* your tastes have changed. In the second, demonstrate *how* they have changed. In the third, contrast specifically your reading tastes in high school with your reading tastes in college.

PARAGRAPHS FOR STUDY

The following paragraphs illustrate some of the elements of good paragraph structure:

(1)

After the coffee is picked it is brought home in sacks, measured, and run through the dispulper, a machine that removes the tough red, outer skin. Every berry (except the pea berry—a freak) is composed of two beans, and these are covered with a sweet, slimy substance known as the "honey," which has to ferment and rot be-

fore the beans may be washed. Washing simply removes the honey
and those pieces of the outer skin that have escaped the teeth of the
machine and flowed from the front end where they weren't wanted.
Four or five changes of water are made in the course of the opera-
tion, and toward the last, when the rotted honey has been washed
away, leaving the beans hard and clean in their coverings of parch-
ment, one of the men takes off his trousers, rolls up his drawers, and
knee deep in the heavy mixture of coffee and water drags his feet
as rapidly as he can around the cement washing tank until the whole
mass is in motion with a swirling eddy in the center. Into the eddy
gravitate all the impurities—the foreign substances—the dead leaves
and twigs and unwelcome hulls, and when they all seem to be
there, the man deftly scoops them up with his hands and tosses
them over the side. Then, if it be a fine hot day, the soggy mess is
shoveled on the asoleadero (literally, the sunning place), an immense sloping stone platform covered with smooth cement, and
there it is spread out to dry while men in their bare feet constantly
turn it over with wooden hoes in order that the beans may receive
the sun equally on all sides.

—C. M. FLANDRAU, *Viva Mexico!*

(2)

It is now over a hundred years since the *Communist Manifesto*,
and the course of history has not gone as Marx planned. It is true
that the capitalist business cycle of prosperity and depression has
gone on, and that possibly depressions have grown worse. There has
certainly been a tendency toward the concentration of capital in
giant industry, but it has not been uniform even in the German,
British, and American economies. The formula that the rich are
growing richer and the poor are growing poorer has certainly not
proved true. Government is intervening to regulate industry even
in the United States, and in all industrial countries there has been a
tendency to some degree of what is often called "state socialism."
And, of course, there was in 1917 in industrially backward Russia—a
country Marx himself disliked—the one major revolutionary movement to come to power under Marxist auspices. The Russians have
established the dictatorship of the proletariat, but there are as yet
not the slightest signs of the withering away of the Russian state.
Marx, indeed, supposed that once the revolution was successful in a
great nation—he apparently thought it would come first in the most
advanced one of his day, Great Britain—it would spread at least
to all the rest of Western society, and therefore throughout the

world. Faithful Marxists can, of course, point out that until the revolution is world-wide, the state cannot possibly be expected to wither away in beleaguered Russia.

—CRANE BRINTON, *Ideas and Men: The Story of Western Thought*

(3)

Philosophers, scholars, and men of science exhibit a common sensitiveness in all decisions in which their *amour propre* is involved. Thousands of argumentative works have been written to vent a grudge. However stately their reasoning, it may be nothing but rationalizing, stimulated by the most commonplace of all motives. A history of philosophy and theology could be written in terms of grouches, wounded pride, and aversions, and it would be far more instructive than the usual treatments of these themes. Sometimes, under Providence, the lowly impulse of resentment leads to great achievements. Milton wrote his treatise on divorce as a result of his troubles with his seventeen-year-old wife, and when he was accused of being the leading spirit in a new sect, the Divorcers, he wrote his noble *Areopagitica* to prove his right to say what he thought fit, and incidentally to establish the advantage of a free press in the promotion of Truth.

—JAMES HARVEY ROBINSON, *The Mind in the Making*

(4)

It is difficult both to define slang and to indicate its relation to other linguistic phenomena. Popular impressions about it are often erroneous: there is no necessary connection, for example, between the slangy and the vulgar, or between the slangy and the ungrammatical; further, there is nothing new about the phenomenon of slang, nor is it anything peculiarly American. Some of these misconceptions we shall return to. In addition, it may be asserted that entirely competent treatments of slang sometimes take in too much territory. One such treatment, Krapp's discussion in *Modern English,* will serve as our point of departure. Incidentally, it is striking testimony to the ephemeral character of a great deal of slang that Krapp's illustrations, brought together only forty-odd years ago, impress the reader as antiquarian specimens, for the most part. Truly, there is nothing so completely dead as last year's slang.

—STUART ROBERTSON and FREDERIC G. CASSIDY, *The Development of Modern English* (Second Edition)

(5)

Let us spend one day as deliberately as Nature, and not be
thrown off the track by every nutshell and mosquito's wing that
falls on the rails. Let us rise early and fast, or break fast, gently
and without perturbation; let company come and let company go,
let the bells ring and the children cry,—determined to make a day
of it. Why should we knock under and go with the stream? Let us
not be upset and overwhelmed in that terrible rapid and whirl-
pool called a dinner, situated in the meridian shallows. Weather this
danger and you are safe, for the rest of the way is down hill. With
unrelaxed nerves, with morning vigor, sail by it, looking another
way, tied to the mast like Ulysses. If the engine whistles, let it
whistle till it is hoarse for its pains. If the bell rings, why should
we run? We will consider what kind of music they are like. Let us
settle ourselves, and work and wedge our feet downward through
the mud and slush of opinion, and prejudice, and tradition, and
delusion, and appearance, that alluvion which covers the globe,
through Paris and London, through New York and Boston and
Concord, through church and state, through poetry and philosophy
and religion, till we come to a hard bottom and rocks in place,
which we can call *reality*, and say, This is, and no mistake; and
then begin, having a point d'appui, below freshet and frost and fire,
a place where you might found a wall or a state, or set a lamppost
safely, or perhaps a gauge, not a Nilometer, but a Realometer, that
future ages might know how deep a freshet of shams and appearances had gathered from time to time. If you stand right fronting
and face to face to a fact, you will see the sun glimmer on both
its surfaces, as if it were a cimeter, and feel its sweet edge dividing
you through the heart and marrow, and so you will happily conclude your mortal career. Be it life or death, we crave only reality.
If we are really dying, let us hear the rattle in our throats and feel
cold in the extremities; if we are alive, let us go about our business.
                                    —HENRY DAVID THOREAU, *Walden*

(6)

One evening he and she went up the great sweeping shore of
sands towards Theddlethorpe. The long breakers plunged and ran
in a hiss of foam along the coast. It was a warm evening. There
was not a figure but themselves on the far reaches of sand, no noise
but the sound of the sea. Paul loved to see it clanging at the land.
He loved to feel himself between the noise of it and the silence of

the sandy shore. Miriam was with him. Everything grew very intense. It was quite dark when they turned again. The way home was through a gap in the sandhills, and then along a raised grass road between two dykes. The country was black and still. From behind the sandhills came the whisper of the sea. Paul and Miriam walked in silence. Suddenly he started. The whole of his blood seemed to burst into flame, and he could scarcely breathe. An enormous orange moon was staring at them from the rim of the sandhills. He stood still, looking at it.

—D. H. LAWRENCE, *Sons and Lovers*

(7)

Nick laid the bottle full of jumping grasshoppers against a pine trunk. Rapidly he mixed some buckwheat flour with water and stirred it smooth, one cup of flour, one cup of water. He put a handful of coffee in the pot and dipped a lump of grease out of a can and spread it sputtering across the hot skillet. On the smoking skillet he poured smoothly the buckwheat batter. It spread like lava, the grease spitting sharply. Around the edges the buckwheat cake began to firm, then brown, then crisp. The surface was bubbling slowly to porousness. Nick pushed under the browned under surface with a fresh pine chip. He shook the skillet sideways and the cake was loose on the surface. I won't try to flop it, he thought. He slid the chip of clean wood all the way under the cake, and flopped it over onto its face. It sputtered in the pan.

—ERNEST HEMINGWAY, "Big Two-Hearted River"

(8)

He saw, facing him across the spring, a man of under size, his hands in his coat pockets, a cigarette slanted from his chin. His suit was black, with a tight, high-waisted coat. His trousers were rolled once and caked with mud above mud-caked shoes. His face had a queer, bloodless color, as though seen by electric light; against the sunny silence, in his slanted straw hat and his slightly akimbo arms, he had that vicious depthless quality of stamped tin.

—WILLIAM FAULKNER, *Sanctuary*

(9)

It was all over though. The big cat lay tangled in the willows, his head and shoulder raised against the red stems, his legs reaching and his back arched downward, in the caricature of a leap, but loose and motionless. The great, yellow eyes glared balefully up through the willows. The mouth was a little open, the tongue hanging down from it behind the fangs. The blood was still dripping from the tongue into the red stain it had already made in the snow. High behind the shoulder, the black pelt was wet too, and one place farther down, on the ribs. Standing there, looking at it, Harold felt compassion for the long, wicked beauty rendered motionless, and even a little shame that it should have passed so hard.

—WALTER V. T. CLARK, *The Track of the Cat*

(10)

At school, he was a desperate and hunted little animal. The herd, infallible in its banded instinct, knew at once that a stranger had been thrust into it, and it was merciless at the hunt. As the lunchtime recess came, Eugene, clutching his big grease-stained bag, would rush for the playground pursued by the yelping pack. The leaders, two or three big louts of advanced age and deficient mentality, pressed closely about him, calling out suppliantly, "You know me, 'Gene. You know me"; and still racing for the far end, he would open his bag and hurl to them one of his big sandwiches, which stayed them for a moment, as they fell upon its possessor and clawed it to fragments, but they were upon him in a moment more with the same yelping insistence, hunting him down into a corner of the fence, and pressing in with outstretched paws and wild entreaty. He would give them what he had, sometimes with a momentary gust of fury, tearing away from a greedy hand half of a sandwich and devouring it. When they saw he had no more to give, they went away.

—THOMAS WOLFE, *Look Homeward, Angel*

PARAGRAPH REVIEW EXERCISE. Discuss the following papers in terms of their over-all and paragraph organization:

SPECIMEN PAPER 4

THE CRISIS

I have lived through two wars. The First World War came to a close in 1918. This was to be the war that ended all wars. Capable leaders in our government were sincere and honest men. They formed a League of Nations just as the United Nations was formed after World War II. But mankind was not ready for it. The same factions pooled their resources, distrust and dishonesty so it was not possible to cultivate the qualities of trust and love for individuals Individuals make up a nation.

Humanity's crying needs are for these simple virtues.

The United Nations has done much good. We as individuals can do much to support it. It has certainly held together longer than the League of Nations, and this is very encouraging.

But as a whole the world seems to be hesitating. I believe this is a crisis, a turning point.

This crisis may be a good thing. We are threatened on one hand with atomic bombs and possible destruction. On the other hand, we can discard our worldliness and force ourselves out of our material way of thinking. We are being forced to accept our true selves and live decently with one another, not only in the United States, but throughout the whole world.

In my own experience I have lost a lot of the material and selfish way of looking at things and now try to look at life objectively.

When the whole world does this, we may find our salvation.

SPECIMEN PAPER 5

COMIC BOOKS

There are many types of comic books. The four main types are
the western, detective, fantastic, and humorous. The stories in each
type are very similar. If you have read one, you have read them all.
The cowboy hero is practically perfect. He always captures the
rustlers single-handed and wins the love of the girl. The detective
always gets his man with little or no help. The hero in the fantastic
comic can do everything imaginable. He flies and moves buildings,
mountains, or countries. The humorous type are very silly and have
no point to them, but they are probably the best of the four types.

Most children read comic books because they are inexpensive
and they are full of pictures. They don't have to read much to
get the story. Also, stories about cowboys, detectives and talking
animals appeal to children. Adults probably read comic books because they are very short. They can sit down and read a comic book
in a few minutes.

Reading comic books may have a bad effect on some people. It is
said that they promote crime because the gangster is built up to be
a hero. Some children fail to remember that the gangster is always
captured at the end of the story. Some children try to do the things
they read about. This practice sometimes leads to trouble. Many
times children spend time reading comic books that could be used
to read good books. They also stay inside reading when they should
be outside getting exercise and fresh air.

There is a good side to reading comic books. They are inexpensive
and very short. They try to teach that crime does not pay. The effect
they have depends on the person who reads them because some people are
more impressed by what they read than others.

SPECIMEN PAPER 6

THE PRICE SUPPORT PROGRAM

The farm price support program is essential to the farmer of America. He must compete with other groups that have nearly the same thing as the price support program. For example, the manufacturer has tariffs to help him keep his prices up, and the wage earner has a minimum wage to keep him in some security. If the farmer did not have a price support program he would have to sell his products in a cheap market and buy his products in an expensive one. He would be completely at the mercy of the manufacturer and the businessman.

I fully realize the tremendous cost of the farm price support program, and I am willing to admit that it could be improved, but I am not willing to see it done away with. The farmer has to have some protection against too much food and over-supply, a situation which pushes his prices down and down. And there is no doubt that the price support program has worked, at lease in a degree. We have only to compare our recent years with the years just after World War I, when thousands of farmers went bankrupt. When agriculture suffers, the whole national economy suffers, for the production of food is still the greatest industry in this country.

My suggestion is not to argue about the necessity of a farm price support program, but to admit the necessity and then go about finding a way to improve the program we have. We can't let the patient die while we are debating ways of saving him.

"WHOLE COMPOSITION" REVIEW EXERCISE. (1) After study-
ing the tentative thesis statement and tentative outline below, write
a more satisfactory thesis statement and make a complete (and
formal) sentence outline.

Tentative thesis statement: A large city is a better place to live than
a small town.

Tentative (rough) outline:

Bigger
Many more activities
Location
Daily newspaper
More stores and shops
Better schools
Less prying by neighbors
Better jobs available
Transportation to and from is better
Well known
Cultural services better
Better library
More social activities
Medical care better
Organized athletics
More movie theaters
Cleaner
Post high school training available
More interesting people

(2) After completing the first part of the assignment, pick out one
major section of the sentence outline and incorporate the information
into at least one paragraph.

Effective Sentences = EF

THERE IS A HIGH ORDER OF CORRELATION BETWEEN
BEAUTY AND CLARITY OF EXPRESSION. A SLOVENLY DE-
SIGNED AND CONSTRUCTED SENTENCE IS AN UNSAFE
CONTAINER OF KNOWLEDGE.

—JOHN J. O'NEILL

IN EXPLAINING why he left "civilized" life for two years, Henry
David Thoreau wrote:

> I went to the woods because I wished to live deliberately, to front
> only the essential facts of life, and see if I could not learn what it
> had to teach, and not, when I came to die, discover that I had not
> lived.

We call this a well-written sentence, and we use words like *clear,
compact, effective* to describe it. But why is it all these? A close examination will give the answer and incidentally provide us with
some useful principles of sentence writing.

First, the sentence expresses a single thought ("I wished to live
deliberately"), on which all the other statements impinge directly
—"front the essential facts," "learn what it had to teach," and "not
discover that I had not lived." The main thought is clear and consistently held to; the contributing details never obscure it. To use
a rhetorical term now familiar, the sentence has *unity*.

Second, the sentence is *continuously* clear; we always know
where we are. The pronoun "it" refers clearly to "life" and links up
the second half of the sentence with the first. The phrases beginning "to live" and "to front" are connected by a parallel grammatical

construction. The major transition "and" introduces an expansion of the main idea; yet the two parts of the sentence are closely tied by the relationship of the verbs "live" and "die," "front" and "learn." Because all parts of the sentence are clearly related, the sentence has *coherence.*

Third, the parts of the sentence are arranged effectively. The principal idea, "I wished to live deliberately," gets an emphatic position at the beginning. The least emphatic part of the sentence, the middle, is devoted to supplementary statements. The repetition of the main idea, with its effective balance of "die" and "not lived," gets the most strategic position of all, the end of the sentence. And the words "not lived" provide a stylistic as well as an actual conclusion to the sentence. The sentence has *emphasis.*

Unity, coherence, and *emphasis* are therefore useful terms for judging the effectiveness of a sentence. And the "rules" of effective sentence writing which appear on the succeeding pages are statements of the specific qualities of effective sentences. They will often tell us where our own sentences go wrong. But we must remember that "effectiveness" is not a mechanical matter. There is no way of divorcing a sentence from the idea it expresses. The idea constructs the sentence, not vice versa. A clumsy sentence is really a badly thought-out idea, and to revise it means, first, to rethink it.

EXERCISE 1. Analyze the following sentences just as your editors analyzed the one above:

(1) Here, more than anywhere else in the world, the daily panorama of human existence—the unending procession of governmental extortions and chicaneries, of commercial brigandages and throat-slittings, of theological buffooneries, of aesthetic ribaldries, of legal swindles and harlotries—is so inordinately extravagant, so perfectly brought up to the highest conceivable amperage, that only the man who was born with a petrified diaphragm can fail to go to bed every night grinning from ear to ear, and awake every morning with the eager, unflagging expectations of a Sunday-school superintendent touring the Paris peep-shows.

—H. L. MENCKEN

(2) Every sentence is the result of a long probation [and] should read as if its author, had he held a plough instead of a pen, could have drawn a furrow deep and straight to the end.

—HENRY DAVID THOREAU

166

(3) Whenever you hear much of things being unutterable and indefinable and impalpable and unnamable and subtly indescribable, then elevate your aristocratic nose towards heaven and snuff up the smell of decay.

—G. K. CHESTERTON

(4) Farmers are interested in science, in modern methods, and in theory, but they are not easily thrown off balance and they maintain a healthy suspicion of book learning and of the shenanigans of biologists, chemists, geneticists, and other late-rising students of farm practice and management.

—E. B. WHITE

14. SUBORDINATION = SUB

The most important idea in the sentence should be
expressed in the main clause, lesser ideas in subordinate clauses or phrases.

Some sentences have two or more ideas which are co-ordinate, or
of equal rank. But more often one idea is dominant, the others of
lesser significance. The main clause of the sentence is reserved for
the main idea; subordinate clauses are reserved for subordinate
ideas.

14a. A false co-ordination results if a subordinate or unrelated idea is joined to a main clause by a co-ordinating conjunction.

(1) If *and* is used to join a subordinate idea to the main clause,
it immediately gives the subordinate idea the status of an independent one.

INEXACT   The traffic was heavy *and* we arrived late at the party.
REVISED   *Because* the traffic was heavy, we arrived late at the
          party. (The lesser idea is subordinated.)
INEXACT   I saw the lost dog *and* I whistled to him.
REVISED   *When* I saw the lost dog, I whistled to him. (The lesser
          idea is subordinated.)

(2) The co-ordination of unrelated ideas results in a poorly
unified sentence. In such sentences it is difficult to tell which idea
was intended as dominant (see also 14c).

UNRELATED   My Uncle Bert was a golf instructor and moved here
            from New Mexico in 1943.
REVISED   My Uncle Bert, a golf instructor, moved here from
            New Mexico in 1943.

168

REVISED   My Uncle Bert, who moved here from New Mexico in 1943, was a golf instructor.

A sentence of this sort is often a sign of bad organization. Very likely the ideas belong in entirely different sentences or in different paragraphs.

(3) Another frequent cause of improper co-ordination is the writer's leaving out logical steps which perhaps seem so evident to him that he neglects to put them down.

UNRELATED   He was in the army, but he didn't have enough money to finish college.

REVISED   Although his service in the army entitled him to some schooling under the GI Bill, he didn't have enough money to finish college.

(4) Some writers make mistakes in co-ordination when they attempt to pack miscellaneous information into a short space.

"Light-Horse Harry" Lee lived from 1756 to 1818 and was an officer in the Revolutionary War. His army was responsible for quelling the Whiskey Rebellion in Pennsylvania, and he also served his country as governor of Virginia and as a member of Congress. It was "Light-Horse Harry" who described Washington as "first in war, first in peace, and first in the hearts of his countrymen," and was the father of Robert E. Lee.

Such information should be examined carefully for relevance. There is usually little reason for a collection of slightly related facts except in a reference book. However, if such a compendium is felt to be appropriate, smooth and logical subordination is essential:

The author of the description of Washington as "first in war, first in peace, and first in the hearts of his countrymen," was "Light-Horse Harry" Lee, father of Robert E. Lee. "Light-Horse Harry," having made a reputation as an officer in the Revolutionary War, later became governor of Virginia and led the army which quelled the Whiskey Rebellion.

(5) Illogical co-ordination results when items which are not logically of the same kind are joined with a co-ordinate conjunction.

169

ILLOGICAL   Entered in the pet show were several dogs, a parrot, a monkey, and a rather mangy cocker spaniel.

REVISED   Entered in the pet show were a parrot, a monkey, and several dogs, one of which was a rather mangy cocker spaniel.

EXERCISE 2. Revise those sentences below which contain clauses that should be subordinated:

(1) We searched for nearly an hour, and we at last found the missing necklace.

(2) It began to rain, and we ate our picnic dinner indoors.

(3) I did not see the traffic sign and I did not stop.

(4) We were tired and the sun was hot, but we did not look for shelter.

(5) The dog yelped and then he circled the tree, and the raccoon scrambled to a higher branch.

(6) The city was lax in its collection of taxes, and the fire department was unable to cope with several large fires.

(7) The Huron Indians were Iroquoian, and they were hated by the main body of the Iroquois.

(8) All the miners called the child "The Luck," and were completely transformed by the presence of a baby in a rough mining settlement.

(9) "The Star-Spangled Banner" was set to music written by an Englishman, John Stafford Smith, and was used by the army and navy long before it became the national anthem in 1931.

(10) Melville served in the navy, and his novel *White-Jacket* exposed many abusive practices in the navy and led to reforms of those abuses.

(11) I like any kind of vacation, whether it is to the seashore, to the mountains, or merely over a holiday weekend.

(12) In the will he was made heir to a collection of rare stamps, a number of carpentry tools, an old automobile, and his grandfather's favorite handsaw.

(13) The last Chief of the Army General Staff under Hitler was General Heinz Guderian, and he was largely responsible for building up the panzer force.

(14) He said that he was disgusted with his job of writing propaganda, and that he spent all his time reshuffling ideals to meet the demands of power-politics.

(15) The Indian Highway was formerly an Indian trail, but it is now an important thoroughfare, and it is a scenic as well as useful route.

14b. A principal idea should not be put in a subordinate construction.

This practice, called "upside-down" subordination, is the result of fuzzy thinking.

INEFFECTIVE	The octopus momentarily relaxed its grip, when the diver escaped.
REVISED	When the octopus momentarily relaxed its grip, the diver escaped.
INEFFECTIVE	He happened to glance at the sidewalk, noticing a large diamond practically at his feet.
REVISED	Happening to glance at the sidewalk, he noticed a large diamond practically at his feet.

EXERCISE 3. Revise the following sentences by putting principal ideas in main clauses and by subordinating lesser ideas:

(1) He studied hard for his examinations, making high grades.

(2) She seized the child as he began to sink, saving him from drowning.

(3) My hands trembled and the gun moved, causing me to miss the deer.

(4) Mrs. Wood opened the door of the bird cage, when her pet canary escaped.

(5) We formed a bucket brigade, putting out the fire.

(6) According to the popular ballad, Casey Jones attempted to arrive in "Frisco" on schedule, being prevented by a head-on collision with another train.

(7) The original Madison Square Garden, run by P. T. Barnum, was also an auditorium in New York City.

(8) William H. Vanderbilt, who once said, "The public be damned," indicated by that statement the attitude which characterized the maneuvers that had made his father, Cornelius Vanderbilt, and himself rich.

(9) James Fenimore Cooper was reading a novel to his wife when she challenged his claim that he could write a better one and set him off on his literary career.

171

(10) Our parting at the station consisted of some thirty minutes of kissing, sobbing and exchanging good wishes, and ended with our returning to the house together, since I had missed the train.

14c. The "primer style" should be avoided unless it serves a specific function.

The "primer style" is a series of short, simple sentences of similar structure (*e.g.*, subject is followed immediately by predicate, clauses are joined by *and*). (See "Variety," Section 27.) In such sentences all actions and perceptions have equal weight and importance. The skilled narrative writer sometimes uses the "primer style" deliberately and effectively:

> I was in under the canvas with guns. They smelled cleanly of oil and grease. I lay and listened to the rain on the canvas and the clicking of the car over the rails. There was a little light came through and I lay and looked at the guns. They had their canvas jackets on. I thought they must have been sent ahead from the third army. The bump on my forehead was swollen and I stopped the bleeding by lying still and letting it coagulate, then picked away the dried blood except over the cut. It was nothing. I had no handkerchief, but feeling with my fingers I washed away where the dried blood had been, with rain-water that dripped from the canvas, and wiped it clean with the sleeve of my coat. I did not want to look conspicuous. I knew I would have to get out before they got to Mestre because they would be taking care of these guns. They had no guns to lose or forget about. I was terrifically hungry.
>
> —ERNEST HEMINGWAY, *A Farewell to Arms*

But the clumsy use of short, simple sentences and *and* sentences is a sign of immaturity.

(1) *Short, simple sentences.* A series of such sentences is likely to be monotonous, to give the effect of choppiness. No distinction is indicated between important and unimportant ideas.

> CHOPPY   He stood on a street corner. The wind was blowing. He peered into the darkness. He was a stranger. He realized that he had no place to go.
>
> REVISED   Standing on a windy street corner and peering into the darkness, the stranger realized that he had no place to go.

(2) *"And" sentences.* "And" sentences are what the phrase implies: short simple sentences joined by *ands.* Lazy writers vainly attempt to cure choppiness by thus linking sentences together.

And SENTENCE   We approached the river and we looked down from the bluff, and we could see the silvery stream and it wound below in the valley.

REVISED   When we approached the river and looked down from the bluff, we could see the silvery stream winding below in the valley.

In this revision the first and second co-ordinate clauses have been reduced to a single subordinate clause. The next main clause stands as the dominant idea in the sentence. The final clause has been reduced to an adjective phrase modifying the noun *stream* in the main clause.

EXERCISE 4. Which of the following groups of sentences are effective as they stand? Revise those that could be improved by subordination.

(1) I got up later than usual this morning. I had to wait fifteen minutes for a bus. I was late to class.

(2) The play was very amusing. I was unable to hear some of the actors' speeches. The people sitting behind me talked incessantly.

(3) He entered the hall. He climbed the stairs to the second floor. The door to one of the rooms was partly open. He softly entered.

(4) I heard a loud clamor in the street. I ran to the window. I saw a crowd gathered around a shopkeeper. He was gesticulating wildly. He shouted that his store had been robbed.

(5) We drove onto a sand road. It led into the woods. It was very narrow. We wondered whether it was safe for travel.

(6) I went to a park and sat on a bench, and I fed nuts to the squirrels.

(7) The house was very old and it was painted yellow, and the paint was faded and in some places it was cracked.

(8) A fly buzzed in the window and a clock ticked on the shelf, and there was no other sound in the room.

(9) A car came out of a side road and I pushed hard on the foot

         brake, and I steered sharply to the left and I narrowly avoided a collision.

(10) She crossed the street and she met a policeman and she asked him the way to Monroe Street.

(11) Among his other accomplishments Paul Revere designed paper money. It was called Continental Currency. It was issued by the second Continental Congress. In time it became nearly worthless. That's the source of our phrase, "Not worth a Continental."

(12) One of the early experimenters with submarines and torpedoes was Robert Fulton, and he built the first successful steamboat as well.

(13) John Marshall discovered gold at Sutter's Mill in 1848, and in the gold rush which followed both he and Sutter were financially ruined.

(14) Tristram defeated Morault and saved the kingdom of Cornwall and won the gratitude of King Mark.

(15) The Barbary Coast was a notorious section of San Francisco. The dancing halls and gambling houses were the scene of vice and crime. The section was almost destroyed in the famous San Francisco earthquake.

14d. Sentences should not be overloaded with detail or with excessive subordination.

Unessential details in a sentence have the effect of the chatter of a talkative child who utters indiscriminately every thought that comes into his head. The italicized words in this passage deflect the aim of the writer:

EXCESSIVE   My fishing equipment includes a casting rod *which Uncle Henry gave me many years ago* and which is nearly worn out, and an assortment of lines, hooks, and bass flies, which make good bait *when I can get time off from work to go bass fishing* at Hardwood Lake.

REVISED   My fishing equipment includes an old casting rod and an assortment of lines, hooks, and bass flies. The flies make good bait when I am bass fishing at Hardwood Lake.

This particularly ineffective kind of construction is called the "House-that-Jack-built" sentence. In such sentences one dependent

174

clause is tacked on after another, each seeming to be an after-thought:

HOUSE-THAT-JACK-BUILT The heroine thought the hero was a gambler while he was really a government agent who was investigating the income tax frauds of gamblers who concealed the larger part of their winnings which they took in violation of laws of the state which would arrest them if they made their activity public, which is why she wouldn't marry him, which is why I was disgusted with the movie.

EXERCISE 5. Revise the following sentences by eliminating unessential details and excessive subordination.

(1) While I watched a full moon rise above the trees and the fish splash in a nearby stream, a light breeze fanned the embers of the campfire and it was an experience I shall never forget.

(2) When I left home early in the morning I did not realize that I had forgotten my railroad ticket until I reached the station and boarded the train and the conductor asked to see my ticket.

(3) The policeman stood by the door of the old house, which, I have been told, was once a very handsome dwelling owned by a wealthy importer, and waited for the thief to come home.

(4) The conductor raised his baton and Joe picked up his trumpet, which was an expensive instrument given to him by his parents on his eighteenth birthday, and made ready to play his solo.

(5) My dog, which I bought from Mr. Hill, a real estate broker who raises dogs as a hobby because he likes dogs, can stand on his hind legs.

(6) John Wesley, his brother Charles, and a friend named George Whitefield, were students at Oxford, where they adopted a set of religious exercises which were very precise which is why they were called Methodists, which later became the accepted term for members of the sect which they founded.

(7) As we swung around the curve a truck with glaring headlights which was probably one of the huge cattle trucks carrying

livestock into Chicago and traveling late at night to avoid heavy daytime traffic loomed into view.

(8) Hearst, who began his career by taking charge of his father's newspaper, the San Francisco *Examiner,* probably had a great deal to do with our entry into the Spanish American War, which was fought during 1897 and 1898 and which is often regarded as having been imperialistic, through his attempts to make sensational news stories which would sell his papers and aggravate international friction.

(9) Casting into the lily pads where I often had gigged frogs in the days when I visited Grandfather during my summer vacations from school I snagged one of my best dry flies, a hand tied hackle for which I had paid two dollars, on an overhanging limb.

(10) Having escaped from the pendulum, a crescent shaped blade which was razor sharp and which had descended gradually until it cut the ropes in which he had found himself tied upon awakening, he found that the metal walls of his cell were being heated and were closing in, forcing him toward a pit in the center of the room.

14e. Connectives (*e.g.,* BUT, AS, WHILE) **should be used accurately and clearly.**

Careless use of such conjunctions as *and, as, but, so,* and *while* conceals the exact relationship or shade of meaning which the writer intends. See also "Transitions," Section 23.

(1) As *is ambiguous when it implies both time and cause.*

AMBIGUOUS   As the river rose to flood stage, many people fled to higher ground. (Time or cause?)

REVISED   *When* the river rose to flood stage, many people fled to higher ground. (Time intended.)

REVISED   Because the river rose to flood stage, many people fled to higher ground. (Cause intended.)

(2) As *is inappropriate in the sense of* whether *or* that.

FAULTY   I do not know *as* I want to go tomorrow.

REVISED   I do not know *whether* (or *that*) I want to go tomorrow.

(3) But *should be used to connect contrasted statements.*

176

FAULTY   He was an All-American in college, *but* even today he is in fine physical condition.

REVISED   He was an All-American in college, *and* even today he is in fine physical condition.

(4) *The preposition* like *as a substitute for the conjunctions* as if *or* as though *is not appropriate in formal writing.*

FORMAL   He looks *as if* (or *as though*) he were exhausted.

INFORMAL He looks *like* he is exhausted.

(5) While *is weak and overused in the sense of* and *or* but.

INEFFECTIVE   John is a doctor, *while* Ray is an engineer.

REVISED   John is a doctor *and* Ray is an engineer.

INEFFECTIVE   Monday was a cool day, *while* Tuesday was warmer.

REVISED   Monday was a cool day, *but* Tuesday was warmer.

(6) While *is ambiguous when it implies both time and concession.*

AMBIGUOUS   *While* I was working at night in the library, I saw Jane often. (Time or concession intended?)

REVISED   *When* I was working at night in the library, I saw Jane often. (Time intended.)

REVISED   *Although* I was working at night in the library, I saw Jane often. (Concession intended.)

EXERCISE 6. In the following sentences change any connectives which are used weakly or inaccurately:

(1) He talks like he is happy.

(2) I do not feel as I am qualified for the job.

(3) As the ship struck the rocks, several people jumped overboard.

(4) She likes sugar in her coffee, while I like cream in mine.

(5) Her grape jelly won a prize at the county fair, but it was delicious jelly.

(6) While Leander lived across the Hellespont from Hero, he would swim over often to be with her.

(7) I don't know as I would have enough energy after such a swim to be good company.

(8) The Hellespont is nearly a mile wide at its narrowest point, while a constant current makes swimming very difficult.

(9) It seems like Leander would have lost his way swimming at night.

(10) Hero carried a torch for him on the opposite shore, but he watched that to be sure of his direction.

15. REFERENCE OF PRONOUNS = REF

Pronouns should refer clearly and exactly to their antecedents.

Since the meaning of a pronoun depends upon its reference to a noun or another pronoun, the antecedent should be clear and obvious to the reader. The writer can avoid confusion in meaning (1) by putting pronouns as near as possible to their antecedents, and (2) by making references exact.

15a. Ambiguity results when a pronoun has two possible antecedents.

AMBIGUOUS   Jack told Carl that he was ungrateful. (Does *he* refer to Jack or Carl?)

CLEAR   Jack said to Carl, "You are ungrateful."

CLEAR   Jack said to Carl, "I am ungrateful."

CLEAR   Jack confessed to Carl that he was ungrateful.

CLEAR   Jack accused Carl of being ungrateful.

AMBIGUOUS   He took the orchids from the boxes and put them on the table. (Does *them* refer to the orchids or the boxes?)

CLEAR   He took the orchids from the boxes and put the flowers on the table.

CLEAR   He removed the orchids and put the boxes on the table.

EXERCISE 7. Revise the following sentences by eliminating the ambiguous reference of pronouns:

(1) Carol told her mother that she should go to college.

(2) I dropped a bottle of vinegar on my toe and broke it.

(3) When Aunt Martha visited her sister, she was not feeling well.

(4) He put the clock on the mantel which had been repaired.

(5) The instructor gave Warren a copy of *Hamlet,* which was his favorite play.

(6) George had a dog with fleas which he was always scratching.

(7) With a worm in its mouth the bird flew to the nest and shoved it down the baby's throat.

(8) My children had too many clothes, so I gave them to the Salvation Army.

(9) The American people have elected a number of poor presidents, but Congress has generally kept them from ruining the country.

(10) Professor Donahue wanted to write a biography of Rutherford B. Hayes with the collaboration of his assistant, Dr. Terence, after he won the Larkins History prize.

15b. A reference to a remote antecedent should be avoided.

REMOTE   The birds sang in the forest where the undergrowth was thick, and a brook wound slowly in the valley. *They* were of many colors. (The pronoun *they* is too far removed from its antecedent, *birds.*)

CLEAR   . . . The *birds* were of many colors. (Confusion in meaning avoided by repetition of the noun.)

CLEAR   The *birds,* which were of many colors, sang in the forest. . . . (Elimination of the remote reference by revision of the sentence. The second sentence of the unrevised example has been here changed into a subordinate clause.)

EXERCISE 8. Revise those sentences below in which pronouns are too remote from their antecedents:

(1) Reading is an important means by which a person can acquire an education. Students, business and professional people, and many others find it of great value.

(2) The house belongs to my grandfather. The grounds cover several acres and include vineyards and orchards. It is very old.

(3) Flowers grew profusely on the hillside. Many people strolled along the path at the foot of the hill on Sunday afternoons. Usually they stopped to admire them.

(4) The boy threw the newspaper as he spun headlong down the street on his new bicycle. Making a perfect arc, flying neatly over the fence and between our elm trees, it landed solidly on

the stomach of my father, who was sleeping in a hammock on the porch.

(5) The curtains by the open window had blown back across the desk and knocked a bottle of red ink into a wastebasket. When we saw them later they appeared to be stained with blood.

15c. Vague use of THIS, THAT, or WHICH to refer to the general idea of a preceding clause or sentence should be avoided.

A pronoun should not have a clause or sentence for its antecedent unless the reference is obvious and clear. Although such general antecedents are fairly common in informal English, formal usage prefers that the pronoun refer to a particular word in the sentence.

FORMAL   His *joining* a fraternity, *which* was unexpected, pleased his family. (*Which* refers specifically to *joining*.)

INFORMAL   He joined a fraternity, *which* was unexpected and pleased his family. (The reference is clear, although *which* refers to the entire preceding clause, not to any specific word.)

FORMAL   He pounded my back, an *action that* annoyed me, and I objected strenuously. (*That* refers to *action*.)

INFORMAL   He pounded my back. *That* annoyed me, and I objected strenuously. (*That* clearly refers to the preceding sentence.)

Careless references to a preceding clause or sentence often result in a lack of clarity. Sentences containing vague references can usually be revised (1) by recasting the sentence to eliminate the pronoun, or (2) by supplying a specific antecedent for the pronoun.

VAGUE   The profits from the investment would be large, *which* I realized almost immediately.

CLEAR   I realized almost immediately that the profits from the investment would be large. (The pronoun is eliminated.)

CLEAR   The profits from the investment would be large, a *fact which* I realized almost immediately. (A specific antecedent is supplied for the pronoun *which*.)

EXERCISE 9. Revise those sentences below in which the reference of pronouns is vague:

(1) He makes his own bed every morning, which he learned in the army.

(2) He was unaware of his own pleasant personality. This made people like him.

(3) Some people do not get enough exercise, and they acquire flabby muscles. That will affect their health in later life.

(4) The merchant displays the price on every item of his merchandise, which his customers find helpful.

(5) There is a large lake near our summer cottage, which is convenient.

(6) Jack was very fond of athletics, which influenced him to become a sports writer.

(7) People should always vote on election day. This is an indication of their desire to have good government.

(8) His slice of pie was smaller than mine, which made him angry.

(9) The engine of the car is very noisy, which should be repaired immediately.

(10) The granary is bursting with grain. This is due to the fine rains during the growing season.

15d. The antecedent of a pronoun should ordinarily be a noun which can be logically substituted for the pronoun.

WEAK   Because we put the wire fence around the chicken yard, *they* cannot escape. (*they* cannot logically refer to *chicken*, which here functions as an adjective.)

CLEAR   Because we put the wire fence around the chicken yard, the *chickens* cannot escape.

WEAK   Tom's brother is an engineer, and *this* is the profession Tom wants to study. (*this* cannot logically refer to *engineer*.)

CLEAR   Tom's brother is an engineer, and *engineering* is the profession Tom wants to study.

EXERCISE 10. In the following sentences eliminate where necessary the references to unexpressed antecedents:

(1) There is a fire station near the school, and we called them when we saw smoke in the basement.

(2) Mr. Carson operates a dairy farm, and his son hopes to become one.

(3) Because John had never milked a cow, he supposed it was easy.

(4) She is a good cook, because she learned it when she was only a child.

(5) We removed the fish scales before we fried them.

(6) He suffered a slight heart attack, but after a month's rest it was as good as ever.

(7) When the political refugee asked for police protection, four of them were assigned to guard him.

(8) After reading a book about television engineering, Mr. Foster had great admiration for them.

(9) In his youth he was a skilful fisherman, but now he seldom has time to do it.

(10) Although Brown likes to talk about politics, he has no personal ambition to be one.

15e. Indefinite use of THEY, YOU, and IT should be avoided.

Although the indefinite use of *they, you,* and *it* is fairly common in informal and colloquial usage, it is not appropriate in formal writing, which requires a more exact use of pronouns.

FORMAL   At the state university the rules require all students to take a course in composition.

INFORMAL   At the state university *they* require all students to take a course in composition.

FORMAL   In some states motorists are not permitted to drive faster than fifty miles an hour.

INFORMAL   In some states *you* are not permitted to drive faster than fifty miles an hour.

FORMAL   The newspaper says that Monday will be warmer.

INFORMAL   *It* says in the newspaper that Monday will be warmer.

NOTE. The indefinite use of *it* is appropriate in such idiomatic expressions as *it is cloudy, it seems, it is early.*

EXERCISE 11. Revise the following sentences to avoid the indefinite use of *they, you,* and *it:*

(1) In Iowa they grow a great deal of corn.

(2) When playing golf, you keep your eye on the ball.

(3) In the advertisement it says that the wrist watch is waterproof.

(4) They put these stop lights every place but where they are needed.

(5) In the Middle West you have cold winters and hot summers.

(6) Before you take it, it says to shake the bottle well.

(7) In pioneer times you ground your own flour.

(8) They deal severely with reckless drivers in this community.

(9) In this chapter it states that the Federalists advocated a neutral attitude toward European wars.

(10) According to the Puritan law, if a person committed a crime against the theocracy, you had to pay the penalty.

Φ Δ T

16. PARALLELISM = //

Sentence elements that are parallel in thought should be expressed in parallel grammatical form.

Parallel structure is a method of co-ordination; it puts ideas of equal importance in the same grammatical construction. In the sentence below, for example, the relationship between the *same grammatical construction* and *equal importance* is expressed by a parallel infinitive construction:

> *To put ideas* in the same grammatical construction is *to give them* equal importance.

16a. Co-ordinate elements should be put in parallel form.

If the first co-ordinate element is placed in an infinitive construction, for example, the second element should also be placed in an infinitive construction. Similarly, when other constructions are used; the first sets the pattern to be followed.

AWKWARD	She likes to sew and cooking.
PARALLEL	She likes to sew and cook.
AWKWARD	Sam is tall, with blue eyes, and has a congenial manner.
PARALLEL	Sam is tall, blue-eyed, and congenial.

NOTE: *Parallel structure can be indicated by repetition of words in the parallel sentence elements.* (See also "Emphasis," 24d.)

AMBIGUOUS	He wants to write stories which describe the South and study the habits of the Creoles. (Stories which study the habits of the Creoles?)
REVISED	He wants to write stories which describe the South and to study the habits of the Creoles.

AMBIGUOUS   Mr. Gray helps his wife by cooking and ironing his own shirts. (Cooking his own shirts?)

REVISED   Mr. Gray helps his wife by cooking and by ironing his own shirts.

16b. Faulty parallelism (AND WHO, AND WHICH) should be avoided.

A common example of faulty parallelism is the use of an *and who* or *and which* clause in a sentence that does not have a parallel *who* or *which* clause.

FAULTY   Mary is a graceful dancer, *and who* is also an excellent pianist.

REVISED   Mary is a graceful dancer and also an excellent pianist.

FAULTY   He bought a large farm, *and which* has a productive peach orchard.

REVISED   He bought a large farm which has a productive peach orchard.

EXERCISE 12. In the following sentences, express co-ordinate ideas in parallel structure:

(1) The soldier was told to report to the orderly room and that he was then to do guard duty.

(2) He bought a new automobile with an automatic transmission and having a radio and a heater.

(3) We stopped at West Branch for food supplies and to inquire about the road to North Point.

(4) We did not realize the dangers of the trip, or how long it would take.

(5) Playing tennis is more strenuous than to swim or baseball.

(6) My work consists of planning the menus, purchasing of the food, supervision of the employees, and keeping a check on the perpetual inventory of the food.

(7) Our living room is eighteen feet in length and twelve feet wide.

(8) The policeman warned me to drive slowly and that I should be careful.

(9) The lecture was long, tedious, and could not easily be understood.

(10) The mess sergeant insisted that the pans needed scouring and that the stove be cleaned.

16c. Correlatives should be followed by sentence elements that are parallel in form.

The correlatives are *either—or, neither—nor, not only—but also, both—and, whether—or.*

FAULTY   You are either *late* or *I am early.* (An adjective made parallel with a clause.)

REVISED   Either *you are late* or *I am early.* (Two parallel clauses.)

FAULTY   Jim not only *has been* outstanding in athletics, but also *in* his studies. (A verb made parallel with a preposition.)

REVISED   Jim has been outstanding not only *in athletics,* but also *in his studies.* (Two parallel phrases.)

EXERCISE 13. Revise the following sentences by using the correlatives accurately:

(1) The book was neither informative nor did I find it entertaining.

(2) Pete was undecided whether he should go to the meeting or to stay at home.

(3) Mrs. Boggs stayed both longer and gossiped more than I liked.

(4) Not only was she unhappy, but also she resented our sympathy.

(5) The traffic light was either broken or it had been disconnected.

(6) Not only are the lampreys killing the fish in the Great Lakes but also in adjacent lakes and streams.

(7) Her birthday is either next week or I am mistaken.

(8) The captain was uncertain whether he should ride out the storm or to put in at the nearest port.

(9) He was neither properly trained for the work nor did he want to do it.

(10) The foreman both watched me and criticized my work more than was necessary.

Phi Delt

187

17. COMPARISONS = COMP

Comparison should be logical and complete.

An *illogical comparison* relates items inexactly or attempts to compare items which are incapable of comparison. An *incomplete comparison* omits details which are necessary to the meaning of the comparison.

17a. Illogical use of THAN ANY OF should be avoided.

ILLOGICAL   I like "Mending Wall" better than any of Frost's poems.

REVISED   1 like "Mending Wall" better than any other of Frost's poems.

17b. Illogical use of OF ANY should be avoided.

ILLOGICAL   He is the best singer of any in the chorus.

REVISED   He is the best singer in the chorus.

17c. Items incapable of comparison should not be compared.

ILLOGICAL   The buildings here are as impressive as any other city.

REVISED   The buildings here are as impressive as those in any other city.

17d. Incomplete comparisons should be avoided.

These result when a parenthetical phrase is allowed to determine the grammatical form of the final element of comparison. Sentences of this sort can be tested by seeing what happens when the parenthetical phrase is omitted. (For example, the omission of the parenthetical phrase in the first sentence below results in "He is as strong than I am.") In colloquial English, the use of the incomplete comparison is quite common.

188

(1) *Omission of a necessary* as *or* than.

INCOMPLETE	He is as strong, if not stronger, than I am.
REVISED	He is as strong as, if not stronger than, I am.
REVISED	He is as strong as I am, if not stronger.

(2) *Incomplete use of the superlative.*

| INCOMPLETE | She is a very kind, if not the kindest, woman I know. |
| REVISED | She is one of the kindest women I know, if not the kindest. |

17e. Both terms of the comparison should be given.

INCOMPLETE	I admire her more than Jane.
REVISED	I admire her more than I admire Jane.
REVISED	I admire her more than Jane does.

17f. The basis of comparison should be stated.*

| INCOMPLETE | Our new automobile uses less gasoline. |
| REVISED | Our new automobile uses less gasoline than our old one did. |

EXERCISE 14. In the following sentences make comparisons logical and complete:

(1) She is as tall, if not taller, than her husband.

(2) I like "On, Wisconsin" better than any college victory song.

(3) I respect him more than John.

(4) Her gestures are like an actress.

(5) Air travel is much faster.

(6) He is the best dancer of any.

(7) The students here are as friendly as any other college.*

(8) Ellen's new boy friend is much more courteous.

(9) Mr. Martin's new television set is as good, if not better, than any I ever saw.

(10) Henry's "hot rod" will go faster than any of the fellows.

* Advertisers are especially—and persistently—guilty of violating this rule. The comparison in "Smoke 'Dromedaries'—they're better!" is allowed to stand incomplete for obvious reasons. In colloquial English, the basis of comparison is often omitted.

18. MISPLACED PARTS = MIS PT

Modifiers should be placed as close as possible to
the words they modify: related sentence elements
should not be needlessly separated.

Modern English, unlike German or Latin, has few inflections, or
special endings, to show the relation between words. For example,
the Latin sentences *Puella amat agricolam* and *Agricolam amat
puella* have roughly the same literal meaning: *the girl loves the
farmer.* But if the English equivalents of the Latin words are similarly reversed, so is the English meaning: *the girl loves the farmer;
the farmer loves the girl.* In English, therefore, the relation between
word order and clear meaning is fundamental, and one of a writer's
major concerns is how best to arrange his words and groups of
words within the sentence. An awkward or illogical placing of words
will obscure or change his meaning.

For example, logic and clarity require that a modifier be placed
next to the word it modifies, or at least as close as possible. Moreover, there must be no ambiguity about its relation to words that
precede or follow it. Sometimes the unconscious violation of this
principle has humorous results:

He bought a horse from a stranger *with a lame hind leg.*

18a. Adverbs such as ALMOST, EVEN, HARDLY, JUST, MERELY, ONLY,
NEARLY, SCARCELY **should refer clearly and logically to the
words they modify.**

The misplacement of modifiers—particularly *only*—does not always result in confusion. The misplaced *only* is rather common in
informal English, and the reference is usually clear, though not
exact.

INFORMAL	We *only* caught three fish.
FORMAL	We caught *only* three fish.
ILLOGICAL	She *nearly* blushed until she was purple.
CLEAR	She blushed until she was *nearly* purple.
MISPLACED	I *almost* read half the book. (Was this a lucky escape or a triumph?)
CLEAR	I read *almost* half the book.

EXERCISE 15. Revise the following sentences by putting the adverbs near the words they modify:

(1) I just arrived here last week.

(2) She almost seemed tired.

(3) We only have club meetings once a month.

(4) She merely declined my invitation because she wished to be spiteful.

(5) Since I had never attended an opera before, I nearly was sick with excitement when it began.

(6) Tickets will only be sold on the day of the game.

(7) The pioneers needed men to clear the forests badly.

(8) The brass band nearly entertained us for two hours.

(9) We scarcely harvested any apples on the farm last year.

(10) For a year we almost heard nothing from our former neighbors.

18b. Modifying phrases should refer clearly to the words they modify.

ILLOGICAL	Who is the woman who gave you the candy *in the pink dress?*
CLEAR	Who is the woman *in the pink dress* who gave you the candy?
ILLOGICAL	This poison attracts mice *with the smell of cheese.*
CLEAR	This poison *with the smell of cheese* attracts mice.

EXERCISE 16. Revise the following sentences by putting modifying phrases near the words they modify:

(1) We sat and watched the moon rise without saying a word.

(2) The roof collapsed soon after we left the building with a great crash.

(3) I returned to school after a week's vacation on Monday.

(4) Betty looked at the boy eating the sundae with envious eyes.

(5) George said that his father was a boy prodigy at my party last week.

(6) The yellow cat slowly crept up behind the bird with a bell on his collar.

(7) The escaped lion was captured before anybody was clawed or eaten by its keepers.

(8) The children looked forward to celebrating Christmas for several weeks.

(9) We hope that you will notify us if you can attend the banquet on the enclosed post card.

(10) The searchers found the cocker spaniel in a vacant garage with a broken leg.

18c. Modifying clauses should refer clearly to the words they modify.

ILLOGICAL	She borrowed an egg from a neighbor *that was rotten*.
CLEAR	From a neighbor she borrowed an egg *that was rotten*.
ILLOGICAL	There was a canary in the cage *which never sang*.
CLEAR	In the cage there was a canary *which never sang*.
ILLOGICAL	A dog is good company *that is well trained*.
CLEAR	A dog *that is well trained* is good company.

EXERCISE 17. Revise the following sentences by putting modifying clauses near the words they modify:

(1) I heard the train whistle at the crossing that was going to Denver.

(2) This book does not describe the Indian wars that I borrowed from the library.

(3) The boys bought an old car from a dealer that had no fenders.

(4) She put a green bonnet on her head which she had bought at an auction.

(5) He secured a job with a department store after he graduated from college which lasted for nearly twenty years.

(6) He bought an English setter from a neighbor that was beautifully trained.

(7) The fisherman paused to take an artificial fly from his tackle box which had never failed to catch a trout.

(8) We listened to the baseball game on the radio which the Yankees won.

(9) Dan showed me some beautiful pictures of his trip which he had made with his new enlarger.

(10) He told the clerk he wanted to buy a book for his mother that he thought was good.

18d. "Squinting" modifiers should be avoided.

A "squinting" modifier is a construction that may modify either a preceding or a following word. It squints at the words on its right and left, and the reader is left confused.

SQUINTING	His physician told him *frequently* to exercise.
CLEAR	His physician *frequently* told him to exercise.
CLEAR	His physician told him to exercise *frequently*.

EXERCISE 18. Recast the following sentences to eliminate squinting modifiers:

(1) I invited her occasionally to visit me.

(2) Religious faith without doubt is a great comfort to many people.

(3) He asked me the following day to pay my grocery bill.

(4) A dog that can do this trick well deserves to be praised.

(5) He said today the game would be played.

18e. The awkward splitting of infinitives should be avoided.

An infinitive is split when an adverbial modifier separates the *to* and the verb. There is nothing ungrammatical about splitting an infinitive, and sometimes a split is necessary to achieve clarity. But most split infinitives are awkward and unnecessary.

AWKWARD	She tried *to* not carelessly *hurt* the kitten.
CLEAR	She tried not *to hurt* the kitten carelessly.
AWKWARD	You should try *to,* if you can, *take* a walk every day.
CLEAR	If you can, you should try *to take* a walk every day.
CLEAR	Needing an advantage in the race, he expected *to* more than *gain* it by diligent practice. (Awkwardness results if *more than* is moved to any other position in the sentence.)

AWKWARD   Needing an advantage in the race, he more than ex-
             pected *to gain* it by diligent practice.

EXERCISE 19. Revise the following sentences by eliminating awkward split infinitives:

(1) He promised to never again go swimming in the old quarry.

(2) We agreed to once and for all dissolve our partnership.

(3) We expect our guests to not purposely damage our furniture.

(4) The general ordered the enemy to completely and uncondi-
    tionally surrender.

(5) The boys intend to, if the weather is fair, play ball tomorrow.

(6) After dinner they decided to some day in the near future meet
    at the same restaurant.

(7) Because they quarreled so much they decided to permanently
    separate.

(8) Just as I was about to triumphantly and gleefully slip the net
    under the biggest trout I have ever seen, he made one last
    lunge and escaped the hook.

(9) There is a legend that Shakespeare had to suddenly and igno-
    miniously leave his boyhood home because of his deer poach-
    ing.

(10) The marines were able to for three days repel the enemy as-
     saults on Glory Ridge.

18f. Subject and verb, verb and object, or parts of verb phrases should not be awkwardly separated.

The separation of basic sentence elements by less important parts,
though sometimes effective, often results in awkwardness.

EFFECTIVE SEPARATION   The *captain,* seeing the ominous storm
                          clouds gathering overhead, *ordered* the
                          crew to take in the sail.

EFFECTIVE SEPARATION   And so Pilate, *willing to content the peo-
                          ple,* released Barabbas unto them, and de-
                          livered Jesus, *when he had scourged him,*
                          to be crucified. (St. Mark, 15, 15)

EFFECTIVE SEPARATION   Only when a man is safely ensconced un-
                          der six feet of earth, *with several tons of
                          enlauding granite upon his chest,* is he in

194

a position to give advice with any cer-
tainty, and then he is silent.

—EDWARD NEWTON

AWKWARD SEPARATION | She *found,* after an hour's search, the *money* hidden under the rug.

CLEAR | After an hour's search, she *found* the **money** hidden under the rug.

AWKWARD SEPARATION | At the convention I saw Mr. Ward, **whom** I *had* many years ago *met* in Chicago.

CLEAR | At the convention I saw Mr. Ward, **whom** I *had met* many years ago in Chicago.

EXERCISE 20. Revise the following sentences by eliminating the unnecessary separation of related sentence elements:

(1) I, realizing that I was in danger, looked for a means of escape.

(2) In the spring we saw the songbirds which had some time during the autumn flown south.

(3) We shall, if we ever happen to be in St. Louis, call on you.

(4) I wrote, after several hours of deliberation, a letter to the president of the corporation.

(5) In a pleasant house in Concord, Emerson, who was a neighbor of Thoreau, lived.

(6) He discovered, after many years of restless voyaging, an enchanted island in the South Seas.

(7) We visited the little park where we had during our childhood lived.

(8) The greenhorn was, because he had not been warned against the racketeer's plot, easily fleeced of his money.

(9) I sold, although I did not want to do so, my movie camera.

(10) At last the scientist perfected the formula which he had been for years and years seeking.

19. DANGLING CONSTRUCTIONS = DGL

A modifying phrase or clause should be related logically and grammatically to some word in the sentence.

A modifier is said to dangle if it modifies nothing in the sentence or appears to modify a word to which it is not logically related. The result is frequently humorous:

> Plastic sheeting is used to keep a baby on the rear seat of a car from rolling off and also to protect the seat itself. The sheeting is fashioned to fit the seat and extend upward at the front to fasten to window frames. *Being transparent, the sleeping baby is always visible.*
>
> *or*
>
> Having been shot in the stern, the captain ordered the ship towed back to the port.

Dangling constructions, usually a result of carelessness or inexact thinking, can be revised (1) by making the dangling modifier apply to the subject of the main clause, or (2) by expanding the phrase into a subordinate clause.

19a. Dangling participles should be avoided.

Although a participle does not make an assertion, it implies an actor. Clarity requires that the actor be unmistakably identified, unless the participle appears in an idiomatic construction (*e.g.*, "Generally speaking, August is one of the hottest months").

> DANGLING *Driving* through the mountains, several bears were seen. (The participle *driving* modifies nothing, although it appears to modify *bears,* to which it is not logically related.)
>
> REVISED *Driving* through the mountains, *we* saw several bears. (*Driving* clearly modifies *we,* the subject of the main clause.)

196

REVISED   When *we drove* through the mountains, *we saw* several
              bears. (The modifying phrase is expanded into a sub-
              ordinate clause.)

DANGLING   *Riding* my bicycle, a dog chased me. (*Riding* modifies
              nothing; it cannot logically modify *dog*.)

REVISED   *Riding* my bicycle, I was chased by a dog. (Riding
              clearly modifies *I*, the subject of the main clause.)

REVISED   While *I was riding* my bicycle, a dog chased me. (The
              modifying phrase is expanded into a subordinate clause.)

EXERCISE 21. Revise the following sentences to eliminate the dangling participial phrases.

(1) My supper was cold, having come home late.

(2) Being made of stone, the builder expected the house to stand
    for a century.

(3) Working in the cotton field, the day passed slowly.

(4) Sitting in the bus, it was fun watching the passengers.

(5) The train ride was tiresome, waiting for morning to come.

(6) Expecting dad to send money, the postman brought only dis-
    appointment.

(7) The house was dark, coming home late last night.

(8) Knowing little algebra, the equation was difficult.

(9) Watching from the canoe, the moose approached the water's
    edge.

(10) Circling the bend of the river, the bridge loomed before us.

19b. Dangling gerunds should be avoided.

For a definition of gerund see "Index of Grammatical Terms,"
Section 50.

DANGLING   After *putting* a worm on my hook, the fish began to bite.

REVISED   After *putting* a worm on my hook, *I* found that the fish
              began to bite. (*Putting* clearly refers to *I*, the subject of
              the main clause.)

DANGLING   Before *exploring* the desert, our water supply was re-
              plenished. (*Exploring* cannot logically refer to *supply*,
              the subject of the main clause.)

REVISED   Before *exploring* the desert, *we* replenished our water
              supply. (*Exploring* refers to *we*, the subject of the main
              clause.)

EXERCISE 22. Revise the following sentences to eliminate the dangling gerund phrases:

(1) On entering the cave, the bones of a wild animal were seen.

(2) By studying hard, his grades improved.

(3) On receiving the telegram, our hopes were shattered.

(4) By keeping a budget, my bank account increased.

(5) In drawing our house plans, a back porch was omitted.

(6) After opening the door, the coat rack stood squarely in front of me.

(7) In packing the car, a suitcase was forgotten.

(8) By working every day, the barn was soon completed.

(9) After flying for three hours, the Hudson River appeared in the distance.

(10) Before washing the windows, a strong ladder must be obtained.

19c. Dangling infinitives should be avoided.

DANGLING   *To write* effectively, practice is necessary. (*To write* cannot logically refer to *practice*, the subject of the main clause.)

REVISED   *To write* effectively, *one* must practice. (*To write* logically refers to *one*, the subject of the main clause.)

REVISED   If *one wishes to write* effectively, practice is necessary (*or* he must practice).

DANGLING   *To examine* the brakes, the wheel must be removed. (*To examine* cannot logically refer to *wheel*.)

REVISED   *To examine* the brakes, *one* must remove the wheel. (*To examine* refers to *one*.)

REVISED   If *you wish to examine* the brakes, the wheel must be removed (*or* you must remove the wheel).

EXERCISE 23. Revise the following sentences to eliminate the dangling infinitive phrases:

(1) To be a successful salesman, people must like your personality.

(2) To become a lawyer, several years of study are required.

(3) To grow tomatoes, the plants should be watered regularly.

(4) To be really scoured, you have to scrub the pans with strong soap.

198

(5) To be well baked, you should leave the potatoes in the oven for forty minutes.

(6) To learn how to sing, a good voice teacher should be engaged.

(7) To find the trouble, the problem must be carefully studied.

(8) To be completely soaked, you have to immerse the sponge in water.

(9) To be a financial success, the public must buy a thousand tickets to the class play.

(10) To make a good impression, a clean shirt should be worn to the interview.

19d. Dangling elliptical clauses should be avoided.

An elliptical clause is one in which the subject or verb is implied rather than stated. The clause dangles if its implied subject is not the same as the subject of the main clause. Sentences containing dangling elliptical clauses can be revised (1) by making the dangling clause agree with the subject of the main clause, or (2) by supplying the omitted subject or verb.

DANGLING   *When a baby,* my grandfather gave me a silver cup.

REVISED   *When a baby, I* was given a silver cup by my grandfather. (The subject of the main clause agrees with the implied subject of the elliptical clause.)

REVISED   *When I was a baby,* my grandfather gave me a silver cup. (The omitted subject and verb are supplied in the elliptical clause.)

DANGLING   *While rowing on the lake,* the boat overturned.

REVISED   *While rowing on the lake,* we overturned the boat. (The subject of the main clause agrees with the implied subject of the elliptical clause.)

REVISED   *While we were rowing on the lake,* the boat overturned (*or* we overturned the boat). (The elliptical clause is expanded into a subordinate clause.)

EXERCISE 24. Revise the following sentences to eliminate the dangling elliptical clauses:

(1) While washing the dishes, somebody knocked on the front door.

(2) When well stewed, you remove the bones from the chicken.

(3) If found, I shall pay a reward for the dog.

(4) While counting the ballots, an argument began at the polling place.

(5) If attacked, a planned retreat will be made by the battalion.

(6) While shopping, the house burned down.

(7) My shoelace broke while hurrying to class.

(8) Just after rinsing out the nylon hose, her boy friend rang the doorbell.

(9) While flying a kite, the wind stopped.

(10) If overstuffed, I will buy the chair.

20. OMISSIONS AND INCOMPLETE CONSTRUCTIONS = OM

Words and phrases necessary to the clarity of the sentence should not be omitted.

Many sentences fail to communicate clearly because the writer has left out necessary words, either carelessly or ignorantly. The following sentences illustrate such omissions:

(1) Learning by imitation is one of the most common in early life.

(2) Television has become a dominating factor in today's children.

(3) The opportunities for men the popcorn business are varied.

Sentences (1) and (2) are totally confusing as they stand. Sentence (1) needs a phrase like *methods of learning* after *common;* sentence (2) needs a phrase like *the lives of* after *in.* What happens in this kind of sentence is that the writer completes the construction in his head but does not bother to put it on paper for his reader, who is thus left completely at sea. In sentence (3) the omission of *in* after *men* is a mechanical error that often occurs when speedily written first drafts are allowed to stand unchecked. The writer's hand is trying too eagerly to catch up with his thought, and words —usually articles, prepositions, and conjunctions—get left out.

20a. Papers should be carefully proofread to catch any careless omissions.

CARELESS	The ball sailed over back fence and out of sight.
CORRECTED	The ball sailed over *the* back fence and out of sight.
CARELESS	The officers of the fraternity were brought before the dean and asked explain the incident.
CORRECTED	The officers of the fraternity were brought before the dean and asked *to* explain the incident.

201

Some such omissions are acceptable in familiar speech but not in written English:

SPOKEN   We became friends our junior year in high school.

WRITTEN   We became friends *during* our junior year in high school.

SPOKEN   I have great interest in the field of medicine.

WRITTEN   I have *a* great interest in the field of medicine.

EXERCISE 25. Supply the words now omitted in the sentences below. Comment on any omission which you think may pass as acceptable in informal speech.

(1) Orientation week gave the student an idea what was ahead.

(2) This type error is difficult to analyze.

(3) Since the money was not given me, I had to work my way through college.

(4) I was not brought up a rich family.

(5) Hard work is the best to earn good marks.

(6) Some students make great fuss over having to work hard.

(7) World War II was the most costly war in the world.

(8) Some people think an athlete does not need sacrifice anything to become a star.

(9) Many millions people were unemployed the last depression.

(10) Scientific advancement the last twenty years has given us new way of life.

20b. Constructions necessary to the clarity of a sentence should not be omitted or left incomplete.

INCOMPLETE   To go to college for its practical value is a difficult choice in the face of the present economic situation.

COMPLETE   To go to college for its practical value *or to stay at home and take a job in industry is* a difficult choice in the face of the present economic situation.

INCOMPLETE   A period of happiness never lasts long but is interrupted.

COMPLETE   A period of happiness never lasts long but is *inevitably* interrupted *by pain or grief.*

Quite often the best way to deal with an incomplete construction is not to complete it but to omit it altogether. For instance, the sentence given as an example just above would be fully as meaning-ful if it were written *A period of happiness never lasts long.*

EXERCISE 26. Improve the sentences below:

(1) To make the change from glutton to connoisseur, one must know the difference.

(2) The first impression I had when I glanced at the front page of the *Times* was the difference in headlines.

(3) The effect of good looks or personality on the total character of an individual is not the only thing.

(4) Going into the army is something I never thought would hap-pen.

(5) While reading this book I found myself looking at a dictionary to help me understand what I was reading.

(6) In college, as compared with high school, teachers are more on an equal basis with students instead of a statue on a high pedestal.

(7) Being in class all day is bad, for by the end of the day when a student begins his homework he has forgotten.

(8) Having spent most of my first year in college in mathematics and chemistry has made me a bit wary of English courses.

(9) At the close of the summer vacation my mind was made for forestry.

(10) If you miss chapel, either because of sickness or will power, you have to account for your absence.

(11) The competition in business is very keen and requires lots of hard work to keep above the failing point.

(12) In running somebody down or building them up when you don't have the facts, you use words with connotations.

21. MIXED CONSTRUCTIONS = MIX

Mixed constructions should be avoided.

A "mixed construction" occurs when a writer begins a sentence with one construction in mind and, while writing, changes to another.

> We walked slowly up the hill, through the woods to the house stands like a lonely sentinel on the hilltop.

The writer was so taken with the beauty of what he was describing that he forgot that *house* was not the subject of the sentence but the noun in a prepositional phrase. What he meant was *the house which stands,* but what he meant and did not say will not excuse him with his readers.

Generally, as in the example above, the shift from one construction to another is absolute; the sentence begins with one construction and ends with another, as in

> The fact that John was a good student he received many offers for well-paying jobs.

Such errors sometimes occur when a writer is caught in a sentence either longer or more complex than the sentences he commonly writes. They are easy to repair, once the error is recognized.

MIXED   Take, for example, in the strip-mines of southeastern Ohio, the blaster has one of the best paying jobs.

REPAIRED   For example, in the strip-mines of southeastern Ohio, the blaster has one of the best paying jobs.

MIXED   If we here in America cannot live peaceably and happily together, we cannot hope that nations who have different living conditions to live peaceably with us.

REPAIRED   If we here in America cannot live peaceably and happily together, we cannot expect that other nations who have different living conditions will live peaceably with us.

MIXED Every few hundred feet a test sample of the layer of earth a bit of it is analyzed to determine the distance from oil.

REPAIRED Every few hundred feet a test sample of the layer of earth is analyzed to determine the distance from oil.

The examples above show a general kind of mixed construction. A more specific kind involves the improper use of the tense of a verb in indirect questions, as

The manager told me that he would have my car for me as soon as he can get the service garage.

Here the problem is one of sequence of tenses (see Section 6a.) The verb *can* should be changed to *could* to correlate with *told* and *would have.*

EXERCISE 27. Eliminate any mixed constructions in the sentences below:

(1) She has a way that makes you feel at home when I am with her.

(2) Much help came from the instructor tried a second time to make the students understand.

(3) With a slap on the back and a few friendly handshakes the next thing I knew I was on the football field during an actual game.

(4) The campus is enormous and one glimpse of it made me feel as a weary traveler must have felt lost in the forbidden mountains.

(5) The attitude of forcing the student to make his own decisions is the only way to go to school and learn something.

(6) I consider social climbing an evil, for you see many girls look for fellows that can offer security in life.

(7) By giving him an education and making him feel wanted will benefit the juvenile delinquent greatly.

(8) I am getting acquainted with new friends here, and the friends I had I see them occasionally.

(9) Being a girl's boarding school I attended, there were no mixed classes.

(10) The law requires you to go to school until of a certain age, besides being an accepted policy that all children go through at least high school.

(11) The forestry courses taught here prepare you for a highly technical profession in which it takes four years of very difficult study in order to graduate.

(12) The clinic here is very busy, but the way it is handled it doesn't seem to inconvenience the patients.

(13) I feel that there is a great need for the integration of education—bring the school, home, and community into a more cooperative program and better understanding of the needs, resources, and meeting the various programs.

(14) Compared to the university where your presence in class is not compulsory makes you want to get to class on time.

(15) By letting the individual develop as a worthwhile member of society instead of as a member of a reform school is in my way of thinking the way to develop good citizenship.

22. GENERAL AWKWARDNESS AND
OBSCURITY = AWK, OBSC

Awkward and obscure sentences should be recast.

Some sentences are so clumsy or so generally meaningless that they cannot be repaired by minor surgery; they have to be rethought and rewritten. They contain so many errors in basic sentence structure that statements like "lack of parallelism," "poor subordination," or "vague reference" only begin to indicate what is wrong. For example, the person who wrote

> The heart, an essential in any organism, to me has the same significance to the organism in comparison with hope and man.

would be wise to draw a heavy line through the whole sentence and start over again.

A second kind of obscurity is one not necessarily awkward, but so absurd or ridiculous as to be meaningless.

> Even though our material possessions are destroyed, we know tomorrow will be different.

This is a perfectly straightforward sentence, grammatically, and no one would accuse it of being awkward. But its meaning is absurd, or at best not clear. If we are being told that material possessions which are destroyed today will be made whole again tomorrow, then we are reading nonsense.

22a. Awkwardly phrased sentences should be recast.

AWKWARD   If people know something about color and design they will avoid buying something that they will later say of, "I just don't look as good in it as I thought I would."

RECAST   If people know something about color and design they will avoid buying clothes of which they will later say, "I don't look as good in this as I thought I would."

AWKWARD	Some farmers plow their land in the fall of the year, and this is better they think.
RECAST	Some farmers prefer to plow their land in the fall.
AWKWARD	An education will enable me to read good books which in turn will provide happiness on my part.
RECAST	An education will provide me with the opportunity to read the good books I feel necessary to my happiness.
AWKWARD	Each student has different problems because each has a different reason for coming and place to live.
RECAST	The problem of each student is different because his home life and his reasons for coming to college are different.

EXERCISE 28. Recast the following sentences:

(1) A fruit substitute for a pastry can make a big difference in our general health if we will do this every day.

(2) In high school there are few if any fraternities to hinder, which they sometimes do, your school work.

(3) The thought of becoming a political scientist was brought up in the discussion, and the answer given by Professor Beal was that one should be able to change his views, if the facts were strong enough on another viewpoint, to become a political scientist.

(4) When I walked through the gates of the university, in the best tradition, I was entering something I knew nothing about and of which I had no knowledge.

(5) A new student entering college will find himself surrounded with a completely new way of life and school.

(6) Can you overcome some of your weaknesses which you had in high school, such as studying, learning to make smart decisions instead of being foolish, and many more weaknesses which I can't think of offhand?

(7) The students in a technical school are very different because most of them are there to learn something instead of because they have to be there.

(8) To me the course in Latin was a real test, proving a will to learn or to be pulled down by weak will power.

(9) In college they don't care if you come to class, which makes a person feel it is his duty to do it, but in high school when they

said you had to be there that just made you want to try to get away with it.

(10) In college I find that there is not the individual help given students as was so in high school.

22b. Sentences whose meaning is obscure or illogical should be re-thought and recast.

(1) It would not do a person any good to boast of a college education if he had accomplished nothing and had nothing at the time.

(2) I have always thought that the present time was a rather unhappy time because there are always worries, but as the time went on I looked back at these times as the only happy times.

The author of sentence (1) may have thought he was saying something profound, but the statement "would not do a person any good" is meaningless in its context. *Good* is too ambiguous a word to be used so loosely. The writer of sentence (2), on the other hand, is tangled in "time." What he wants to say, we suspect, is that experience grows more pleasant in retrospect, but his sentence structure does not permit him to go from the present to the future and then to the past, as he wants to. We would have to say of the sentence, as did the confused young boy trying to give directions to some travelers, "You can't get there from here."

There is a kind of illogical sentence which, in a proper context, may make sense—and in fact strike appreciative readers or listeners as sophisticated and witty. For example, the sentence, "His bad temper is a lot like his father's, only more so," might impress acquaintances of the father and son as an extremely apt description. Similarly, a sentence like, "He is more or less crooked, mostly more," could be either clever or inane, depending on the speaker and the circumstances. But such a sentence as "Our feeling was the closest feeling to love, maybe even closer" is likely to strike readers as absurd. Be sure that your attempted wit reaches its mark.

EXERCISE 29. Recast the following sentences:

(1) While I was a salesman traveling hither and yon I ate better yon than hither.

(2) Her eyes were not set too far apart or too close together, and the two together, apart from her face, were beautiful.

(3) The freshman will always be bewildered at the beginning of school, even if it is high school or college.

(4) A large city is not much different, but it sure is bigger.

(5) The first impression I had of navy life was very noticeable to me.

(6) Most of the unknown facts about psychology are very common; others are complicated.

(7) The United States is making some progress in producing synthetic rubber but not enough is produced if the supply were cut off tomorrow.

(8) The first difference to enter the mind of a recruit is the lack of freedom he has.

(9) When a college teacher has a group of boys and girls of college age, the instructor tends to let them on their own.

(10) College life, as compared with high school, is a very great comparison indeed.

23. TRANSITIONS = TRANS

Transitions in the sentence should be exact and clear.

Transitional words and phrases are often necessary to show how the separate parts of a sentence are related. They are connecting links. When a necessary transition is omitted, the reader loses his way; when a transition is inexact, the reader is misled. See "Subordination," Section 14e.

The misuse (intended, of course) of *but, and though,* and *under it all* in the sentence below shows how surprising to a reader an illogical transition can be:

> [Pittsburgh millionaires] are rough but uncivil in their manners, and though their ways are boisterous and unpolished, under it all they have a great deal of impoliteness and discourtesy.
>
> —O. HENRY

A list of common transitional words and phrases appears in Section 13.

23a. Inexact transitions should be avoided.

INEXACT   Martin Sellers wanted to attend the concert, *and* his wife wanted to see the wrestling matches. (The transition fails to show the contrast between the ideas in the two clauses.)

CLEAR   Martin Sellers wanted to attend the concert, *but* his wife wanted to see the wrestling matches.

EXERCISE 30. Revise the following sentences by using exact transitions:

(1) We unfortunately lost our tickets; however, we did not attend the play.

211

(2) Jack wanted to be a high jumper, and the track coach insisted that he be a hurdler.

(3) I was upset by his anger; besides, I don't blame him for being angry.

(4) The performance was interesting; nevertheless, the second act impressed me most.

(5) All the witnesses emphasized his cowardly behavior, but I was surprised when he took the stand in his own defense.

(6) The sailor's complexion was not dark; moreover, he spent a great deal of time in the tropics.

(7) I enjoy eating roast beef, but I also like pork.

(8) I wanted to carry out the plan, and my conscience said "No."

(9) Most of the football game was unexciting; besides, the second quarter had some thrills.

(10) Two times two equals four, yet four times four equals sixteen.

23b. Necessary transitions should not be omitted.

ABRUPT   She wanted to buy a new hat; she could not afford one. (The close relationship between the two ideas is not indicated by a transition.)

REVISED   She wanted to buy a new hat, *but* she could not afford one.

ABRUPT   The captain had had many adventures; he had once been lost in the African jungle.

REVISED   The captain had had many adventures; *for instance,* he had once been lost in the African jungle.

EXERCISE 31. Revise the following sentences by inserting transitions between closely related ideas:

(1) The cherries were high in the tree; we borrowed a long ladder.

(2) I got up early, went fishing.

(3) The snow was deep; the children played indoors.

(4) I have lived in several large cities, New York and Chicago.

(5) Nancy was ill with pneumonia; she did not attend the party.

(6) There were many rabbits in the woods; the hunter saw only one.

(7) He lives in Florida; the setting of his poems is in Vermont.

(8) When hunting, Jim wears a red jacket; he does not want to be mistaken for a deer.

212

(9) Trout change their diet unexpectedly. Yesterday they were biting on worms; today they want flies.

(10) Wilbur likes to ride in the country; his family enjoys going with him.

24. POSITION OF EMPHATIC
SENTENCE ELEMENTS = EMP

The parts of the sentence should be arranged to give emphasis to important ideas.

24a. Important words should be placed at the beginning or at the end of the sentence.

The most emphatic place in a sentence is its ending; the next most emphatic, its beginning; the least emphatic, its middle.

UNEMPHATIC   The nationalist armies won a decisive victory, according to newspaper reports. (An incidental detail is given the most emphatic position in the sentence.)

EMPHATIC   According to newspaper reports, the nationalist armies won a decisive victory.

UNEMPHATIC   If this account is accurate, the results of the chemical experiment were startling, however.

EMPHATIC   If this account is accurate, however, the results of the chemical experiment were startling.

EXERCISE 32. Revise the following sentences by putting important words in an emphatic position:

(1) The defendant abused his civil liberties, in my opinion.

(2) Moreover, she is a person of wide interests and sympathies, I think.

(3) The outcome of the game was decided by lucky breaks, to a large extent.

(4) It seems to me that men are more interested in scientific subjects than women are, as a rule.

(5) Nevertheless, important scientific discoveries have been made by women, in some cases.

(6) The terms of the treaty are unacceptable, if I understand the problems correctly.

214

(7) As I see it, the trial was unfair, in the first place.

(8) We have an even chance to win the game, if everything goes right.

(9) It appears to me that plane accidents are fatal, generally.

(10) As a boy, Milton had good eyesight, it is said.

24b. Emphasis is achieved by the skillful use of the periodic sentence.

A *periodic sentence* withholds its main idea until the end; a *loose sentence* begins with the main idea and ends with subordinate details. A skillfully written periodic sentence is therefore dramatic; it creates suspense.

> The English poor, broken in every revolt, bullied by every fashion, long despoiled of property, and now being despoiled of liberty, entered history with a noise of trumpets, and turned themselves in two years into one of the iron armies of the world.
>
> —G. K. CHESTERTON

Similarly in the following sentence: the main idea—*i.e.*, praise of the English jury system—is carefully (perhaps too obviously so) withheld until the end.

> In my mind, he was guilty of no error, he was chargeable with no exaggeration, he was betrayed by his fancy into no metaphor, who once said that all we see about us, kings, lords, and commons, the whole machinery of the State, all the apparatus of the system, and its varied workings, end in simply bringing twelve good men into a box.
>
> —HENRY PETER

In the examples below, the periodic sentence is much more effective than the loose one.

PERIODIC   After he had stood for five minutes with his arms hanging limply at his sides, a look of beaten humility on his face, the cowboy suddenly reached for his gun and began firing at the two outlaws.

LOOSE   The cowboy suddenly reached for his gun and began firing at the two outlaws after he had stood for five minutes with his arms hanging limply at his sides, a look of beaten humility on his face.

On the other hand, a writer cannot and should not make all his sentences formally periodic. Too much suspense is wearying. The periodic sentence is effective only when used judiciously—when the subject matter of the sentence warrants it.

PERIODIC AND INEFFECTIVE   At the end of a dark alley, three flights down in a dark basement full of grim and evil-looking sailors, I ate my lunch.

In many instances the *periodic* and *loose* constructions are equally effective.

LOOSE   Balboa reached the Pacific after a long, hazardous journey.

PERIODIC   After a long, hazardous journey, Balboa reached the Pacific.

LOOSE   He will be a good physician, if enthusiasm is a guarantee of success.

PERIODIC   If enthusiasm is a guarantee of success, he will be a good physician.

EXERCISE 33. Change the following loose sentences into periodic sentences:

 (1) Your money will be returned if, after trying this medicine, you are dissatisfied.
 (2) The bear turned about suddenly when he heard a noise in the underbrush.
 (3) Many years ago there was only a wagon trail here, before the highway was built.
 (4) You must pay the fine unless you can prove that no traffic law was violated.
 (5) The tomato plants died, although we tried to protect them from the frost.
 (6) The winning run was scored after two men were out in the last of the ninth inning.
 (7) You may be killed if you walk into the street without looking.
 (8) I saw two cars crash head-on several years ago on a three-lane highway just outside a small town in Kentucky.
 (9) The cavalry force attacked after receiving a message from headquarters telling them to go ahead.

(10) The atomic bomb was not perfected until 1945, although atomic fission had been experimented with for many years.

24c. Items in a series should have a logical order as well as parallel form.

"Logical order" is generally natural or chronological order, as "He ate his dinner, went to a movie, and then retired to his room." But it may sometimes refer to "climactic order"—the arrangement of ideas in rising order of importance. In the natural (and childish) order of things, the best comes first, like dessert before spinach. In rhetorical strategy, the opposite is true; the strongest and most striking comes last.

> UNEMPHATIC   His life was tragic and brief.
> EMPHATIC   His life was brief and tragic.

Violation of this principle often results in the humor of anticlimax.

> Madame, your dinner was superbly cooked, beautifully served, and very good, too.

Perhaps the classic example of humorous anticlimax is the following:

> If once a man indulges himself in murder, very soon he comes to think little of robbery; and from robbing he next comes to drinking and Sabbath-breaking, and from that to incivility and procrastination.
>
> —THOMAS DE QUINCEY

EXERCISE 34. Revise the following sentences by arranging ideas in the order of climax:

(1) During his vacation Ben acquired a coat of tan, a wife, and a secondhand automobile.

(2) Her novel created a furor of controversy and was well written.

(3) In the oratorical contest Alan won a college scholarship and a medal.

(4) Henry is a capable violinist, a renowned surgeon, and a stamp collector.

(5) Mrs. Carey inherited a large farm, some old furniture, and a small insurance policy.

(6) After the earthquake one could see tumbled buildings, twisted water pipes, and mangled automobiles.

(7) Most students study English in high school, college, and elementary school.

(8) Daniel Webster was a great orator and a capable writer.

(9) While in college Harry was an "A" student, a waiter in a fraternity house, and a member of the glee club.

(10) Metzger finally graduated with honors after almost flunking out in his freshman year and making rather poor grades as a sophomore.

24d. Emphasis is achieved by the effective repetition of words and ideas.

For a discussion of how words may be repeated to gain clarity, see Section 32d; for a discussion of ways in which the repetition of words and ideas can serve to link sentences together in a paragraph, see Section 13d. In the rhetoric of sentence structure, effective repetition is chiefly a matter of repeating key phrases or constructions —in many respects a matter of effective parallelism (see Section 16a). For example, note how Dr. Johnson's "I like their" is effectively repeated in the sentence below:

I am very fond of the company of ladies. *I like their* beauty, *I like their* delicacy, *I like their* vivacity and *I like their* silence.

—SAMUEL JOHNSON

The repetition of key constructions in the passage below might strike some modern readers as overly eloquent, but it does serve to illustrate how repetition may be used, not only to give a continuity to what is being said, but also to bring the reader (or listener) to a rhetorical climax.

I would rather have been a French peasant and worn wooden shoes. *I would rather have* lived in a hut with a vine growing over the door and the grapes growing purple in the kisses of the Autumn sun. *I would rather have been that* poor peasant with my loving wife by my side, knitting as the day died out of the sky, with my children upon my knee and their arms about me. *I would rather have been that* man and gone down to the tongueless silence of the dreamless

218

dust than to *have been that* imperial impersonation of force and murder known as Napoleon the Great.

—ROBERT INGERSOLL

EXERCISE 35. Discuss the effectiveness of the repetition of words and phrases in each of the sentences below. (Note how frequently effective repetition and effective parallelism reinforce each other.)

(1) No one can be perfectly free till all are free; no one can be perfectly moral till all are moral; no one can be perfectly happy till all are happy.

—HERBERT SPENCER

(2) There is no mistake; there has been no mistake; and there shall be no mistake.

—DUKE OF WELLINGTON

(3) To know how to say what others only know how to think is what makes men poets or sages; and to dare to say what others only dare to think makes men martyrs or reformers or both.

—ELIZABETH CHARLES

(4) It is true that you may fool all the people some of the time; you can even fool some of the people all the time; but you can't fool all of the people all the time.

—ABRAHAM LINCOLN

(5) We are always doing something for Posterity, but I would fain see Posterity do something for us.

—JOSEPH ADDISON

25. WEAK PASSIVE VOICE = WP

The active voice is usually more emphatic than the passive voice.

The passive voice stresses the importance of the receiver of the verb's action rather than its doer. It has legitimate uses:

PASSIVE (1) He *was struck* on the head by a foul ball.
ACTIVE (2) A foul ball *struck* him on the head.

Sentence (1) emphasizes *who* was struck; sentence (2), *what* struck him. A writer's choice between the two would be determined by which he wished to emphasize; the active voice is not always more effective than the passive. In sentences like these below, the passive construction is more effective than the active:

(1) He *was shot* through the heart.
(2) We *were to be hanged* at midnight.

On the other hand, the use of the passive voice weakens the force of the sentences below:

(1) During the morning the equator *was crossed* by the ship.
(2) A tree *was crashed into* by a car going ninety miles an hour.

Such ineffective use of the passive voice gives rise to the term "weak passive." Its excessive use smothers the life and personality of a writer's style.

EXERCISE 36. In the following sentences replace the passive voice with the active voice:

(1) Waffles and bacon were ordered by us for supper.
(2) Mr. Brown's lawn will be mowed by Johnny on Saturday.
(3) A black cotton dress was bought by Susan.
(4) No moss is gathered by a rolling stone.

(5) My ankles were snapped at by an angry dog.

(6) On the opening day of the season a bear was shot by the hunter.

(7) Next week my vacation will be begun by me.

(8) The radiator of the car became frozen during the cold night.

(9) The bone was devoured by the dog.

(10) The Battle of Waterloo was lost by Napoleon.

26. POINT OF VIEW = PV

Point of view in the sentence should be consistent and logical.

Point of view is a term which describes a writer's use of subject, of person and number, and of verb tense, voice, and mood. Needless shift in point of view not only affects the relationship of sentence elements, but also reveals careless thinking.

26a. A needless shift in subject or voice should be avoided.

FAULTY   Frogs could be heard croaking as we neared the swamp. (The subject shifts from *frogs* to *we*. The verb shifts from passive to active voice.)

REVISED   We heard frogs croaking as we neared the swamp.

FAULTY   Ellen stayed at a mountain resort, and much of her time was spent in painting. (The subject shifts from *Ellen* to *much*. The verb shifts from active to passive voice.)

REVISED   Ellen stayed at a mountain resort and spent much of her time in painting.

EXERCISE 37. Revise the following sentences by eliminating all needless shifts in subject or voice:

(1) When we approached the burning house, smoke was seen.

(2) Mrs. Carey washed the dishes, and then the ironing was done by her.

(3) Tex is a good swimmer, but his strength was not great enough to swim the channel.

(4) He held the ruler on the paper, and a long line was drawn.

(5) After a hot fire was built by the campers, they dried their wet clothing.

(6) We entered our first college classroom, and seats were taken by us.

(7) Mr. Jones practiced daily, and his golf game was improved.

(8) Fish could be seen jumping as we approached the river.

(9) The men decided upon a camp site, and the tent was soon pitched.

(10) Casey Jones mounted to the engine cab, and the throttle was grabbed.

26b. A needless shift in person or number should be avoided.

FAULTY   When *you* have good health, *one* should feel fortunate. (A shift from second to third person.)

REVISED   When *you* have good health, *you* should feel fortunate.

REVISED   When *one* has good health, *he* (or *one*) should feel fortunate.

FAULTY   If a *person* practices diligently, *they* can become an expert archer. (A shift from singular to plural number.)

REVISED   If a *person* practices diligently, *he* can become an expert archer.

EXERCISE 38. Revise the following sentences by eliminating all needless shifts in person or number:

(1) I always carry a pocketknife, because they are often useful.

(2) I took an aspirin tablet, for I knew they would relieve my headache.

(3) If one is willing to help put up the tent, you can get a free ticket to the circus.

(4) Everyone should exercise daily, for you derive great benefit from exercise.

(5) I like an occasional cup of coffee, for they give me that added boost which I need.

(6) After you have finished two sets of tennis, one feels like relaxing in a cool shower.

(7) Every young person should learn to drive an automobile, for they will need the ability later in life.

(8) I enjoy a novel by Dickens because their plots are so involved.

(9) No matter what subject one intends to major in, you should be proficient in writing.

(10) I distrust a public opinion poll because they have often been wrong in the past.

26c. A needless shift in tense or mood should be avoided.

FAULTY   He *sat* down at his desk and *begins* to write. (The verb shifts from past tense to present tense.)

REVISED   He *sat* down at his desk and *began* to write.

FAULTY   *Hold* the rifle firmly against your shoulder, and then you *should take* careful aim. (The verb shifts from imperative mood to indicative mood.)

REVISED   *Hold* the rifle firmly against your shoulder and then *take* careful aim.

EXERCISE 39. Revise the following sentences by eliminating all needless shifts in tense or mood:

(1) When I met Roger at the street corner, he does not recognize me.

(2) First you tie a fisherman's knot, and then you should tighten the loops so that they lie straight in line.

(3) Large clouds are drifting in the sky, and suddenly the moon was hidden from view.

(4) Spade carefully around the tree, and you should take care not to cut the roots.

(5) The book is interesting, although one of the main characters was unrealistic.

(6) After I had finished the long explanation, he says he doesn't understand.

(7) The cats are playing contentedly, but the family dog was in an angry mood.

(8) Heat the grease in the frying pan, and then you should put in the eggs.

(9) Without hesitating, he picks up the ball and shot for the wrong basket.

(10) I had put a nickel in the juke box, and the fun really starts.

27. VARIETY = VAR

The skillful writer avoids monotony by mixing short simple sentences with longer compound or complex sentences and by varying the beginnings of sentences.

27a. The overuse of short simple sentences should be avoided.

See "Subordination," Section 14c.

INEFFECTIVE   Jack approached the mare warily. She saw the bridle in his hand. He stood still. The mare waited. Jack tried to toss the reins over her head. But she galloped away.

REVISED   Jack warily approached the mare, who saw the bridle in his hand. He stood still and the mare waited. But when he tried to toss the reins over her head, she galloped away.

EXERCISE 40. Revise the following sentences to avoid the overuse of short, simple statements.

(1) The bookstore was crowded. Martha finally got the attention of a clerk. She asked the price of her history textbook. The price was three dollars. Martha paid the money and left.

(2) A company of soldiers marched by. They were led by a burly captain. He gave orders in a thunderous voice. He watched his men with a stern eye.

(3) I saw a movement in the deep grass. I stood still. There was a sudden whir of feathers. A pheasant sailed over my head.

(4) The pitcher prepared to deliver the ball. The catcher gave him a signal. The pitcher whirled and threw the ball to the first baseman. The baserunner dived safely back to the base.

(5) The lecturer looked critically at his audience. He shuffled his notes and cleared his throat. He drank a glass of water. He began speaking in a low voice.

(6) Grace is pretty. Her hair is blonde and her eyes blue. She has a fair complexion.

(7) I cast my bait into the reed bed. I had seen a large black bass jump there. I felt a powerful jerk on my line. The battle had begun.

(8) He picked up the letter. He began to read it. A look of pure bewilderment crossed his face. Then he began to smile. The next moment he was waving the letter in the air and shouting something. He was laughing hard. I couldn't make out what he was saying.

(9) The college was small and secluded. It was very old, however. It had an excellent reputation. Its faculty was world famous.

(10) Benjamin Franklin achieved his first success as a printer. He was also a practical inventor. The Franklin Stove is named after him. He was also interested in English spelling. He wanted to reform it.

27b. The overuse of long compound sentences should be avoided. See "Subordination," Section 14c.

INEFFECTIVE   The stagecoach rounded a bend, but two masked horsemen blocked the road, and they covered the driver with their rifles, and then they ordered him to raise his hands.

REVISED   As the stagecoach rounded a bend, two masked horsemen blocked the road. Covering the driver with their rifles, they ordered him to raise his hands. (In this revision the first co-ordinate clause is reduced to a subordinate clause; the third co-ordinate clause is reduced to a phrase; the second and fourth co-ordinate clauses become the main clauses of separate sentences.)

INEFFECTIVE   He was chief of the volunteer fire company, and he was the town's grocer, but he was never too busy in his store to attend a fire.

REVISED   The chief of the volunteer fire company, who was also the town's grocer, was never too busy in his store to attend a fire. (The first co-ordinate clause becomes a noun phrase, the subject of the main clause in the revised sentence; the second co-ordinate clause

226

becomes a subordinate clause; the third co-ordinate clause becomes the predicate of the main clause.)

INEFFECTIVE   She carefully powdered her nose, and then she applied her lipstick, and then she smiled at her reflection in the mirror.

REVISED   She carefully powdered her nose, applied her lipstick, and then smiled at her reflection in the mirror. (The compound sentence is revised to make a simple sentence with a compound predicate.)

EXERCISE 41. Revise the following sentences to avoid excessive co-ordination.

(1) He had frequent headaches, and he realized that he should have his eyes examined, but his meager income did not allow him the expense of an examination.

(2) The Mortons lived in a residence of impressive size, for they believed that large houses were an indication of financial success, and they wanted to show some evidence of their social position.

(3) *Ben Hur* was written by Lew Wallace in 1880, and it is a novel of the time of Christ, and it was widely read in America.

(4) Arthur was an excellent pianist, and he organized a dance orchestra at the university, and he financed his own education, but his long hours of work kept him from making higher grades.

(5) The social centers of the Puritan community were the church and the school, and the Puritans believed that the school should exert a religious influence, and they gave a strong impetus to moral education in America.

(6) I rose early in the morning and I dressed quickly, and then I ate breakfast quickly and rushed off to class.

(7) The German equivalent of the American high school is the Gymnasium, but the word is not connected with athletics, and the education is much more formalized than ours.

(8) The history of the world is the story of the rise of the common man, for the common man has not always enjoyed a voice in government, for he was held down by his rulers, and he had to fight bitterly for his freedom.

(9) The halfback was the star of the game, for after running the

kickoff back for a touchdown, he recovered a fumble and on the next play passed thirty yards for a second touchdown, after which he kicked the extra point.

(10)   Mrs. Tanner talks to my mother over the back fence and they go on for hours never really saying anything, but having a wonderful time, and the dishes sit in the sink and the dust collects and Father wonders where his supper is, and sometimes, I admit, I do too.

27c. A series of sentences each beginning with a subject-noun should be avoided.

The repetition of a subject-noun beginning in a series of sentences is usually monotonous. It is easy to fall into such monotony in a first draft; in revision a number of variations can be effected. We must remember, however, that devices for varying the word order of sentences cannot be applied mechanically. Word order is closely associated with meaning and emphasis, and varying the beginning of a sentence changes, however slightly, its meaning. For illustrations of the way in which the beginnings of sentences may be varied—and the ways in which these variations modify meaning—consider the following:

Deer grazed peacefully in the valley and were unaware of the advancing hunter.

(1) BEGINNING WITH A PREPOSITIONAL PHRASE.

In the valley the deer grazed peacefully and were unaware of the advancing hunter.

(2) BEGINNING WITH A VERBAL PHRASE.

Grazing peacefully, the deer in the valley were unaware of the advancing hunter.

(3) BEGINNING WITH AN EXPLETIVE.

There were deer grazing peacefully in the valley, unaware of the advancing hunter.

(4) BEGINNING WITH A SUBORDINATE CLAUSE.

As they grazed peacefully in the valley, the deer were unaware of the advancing hunter.

228

(5) BEGINNING WITH A CO-ORDINATING CONJUNCTION.

And the deer, grazing peacefully in the valley, were unaware of the advancing hunter.

But the deer, grazing peacefully in the valley, were unaware of the advancing hunter.

EXERCISE 42. Revise the following sentences by varying their beginnings in three of the five different ways suggested above:

(1) The prisoner looked hopefully at his lawyer and awaited the jury's verdict.

(2) Jean hoped her new dress would be pretty and selected the material with great care.

(3) The child lost his way in the wilderness but was rescued by a party of searchers.

(4) The coach rushed out on the field to protest the umpire's decision.

(5) Jumbo was a huge elephant and ate all the peanuts the children gave him.

(6) Air pressure is greater on the water in the glass than on the water in the straw, and therefore forces water down in the glass, up the straw and into your mouth.

(7) The chair appeared stable until the minister sat down in it, but then one leg crumpled, tipping chair and minister into the swimming pool.

(8) We returned home sullen and irritable after a delightful afternoon on the midway.

(9) Norm Holden played a good game in left field, but he spent the next three days in bed.

(10) The upholsterer, his mouth full of tacks and his magnetic hammer swinging like a piece of machinery, stretched and fastened the chaircover with amazing speed.

EXERCISE 43. Rewrite the following paragraph with greater variety in the sentence structures.

Rod felt better as soon as he was out of the house. He sat on the stoop of a nearby apartment house and lighted a cigaret. He knew why his mother screamed at him, and he didn't blame her. She worked a long day, and she spent an hour going and coming on the subway, so naturally she was exhausted when she came home. Rod knew that his mother would be a lot happier if he got a job. He didn't know why he couldn't bring himself to hunt for one, but it seemed as though he couldn't get out of bed before noon. That wasn't the real reason. He was afraid of working because he was afraid he would be fired, like last time. Rod knew that, but he also knew he couldn't tell his mother. They would keep on arguing, and Rod would keep on staying away from home most of the night so that he wouldn't have to face his mother.

EXERCISE 44. Imitate the structures of the following sentences, preserving each grammatical part and keeping the emphasis the same, but substitute different ideas and different words for those given. You may, if you wish, use the prepositions, conjunctions, articles, and demonstratives used in the original sentence.

EXAMPLE: These two pairs of sentences are imitations of those immediately above.

Remember the days of your childhood, nursing each ancient wound and making old victories more glorious, but seek new wounds and new victories without hesitation. Memory can, when it chooses, deaden the spirit, the will, the intent and the effectiveness needed for present action.

Pack the tobacco with your thumb, maintaining even pressure and making the surface flat, but avoid the tight pack or the loose one described in the last paragraph. A pipe will, when packed properly, give the taste, the even draw, the long smoke and the contentment described by seasoned pipe-lovers.

Notice that you may supply or leave out modifying words when you need to. Your sentences need not be related to one another.

1. A sentence is a living thing. (*e.g.* The heat wave was a withering experience.)
2. The good ones have neither too many nor too few parts.
3. And each part, like each organ of a living body, dies when cut off from the source of life.
4. A meaningless fragment shocks the reader as would a dissevered limb.
5. But that same fragment, performing its function in conjunction with the other organs of a good sentence, can be a thing of beauty.

6. Another quality which a sentence shares with an organism is flexibility.

7. With the energetic spurt of a strong verb, with the graceful gesture of an adjective or an adverb, with the persistence of a conjunction or the stubbornness of a noun, a sentence can adapt itself quickly to any demand.

8. Like any living thing, every sentence is a proud individual.

9. Although it is necessarily very much like its neighbors in all essentials, it has a life of its own to lead.

10. To conform mechanically to the structures of surrounding sentences would be an indignity to so capable an individual.

11. It might even be said that a sentence is not only a living organism but also a citizen in a community, its paragraph.

12. Two considerations, then, govern the way it is put together.

13. Its first duty is to do its job, as efficiently as possible, in the communicative work of the paragraph.

14. That every writer will make his sentences do this is taken for granted, but the good writer will, in addition, remember the second consideration.

15. He should be able to make each sentence live with harmony and distinction among the other citizens of the paragraph.

SENTENCE REVIEW EXERCISE. The sentences below contain errors discussed in Sections 14-27. Indicate what strikes you as the principal error in each sentence (faulty parallelism, illogical comparison, etc.) and then revise the sentence accordingly.

(1) The vase was a beautiful and priceless illustration of ancient Cretan art, and it was in a glass display case.

(2) The dog was casually sauntering down the street when he was hit and instantly killed by a speeding car.

(3) While Innis was already deeply in debt, he felt that the bargain was too good to let pass.

(4) The sports writers generally pay more attention to Notre Dame than any team in the midwest.

(5) To make concrete you need cement. This should be of good quality. You also need sand. You should have twice as much sand as concrete. Gravel is the third thing needed. About three times as much gravel as cement goes into concrete. The

gravel should be clean. It should not be mixed with soil or dirt.

(6) Elmer Davis said that Senator Jordan showed much ignorance of Asiatic affairs in his broadcast last night.

(7) Dushard paused a second and then shot with his famous skill and accuracy the puck straight at the goal.

(8) Having been soaked in the experimental pickling solution, the cannery manager decided that the tomatoes had too odd a taste to be used.

(9) While counting the day's receipts, two hold-up men entered the cashier's cage.

(10) Lake Madison was three miles over to the left of Fort Collier, and we had to drive back to pick up Jimmy.

(11) The relief pitcher was a rookie with a good fast ball and who had the coolness and poise of a veteran.

(12) The bear was a formidable creature standing over six feet high, with big sharp teeth, and having eyes that glared red in the dark.

(13) An experienced traffic sergeant took over and gave directions and soon the snarl was unravelled by him.

(14) After looking over the paint charts, Mrs. Cramer decided on light green, and the cottage was finally painted blue.

(15) There had been a skunk in the neighborhood and its scent was soon perceived by us as we walked along.

(16) Carlsbad Caverns are the largest in the United States, and they were discovered by accident in 1912.

(17) After changing her mind several times, Jane finally decided to go to the tea, meeting at it the man she later married.

(18) The Buick was speeding down the Mount Quinlan Road when it got out of control, falling sixty feet over a cliff.

(19) Frank had always wanted to be able to drive the family car like his brother did.

(20) Mr. Ash liked Ike Eisenhower better than any of the American generals.

(21) The Sox will be under a new manager next year and they are bringing up two new catchers from their farm system and there will be changes in the infield and the rookie Ziegler is going to play first base.

(22) Since Vernon had never been nearly as good in chemistry as his sister Ellen, who had won a scholarship in the subject at West Virginia and was now working in the DuPont laboratories in Wilmington, Delaware, he tried to rearrange his schedule by changing his history section so that he would not be in the chemistry section taught by Professor Welsh, who, everyone agreed, was a very stiff marker.

(23) The report was filed an hour ago by the new girl with the red dress in the corner cabinet.

(24) For tonight's campfire we can use, if they are not too green, the oak branches.

(25) Having been fingerprinted and photographed, the guards led Fredericks back into the cell-block.

(26) Rocco had some trouble with Marciano in the first three rounds; finally he was too tough for him.

(27) The chief strode ahead of his warlike tribesmen, and he was brandishing a long spear in his hand.

(28) The canaries lay inert at the bottom of the cage, showing that the mine gallery was filled with dangerous gases.

(29) Although journalism critics praise it a great deal, the *Morning Post* actually has less circulation.

(30) Earl went to work for the Bowman Construction Company after graduating from high school as a bricklayer.

(31) The Morning *Gazette* was against Saunders. It had many editorials attacking him. The *Star* also opposed him. The afternoon papers were against him too. They supported Scanlon, his opponent. Scanlon also had the support of the various civic organizations. But Saunders won.

(32) As the late afternoon sun lengthened over Tressler Field, which was named for John C. Tressler, who gave it to the school, the Harwood team, which had lost five of its seven games during the year, pushed over the touchdown late in the fourth quarter that beat the Minnequa team and knocked them out of the state championship.

(33) Laura sent Bill a letter saying that she had decided not to come; he had planned on this.

(34) First tabulations showed that the majority of the tests contradicted Rinehart's theories, but Randall doubted their accuracy.

(35) This new set has a wider screen than the others, being equipped with a new clarity filter, and comes in a nicer cabinet.

(36) The bobbin of the sewing machine did not work very well; my aunt always has trouble with them.

(37) The melodrama was about a series of murders in an old castle and a Scotland Yard man solved them.

(38) Gorgeous Gus put on an act in which he appeared girlish, and he was a bone-crushing wrestler.

(39) After the cook has put together the other ingredients, salt and seasonings are added by him to the stew.

(40) Captain Hunter watched his inexperienced crew make a confused mess of the mooring gear with many strong and salty observations about today's sailors.

Logic = LOG

IN ANSWERING HE STATES THE QUESTION, AND EX-
POUNDETH THE TERMS THEREOF. OTHERWISE THE DIS-
PUTANTS SHALL END, WHERE THEY OUGHT TO HAVE
BEGUN, IN DIFFERENCES ABOUT WORDS, AND BE BAR-
BARIANS EACH TO THE OTHER, SPEAKING IN A LAN-
GUAGE NEITHER UNDERSTAND.

—THOMAS FULLER, *1642*

I COME FROM A STATE THAT RAISES CORN AND COTTON
AND COCKLEBURS AND DEMOCRATS, AND FROTHY ELO-
QUENCE NEITHER CONVINCES NOR SATISFIES ME. I AM
FROM MISSOURI. YOU HAVE GOT TO SHOW ME.

—WILLARD DUNCAN VANDIVER

**The content as well as the structure of writing
should be logical.**

SENTENCES ARE grammatical frameworks for ideas; these
ideas must be able to bear logical analysis. To put it another
way, correct grammatical structure is not an end in itself but a
vehicle for communicating thought clearly. Clear and purposeful
writing therefore is fundamentally a reflection of logical thinking.
People who complain "My ideas are good, but I can't express them
clearly in writing" are usually fooling themselves. Vague and undirected writing reflects vague and undirected thinking, and the
starting point for revision is in the writer's mind, not on the paper.

The treatment of logic which follows is brief and admittedly over-
simplified. Space permits a discussion of only those matters which
have an obvious relationship to the writing process.

More detailed treatments can be found in the following:

(1) Altick, Richard, *A Preface to Critical Reading.* Revised Edition. New York: Henry Holt and Co., 1951.

(2) Beardsley, Monroe C., *Thinking Straight.* New York: Prentice-Hall, Inc., 1950.

(3) Beardsley, Monroe C., *Practical Logic.* New York: Prentice-Hall, Inc., 1950.

(4) Black, Max, *Critical Thinking.* Second Edition. New York: Prentice-Hall, Inc., 1952.

(5) Chase, Stuart, *The Tyranny of Words.* New York: Harcourt, Brace and Company, 1939.

(6) Cohen, Morris and Ernest Nagel, *An Introduction to Logic and Scientific Method.* New York: Harcourt, Brace and Company, 1934.

(7) Hayakawa, S. I., *Language in Thought and Action.* New York: Harcourt, Brace and Company, 1949.

(8) Johnson, Wendell, *People in Quandaries.* New York: Harper & Brothers, 1946.

(9) Robinson, James H., *The Mind in the Making.* New York: Harper & Brothers, 1921.

(10) Thouless, Robert, *How to Think Straight.* New York: Simon and Schuster, Inc., 1932.

DEFINITION

28a. Terms should be defined when their exact meaning is essential to clear and logical communication.

The failure to define key words—or to use them in a context where their meaning is clear—is the commonest cause of faulty communication. (See "Exactness," Section 31.) The need for definition is especially apparent in argument. Many useless debates would never occur if people would agree on the meanings they were attaching to words like *propaganda, democracy, education, virtue, religion.* Even in general expository writing, definition is often essential, if merely to clear the air and indicate the starting point of the discussion.

(1) *The term being defined should first be put into the class of objects* (genus) *to which it belongs.* This process is called *classification.*

TERM		GENUS
A saw	is	a cutting tool
A carpet	is	a floor covering

In general, the narrower the classification, the clearer the eventual definition.

NOT
A rifle is a *weapon.*
BUT
A rifle is a *firearm.*

Though *weapon* is a legitimate classification for *rifle,* for purposes of definition it includes more than is necessary (*knives, spears, bows and arrows, clubs, etc.*).

(2) *The term being defined should be distinguished from other objects* (genus) *with which it has been classified.* This process is called *differentiation.*

TERM		GENUS	DIFFERENTIATION
A saw	is	*a cutting tool*	*with a thin, flat blade and a series of teeth on the edge.*
A carpet	is	*a floor covering*	*of woven or felted fabric, usually tacked to the floor.*

(3) *The parts of a definition should be cast in parallel grammatical form.* The grammatical structure of the *genus* must be the same as that of the term defined. The use of "is when" or "is where" is illogical.

NOT
A debate *is when* two people or sides argue a given proposition in a regulated discussion.

BUT
A *debate is a regulated discussion* of a given proposition between two matched sides.

237

(4) *The definition should not contain the name of the thing defined or any derivative of it.* Nothing is achieved when words are defined in terms of themselves.

> NOT
> A rifle is a firearm with *riflings* inside its barrel to impart rotary motion to its projectile.
>
> BUT
> A rifle is a firearm with *spiral grooves* inside its barrel to impart rotary motion to its projectile.

Whenever possible, a term should be defined in words more familiar than the term itself. The complexity of Dr. Samuel Johnson's definition of the simple word *network* is notorious:

> *Network:* anything reticulated or decussated, at equal distances, with interstices between the intersections.

Of course in ordinary writing there is not much occasion for defining saws or carpets. Probably, too, every writer defines many terms without being aware of giving them a genus and a differentiation. But it is always possible to check the logic of a definition against such careful definitions as those give above. Consider the following example from a student paper:

> Finally, college is valuable to a person interested in success. By *success* I don't mean what is usually thought of when that word is used. I mean achieving one's goals. Everybody has his own goals to achieve, all of them very different. But whatever they are, college will give one the know-how and the contacts he needs to achieve them successfully.

This definition is obviously unsatisfactory; but the specifications for logical definition will help clarify why and how it breaks down. First, if the statement which this paragraph makes about *success* is isolated, it comes out like this: "Success is the successful achievement of goals which know-how and contacts gained at college help one achieve." But the paragraph contradicts itself in the differentiation, emphasizing as it does that the "goals" one is helped to achieve at college may be anything at all. If my goal were to stay away from college, certainly going to college would not help me achieve it. There are many goals more common than that one which no college can help one reach, or which some colleges, but not "college," might contribute to. We cannot discover much about what the writer meant by success until we know clearly what he intended "goals" to mean and what his definition would be for "know-how" and "contacts." About all the sense we can make of his paragraph is that success means being successful, a definition of little help indeed. Very likely the writer had no very clear idea of what he was talking about and so could not hope to communicate it to his readers. Had he checked the logic of his definition, he would have discovered this fact for himself.

EXERCISE 1. Discuss the validity of the sentences below *as definitions:*

(1) Democracy is a government of the people, by the people, and for the people.
(2) Humor is to say something funny.
(3) Housemaid's knee is a swelling due to the enlargement of the bursa in front of the patella.
(4) Walking is when we use our legs as a means of transportation.
(5) Swimming is propelling yourself forward in water with a swimming motion.
(6) Poetry is when the lines end where they will rhyme with the next one.
(7) A touchdown is where the team with the football crosses the goal line of its opponents.
(8) Diagnosis means to find out what is wrong with something.
(9) A bandsaw is a saw with a cutting blade that revolves in an endless circle.
(10) Winter wheat is a species of wheat which is planted in the fall and harvested in the late spring or early summer.

GENERALIZATION

28b. Generalizations should be adequately supported or qualified.

To generalize is to assert that what is true of several particulars (objects, experiences, people) of the same class (genus) is true of most or all of the particulars in that class. For example, the statement "Drinking coffee in the evening always keeps me awake all night" is a generalization of several particular experiences with drinking coffee on separate evenings. Obviously, generalization is an essential process; without it, there can be no evaluation of experience—only the accumulation of isolated facts. Yet it is equally obvious that generalization has its dangers, some examples of which are treated below.

(1) *Generalizations should be based on adequate evidence.* The temptation to generalize on the basis of a few striking examples is strong, especially when these accord with what we want to believe. The example below illustrates a hasty generalization, a "jumping to conclusion" on the basis of insufficient evidence.

PARTICULAR A	My sister Imogene dented the car's fenders yesterday.
PARTICULAR B	Mrs. Elliott has just driven her car through the rear end of the garage.
PARTICULAR C	Did you see that woman drive through that red light!
HASTY GENERALIZATION	Women can't drive.

When generalizing, writers must remember constantly their obligation to their readers—to support their statements with examples, illustrations, anecdotes, or other evidence. How much evidence is needed depends on the purpose of the paper. Sometimes the listing of three or four examples will suffice; sometimes the evidence itself must be analyzed in detail. (In writing, generalizations often take the form of topic sentences in paragraphs. See "Paragraphs," Section 13a.)

(2) *Such words as* ALWAYS, NEVER, ALL, NONE, RIGHT, WRONG *should be used cautiously in generalizations.* The tendency to generalize too broadly is as constant as the tendency to generalize too quickly. In fact, the two usually spring from the same desire—to reach a conclusion without going through the necessary effort of collecting evidence. A valid generalization is often rendered invalid by the careless use of *never* instead of *seldom,* of *always* instead of *usually.*

OVERSTATED	People who are excessively radical in their youth always become conservative when they acquire power and property.

QUALIFIED   Even the most radical youths are likely to grow con-
                   servative when they acquire power and property.

EXERCISE 2. Discuss the validity of the following sentences *as
generalizations*. Restate those which seem exaggerated.

(1) Only intellectuals have nervous breakdowns.

(2) That dog understands everything I say.

(3) Any man who is honest cannot fail to be successful.

(4) A great deal of "realistic" fiction is based on what average
people would call "indecent" characters.

(5) There isn't a businessman in this country who isn't disgusted
with the red tape of government bureaucrats.

(6) Professors and preachers are men who cannot succeed in
business.

(7) Professors and preachers are men who do not care about making money.

(8) The number of airplane accidents proves that air travel is
not safe.

(9) A dog's disposition is simply the reflection of the disposition
of the people who own him.

(10) American doctors prefer Weedo cigarets.

FAIRNESS

**28c. Arguments should be based on honest evidence and should
be presented fairly.**

Consciously or unconsciously, we tend to falsify, suppress evidence, call names, cheat, and hit below the belt in our arguments
because we wish to seem right.

(1) *Judgments should be made on the basis of what one knows,
not of what one wishes to believe.* Prejudice (prejudgment, or judgment before the facts are examined) is the commonest type of
unfairness. The prejudgments below are cases in point.

PREJUDGMENT   I heard that he didn't get in until one A.M. last night,
                 *and you can bet that he was spending his time in
                 some cheap saloon.*

PREJUDGMENT   Did you hear what Peggy said about her? *It's our
                 duty to ask her to resign from the club immediately.*

(2) *It is unfair to dismiss an argument or an opponent by making a statement that appeals to general prejudice.* Name-calling is an appeal to a reader's emotion, not his reason. It attempts to create prejudice by attaching unpleasant labels to an idea or person. Labels such as "Red," "Fascist," "Atheist," "Low-brow," and "Fellow-traveler" carry a heavy emotional charge but little information; to use them loosely and irresponsibly is to be dishonest.

(a) *Argumentum ad hominem* ("argument to the man"). The argument is sidestepped by an attempt to discredit the man who proposed it.

AD HOMINEM　He has no business talking about the responsibilities of a democracy, *because he has just got out of jail.*

AD HOMINEM　Don't pay any attention to what Milton says about divorce. He just couldn't get along with his wife.

(b) *Argumentum ad verecundiam* (more simply called "transfer"). This method usually involves association of the idea with a great name or movement (or, particularly, with an attractive face or figure, as in advertising) in the hope that the prestige or glamour of attractiveness will be transferred to the proposal being argued. The "transfer" device of course also works in the opposite direction: if a proposal or person can be associated with a movement or name in general disfavor (Communism, economic-royalism, and so on), it or he has very little chance of getting objective and logical judgment.

TRANSFER　If Abraham Lincoln were alive today, I am sure he would devote his full energies to seeing our policy made the law of the land.

TRANSFER　She's lovely! She's engaged! She uses X!

TRANSFER　He believes in a high income tax, just as do the Marxists.

(c) *Argumentum ad populum* ("argument to the people"). An argument is sidestepped by appealing to the instincts and ideas of the crowd, on the assumption that what the crowd believes and feels is right. This is the "bandwagon" device; everyone is urged to climb aboard. Advertisers, of course, are masters of this appeal:

AD POPULUM　Drink X! For 75 years *it has been the favorite drink of the man in the street. You'll like it too.*

AD POPULUM   Decent, upright citizens will not be interested in anything he says.

EXERCISE 3. Discuss the "fairness" of the statements below:

(1) What does Bill know about the responsibilities of businessmen? He never met a payroll in his life.

(2) George Washington, the Father of our Country, made his position on "foreign entanglements" very clear, and what was good enough in Washington's day is good enough for us.

(3) Your neighbor drives a "Wingfoot Special." Why don't you?

(4) He's your hit-and-run driver all right; every morning he goes by our house at sixty miles an hour.

(5) My parents were like yours: plain, simple hardworking folks, and if you vote for me you can be sure that the rights of the common people will be safeguarded.

(6) There is a law against murder in this country, and all murderers ought to pay the full penalty of the law.

(7) Whenever corruption is found in the federal government the people ought to vote another party into power.

(8) I'm sure that Ivan Ivanovitch is a Communist. With a name like that how could he be anything else?

(9) Every ambitious citizen should aspire to own a large home because people measure a man's prestige and respectability by the size of his house.

(10) The state university has no business using the taxpayers' money to buy books for the library. They haven't read a lot of the books that are already in the library.

SOUND REASONING

28d. Statements involving cause and effect relationships should be logically sound.

Some of the defects of thinking arise not from prejudice, unfairness, or ignorance of the facts, but from lack of training in basic logical processes. Such training cannot be offered in this brief space, but a few of the commonest errors in logic can be described.

(1) *A cause and effect relationship between two facts should not be assumed merely because one follows the other in time.* This fal-

lacy is known as *post hoc, ergo propter hoc* ("after this, therefore because of this").

POST HOC   Industrialism was not established until after the Protestant Revolution; therefore Protestantism was the cause of industrialism.

POST HOC   I won't say she's to blame, but I do know that he didn't drink before he married her.

(2) *A mere inference should not be mistaken for a logically sound conclusion.* This fallacy is known as *non-sequitur* ("it does not follow").

NON-SEQUITUR   This is the best play I have seen this year and should win the Pulitzer Prize.

(Have you seen *all* the plays produced this year? Are you qualified to judge the qualities that make a Pulitzer Prize play? Does it follow that just because a play is the best you have seen this year, it should therefore win the Pulitzer Prize?)

NON-SEQUITUR   Steven will never get anywhere; he's got his head in the clouds.

(3) *A writer should not assume the truth of something he is trying to prove.* This fallacy is known as "begging the question."

BEGGING THE QUESTION   His handwriting is hard to read because it is almost illegible.

BEGGING THE QUESTION   I like Buicks because they are my favorite automobiles.

BEGGING THE QUESTION   I don't care what he's done; if he's in jail he's done *something* wrong. Good people don't go to jail.

(4) *A writer cannot assume that because two circumstances or ideas are alike in some respects, they are alike in all others.* This is the fallacy of "false analogy"—and perhaps the principal cause of shoddy political thinking.

FALSE ANALOGY   Of course he'll make a good Secretary of Agriculture—hasn't he lived on a farm all his life and hasn't he succeeded in making a profitable business of raising livestock!

(Undoubtedly, the Secretary of Agriculture should have experience with farmers' problems, and undoubtedly he should be a competent man. But a farming background and success in raising livestock are not in themselves proof that a man will be a good administrator or know what is best for all farmers.)

(5) *A writer should avoid self-contradiction.* This fallacy occurs when a writer is unwilling or unable to establish a clear conclusion or opinion. He wants to have his cake and eat it too.

SELF-CONTRADICTION   Democracy and communism are widely different political systems, although communism is really an economic system.

EXERCISE 4. Discuss the validity of the reasoning in the sentences below:

(1) Good Englishmen should oppose socialized medicine because it violates established British tradition.

(2) Democracy has never succeeded in China; therefore immigrant Chinese do not make good American citizens.

(3) Don't swap horses in the middle of a stream; don't change presidents during a crisis.

(4) Harvey likes reading because books are his favorite pastime.

(5) I know a man who had seven years' bad luck because he broke a mirror.

(6) Bill's success as a real estate broker is assured; he has a good sense of values.

(7) Gentlemen prefer blondes because they are attracted to women with fair hair.

(8) The Confederate and Northern states became a united nation after the Civil War. Civil wars are always a unifying force in a country's development.

(9) In the state primary election Governor Cameron got the largest number of votes a gubernatorial candidate ever received in this state. This proves that he is the most popular governor in the state's history.

(10) Our football team never lost more than three games in a season until last year, when we lost five. It is obvious that the new coach, who came last year, is not as good a coach as his predecessors.

245

EXERCISE 5. Comment on the logic in the following conversation:

MR. JONES: Newspapers today coddle and spoon-feed the public by such devices as cheesecake, one-syllable words, clichés, jargon, etc. Don't you think it's about time that the public did something about this? It seems to me that our standards of literacy are getting lower and lower. Newspapers used to have a higher standard. They stood for something. Now they depend almost exclusively on cheap devices and sensationalism. All papers must follow this policy if they are to survive.

MR. SMITH: What you're saying is, "Let's go back to the covered wagon era." You don't want to progress. Don't you think automobiles are a sign of progress? I do. Similarly, with newspapers. Today they reach many more people than they used to. Anyone can read and understand a newspaper today. That's more than they could do a hundred years ago. If that isn't progress, then nothing is.

EXERCISE 6. Comment on the logic (generalization, fairness, reasoning, etc.) of the following selection:

SPORTS VERSUS THE SPORTSWRITER

The trouble with sports is the sportswriters. These tin-horn sports, these semi-literate dealers in clichés, cram the daily newspapers with misinformation and moronic opinions about athletes, coaches, and sports themselves. The day after a sports contest sees the poor sports lover once again a victim in another of the eternal successions of "mornings-after"—when sportswriters begin again their assault on the English language, good taste, and common sense.

One would think that people who pretend to know so much about the secret workings and inside strategy of sports would be able to report on a football or baseball game with some objectivity and penetration. But no! The sportswriter goes to great pains to tell us what we already know: that Old Siwash won. He tells us further that it is his considered opinion that Old Siwash played the better game. He then proceeds to indulge in assorted bits of irrelevancy and viciousness, according to the state of his ulcers. He gives us the startling news that Old Siwash's supporters were eager to win the game; that Halfback Haggerty would not have fumbled the kickoff if he had caught it instead.

But a sportswriter in front of a typewriter is only an idiot; a sportswriter in front of a microphone is a jabbering idiot. The next time you listen to a radio broadcast of a football game, force yourself to listen to the half-time interviews. Listen to the sportswriters gather to tell one another, in their own substandard idiom, what marvelous jobs they have done in "bringing you the game." Listen to them inform you, in voices choked with emotion and borrowed Scotch, that the game isn't over until the final gun sounds—"that anything can happen." This is undoubtedly what sportswriters mean when they speak of "inside dope."

Words = WDS

DICTIONARIES ARE LIKE WATCHES; THE WORST IS BETTER
THAN NONE, AND THE BEST CANNOT BE EXPECTED TO GO
QUITE TRUE.

—SAMUEL JOHNSON

29. THE DICTIONARY

THE STUDY of words begins with the dictionary, the great storehouse of linguistic information. A good dictionary is a biography of words, recording the spelling of a word, its pronunciation, its part of speech, its etymology, its meaning, and when necessary its principal parts, or plurals, or other forms. Very often it includes other information—lists of abbreviations, rules for punctuation and spelling, condensed biographical and geographical information, the pronunciation and source of many given names, and frequently a vocabulary of rhymes. For writers and readers, therefore, a dictionary is indispensable.

UNABRIDGED DICTIONARIES

For English the great standard work is the *New English Dictionary,* sometimes called the NED, a work issued in ten volumes and a supplement between 1888 and 1933 by the Clarendon Press, Oxford, England, and reissued in 1933 as the *Oxford English Dictionary* (OED). A historical work, this dictionary traces the progress of a word through the language by the use of dated quotations which illustrate its meaning and spelling at particular times in history. Often many pages are devoted to a single word. *Set,* for example, is given twenty-three pages of closely printed type. Under one of the 150-odd definitions of *set*—"to fix or appoint (a time) for the transaction of an affair"—there are illustrative sentences taken from writings dated 1056, 1250, 1290, 1300, 1387, 1470-85, 1548-77, 1633, 1693, 1753, 1810, 1890, and 1893.

Another unabridged dictionary is *Webster's New International Dictionary of the English Language,* first published in 1909 and then reissued in a second edition in 1934 by the G. and C. Merriam Company of Springfield, Massachusetts, a long-established house and the legal inheritor of Noah Webster's copyright. The Merriam-Webster entries are scholarly and exact, though by no means as exhaustive as the OED's. A specimen entry is given below.

> **jail** (jāl), *n.* Also **gaol** (jāl). [ME. *jaile, gail, gayhol,* fr. OF. *jaiole* (F. *geôle*), ONF. *gaiole,* fr. VL. *caveola,* dim. fr. L. *cavea* cage. See CAGE.] **a** Orig., and still often, a prison. **b** A building for the confinement of persons held in lawful custody, esp. for minor offenses or with reference to some future judicial proceeding; a lockup.
> ☞ COMBINATIONS: **jail′keep′er, jail′mate′, jail′yard′.**
> **jail,** *v. t.;* JAILED (jāld); JAIL′ING. Also **gaol.** To confine in or as in a jail; to imprison; to lock up. "[Bolts] that *jail* you from free life."   *Tennyson.*

Dictionaries must say much in little space; hence the use of abbreviations and cryptic entries. These will be troublesome unless we take time to read the explanatory pages.

Concerning the specimen above, the explanatory notes tell us that the word *jail* is entered first as a noun (*n.*) and then as a transitive verb (*v.t.*). The pronunciation is indicated by (jāl); by referring to the bottom of the page of the dictionary we see that *ā* is to be sounded as *a* in *ale.* The variant *gaol,* pronounced exactly as *jail,* is a secondary spelling (as in Oscar Wilde's *Ballad of Reading Gaol*). The material between the brackets shows the origin or etymology of the word: *jail* comes from a word in Middle English (ME.) which was variously spelled *jaile, gail, gayhol.* These forms in turn came from Old French (OF.) *jaile* and Old Norman French (ONF.) *gaile.* In modern French the word is now *geôle.* These old French words in turn came from the vulgar Latin (VL.) *caveola,* a diminutive (dim.) formation of the Latin (L.) *cavea,* which meant *cage.* The editors then suggest that we refer to the word *cage* itself for fuller information. The use of *a* and *b* to number the definitions instead of *1* and *2* indicates that the two meanings are closely related. Because neither of the definitions carries a label (*Brit., U. S., Law,* etc.) we know that each is used in general speech or writing. The final item lists combination forms: in each case the main accent (´) falls on the first syllable, the secondary accent (´) on the last.

The second entry is devoted to the verb *jail.* We know at once that it is pronounced in the same way as the noun; otherwise a different pronunciation would be indicated. We learn also that the past tense (and past participle, since no past participle form is given) is *jailed,* the present participle *jailing.* Further, we find that the verb *jail* has the secondary spelling *gaol,* as has the noun. Finally, the meaning of the verb is illustrated by a quotation from the works of the English poet Alfred Tennyson.

DESK DICTIONARIES

Unabridged dictionaries are useful as reference works. For everyday purposes a good abridged or desk dictionary is more practical. Some of the leading desk dictionaries, with specimen entries, are given below.

(1) *Webster's New Collegiate Dictionary,* G. and C. Merriam Company, Springfield, Massachusetts, 1949. This is the successor to *Webster's Collegiate Dictionary,* 1941, and like its predecessor is carefully edited and conservative. Its etymologies are especially complete. Insofar as possible, the order of definitions under any one word is historical: the original meaning is given first, the second meaning next, and so on.

> **jail** (jāl), *n.* Also **gaol** (jāl). [OF. *jaiole,* ONF. *gaiole,* fr. VL. *cabeola,* dim. fr. L. *cavea* cage.] A building for the confinement of persons held in lawful custody, esp. for minor offenses or pending judicial proceeding; a lockup. — *v. t.* To confine in or as in a jail.

(2) *The American College Dictionary,* Harper and Brothers, New York and London, 1947. This dictionary, which is being revised continuously, is edited by a group of outstanding American linguists who recognize that Middle American, Western, and Southern pronunciation and usage contribute as much to the character of the

American language as do the pronunciation and usage of New England or the Atlantic seaboard. The word "American" on the title page, therefore, has real significance.

> **jail** (jāl), *n.* **1.** a prison, esp. one for the detention of persons awaiting trial or convicted of minor offenses; gaol. —*v.t.* **2.** to take into or hold in custody. Also, *Brit.,* **gaol.** [ME *jaiole,* t. OF: prison, cage; ult. der. L *cavea* cavity, enclosure, cage. See GAOL] —**jail′less,** *adj.* —**jail′like′,** *adj.*
>
> By permission. From *The American College Dictionary*
> Copyright, 1947, 1949, by Random House.
> Text edition, copyright, 1948, by Harper & Brothers.

(3) *New College Standard Dictionary,* Funk and Wagnalls Company, New York, 1947. This dictionary is especially helpful with technical words and simplified spelling forms.

> **JAIL** *noun* A building or place for the confinement of arrested persons or those guilty of minor offenses. — *tr. verb* To put in jail; imprison; incarcerate. Also spelled *gaol.* [<OF. *jaiole, gaiole*]
>
> By permission. From *The New College Standard Dictionary*
> Copyright, 1947, by Funk & Wagnalls Co.

(4) *The Winston Dictionary,* College Edition, The John C. Winston Company, Philadelphia, 1945. The *Winston* stresses a readable typographical arrangement and straightforward, nontechnical definitions.

> **jail** (jāl), *n.* [< O.F. *jaiole,* prison, cage < L.L. *gabiola,* cage, dim. of L.L. *gabia,* for Lat. *cavea,* cage < *cavus,* hollow], a prison; especially, a place where persons guilty of minor offenses are confined: **jail fever,** typhus fever, formerly common in certain jails:—*v.t.* to imprison. Also, *Br.,* **gaol** (jāl).
>
> By permission. From *The Winston Dictionary*
> Copyright, 1945, by the John C. Winston Co.

(5) *Thorndike-Barnhart Comprehensive Desk Dictionary,* Doubleday and Company, Inc., 1951. This is handy-sized and inexpensive, yet reliable and up-to-date.

> **jail** (jāl), *n.* **1.** Also, *Brit.* **gaol.** prison for people awaiting trial or being punished for minor offenses. **2. break jail,** escape from jail. —*v.* put in jail; keep in jail. [< OF *jaiole,* ult. < L *cavea* coop] —**jail′less,** *adj.* —**jail′like′,** *adj.*
>
> By permission. From *Thorndike-Barnhart Comprehensive Desk Dictionary.* Copyright, 1951, by Doubleday & Company, Inc.

(6) *Webster's New World Dictionary*, The World Publishing Company, Cleveland, 1953. This is the largest and most recently published of the present group of reliable desk dictionaries.

> **jail** (jāl), *n.* [ME. *jaile, gaile, gayhol;* OFr. *jaiole, jaole, gaole,* a cage, prison; LL. *caveola,* dim. of L. *cavea,* a cage, coop], a building for the confinement of people who have broken the law or are awaiting trial; prison, especially for those convicted of minor offenses. *v.t.* to put or keep in jail; imprison. Also, British, **gaol.**
>
> By permission. From *Webster's New World Dictionary.* Copyright, 1953, by The World Publishing Company.

THE USES OF A DICTIONARY

(1) *Spelling.* A word is listed in the dictionary under the spelling the editors find most common. We can usually come close enough to the spelling of a doubtful word to find it. We ought to remember, however, the vagaries of English spelling: particularly that *c* and *s* and *sc* are sometimes pronounced alike. When usage in spelling is divided, the preferred form is usually given first. The secondary spelling is usually British (as *humour*), or foreign (as *manoeuvre*), or simplified (as *altho, thru*). In any event we should avoid the secondary spelling except when special circumstances call for it.

The spelling entry also divides the word into syllables, showing us how to separate it properly at the ends of lines (see "Syllabication," Section 11). The proper spelling of compound words is also given—whether the editors found them more often written as two single words (*half brother*), as a hyphenated compound (*quarter-hour*), or as one word (*drugstore*). Foreign words not yet anglicized and thus requiring italics (in manuscript, underlining) are indicated with special symbols. The *New Collegiate* marks such words with two vertical bars (||); *American College* and *Thorndike Barnhart* as Latin, French, etc.; *College Standard* with the abbreviation [L.], [F.]; *Winston* with the asterisk (*); and *Webster's New World* with the double dagger (‡).

EXERCISE 1. What is the preferred spelling of each of these words?

aeroplane	criticise	humour
aesthetic	daemon	medieval
canceled	enclose	Shakspere
cheque	judgement	theatre

EXERCISE 2. Which of the following compounds should be written as they are, which hyphenated, and which written as separate words?

ablebodied	selfmade
cleancut	stepson
iceboat	tonguetied
illbred	uptodate
onesided	upperclassmen

EXERCISE 3. Which of the following foreign words are not yet anglicized and thus require italics (underlining)?

coiffeur	matinee
coup d'état	nouveau riche
debonair	résumé
debut	sine qua non
ibidem	status quo

(2) *Pronunciation.* Dictionaries indicate the pronunciation of words by respelling them with special symbols and letters. Explanation of the symbols is given either at the bottom of the page on which the entry appears or in the prefatory pages or both.

Indicating pronunciations is the most difficult of all the tasks of dictionary editors. *Correct pronunciation* is a very flexible term. Generally speaking, it is the standard of pronunciation prevailing among educated people, but often correctness is a theory rather than a reality. Does a Southerner mispronounce *I* when he says *Ah?* Is a Bostonian incorrect in saying *pa'k* for *park?* Dictionaries do not even attempt to list all the variant pronunciations in use.

The pronunciation of words, moreover, is influenced by the situation in which they are pronounced. In formal speech, syllables are likely to be more deliberately sounded than in informal speech. Further, the pronunciation of a word is affected by its position in the sentence and by the meaning it carries. Yet dictionaries have no choice but to deal with each word as an individual entity. They record its formal, or full, pronunciation—what may be referred to as "platform" pronunciation. Certainly, to pronounce every word in our conversation as deliberately as the dictionary recommends would make our speech stilted and pompous.

Dictionaries do, however, make an attempt to show divided usage in pronunciation. Ordinarily, the first pronunciation given is to be preferred, though occasionally the second pronunciation is as acceptable or as "correct" as the first. In the last analysis our preference will be determined by the pronunciation heard in cultivated conversation around us.

EXERCISE 4. What is the pronunciation of the following words?

alias	exquisite	heinous
bestial	forehead	hyperbole
clique	formidable	mischievous
deference	genuine	municipal
epitome	gondola	superfluous

EXERCISE 5. Is usage divided in the pronunciation of the following words? If so, which pronunciation seems more acceptable to you? Why?

acclimate	illustrated
adult	inquiry
amateur	interesting
apparatus	precedence
decorous	process
Don Juan	program
Don Quixote	research
envelope	vaudeville

(3) *Etymology.* The etymology of a word is its origin and derivation. Such information often clarifies for us the present meaning and spelling of a word. Sometimes the information is interesting or amusing in its own right. But we must not forget that the original meaning of a word is not necessarily its present meaning. The course of history changes or restricts or extends the meanings of many words. Many original meanings have been lost completely. *Presently,* for example, formerly meant *at once, immediately;* because of the human tendency to procrastinate, it now means *shortly, in a little while.*

EXERCISE 6. Trace the etymology of each of the following words:

assassin	nay
bedlam	neighbor
chapel	priest
draggle	screech
egg	shirt
edge	skirt
familiar	slogan
incisive	squelch

EXERCISE 7. What specific places or persons have given us the following words?

ampere	macadam
boycott	quisling
chauvinism	shrapnel
dunce	ulster
gardenia	watt

EXERCISE 8. From what language did each of the following words come?

almanac	dory	jute	piano	tulip
canoe	goulash	kerosene	rucksack	turban
cruise	huckster	persimmon	squadron	tycoon

(4) *Meaning.* Strictly speaking, dictionaries do not "define" words; they record the meaning or meanings which actual usage, past and present, has attached to words. When more than one meaning is recorded for a single word, the Merriam-Webster dictionaries list them in order of historical use. Most other dictionaries list the more general and present meaning first. Special and technical meanings are clearly labeled. Choosing the appropriate meaning out of the many that are offered is not difficult if we read them *all* and understand their order of arrangement, a discussion of which appears in the prefatory pages of the dictionary.

EXERCISE 9. How many different meanings can you find for each of the following words?

cut	open
give	out
go	run
hit	sit
light	strike

EXERCISE 10. Trace the changes in meaning that have taken place in each of the following words:

ban	humor
complexion	intern
engine	machine
fond	manufacture
gossip	sincere

256

EXERCISE 11. Distinguish between the meanings of the words in each of the following groups:

> ambitious, aspiring, enterprising
> apt, likely, liable
> common, mutual
> deface, disfigure
> diplomatic, politic, tactful
> eminent, celebrated
> enormous, immense
> equanimity, composure
> restive, restless
> voracious, ravenous

(5) *Grammar.* Good dictionaries indicate the part or parts of speech of a word. They also give the principal parts of verbs, the plurals of nouns, and the comparative and superlative degrees of adjectives and adverbs, but only when these forms are irregular or present spelling difficulties. The past tense and present participle of a verb are not given when they are regularly formed by adding *-ed* and *-ing* (*walked, walking*). Plurals ending in *s* or *es* (*cats, dishes*) are not usually given. And comparatives and superlatives formed by adding *more, most,* or *less, least,* or *-er, -est* are not given, unless the addition of the *-er, -est* endings presents a spelling difficulty (*heavy, heavier, heaviest*).

EXERCISE 12. What are the past tense and the present participle of each of these verbs?

be	prove
broadcast	rely
focus	set
get	teach
lend	wring

EXERCISE 13. What is the plural (or plurals) of each of the following?

alumna	deer
beau	index
bus	madame
crisis	phenomenon
daisy	volley

EXERCISE 14. Write the comparative and superlative forms of each of the following:

bad	often
ill	red
little	refined
lengthy	shyly
much	well

(6) *Labels.* Dictionaries do not label words that belong to the general vocabulary. The absence of a label therefore means that the word is proper for formal and informal speaking and writing. Other words may have one of three kinds of labels:

Subject labels, indicating that the word belongs to a special field: law, medicine, baseball, finance, and so on.

Geographical labels, indicating that the use of the word is generally restricted to a particular region or country: U. S., British, Australian, New England, Southern U. S., and so on.

Usage labels, indicating that the word is classified as archaic, colloquial, dialectal, obsolete, or slang. *Archaic* means that the word is old-fashioned (as *mayhap*); *colloquial* that the word is more suitable for loosely informal than formal use (as *boss*); *dialectal* that the word is restricted to local or provincial use (as *hoecake*); *obsolete* that the word has passed out of use (as *gantelope*); *slang* that the word has not yet been dignified by inclusion in the general vocabulary (as *blockhead*); *illiterate* that the use of the word is limited to vulgar speech (as *ain't*).

EXERCISE 15. Which of the following are standard English, which colloquial, and which slang?

enthuse	milksop
hindsight	natty
jam session	pal
kibitzer	perky
kill-joy	playboy

EXERCISE 16. In what areas of the world are we likely to hear the following?

batsman	mavourneen
billycan	mudcat
coulee	petrol
hoecake	pukka
laager	sourdough

EXERCISE 17. The following questions are designed to test your ability to use the whole dictionary—not only its vocabulary entries but also its various appendices. Any of the desk dictionaries discussed previously will help you find the answers.

(1) What is the orthography of the word *embarrass?*

(2) What is the preferred orthoëpy of the noun *envelope?*

(3) What is the etymology of the word *precise?*

(4) What are two homonyms for the word *reign?*

(5) What are some antonyms for the word *concise?*

(6) What is the syllabication of the word *redundant?*

(7) What are some synonyms for the adjective *correct?*

(8) Give the words for these abbreviations: *syn., v., mus., R.C.Ch.*

(9) What do the following phrases mean? *finem respice, ars longa vita brevis, de frofundis, honi soit qui mal y pense.*

(10) What is the population of Birmingham, Michigan?

(11) What is the meaning of the symbol B/E?

(12) How long is the Cumberland River?

(13) Who was the oldest of the Brontë sisters?

(14) From what language does the proper name *Nahum* come?

(15) List six words that rhyme with *mince.*

SPECIAL DICTIONARIES

Specialized information about words is occasionally necessary. One of the following dictionaries may provide this information.*

(1) *Chambers's Technical Dictionary.* Revised Edition with supplement. New York: The Macmillan Company, 1944.

(2) *Abbrevs: (A Dictionary of Abbreviations).* Compiled by H. J. Stephenson. New York: The Macmillan Company, 1945.

(3) *New Rhyming Dictionary and Poet's Handbook.* Ed. Burgess Johnson. New York and London: Harper & Brothers, 1931.

(4) *A Dictionary of Slang and Unconventional English.* Ed. Eric Partridge. New York: The Macmillan Company, 1937.

(5) *The American Thesaurus of Slang.* Ed. Lester V. Berry and Melvin Van Den Bark. New York: Thomas Y. Crowell Company, 1942.

* See also the list under *Reference Books* ("2. Dictionaries, Word Books") in Section 48.

(6) *Dictionary of Synonyms.* Springfield, Massachusetts: G. and C. Merriam Company, 1942.

(7) *A Pronouncing Dictionary of American English.* Ed. J. S. Kenyon and T. A. Knott. Springfield, Massachusetts: G. and C. Merriam Co., 1944.

30. VOCABULARY

> THE DIFFERENCE BETWEEN THE RIGHT WORD AND THE
> ALMOST-RIGHT WORD IS THE DIFFERENCE BETWEEN
> LIGHTNING AND THE LIGHTNING BUG.
> —ATTRIBUTED TO MARK TWAIN

The number of English words is well over a million. Of these, about two-fifths belong almost exclusively to special fields: *e.g.,* zoology, electronics, psychiatry. Of the remaining, the large dictionaries list about 600,000, the desk dictionaries about 200,000. Such wealth is both a blessing and a curse. On the one hand, many English words are loosely synonymous, sometimes interchangeable, as in *buy* a book or *purchase* a book. On the other hand, the distinctions between synonyms are fully as important as their similarities. For example, a family may be said to be living in *poverty,* or in *penury,* or in *want,* or in *destitution.* All these words are loosely synonymous, but only one will describe the family exactly as the writer sees it and wishes you to see it. In short, the writer of English is obligated to use his resources wisely.

ACTIVE AND *PASSIVE* VOCABULARY

Our *passive* or *recognition* vocabulary is made up of words we recognize in the context of reading matter but do not actually use ourselves. Our *active* vocabulary consists of our *"working"* words— those we use daily in our own writing and speaking. In the passage below, the meaning of the italicized words is fairly clear (or at least can be guessed at) from the context. But how many belong in your *active* vocabulary?

Has it been duly marked by historians that the late William Jennings Bryan's last *secular* act on this globe of sin was to catch flies?

A curious detail, and not without its *sardonic overtones*. He was the most *sedulous* fly-catcher in American history, and in many ways the most successful. His *quarry*, of course, was not *Musca domestica* but *Homo neandertalensis*. For forty years he tracked it with coo and bellow, up and down the *rustic* backways of the Republic. Wherever the *flambeau* of Chautauqua smoked and guttered, and the bilge of Idealism ran in the veins, the Baptist pastors damned the brooks with the *sanctified,* and men gathered who were weary and heavy laden, and their wives who were full of Peruna and as *fecund* as the shad (*Alosa sapidissima*)—there the *indefatigable* Jennings set up his traps and spread his bait.

—H. L. MENCKEN, *Selected Prejudices*

MEASURING VOCABULARY

Measuring a person's vocabulary range with any accuracy is extremely difficult. For one thing, the estimates of the number of words in a normal person's vocabulary vary considerably, from eight to twenty thousand. For another, vocabulary tests themselves are based on "word-frequency counts" which cannot take into account the special vocabulary (business, medicine, engineering, law, and so forth) that almost every individual person has.

The following test* is based on Thorndike's list of the 10,000 words that occur most frequently, grouped in order of their difficulty. It is assumed that a person who knows all (111) the words has a vocabulary of at least 10,000 words; a person who knows only 12 has a vocabulary of about 3,000. This table will help you estimate the size of your own vocabulary:

12	3,000	76	6,500
26	4,000	86	7,000
41	5,000	95	8,000
56	5,500	103	9,000
67	6,000	111	10,000

Select in each series the word or word-group which is closest in meaning to the word italicized in the phrase and insert its number in the blank:†

* From *Concerning Words*, Revised Edition, by J. E. Norwood. Copyright, 1938, 1941, by Prentice-Hall, Inc., and reprinted with their permission.

† Your instructor may wish you to write your answers to this test on a separate paper. Ask for his instructions before you proceed.

1. A *blissful* moment
   —— 1. lovely 2. holy
   3. happy 4. uncomfortable 5. sad

2. The crowd was *boisterous*.
   —— 1. quiet 2. bold
   3. noisy 4. meddlesome
   5. subdued

3. The men began to *brawl*.
   —— 1. quarrel 2. sing
   3. shake hands 4. embrace 5. scrimmage

4. The *brevity* of his reply added to its force.
   —— 1. sharpness 2. humor
   3. shortness 4. contrast
   5. prolixity

5. A vote of *censure*
   —— 1. blame 2. confidence
   3. census counting
   4. appropriation
   5. commendation

6. *Cherish* the traditions of your school.
   —— 1. revive 2. learn
   3. improve 4. question
   5. hold dear

7. A great *clamor* broke out.
   —— 1. sweat 2. fight
   3. protest 4. outcry
   5. fire

8. A plea for *clemency*
   —— 1. a reprieve 2. justice
   3. mercy 4. extension of time 5. partiality

9. The *cloister* of the monastery
   —— 1. roof 2. pillar
   3. covered passage
   4. ceiling 5. arches

10. An *implacable* enemy
    —— 1. weak 2. unknown
    3. passive 4. disposed to forgive 5. not disposed to forgive

11. *Adequate* facilities
    —— 1. insufficient 2. comfortable 3. convenient
    4. sufficient
    5. additional

12. In a *dilemma*
    —— 1. frenzy 2. melancholy state 3. stupor 4. fever
    5. state of perplexity

13. To *comprehend* the terms of the treaty
    ——1. accept 2. understand 3. reject 4. reveal 5. revise

14. His *conjecture* was better than mine.
    ——1. gesture 2. plea 3. experience 4. knowledge 5. surmise

15. *Coy* girls
    ——1. bold 2. mealy-mouthed 3. immodest 4. coquettish 5. pleasing

16. *Deferred* payment
    ——1. prompt 2. postponed 3. easy 4. monthly 5. cash

17. The race had *degenerated*.
    ——1. deteriorated 2. gone native 3. improved 4. disappeared 5. changed

18. Labor under a *delusion*
    ——1. fancy 2. bondage 3. grievance 4. loss 5. misconception

19. *Extol* his virtues
    ——1. minimize 2. praise 3. exaggerate 4. recount 5. call in question

20. *Fallow* ground
    ——1. marginal 2. planted 3. sandy 4. fertile 5. uncultivated

21. The accused man was *absolved*.
    ——1. unjustly accused 2. insolvent 3. acquitted 4. neglected 5. locked up

22. The question is an *abstract* one.
    ——1. moral 2. concrete 3. long drawn out 4. theoretical 5. difficult

23. Food was *abundant* that year.
    ——1. scarce 2. expensive 3. cheap 4. inspected 5. plentiful

24. To *acknowledge* a mistake
    ——1. admit 2. understand 3. repeat 4. deny 5. repent

25. The jury *acquitted* the accused.
———1. pronounced not guilty
2. found guilty   3. heard evidence against
4. questioned   5. held for trial

26. *Adhere* to the principles of democracy.
———1. desert   2. change
3. hold firmly   4. add
5. re-examine

27. An *eccentric* old man
———1. kindly   2. courteous
3. queer   4. humorous
5. rich

28. The lecturer *reaffirmed* the doctrine.
———1. denied again   2. repeated   3. re-established
4. strengthened   5. re-asserted as valid

29. She was *agitated* by the words.
———1. surprised   2. pleased
3. angered   4. perturbed
5. calmed

30. The *alleged* difficulties
———1. legal   2. unacknowledged   3. increased
4. fictitious   5. asserted

31. A state of *anarchy*
———1. lawlessness   2. unhappiness   3. rule of one man   4. rigid enforcement of law
5. peacefulness

32. Mental *anguish*
———1. perplexity   2. satisfaction   3. cruelty
4. distress   5. joy

33. A worthy *antagonist*
———1. sufferer   2. beginner
3. friend   4. opponent
5. revolutionist

34. A strange *apparition*
———1. phantom   2. situation
3. division   4. pair
5. happening

35. To *appease* the crowd
———1. displease   2. arouse
3. feed   4. bless
5. conciliate

36. *Arrogant* in bearing
———1. gracious   2. doubtful

3. humble   4. haughty
5. confident

37. To speak in an *artificial* manner ——1. natural   2. cultivated
3. plain   4. affected
5. unpleasant

38. Vigorously *assailed* the proposal ——1. questioned   2. carried
through   3. explained
4. supported
5. attacked

39. A system of *barter* ——1. drinking   2. exchanging   3. gambling
4. exclusion   5. borrow-
ing

40. *Scrupulous* in all things ——1. persistent   2. careless
3. miserly   4. con-
scientious   5. distrustful

41. The juror showed no *bias*. ——1. contempt   2. enmity
3. friendliness   4. preju-
dice   5. interest

42. He *supplanted* his friend. ——1. criticized   2. supported   3. insulted
4. took the place of
5. worked under

43. In a *gruff* voice ——1. loud   2. soft
3. harsh   4. unpleasant
5. pleading

44. Persuaded by *guile* ——1. profit   2. trickery
3. eloquence   4. magic
5. affableness

45. Held as *hostage* ——1. communist   2. alien
3. unfriendly person
4. pledge for payment
5. indorser

46. Tried to conceal her *humiliation* ——1. pride   2. discomfort
3. mortification   4. anger
5. humble origin

47. The man seemed *incredulous*. ——1. skeptical   2. believing
3. gullible   4. believable
5. in a poor financial
condition

48. *Impartial* judge —— 1. unfair   2. biased   3. honest   4. uninformed   5. fair

49. Of an *impetuous* temperament —— 1. competitive   2. impulsive   3. lazy   4. stubborn   5. phlegmatic

50. *Implied* criticism —— 1. deserved   2. undeserved   3. hinted   4. outspoken   5. useful

51. Ashamed of his *indolence* —— 1. poverty   2. grief   3. ignorance   4. laziness   5. incoherence

52. She has *ruddy* cheeks. —— 1. wrinkled   2. red   3. pale   4. splotchy   5. fat

53. The *intercession* of a friend —— 1. reciprocation   2. concession   3. betrayal   4. forgiveness   5. mediation

54. Decide the *issue* —— 1. next step   2. point in debate   3. result   4. lawsuit   5. problem

55. A *judicious* statement —— 1. unwise   2. harsh   3. serious   4. legal   5. wise

56. *Latitude* of thought and speech —— 1. freedom   2. indecency   3. sinfulness   4. slowness   5. boundaries

57. His manner was *solemn*. —— 1. haughty   2. grave   3. insolent   4. weary   5. nervous

58. The argument lacks *relevancy*. —— 1. justice   2. vigor   3. applicability   4. consistency   5. importance

59. A *ludicrous* situation —— 1. embarrassing   2. pleasant   3. tragic   4. laughable   5. exciting

60. *Reconcile* differences —— 1. change   2. abandon

3. consult about
4. agree to 5. adjust

61. Felt no *remorse*

———1. hatred 2. intuition
3. bitter repentance
4. sense of failure
5. revengeful feelings

62. The prince *renounced* his prerogatives.

———1. demanded 2. resigned
3. mistook 4. reclaimed
5. announced

63. Interrupted her *reverie*

———1. musing 2. prayer
3. revelry 4. spinning
5. slumber

64. A *rift* in the Democratic Party

———1. change 2. reversal
3. harmony 4. splitting
5. discussion

65. *Robust* spirit

———1. gentle 2. calm
3. strong 4. brave
5. bullying

66. *Ruthless* treatment

———1. ingenuous 2. dishonest 3. merciful
4. considerate 5. cruel

67. A *sane* mind

———1. just 2. ethical
3. irrational 4. sound
5. consistent

68. To *scoff* at the speaker

———1. mock 2. shout
3. be annoyed 4. disagree with 5. kick

69. Lived a *secluded* life

———1. immoral 2. selfish
3. hard 4. isolated
5. snobbish

70. A *serene* mood

———1. serious 2. gay
3. artificial 4. tranquil
5. sad

71. She *shammed* sickness.

———1. feared 2. escaped
3. feigned 4. showed
signs of 5. was embarrassed by

72. *Specious* reasoning

———1. quick 2. plausible
3. logical 4. specialized
5. specific

73. *Sprawled* on the desk   ——1. loafed 2. wrote
    3. lay awkwardly
    4. fought 5. crawled

74. The *stark* narrative   ——1. vulgar 2. gloomy
    3. tragic 4. thrilling
    5. unadorned

75. An unusual *stratagem*   ——1. plan to entrap
    2. layer of rock 3. jewel
    4. climax 5. combination

76. *Strenuous* objections   ——1. thoughtful 2. vigorous
    3. tenuous 4. weak
    5. factitious

77. A *subtle* argument   ——1. bold 2. unexpected
    3. dull 4. detailed
    5. ingenious

78. A *sullen* mind   ——1. evil 2. stupid
    3. morose 4. pleasant
    5. menacing

79. The commentary is *superfluous.*   ——1. essential   2. excessive
    3. fluent 4. detailed
    5. extraordinary

80. Your *surmise* is correct.   ——1. attitude 2. censure
    3. suggestion 4. con-
jecture 5. information

81. The king dismissed the *suppli-ants.*   ——1. ministers 2. supply
men 3. candidates
    4. petitioners
    5. intriguers

82. A *magnanimous* act   ——1. generous 2. selfish
    3. incredible 4. involv-
ing many people
    5. important

83. A *monotonous* tone of voice   ——1. resonant 2. flexible
    3. low 4. unvarying
    5. high pitched

84. Try to avoid *pedantry.*   ——1. lowmindedness
    2. sales talk 3. effem-
inacy 4. scholarliness
    5. display of learning

85. Showed *pique* at his remark   ——1. lack of interest

                                                     2. resentment   3. fear
4. interest   5. pleasure

86. A *pompous* manner   ——1. mild   2. insincere
3. absurd   4. awkward
5. pretentious

87. A *portentous* statement   ——1. invalid   2. important
3. ominous   4. unimportant   5. exaggerated

88. The judgment of *posterity*   ——1. old people   2. future
3. tradition   4. ancestors
5. successful people

89. A *presumptuous* statement   ——1. overbold   2. modest
3. frank   4. false
5. misunderstood

90. *Nettled* by his remark   ——1. puzzled   2. irritated
3. exalted   4. illuminated
5. mollified

91. Your fears are *chimerical.*   ——1. imaginary   2. real
3. childish   4. hysterical
5. morbid

92. A *thrifty* housewife   ——1. frugal   2. careful
3. stingy   4. cheerful
5. tasteful

93. *Tranquil* beauty of Greek sculpture   ——1. simple   2. cold
3. quiet   4. fragile
5. restless

94. This *transitory* life   ——1. sad   2. fleeting
3. uninteresting
4. transitional   5. long

95. A *trivial* matter   ——1. complex   2. petty
3. important   4. boring
5. unpleasant

96. *Ultimate* success   ——1. at last   2. complete
3. ulterior   4. present
5. easily achieved

97. *Unscrupulous* competition   ——1. zealous   2. untiring
3. fair   4. unprincipled
5. unintelligent

98. *Usurp* authority   ——1. seize   2. give up

3. weaken   4. hold
5. defy

99. Spoke kindly to the *vagrant* ———1. tenant   2. vagabond
3. peddler   4. country-
man   5. beggar

100. The *venom* of his glance ———1. secretiveness
2. weariness   3. fierce-
ness   4. malignity
5. displeasure

101. His popularity is *waning.* ———1. increasing
2. decreasing   3. short
lived   4. well-deserved
5. wavering

102. Not *averse* to taking the position ———1. disinclined   2. inclined
3. eager   4. fitted
5. unfitted

103. The *excerpt* is typical. ———1. condition   2. extract
3. exception   4. choice
5. symptom

104. His desire was *frustrated.* ———1. fulfilled   2. disregarded   3. increased
4. thwarted   5. lessened

105. The *tenets* of his faith ———1. brethren   2. teachers
3. beliefs   4. sources
5. problems

106. *Immutable* destiny ———1. cruel   2. unknown
3. blind   4. unchange-
able   5. fickle

107. Known for his *garrulity* ———1. kindness   2. artistic
sense   3. quiet manner
4. sternness
5. talkativeness

108. His reasoning was *fallacious.* ———1. logical   2. weighty
3. obvious   4. sensible
5. misleading

109. Displayed *chagrin* at the report ———1. pain   2. excitement
3. courage   4. vexation
5. amusement

110. An *affable* person ———1. foolish   2. friendly

3. impulsive
4. insincere   5. careless

111. *Circumspect* behavior   ———1. annoying   2. strange
3. cautious   4. austere
5. courteous

Number of words marked correctly ————.
Corresponding vocabulary range ————.

INCREASING VOCABULARY

"Five easy lessons to word mastery" is a delusion. There are no magical short cuts to word power. A good vocabulary is the incidental product of years of serious reading, of listening to intelligent talk, and of seeking to speak and write forcefully and clearly. All this does not mean that devices and methods for vocabulary-building are useless. But it does mean that getting a good vocabulary is inseparable from getting educated in general.

(1) *Increasing recognition vocabulary.* English has many words based on a common root form, to which different prefixes or suffixes have been added. The root form *spec-*, for example, from the Latin *specere* (to look) appears in *specter, inspection, perspective, aspect, introspection, circumspect, specimen, spectator.* Knowing the common prefixes and suffixes will help us get the meaning of many words whose roots are familiar.

(a) *Prefixes.*

PREFIX	MEANING	EXAMPLE
ab-	away from	absent
ad*-	to *or* for	adverb
com*-	with	combine
de-	down, away from, *or* un-doing	degrade, depart, dehumanize
dis*-	separation *or* reversal	disparate, disappoint
ex*-	out of *or* former	extend, ex-president
in*-	in *or* on	input
in*-	not	inhuman
mis-	wrong	mistake
non-	not	non-Christian
ob*-	against	obtuse

* See note on next page.

272

PREFIX	MEANING	EXAMPLE
pre-	before	prevent
pro-	for *or* forward	proceed
re-	back *or* again	repeat
sub*-	under	subcommittee
trans-	across	transcribe
un-	not	unclean

EXERCISE 18. Write words denoting *negation* from the following:

artistic	mutable
attached	revocable
essential	tenable
explicable	workable
honest	

EXERCISE 19. Write words denoting *reversal* from the following:

centralize	persuade
do	please
inherit	qualify
integrate	ravel
magnetize	

(b) *Suffixes.* These fall into three groups: noun suffixes, verb suffixes, adjectival suffixes.

Noun suffixes denoting "act of," "state of," "quality of."

SUFFIX	ROOT WORD	EXAMPLE
-dom	free	freedom
-hood	a man	manhood
-ness	dim	dimness
-ice	coward	cowardice
-ation	flirt	flirtation
-ion	intercede	intercession
⎰ -sion	scan	scansion
⎱ -tion	corrupt	corruption
-ment	argue	argument
-ship	friends	friendship

* The spelling of these prefixes varies, usually to make pronunciation easier. *Ad* becomes *ac* in *accuse, ag* in *aggregate, at* in *attack.* Similarly, the final consonant in the other prefixes is assimilated by the initial letter of the root word: *colleague* (*com + league*); *illicit* (*in + licit*); *offend* (*ob + fend*); *succeed* (*sub + ceed*).

SUFFIX	ROOT WORD	EXAMPLE
-ance	continue	continuance
-ence	precede	precedence
-ancy	flippant	flippancy
-ency	current	currency
-ism	baptize	baptism
-ery	brave	bravery

Noun suffixes denoting "doer," "one who."

SUFFIX	EXAMPLE	MEANING
-eer (male)	auctioneer	*one who* auctions
-ess (female)	poetess	*a woman who* writes poetry
-ist	fascist	*one who* believes in fascism
-or	debtor	*one who* is in debt
-er	worker	*one who* works

Verb suffixes denoting "to make" or "to perform the act of."

SUFFIX	EXAMPLE	MEANING
-ate	perpetuate	*to make* perpetual
-en	soften	*to make* soft
-fy	dignify	*to make* dignified
-ize, -ise	sterilize	*to make* sterile

Adjectival suffixes.

SUFFIX	MEANING	ROOT	EXAMPLE
-ful	full of	hate	hateful
-ish	resembling	fool	foolish
-ate	having	affection	affectionate
-ic, -ical	resembling	angel	angelic
-ive	having	prospect	prospective
-ous	full of	zeal	zealous
-ulent	full of	fraud	fraudulent
-less	without	father	fatherless
-able, -ible	capable of	peace	peaceable
-ed	having	spirit	spirited
-ly	resembling	woman	womanly
-like	resembling	child	childlike

EXERCISE 20. Write nouns denoting "act of," "state of," or "quality of" from the following words:

arrange   judge
buoy   locate

occur   promote
pauper   separate
peace

EXERCISE 21. Write nouns denoting "doer" from the following words:

advise   procrastinate
conservation   profit
help   ●   save
manipulate   see (*give masculine and feminine*)
plan

EXERCISE 22. Write verbs denoting "to make" or "to perform the act of" from the following nouns:

capital   moral
captive   peace
editorial   verse
heart   victim
liquid

EXERCISE 23. Make adjectives of the following words by adding a suffix:

humor   talk
irony   thwart
mule   wasp
rest   whimsey
speed

(c) *Combining forms*. Linguists refer to these as "bound forms." They appear generally, but not always, as prefixes.

COMBINING FORM	MEANING	EXAMPLE
anthropo-	man	*anthropo*logy
arch-	ruler	*arch*duke, mon*arch*
auto-	self	*auto*mobile
bene-	well	*bene*ficial
eu-	well	*eu*logy
graph-	writing	mono*graph*, bio*graphy*
log-, logue-	word, speech	mono*logue*
magni-	great	*magni*ficent
mal-	bad	*mal*ady
mono-	one	*mono*tone

COMBINING FORM	MEANING	EXAMPLE
multi-	many	*multi*plication
neo-	new	*neo*-classic
omni-	all	*omni*bus
pan-, pant-	all	*pan*hellenic
phil-	loving	*phil*osophy
phono-	sound	*phono*graph
poly-	many	*poly*gamy
pseudo-	false	*pseudo*nym
semi-	half	*semi*formal

(2) *Increasing active vocabulary.* Another way to increase word power is to keep transferring words from a *recognition* to an *active* vocabulary. This process presupposes a system, at any rate the cultivation of a habit, such as transferring one word a day from your reading to your conversational vocabulary. Another method is to enter new words on small cards: put the word on one side, the definition on the other, with a sentence illustrating its correct use. In spare moments during the day quiz yourself and check your own answers.

EXERCISE 24. Define each of the following words and use it correctly in a sentence:

extenuate	ostentatious	sensuous
inscrutable	fortuitous	calumny
homogeneous	ritual	finite
disparage	predatory	collate
intrinsic	officious	facetious
prodigious	taciturn	corpulent
palliate	malign	exacerbate

(3) *Strengthening active vocabulary.* Are you sure that *aggravate, enervate, transpire* mean what you think they mean? Of course you know that *deadly, mortal,* and *fatal* are very much alike in meaning—but do you know the exact distinctions between them? It is wise to check on yourself occasionally, to see whether some of the words in your vocabulary have the precise meaning you think they do. Good dictionaries frequently group synonyms and point out their differences. Both the Merriam-Webster *New Collegiate* and *The American College Dictionary* are excellent in this respect. The Merriam-Webster *Dictionary of Synonyms* is devoted exclusively to the grouping and differentiating of synonyms. The various

editions of Roget's *Thesaurus* must be used cautiously. They do not point out distinctions in meaning but simply group synonymous words.

The following entry, which appears in the Merriam-Webster *New Collegiate* under *able,* is an example of synonym grouping and differentiation that is provided by a good standard dictionary:

a′ble (ā′b'l), *adj.;* A′BLER (ā′blĕr); A′BLEST (-blĕst; -bl'ĭst). [OF., fr. L. *habilis* that may be easily held or managed, apt, fr. *habere* to have, hold.] **1.** Having sufficient power, skill, or resources of any kind to accomplish an object; capable; competent. **2.** Having intellectual qualifications, or strong mental powers; showing mastery in some department of knowledge or affairs; talented; clever.
Syn. Able, capable, competent, qualified come into comparison when they mean having power or fitness for work. **Able** suggests ability above the average as revealed in promise or performance; **capable** stresses qualities which fit one for work but seldom imply a special ability; **competent** and **qualified** imply the experience or training for a definite employment. — **Ant.** Inept.

By permission. From *Webster's New Collegiate Dictionary*
Copyright, 1949,
by G. & C. Merriam Co.

EXERCISE 25. Indicate the distinctions in meaning between the words in each group:

(1) anger, ire, rage, fury, indignation, wrath

(2) enthusiast, fanatic, zealot, bigot

(3) correct, accurate, exact, precise

(4) punish, chastise, castigate, chasten, discipline

(5) necessary, requisite, essential

(6) accidental, casual, fortuitous, contingent, incidental, adventitious

(7) ghastly, grisly, gruesome, macabre, grim

(8) fool, idiot, imbecile, moron, simpleton

(9) abuse, misuse, mistreat, maltreat, ill-treat

(10) fragrance, perfume, scent, incense, redolence, bouquet

(11) obstruct, hinder, impede, bar, block, dam

(12) arise, spring, originate, derive, issue, stem

(13) design, plan, scheme, plot

(14) benevolent, humane, humanitarian, altruistic, charitable

(15) grim, implacable, unrelenting

(16) sin, vice, scandal, crime

(17) recede, retreat, retract

(18) gift, present, gratuity, favor

(19) breeding, cultivation, poise, refinement

(20) motive, impulse, incentive

31. EXACTNESS = EX

CARE SHOULD BE TAKEN, NOT THAT THE READER MAY
UNDERSTAND, BUT THAT HE MUST UNDERSTAND.
—QUINTILIAN

Exactness in writing is the result of choosing words which accurately and idiomatically convey the meaning intended.

Exactness, or precision in writing, requires a knowledge of both the denotative and connotative meanings of words. *Denotation* is the core of a word's meaning, sometimes called the "dictionary" or literal meaning, as a *tree* is "a woody perennial plant having a single main axis or stem commonly exceeding ten feet in height." *Connotation* refers to the reader's emotional response to a word and to the associations the word carries with it. Thus, *tree* connotes shade or coolness or shelter or stillness, sometimes all of these together. Obviously, the connotation of a word cannot be fixed, for individual responses differ. Some words have fairly standardized associations (flag > the emotion of patriotism; home > security, the sense of one's own place), but even these words have other and less orthodox connotations. In fact, poets get many of their finest effects by avoiding standardized connotations. "Evening," for example, connotes for most of us some quality of beauty, but T. S. Eliot jolts us out of our normal response by seeing

> . . . the evening . . . spread out against the sky
> Like a patient etherised upon a table.

But when one is learning to write prose he must not violate generally accepted connotations without knowing exactly what he is

278

doing. And he must take pains to see that the connotations of his words reinforce and are consistent with their denotative meanings. For example, one of the denotative meanings of *smack* is "to give a hearty kiss," but no one (unless he is trying to be funny) will write

> He looked deep into her eyes, whispered endearing words, and *smacked* her on the ear.

Moreover, many words stand for abstractions: *democracy, truth, beauty,* and so on. Because their connotations are both vague and numerous, the exact writer states specifically what he means by them or so uses them that they are clear in their context. In short, the denotation of a word not only *suggests* its connotation; it ought to *control* that connotation as well. Otherwise, the reader misunderstands the writer's terms, or—what is worse—*thinks* he understands them, when he does not.

31a. Words nearly synonymous should be carefully distinguished from one another.

The meanings of many words are so similar that occasionally one may be substituted for another (see "Vocabulary," Section 30). But "occasionally" does not mean "all the time." A loose use of synonyms is one of the chief characteristics of inexact writing.

Sometimes loose synonyms are the result of careless thinking or expression; the writer of the following sentence probably wrote what came to his mind first, without bothering to hunt for the right word:

> The daughter of an army officer is in an excellent *condition* for finding a husband. (*situation* would be more exact.)

More often, the wrong word is a product of sheer ignorance.

> The minister *instigated* love and charity throughout the community. (The writer probably meant *inspired*.)

> We admired the speaker for his *sententious* appeal for funds. (*eloquent* was probably intended.)

EXERCISE 26. Replace the italicized words in the following sentences with more exact ones. Explain why the italicized word is inappropriate.

(1) His characters are *garish* and alive; they are people you will remember as old friends.

(2) His *obstinancy* in the face of danger saved us all.

(3) The ambassador, being treated like a common tourist, sputtered in *intimidation*.

(4) We can't blame Margaret for leaving him; certainly she had an ample *pretext*.

(5) The school's most honored professor was without fault; a wise mentor to his students, and in addition a scholar recognized as *pedantic* and profound.

EXERCISE 27. Explain the differences in meaning between the italicized words in each of these groups:

(1) between an *ignorant,* an *illiterate,* an *unlettered,* an *uneducated* person.

(2) between a *detached,* a *disinterested,* an *indifferent,* an *unconcerned* attitude.

(3) between *to condone, to excuse, to forgive, to pardon* a person's actions.

(4) between an *insurrection,* a *mutiny,* a *rebellion,* a *revolution.*

(5) between a *barbarous,* a *cruel,* a *fierce,* a *ferocious,* an *inhuman,* a *savage* character.

31b. Words of similar sound or spelling but of different meaning should not be confused.

Most of these words are approximate *homonyms:* words having the same pronunciation but different meanings (*idol, idle, idyll; aisle, isle*). Sometimes they are confused because the writer does not know their correct spelling (see "Spelling," Section 35d); sometimes because he does not know the difference in their meaning.

EXERCISE 28. What is the difference in meaning between the words in the following groups?

(1) adapt, adept, adopt	(7) arraign, arrange
(2) alley, ally	(8) bloc, block
(3) allude, elude	(9) borne, born
(4) anecdote, antidote	(10) calvary, cavalry
(5) anesthetic, antiseptic	(11) cannon, canon
(6) angel, angle	(12) canvas, canvass

(13) carton, cartoon	(22) historic, historical
(14) chord, cord	(23) human, humane
(15) climactic, climatic	(24) ingenious, ingenuous
(16) confidently, confidentially	(25) marital, martial
(17) costume, custom	(26) morality, mortality
(18) elicit, illicit	(27) prescribe, proscribe
(19) epic, epoch	(28) receipt, recipe
(20) flaunt, flout	(29) statue, statute
(21) genteel, gentile	(30) waive, wave

31c. "Invented" words should generally be avoided.

A "coined" word is a new and outright creation (like Gelett Burgess' *blurb*). A "neologism" is either a new word or a new use of an old word or words (like Winchell's *reno-vated, middle-aisled*). A "nonce-word," literally "once-word," is a word made up to suit a special situation and is generally not used more than once, as "My son," he said, "suffers from an acute case of *baseballitis*." Because English is an ever-growing language, new words and new functions for words constantly work their way into it. But the beginning writer had best leave word-invention to others and concentrate on developing the vocabulary already at hand. He should particularly rid his speech and writing of "unconscious" inventions—words he invents because of spelling errors or an inexact knowledge of word forms (*understandment* for *understanding, multification* for *multiplication,* and the like).

EXERCISE 29. Which of the italicized words in the sentences below seem "needless inventions"?

(1) His failure to pay that bill is only one of his many *non-responsible* acts since he became a campus hero.

(2) He has spent most of his life studying Indian culture and is now preparing a book on the effects of *savagism* on modern civilization.

(3) The senator argued that teachers should be *unpolitical* animals; what he really meant was that they should stop campaigning for his opponent.

(4) Lu described the universe before creation as a tremendous stretch of *unstuff.*

(5) The weather bureau reported that because of conditions tomorrow's weather was *unforecastable.*

(6) The newspapers have been full of the *disappearation* of the young man, and no one seems to have any idea where he might be.

(7) William Henry has a very *Trumanesque* temper and a very *Swiftian* tongue.

(8) Joe considered his older brother a very *affectated* young man and would have nothing to do with him.

(9) He's never been able to outgrow his *schoolteacherish* attitude toward me, in spite of the fact that I'm now his superintendent.

(10) His manner of pronunciation is very *peculiaristic*, to say the least, and sometimes I don't know whether he's speaking English or his native language.

31d. Improprieties should be avoided.

An impropriety is a legitimate word wrongly used. In the sentence "He *opinioned* that Edwin was guilty" the word *opinion* is used as a verb, a grammatical function to which it is not accustomed.

IMPROPER   He *carpentered* the doghouse together in less than an hour.

PROPER   He *made* (or *constructed,* or *put together*) the doghouse in less than an hour.

Many words, of course, can function legitimately as more than one part of speech.

PROPER   That garage gives excellent *service.*

PROPER   That garage has agreed to *service* my car.

When in doubt about the grammatical function of a word, the writer should consult a dictionary.

EXERCISE 30. Which of the italicized words in the sentences below are improprieties?

(1) His fussing at me all the time *aggravates* me.

(2) Are you trying to *infer* by that remark that I'm ignorant?

(3) In the third grade they *learned* me all the English I need.

(4) Mike said his family *raised* him to be a doctor but that the best he could do was pass the third grade.

(5) The highway was *stop-lighted* all the way between Seattle and Tacoma and I thought we'd never arrive.

(6) The carpenter wanted *to roof* the place before the weather turned cold.

(7) The program was *videoed* from coast to coast via the new national cable.

(8) We were out *holidaying* when we ran into Ed and Bill and decided to make a foursome of it.

(9) The engineer said we could *bull-doze* a clearing on the hillside in a half a day if we could find a way to start the motor.

(10) The carpenter *doweled* the joints with half-inch dowels and said they'd never come apart.

31e. A change in a word's suffixal form sometimes changes its meaning.

A roommate whom I *like* is not necessarily a *likable* roommate, nor is a *matter of agreement* an *agreeable matter*. Moreover, many words have two, sometimes three adjectival forms; *e.g.,* a *changeable* personality, a *changing* personality, a *changed* personality. One form cannot be substituted for another.

ILLOGICAL	The cook served our *favorable* dessert last night.
LOGICAL	The cook served our *favorite* dessert last night.
ILLOGICAL	He is a good student; he has a very *questionable* mind.
LOGICAL	He is a good student; he has a very *questioning* mind.

EXERCISE 31. Point out the differences in meaning between the italicized words in the following groups:

(1) an *arguable* point
an *argued* point

(2) a *practical* solution
a *practicable* solution

(3) a *hated* person
a *hateful* person

(4) a *liberal* foreign minister
a *liberated* foreign minister

(5) a *single* effect
a *singular* effect

(6) an *intelligible* writer
an *intelligent* writer

(7) a *godly* man
a *godlike* man

(8) an *informed* teacher
an *informative* teacher

(9) a *peaceful* nation
a *peaceable* nation

(10) a *workable* arrangement
a *working* arrangement

(11) an *amicable* teacher
an *amiable* teacher

(12) a *yellow* piece of paper
a *yellowed* piece of paper

31f. "Elegant variation" should be avoided.

The use of synonyms and pronouns to avoid awkward repetition is frequently necessary. But when a writer's desire to avoid repetition is so overwhelming that he finds a synonym or epithet for almost every word he has used previously, he is guilty of "elegant variation."

> Pee Wee Pearce, *the Chicago second-baseman,* got three hits yesterday. The *tiny infielder* came up in the first frame and lashed a one-base blow to right field. In the third inning *the diminutive keystone sacker* knocked a single through the box. In the seventh *the little ballhawk* reached first safely on a screaming drive to the outer garden.

Here, in the short space of four sentences, we have well over a dozen examples of "elegant variation":

Pee Wee	second-baseman	hits	first frame
tiny	infielder	one-base blow	third inning
diminutive	keystone sacker	single	seventh
little	ballhawk	safety	

lashed	right field
knocked	box
sent screaming drive	outer garden

In the first of the examples below, the use of the simple pronoun *he* would have made unnecessary the frantic search for synonyms for *king.* In the second, *visitor* could be omitted and *Two of the other people in attendance* changed to *Two others.*

> The *King* appeared yesterday at the Navy Barracks. *His majesty* was in full dress and escorted by the Home Guards. After inspecting the cadets, the *royal guest* was entertained at the Officers' Club.

> I saw many of my old classmates at your garden party. Two of your *guests* were my fraternity brothers. Another *visitor* played on the same football team with me. *Two of the other people in attendance* were brothers of my old girl friend.

EXERCISE 32. Find a specimen of "elegant variation" in a newspaper or popular magazine and explain to the class how the variation could be avoided.

EXERCISE 33. Comment on the "elegant variation" in the passage on the following page:

The outcome of the game was a personal victory for All-American Marty Jerome. The diminutive halfback scored ten times for the Mustangs, five of these coming in the final frame. In the first quarter the pint-sized wingback ran 10 yards for one score, scampered 45 for another, and actually bulled his way over for a third from the two yard stripe. In the second period the little fellow galloped half the length of the field for a marker after intercepting a Longhorn pass on his own fifty. In the third frame the mighty mite was held to one touchdown—that one coming on the last play of the period and featuring a series of fumbles. Lou Zamberg, Longhorn fullback, dropped the ball as he came through the line; Joe Harris, the Mustangs' giant tackle, picked it up, was hit from behind and fumbled. Like a streak of light the tiny Jerome grabbed it just before it hit the ground and dashed 85 long and magnificent yards to paydirt. The last frame was all Jerome's. In a display of ability seldom, if ever, seen the little man ran for five tallies, one of them a 105 yard kickoff return. He scored again on an intercepted pass, then on a 20 yard rabbit-run through center, and twice more on bullet-like plunges from the 5 yard line to home base.

31g. Words not idiomatic in the phrases in which they appear should be avoided.

Idiomatic writing means writing which strikes a reader as natural, smooth, unaffected. It means that things are said in an English (or American) way. A Frenchman says *un cheval blanc* and *il fait froid,* but the literal translations, *a horse white* and *it makes cold,* are unidiomatic to us, who say *a white horse* and *it is cold. Idiomatic* also describes phrase-forms which are justified by custom rather than by logic or grammar, as *look up an old friend, strike a bargain, go down to the sea in ships.* Generally, native users of English speak and write idiomatically without being conscious of the fact, though all of us find it hard sometimes to hit upon the right idiomatic prepositions or infinitives or gerunds (as *capable of passing the course, able to pass the course,* and so on). Hitting the right *idiom* is largely a matter of experience—either our own or somebody else's. The following list may be helpful.

(1) ABSOLVE BY, FROM   I was *absolved by* the dean *from* all blame.

(2) ACCEDE TO   He *acceded to* his father's demands.

(3) ACCOMPANY BY, WITH   I was *accompanied by* George. Th
terms were *accompanied with* a ple
for immediate peace.

(4) ACQUITTED OF   He was *acquitted of* the crime.

(5) ADAPTED TO, FROM   This machine can be *adapted to* farm
work. The design was *adapted from*
previous invention.

(6) ADMIT TO, OF   He *admitted to* the error. The plan
will *admit of* no alternative.

(7) AGREE TO, WITH, IN   They *agreed to* the plan but *disagreed
with* us. They *agreed* only *in* principle

(8) ANGRY WITH, AT   She was *angry with* me and *angry a*
the treatment she had received.

(9) CAPABLE OF   He is *capable of* every vice of the ig
norant.

(10) COMPARE TO, WITH   He *compared* the roundness of th
baseball *to* that of the earth. He *com
pared* the economy of the Ford *with*
that of the Plymouth.

(11) CONCUR WITH, IN   I *concur with* you *in* your desire to use
the revised edition.

(12) CONFIDE IN, TO   He *confided in* me. He *confided to* m
that he had stolen the car.

(13) CONFORM TO, WITH   The specifications *conformed to* o
      CONFORMITY WITH   *with* his original plans. You must ac
in *conformity with* our demands.

(14) CONNECT BY, WITH   The rooms are *connected by* a corri
dor. He is officially *connected with* th
university.

(15) DIFFER ABOUT, FROM,   We *differ about* our tastes in clothes
      WITH   My clothes *differ from* yours. We *dif
fer with* one another.

(16) DIFFERENT FROM*   Our grading system is *different from*
yours.

* *Different than* is colloquially idiomatic when the object of the prepositiona
phrase is a clause.
FORMAL   This town looks *different from* what I had remembered.
COLLOQUIAL   This town looks *different than* I had remembered it.

(17) ENTER INTO, ON, UPON — *He entered into* a new agreement and thereby *entered on* or *upon** a new career.

(18) FREE FROM, OF — He was *freed from* his mother's domination and now he is *free of* her.

(19) IDENTICAL WITH — Your reasons are *identical with* his.

(20) JOIN IN, TO, WITH — He *joined in* the fun *with* the others. He *joined* the wire cables *to* each other.

(21) LIVE AT, IN, ON — He *lives at* 14 Neil Road *in* a Dutch Colonial house. He *lives on* Neil Road.

(22) NECESSITY FOR, OF — NEED FOR, OF — There was no *necessity (need) for* you to lose your temper. There was no *necessity (need) of* your losing your temper.

(23) OBJECT TO — I *object to* the statement in the third paragraph.

(24) OBLIVIOUS OF — When he held her hand he was *oblivious of* the passing of time.

(25) OVERCOME BY, WITH — I was *overcome by* the heat. I was *overcome with* grief.

(26) PARALLEL BETWEEN, TO, WITH — There is a *parallel between* your attitude and his. This line is *parallel to* or *with* that one.

(27) PREFERABLE TO — A leisurely walk is *preferable to* violent exercise.

(28) REASON ABOUT, WITH — Why not *reason with* him *about* the matter?

(29) VARIANCE WITH — This conclusion is at *variance with* your facts.

(30) VARY FROM, IN, WITH — The houses *vary from* one another *in* size. People's tastes *vary with* their personalities.

(31) WORTHY OF — She is not *worthy of* your trust.

EXERCISE 34. Provide the idiomatic prepositions needed in the sentences on the following page:

* In many phrases, *on* and *upon* are interchangeable: *depend on* or *depend upon; enter on* or *enter upon.*

(1) Many students are oblivious ——— the criteria implicit ——— his criticisms.

(2) He confided ——— me that he thought me different ——— what he had expected.

(3) I agreed ——— his proposal, which had been adapted ——— one I had made previously.

(4) The jury absolved Robbins ——— all blame; hence he was ac quitted ——— the charge.

(5) Lois Bowers said she was angry ——— him because his action did not conform ——— those of a gentleman.

(6) The fence was built parallel ——— the street and connected ——— his neighbor's stone wall.

(7) Having been freed ——— his parents' supervision, he saw n necessity ——— (keep or keeping) them informed of hi whereabouts.

(8) She is not capable ——— (budget or budgeting) her own in come, for she is unable ——— (add) 4 and 4 and get 8.

(9) My father would admit ——— no disagreement ——— hi wishes, and I had to accede ——— his demand that I leave th party at midnight.

(10) We entered ——— a contract to buy the house after Mr. Jone agreed ——— our request for a twenty-year mortgage.

EXERCISE 35. Each of the following sentences violates a principl of *exactness*. Find and correct the error, after giving reasons for th correction.

(1) I often wondered why I didn't exert more enthusiasm towar my studies.

(2) Percival never got accustomed to one respect of college life— the calling of students by "Mr." or "Miss."

(3) While in high school I was always challenged to learn by con stant threats.

(4) I have seen students regardlessly ignore the instructor's lectur and then wonder why they flunked the course.

(5) He hadn't been in the army two days when he discovered tha his sleeping habits were going to be much shorter.

(6) A person has to earn a living in his chosen field if he is going to derive any satisfaction out of it.

(7) The first impression I encountered from the neighbor's dog was one of enmity.

(8) In spite of his round little face and twinkling eyes the preacher was a very serious and godlike man.

(9) "The Charge of the Light Brigade" is a poem about a disaster-full calvary charge in the Crimean War.

(10) He went to bed before all the election returns were in, but his confidential manner led us all into believing that he would be the winning candidate.

31h. The specific word is preferable to the general, "omnibus" word.

A general word stands for generalized qualities or characteristics, as *color, beast, vehicle.* A *specific* word singles out more definite and individualized qualities, as *red, lion, tricycle.* The distinction between specific and general words is not arbitrarily fixed; it depends on the context in which the word appears. For example, *man* is a general word in relation to *Leonard Chapman* and *Barney Rider,* but a specific word in relation to *mammal.* And *beast* is less specific than *lion* but more specific than *creature.*

The skillful writer tries constantly to express his thought—which is an abstraction—in concrete and unambiguous terms; hence his preference for specific details.

GENERAL   An old man walked slowly down the street.

SPECIFIC   A wizened beggar shuffled along Main Street.

GENERAL   They had a picnic under the shade of a tree.

SPECIFIC   They ate pickles and drank lemonade under the shade of an old elm.

SPECIFIC   Mateo was a stocky man, with clear eyes and a deeply tanned face. His skill as a marksman was extraordinary, even in Corsica, where everyone is a good shot. He could kill a ram at one hundred and twenty paces, and his aim was as accurate at night as in the daytime.

MORE   Picture a small, sturdy man, with jet-black, curly hair,
SPECIFIC   a Roman nose, thin lips, large piercing eyes, and a weather-beaten complexion. His skill as a marksman was extraordinary, even in this country, where everyone is a good shot. For instance, Mateo would never fire on a wild

ram with small shot, but at a hundred and twenty paces
he would bring it down with a bullet in its head or shoulder, just as he fancied. He used his rifle at night as easily
as in the daytime, and I was given the following illustration of his skill, which may seem incredible, perhaps, to
those who have never travelled in Corsica. He placed a
lighted candle behind a piece of transparent paper as big
as a plate, and aimed at it from eighty paces away. He
extinguished the candle, and a moment later, in utter
darkness, fired and pierced the paper three times out of
four.

—PROSPER MÉRIMÉE, *Mateo Falcone*

The need for specificity is not limited to descriptive writing. Even
in general informative writing, a good writer leads into a generalization through images, illustrations, and examples. Note how
concretely Bill Mauldin—no "literary" writer—deals with the abstraction "immigration."

But us champeens of the teeming shores aren't doing a new thing.
The immigration battle has been going on in this country ever since
the flag had thirteen stars. Every generation for 170 years has produced two schools for thought about immigration: One has been convinced that the country has reached its saturation point, that more
material for the human melting pot that produces Americans will
result only in lowering the standard of living, reducing wages, and
producing a crop of "furrin ideas." The other group believes—
rightly, I think—that when a country reaches the stage where it
can't expand its population, add new blood, and realize fresh po-
tentialities, it might as well fold its flag because it has reached the
summit and can only go downhill until it expires.

—BILL MAULDIN, *Back Home*

"OMNIBUS" WORDS

Perhaps the chief impediment to exactness among inexperienced
writers is their heavy dependence on "words-of-all-work" like *aspect,
case, cute, factor, field, fine, important, nice, point, swell, thing, type,
wonderful.* These are so general and inclusive in meaning that they
are called "omnibus" words. They have legitimate uses:

ACCURATE USE   The perfection of the assembly line was an *important factor* in the development of mass-production
industries.

290

ACCURATE USE   One interesting *aspect* of Robbins' *case* was the fervency with which the defense attorney addressed the jury.

But "omnibus" words tempt the writer who is too lazy to find the specific word he needs. His dependence on them becomes a form of triteness; he is too tired to see things with any freshness or to describe them with any energy. (See "Triteness," 33c.)

LOOSE   My job has certain *aspects* which I dislike.
REVISED   My job has certain *responsibilities* which I dislike.
LOOSE   He has a *nice* home overlooking Lake Washington.
REVISED   He has a (*large, comfortable, modern, rambling, expensive,* etc.) home overlooking Lake Washington.

EXERCISE 36. Find at least four words which express more specifically the meaning of each of the italicized words.

SAMPLE: *walked*—trudged, shuffled, sauntered, ambled

(1) *spoke* (verb)   (6) *led*
(2) *wrote*   (7) *eat*
(3) *hit* (verb)   (8) *correct* (verb)
(4) *cried*   (9) *break*
(5) *built*   (10) *run*

32. DIRECTNESS = DIR

IN COMPOSING, AS A GENERAL RULE, RUN YOUR PEN
THROUGH EVERY OTHER WORD YOU HAVE WRITTEN;
YOU HAVE NO IDEA WHAT VIGOR IT WILL GIVE YOUR
STYLE.

—SIDNEY SMITH

**Directness in writing is the result of choosing words
which economically and precisely convey the meaning intended.**

The challenge to *directness* comes from two fronts—wordiness
and vagueness. A wordy writer uses more words than are necessary
to convey his meaning.

WORDY   He attacks the practice of making a profitable business
out of college athletics from the standpoint that it has a
detrimental and harmful influence on the college students, and, to a certain degree and extent, on the colleges and universities themselves.

IMPROVED   He attacks commercialization of college athletics as detrimental to the students, and even to the universities
themselves.

A vague writer fails to convey his meaning sharply and clearly.

VAGUE   The report asserts the danger from unguarded machines
which may lessen the usefulness of workers in later life
as well as reducing their life expectancy.

IMPROVED   The report asserts that unguarded machines may severely injure or even kill workers.

Vagueness and wordiness are sometimes indistinguishable, as in the preceding examples. The weight of unnecessary words tends to obscure meaning. But very often wordiness is just awkwardness. The meaning is clear, but the expression is clumsy.

AWKWARD   The notion that Communists are people who wear long black beards is a very common notion.

IMPROVED   The notion is common that Communists are people who wear long black beards.

32a. "Deadwood" can often be eliminated by reducing clauses to phrases, phrases to single words.

"Deadwood" describes words which add nothing to the meaning of a sentence. In the sentence "The football captain, who is an All-American player, played his last game today," *who is* and *player* are deadwood. Sometimes deadwood can be eliminated by changing the position of important words. *"Yesterday's* snow is melting" is more concise than "The snow, *which fell yesterday,* is melting." The practice of reducing clauses to phrases and phrases to single words whenever possible will give sentences a tighter structure and hence more directness.

DEADWOOD   When the time to go had arrived, Jay picked up his suitcase and went to the door.

REVISED   When it was time to go, Jay picked up his suitcase and went to the door.

DEADWOOD   After the close of the war, Phipps Ford entered the university as a special student.

REVISED   After the war, Phipps Ford entered the university as a special student.

DEADWOOD   She is attractive in appearance, but she is a rather selfish person.

REVISED   She is attractive, but rather selfish.

DEADWOOD   There were instances of aggression on the country's frontier in many cases.

REVISED   There were many instances of aggression on the country's frontier.

One kind of deadwood is *circumlocution* (literally *talking around*) —the use of several words where a single exact one will do. "In this day and age" is a longer "today"; "call up on the telephone" a longer "telephone"; "destroyed by fire" a longer "burned"; "was made the recipient of" a longer "was given."

EXERCISE 37. Revise the following sentences by eliminating the deadwood:

(1) He is an expert in the field of labor relations.

(2) He hopes his essay will reinstate in the minds of the people the primary and fundamental purpose of our higher educational schools and colleges.

(3) After we had cleaned up the cabin, we explored the surrounding territory for good fishing spots.

(4) Blacky Hildreth is a peculiar character; he is interested in several aspects of witchcraft.

(5) The fastest type of automobile requires the best quality of gasoline.

(6) People have to be educated as to how to plan delicious, inexpensive menus that will meet their nutritional needs.

(7) Social life seems to be a very important thing to college students.

(8) The rain, which has been coming down steadily for two weeks now, is washing away the young seedlings I planted in the ground last month.

(9) After spending four hours of time waiting for his train to come in, I went home and then to bed.

(10) Edison spent the majority of the hours of each day tinkering in his laboratory.

32b. The substitution of two or more "approximate" words for one exact word should be avoided.

Deadwood and circumlocutions make sentences clumsy, but they do not always interfere seriously with communication. A more serious violation of directness is the substitution of two or more loose synonyms for a single precise word.

LOOSE   His *temperament* and *personality* are not very pleasant.

REVISED   His *disposition* is not very pleasant.

LOOSE   He spoke entertainingly of his *deeds* and *doings* as a foreign correspondent.

REVISED   He spoke entertainingly of his *adventures* as a foreign correspondent.

EXERCISE 38. Find a single synonym to express the meaning of
the following pairs:

real and *true*	*amazed* and *surprised*
plays and *poems*	*severe* and *strict*
life and *times*	*flat* and *even*
love and *regard*	*proud* and *vain*
costly and *dear*	*conscientious* and *honest*

32c. Words which needlessly repeat the meaning of other words should be avoided.

This clumsiness is known as *redundancy* or *tautology,* and is best
illustrated by the expressions "seen by the eyes" and "audible to
the ears."

NOT   He advanced *forward* and told the sergeant that he had captured four enemy spies.

BUT   He advanced (or came forward) and told the sergeant that he
had captured four enemy spies.

NOT   Battalion A retreated *back* to the river bank.

BUT   Battalion A retreated to the river bank.

NOT   One of the first assignments in English was to write *my own*
autobiography.

BUT   One of the first assignments in English was to write an autobiography.

Single words become tautologies when superfluous prefixes, suffixes, or other unnecessary additions are attached to them. *Irregardless* is merely a longer *regardless; preventative* a longer *preventive.*
Even when the longer form does exist, as *truthfulness* and *virtuous-
ness,* the shorter form (as *truth, virtue*) can often be substituted.

SUPERFLUOUS   He is a very *pre-eminent* man, having a reputation as
the country's greatest surgeon.

REVISED   He is an *eminent* man, reputed to be the country's
greatest surgeon.

SUPERFLUOUS   In *summarization,* Lewis Doser spoke of the need for
a larger library.

REVISED　　　　　　In *summary,* Lewis Doser spoke of the need for a larger library.

EXERCISE 39. Revise the following sentences to eliminate any redundancies or tautologies:

(1) Mrs. Hissong's talk made me realize for the first time in my life the important essential of getting a college education.

(2) Barbara Linger's limousine sedan, black in color, has been seen an uncountless number of times parked in front of Blickle's fruit market.

(3) The modern business of today is usually a corporation; businesses owned in joint partnership are decreasing in number.

(4) It is the consensus of opinion that the total effect of all this government spending, enormous in amount, will not achieve any real prosperity.

(5) As a usual rule, the child is in his playpen by nine A.M. in the morning.

(6) The life of Thomas Edison provides a good example to illustrate the truth of the old saying, "Genius is ten per cent inspiration and ninety per cent perspiration."

(7) I like exciting scenery as well as the next person, but I know that very shortly I would become tired of it, and it would become boring.

(8) In good writing there is always a great deal of sincerity in the writer's use of words and phrases.

(9) John Dos Passos employs many unconventionalities in his writing, as well as a number of radical and peculiar tricks and devices of style.

(10) So far as understanding his meaning is concerned, I would classify James Joyce as a very difficult author to read.

32d. Awkward repetition should be avoided.

Only *awkward* repetition makes a sentence wordy; effective repetition is a legitimate way of securing emphasis.

EFFECTIVE REPETITION　　All *dullness* is in the mind; it comes out thence and diffuses itself over everything round the *dull* person, and then he terms everything *dull,* and thinks himself the victim of *dull* things.—C. E. MONTAGUE

EFFECTIVE REPETITION   Don't *join* too many gangs. *Join* few if any. *Join* the United States and *join* the family —but not much in between, unless a college.—ROBERT FROST

EFFECTIVE REPETITION   A *moderately* honest man with a *moderately* faithful wife, *moderate* drinkers both, in a *moderately* healthy house: that is the true middle class unit.—G. B. SHAW

Awkward repetition is usually unintentional and can be detected by reading aloud the first draft.

AWKWARD REPETITION   Methods of using the harvesting equipment are being *improved* constantly to *improve* efficiency.

AWKWARD REPETITION   The investigation revealed that the *average teacher teaching* industrial arts in California has an *average* working and *teaching* experience of five years.

AWKWARD REPETITION   The *important subject* on which I am going to speak is the *subject* of fraternity affairs, a *subject* of great *importance* to college students.

EXERCISE 40. Revise the following sentences to eliminate awkward repetition:

(1) I was late in leaving the house this morning and so was late for class.

(2) He is an industrial engineering student studying the principles of time and motion study.

(3) The final chapter of the book is devoted to recounting what happens to the heroine of the book.

(4) Undoubtedly the world's tallest building is the Empire State Building.

(5) The weather stripping on the door should provide good protection against the cold weather.

(6) People who graduated during the depression found many hardships in the way of finding jobs with adequate pay.

(7) The writer's point about the need of making a college education more difficult is one of our points of agreement.

(8) I was compelled to read the essay three times before I was prepared to make any kind of decision about the effectiveness of the ideas he presents in his essay.

(9) After appearing in the movie "The Four Horsemen," Rudolph Valentino was hounded the rest of his life by autograph hounds.

(10) The formal usage of language is restricted pretty generally to use in academic and technical writing, or what we used to call old-fashioned eloquence.

32e. The simple and direct expression is preferable to the needlessly complex one.

The qualification "needlessly" is important. Sometimes a complex idea requires a complex language and sentence structure. Much philosophic and scientific thought, for example, is inexpressible in a continuously simple language.

> One of the simplest ways of evolving a favorable environment concurrently with the development of the individual organism, is that the influence of each organism on the environment should be favorable to the *endurance* of other organisms of the same type. Further, if the organism also favors *development* of other organisms of the same type, you have then obtained a mechanism of evolution adapted to produce the observed state of large multitudes of analogous entities, with high powers of endurance. For the environment automatically develops with the species, and the species with the environment.
>
> —A. N. WHITEHEAD, *Science and the Modern World* [his italics]

On the other hand, the direct writer is not ashamed to express a simple idea in simple language. He does not subscribe to the notion that the use of complicated language is the sign of a superior intelligence. (See "Appropriateness," Section 33d.)

NEEDLESSLY COMPLEX   Not a year passes without some evidence of the fundamental truth of the statement that the procedures and techniques of education are more complicated and complex than they were two decades ago.

MORE DIRECT   Each year shows how true it is that methods of education are more complex than they were twenty years ago.

Mr. Edgar Dale, in his "Art of Confusion," a selection from which appears below,* has satirized the notion that language must be difficult to be "intelligent."

Young Alvin H. Harrison hesitatingly entered the office of Dr. Maxim S. Kleeshay and timidly inquired about his master's thesis. "What did you think of it?" he asked.

"A worthy endeavor," replied the Doctor, "but it has one major defect. It is written at too elementary a level. I would like to offer somewhat tentatively the pertinent observation that graduate students, research workers, and professors will find it too easy and effortless to read—no disciplinary value. Remember that Chancellor Hutchins once said that good education is painful. Furthermore, you haven't stated any significant challenges in your introductory paragraphs."

"I didn't want to offer any challenges. I just wanted to make my ideas clear."

"That's a worthy primary objective, young man. But no educational writing today should fail to point out that the world is in peril, in flux, in conflict, changing, disordered, and disunited. It's either one world or two, you know.

"And another thing—it is interesting to note that you have a mistaken notion about communication on the scholarly level. It is obvious that you are unaware of the appropriate technical terminology in education. Your thesis is too sprightly, too simple."

"You mean that if I am dull enough and labored enough, I'll sound scholarly?"

"A very unfortunate and inaccurate way to put it, young man. I trust that it is not inappropriate to note some examples from your own thesis and to offer some suggestions (tentative, of course) as to how these examples might be shifted into more precise and scholarly language.

"You say on page 59, 'It will be hard to provide enough schools for the three million children entering in 1950.' It would have sounded much better if you had said, 'The phenomenon of fecundity has confronted American education with a challenge of Herculean proportions. An evaluation of the implication to the tax structure of state governments in providing adequate educational facilities is a difficult and complex task.'

* Reprinted with permission from *The News Letter* (XIV, No. 3), a publication of the Bureau of Educational Research, The Ohio State University, Columbus, Ohio.

"Let me make another point. A critical analysis of your thesis discloses that you are making little use of what is called the adjectival approach in education. You speak of 'thinking.' It would be much better to refer to 'critical thinking.' Change 'an approach to the problem' to 'a constructive approach to the problem.' Instead of 'world citizens' say 'functional world citizens.' At one point here, you say that the teacher is given 'help in working on her problems.' I would say that she had been given 'rather definite assistance in attacking specific difficulties.' You speak of 'reading practices.' Make it 'sound reading practices.' Utilize 'basic fundamentals' and 'desirable goals' a little more. Don't use the word 'function' alone. Say 'basic function.' "

EXERCISE 41. Find a paragraph or two of "complex" writing in one of your textbooks and explain to the class why you think the specimen is "needlessly complex."

EXERCISE 42. Each of the sentences below violates a principle of *directness*. Find and then correct the error.

(1) We of the United States cannot expect to spread peace throughout other nations and countries until we can teach and educate our own people to respect each other as equal individuals.

(2) Professor Harding respects the ability of students to be able critics.

(3) By learning to live with his physical problem, the life of the retarded child is improved, which is in itself a step forward toward recovery.

(4) This has been a problem of growing importance which has bothered and troubled the physicists and engineers for a period of over one and one-half decades.

(5) During the entirety of the whole fishing trip Morris continually went on thinking about those nice big trout he had caught during the summer before this present one.

(6) They were the most beautiful looking fish he had ever seen before in his life.

(7) Mr. Walleck used certain words to compliment the Republican Party and other types of words to slander the other party.

(8) It has just been in the past couple of years that the Southern colleges have begun to open their doors to the Negro.

(9) It was very evident that Pedersen's intention in writing the

letter lies in the fact that not enough loyal brothers of the fraternity have been contributing to the upkeep of the fraternity.

(10) Individuals who hold low standards of success are generally envious of people who have attained prominence and are constantly dissatisfied with their less fortunate existence which the lack of material success has forced upon them.

33. APPROPRIATENESS = APPR

A SPEECH IS COMPOSED OF THREE THINGS: THE SPEAKER,
THE SUBJECT ON WHICH HE SPEAKS, AND THE AUDIENCE
HE IS ADDRESSING.

—ARISTOTLE, *Rhetoric*

Appropriateness in writing is the result of choosing words which are suitable to the subject, to the audience, and to the writer.

Aristotle's statement above is as true of writing as it is of speaking. Appropriate English meets three requirements simultaneously. It fits the personality of the speaker or writer; it accords with the nature of his subject matter; and it impresses his listeners or readers as exact and proper.

33a. Slang should generally be avoided.

Webster's New Collegiate Dictionary defines *slang* as "language comprising certain widely current terms having a forced, fantastic, or grotesque meaning, or exhibiting eccentric humor or fancy." Sometimes *slang* results from an intentional mispronunciation, as *hoss, dawg;* sometimes from an intentional shortening of a regular word, as *prof, gent;* sometimes from making a counter-word (a word of all work) of a regular word, as *lousy, swell, sharp, tough, rugged.* But usually a slang word is an exaggerated metaphor, as *fishface, blockhead, highbrow, cash in your chips, ball and chain.*

The notion that any use of slang is vulgar* is excessively fastidious, if not unrealistic. The creation of slang is a fundamental linguis-

---

* A slang word is *not* a profanity, an illiteracy, or a provincialism. Not one word in the following sentence is slang: "I reckon them damn apples is rotten."

tic process and will continue as long as English is a living language. Many respectable words started their careers as slang (*rascal, parry*). And the use of clipped forms like *auto, ad, gym, phone, taxi,* though not in universal good repute, is seldom objected to in informal writing. In fact, skillful writers can use slang effectively.

> The admiral jumped from his chair and cleared his throat, his mouth forming a straight, tight line; if anything, the corners turned downward. Clenching his fists, he apparently tried to look as severe and angry as possible. But before he could say anything he lost control and broke into a grin. A second later he started laughing so hard that he couldn't stand up. He chewed on his napkin to try to shut up, but he couldn't stop roaring. The party turned into a wing-ding and we practically blew the roof off the place.
>
> —WILLIAM LEDERER, *All the Ship's at Sea*

But slang has two serious limitations seldom appreciated by youthful writers: (1) a little of it goes a long way, and (2) it is not always appropriate. Even a good new slang word is soon rendered lifeless by repetition. Nothing is so stale as yesterday's slang. Who remembers *Twenty-three skiddoo* and *Oh, you kid*? Moreover, the basis of slang is humor, or at least an anti-seriousness; slang is therefore unsuited for serious writing. A reader is especially irritated when he finds slang and respectable words tactlessly mixed in the same sentence:

> In meeting today in a special session to approve the governor's request for an investigation of the liquor board, the legislators decided to blow the whole shebang sky high.

EXERCISE 43. Almost everyone has his favorite "counter-words," without which he would be almost speechless—*swell, lousy, grand, awful,* and so on. Make a list of your own counter-words and compare the list with those of your classmates—to see how "original" your own slang is.

EXERCISE 44. Can you think of a situation or general context in which the sentences below might be appropriate? Explain.

(1) The distinguished envoy to the peace conference finished his address by blowing his top.

(2) The concert was unfortunately interrupted when a piece of plaster fell near the podium and conked one of the violinists on the noggin.

(3) During the congregational meeting the Reverend Mr. Hildreth was called upon to put in his two cents' worth.

(4) The beauty of the painting was marred by the artist's tendency to foul up the backgrounds with screwy designs.

(5) When heat was applied to the chemical mixture, small particles of zinc were dispersed like crazy.

33b. Substandard English should be avoided except in circumstances appropriate for it.

Substandard, or *vulgate,* speech consists largely of *profanity, provincialisms* (sometimes called *localisms* or *dialecticisms*), and *vulgarisms.* The use of *profanity* does not always suggest a limited vocabulary. The purpose of profanity is to provide an emotional release, not to communicate information. An excessively profane person needs a psychiatrist, not a dictionary or a preacher. A *provincialism* is a word restricted generally to a particular region, as *tote* for *carry; poke* for *bag; spider* for *frying pan; gumshoes* for *overshoes; draw* for *small valley.* A *vulgarism* is an illiteracy: *ain't, could of, he done, we was,* and so on. Double negatives (*can't hardly, can't help but, not never*) are considered vulgarisms by many people, though *I cannot help but be confused* is hardly so objectionable an expression as *I can't never seem to git the point.* The vulgarisms that creep most frequently into writing are the *improprieties,* good words incorrectly used (see Section 31d). For example, *accept* is often confused with *except,* as in *I except your invitation.*

SUBSTANDARD	He *didn't ought to have* spent the money.
REVISED	He shouldn't have spent the money.
SUBSTANDARD	I wish Irving *had of drove more careful.*
REVISED	I wish Irving had driven more carefully.
SUBSTANDARD	*Let's don't* study tonight.
REVISED	Let's not study tonight.

Of all substandard English forms, the double negative (*can't hardly, scarcely none, don't* want *no,* and so on) is perhaps the most controversial. The objection to it arose in the 18th century, when many Englishmen assumed that the mathematical principle—two negatives make a positive—should also be applied to grammar. The argument then was that a person saying *I don't want nothing to do with you* was really saying *I want something to do with you.* The argument is of course rather unrealistic. The double (or triple) negative is primarily a way of being emphatic. But because society has been conditioned against the double negative, writers must dispense with it or expose themselves to the charge of ignorance.

EXERCISE 45. Find at least five examples of *provincialisms* (as "The cat wants in") and describe the circumstances under which they could be used appropriately.

EXERCISE 46. If you are a native of the region in which your college is located, ask a classmate from another region to give you a list of ten words or expressions that strike him as being provincialisms in your speech. If you come from another region yourself, make up your own list of provincialisms of the college area and compare it with your classmate's.

33c. Trite expressions should be avoided.

A trite expression, sometimes called a *cliché,* a *stereotyped* or *hackneyed* phrase, is one worn out by constant use, as "burning the midnight oil," "Father Time," "raving beauties," "man about town." Words in themselves are never trite—they are *used* tritely. Thus, neither *break* nor *dawn* is trite; *break of dawn* is. One cannot avoid trite expressions entirely; they sometimes describe a situation accurately.* If they were not so useful, they would not have become trite. But the writer who uses many trite expressions is suspected of being a trite thinker. His readers assume that his ideas as well as his phrases are secondhand. What would be your estimate of a person who said the following?

A college education develops a *well-rounded personality* and gives the student an appreciation of *the finer things of life.*

Effectively used, triteness can be humorous. Note how the string of trite expressions in the example below explodes into absurdity

---

* More fundamentally, of course, triteness is a disease of the personality. If people are conditioned to react to situations in stereotyped ways, their writing is bound to reflect this fact. The next time you prepare a paper on "Why I Came to College" or "What I Expect to Do After Graduation," write what you *really* mean. Triteness will probably disappear.

when the writer transposes the words in the two clichés in the last clause.

A pair of pigeons were cooing gently directly beneath my window; two squirrels plighted their troth in a branch overhead; at the corner a handsome member of New York's finest twirled his nightstick and cast roguish glances at the saucy-eyed flower vendor. The scene could have been staged only by a Lubitsch; in fact Lubitsch himself was seated on a bench across the street, smoking a cucumber and looking as cool as a cigar.

—S. J. PERELMAN, *Keep It Crisp*

EXERCISE 47. In the selection below a number of trite expressions are strung together. How many can you identify?

The wily Indians, wishing to strike while the iron was hot, converged on the wagon-train at the break of dawn. The hardy pioneers, firing in unison, presented the attacking force with a veritable hail of bullets. Dozens of the pesky red-skins keeled over and bit the dust. The rugged frontiersmen continued to give a good account of themselves until broad daylight. Then the Indians broke through the ramparts. The defenders, their backs against the wall, were slaughtered mercilessly. When the dust had risen from the battlefield and when the smoke had cleared away, the carnage was frightful. Every single white man had gone to meet his maker.

EXERCISE 48. Read the following passage, circling all the clichés and the expressions which are longer or more involved than they need be.

The American Way is the only feasible route for educational personnel to tread in our educational institutions of learning. Despite its humble origins, this child of adversity, born in a log cabin, has beyond a shadow of a doubt reached the summits in this fair country of ours.

There is too much of a tendency to view this great institution with alarm. But on the other hand people who live in glass houses, which is the type most inclined to cast aspersions and generally be wet blankets, are usually the ones by whom the criticisms are made.

Now I'm just an ordinary schoolteacher, and don't have any complicated ideas on how our schools should be run, but I know that Abe Lincoln, if he were alive, would disapprove of the newfangled techniques that are making a shambles of our educational system.

Foreigners are at the bottom of the attack on our American herit-

age and the American Way in education. These notorious radicals
have wreaked havoc with our boys and girls.

33d. Jargon should be avoided in general writing.

Jargon has several meanings. In a famous essay entitled "On
Jargon," Sir Arthur Quiller-Couch defined the term as speech or
writing which is vague and "woolly" because it consists of abstract
words, elegant variation, and "circumlocution rather than short
straight speech." Linguists often define jargon as hybrid speech or
dialect formed by a mixture of languages. An example would be the
English-Chinese jargon known as pidgin-English. But to most people, *jargon* is a term of at least mild derision applied to the technical
or specialized vocabulary of a trade or profession—for example, *engineering jargon* or *educational jargon.* As an instrument of communication among people in the same field, jargon undoubtedly has its uses.
Because both writer and readers understand that single words stand
for a body of ideas and concepts, communication can be clear and
accurate. But too frequently, jargon creeps into writing meant for
a general audience. Readers find it either unintelligible or needlessly complex (see "Directness," Section 32).

Unfortunately, many readers dislike to admit that any writing is
unintelligible to them. So jargon persists in general writing, and
writers of jargon get respect when they deserve contempt. There is
a lesson for all of us in the illustration below:

THE TURBO-ENCABULATOR IN INDUSTRY

. . . Work has been proceeding in order to bring to perfection the
crudely conceived idea of a machine that would not only supply in-
verse reactive current for use in unilateral phase detractors, but
would also be capable ot automatically synchronizing cardinal grammeters. Such a machine is the Turbo-Encabulator. . . . The original
machine had a base plate of prefabulated amulite surmounted by a
malleable logarithmic casing in such a way that the two spurving
bearings were in a direct line with the pentametric fan. . . . The
main winding was of the normal lotus-o-delta type placed in a
panendermic semiboloid slot in the stator, every seventh conductor
being connected by a non-reversible tremie pipe to the differential
girdlespring on the "up" end of the grammeters. . . . *

* Reprinted by permission of the publishers, Arthur D. Little, Inc., Cambridge, Mass.

This new mechanical marvel was a joke, the linguistic creation of an engineer at the famous research firm of Arthur D. Little, Inc., who was tired of reading jargon.

> EXERCISE 49. Make a list of words, terms, phrases which seem to constitute the "jargon" in a field that you know. Define these terms in a way that a general reader can understand; then justify the use of the terms among people in your field.

33e. An artificial or stilted diction and "fine writing" should be avoided.

Artificiality is not inherent in words themselves but in a kind of use that is made of them. The statement "The edifice was consumed by fire" contains words that have legitimate uses, but the sentence is pompous because it is a self-conscious assertion of a simple fact —"The house burned down." Similarly, in the sentence "We were unable to commence our journey to your place of residence due to inclement weather conditions," the writer is more concerned with the manner of his statement than with the fact that he wants to say, "We could not come because it was snowing." *

Many inexperienced writers believe, mistakenly, that an artificial diction makes for "good writing." They shift gears, so to speak, when they go from speaking to writing. They try to make their writing sound like the speech of a Hollywood version of a college professor. They write "The athletic contest commenced at the stipulated time," instead of "The game began on time"; or "I informed him that his advice was unsolicited," instead of "I told him to mind his own business."

Writing which relies on a continuously artificial diction is called "fine writing." The passage below, for example, cheapens a worthwhile sentiment ("I am a crusader for international peace") by overdressing it:

> Whenever the press of daily events and duties relaxes its iron grip on me, whenever the turmoil of my private world subsides and leaves me in quiet and solitude, then it is that I feel my crying responsibility

---

* Some time ago, at an important heavyweight fight in Madison Square Garden, the referee ended his instructions with "and may the superior participant emerge victorious!"

as one of God's creatures and recognize the need to speak out loudly and boldly against the greed and intolerance that carry humanity into the terrible destruction of armed conflict.

EXERCISE 50. Find an example of "fine writing" in a newspaper or popular magazine and explain in a short paper why you think it ineffective.

33f. Mixed and incongruous metaphors and other illogical comparisons should be avoided.

In every language one of the most respected and ancient means of reinforcing and enlivening communication is the use of comparisons.

> The teacher shook her finger in my face as she might shake a clogged fountain pen.

An apt figure of speech can be a condensed and effective way of making one experience understandable in terms of another, as the comparison above implies that the reprimanding finger is shaken with the fussy, ineffectual, frustrated motion familiar to everyone who has ever tried to unclog a fountain pen.

But there are dangers in using figurative language. Some figures, for the very reason that they once *were* expressive and meaningful, have been used until they have become tired and trite (see Section 33c). When a word or phrase has been used so long in a metaphorical sense that it has lost all power of reminding us of the original comparison (as the word *stale* in *stale news*), it is likely to be used in a way that violates the logic of the comparison. The student who wrote:

> Every field of study is pursued in the hope of finding a universal panacea.

violated logic and idiom because he did not think of a *field* as a *field,* and therefore as something which cannot be *pursued.* The violation is more disturbing when the figures are less a part of the idiom than *field of study.* The following hodgepodge consists of triteness compounded with nonsense:

> Socialists are snakes in the grass, gnawing at the roots of the ship of state.

The usual mixed metaphor is of this kind. The writer is thinking in trite terms, hence does not notice his own illogicality. A writer who uses a fresh figure of speech is more likely to develop it consistently than one who accepts unthinkingly a timeworn resemblance.

But the writer who tries too hard to find a fresh comparison is likely to use a figure which is inappropriate to the tone of what he is trying to say:

> The minister was not too proud to spend his days visiting the sick and the needy and those rejected by society. He was as little concerned with personal contamination as a pig in a mud puddle when the Lord's work was to be done.

Incongruous figures such as this should either be replaced by more appropriate and logical figures of speech, or simply dispensed with.

> EXERCISE 51. Recast the following sentences to eliminate mixed or incongruous figures of speech:
>
> (1) The enemy threw everything at us but the kitchen sink, keeping us on pins and needles.
>
> (2) My father was usually on top of the world when he brought home the bacon.
>
> (3) Although the first draft of the treaty had received provisional ratification by most of the countries concerned, the diplomats were busy as beavers tidying up the last details.
>
> (4) He had to be on the rocks before he would turn over a new leaf.
>
> (5) Grandmother's tiny, dried fingers seemed to stitch the material with the rapidity of a pneumatic drill.
>
> (6) She may be the last rose of summer, but she's got some vinegar in her yet.
>
> (7) It wasn't until Copernicus began reexamining an old cosmology completely in conflict with the Ptolemaic system that he really hit the nail on the head.
>
> (8) Table tennis is a good game for you sharp yearlings, but when you're blind as a bat it's a horse of a different color.
>
> (9) By a series of such victories, the team was able to roll up a very good foundation for a national reputation.
>
> (10) They decided to play the field until the chips were down and then to get behind a single candidate with both barrels.

EXERCISE 52. After defining the "Audience" (English teacher, classmates, group of businessmen, parents, etc.) comment on the "appropriateness" of the language in the following selection:

Like many other just plain "guys," I just graduated from high school. Being like most of these other guys, I naturally didn't really accomplish much during my previous school years. Yes, I got fair grades, met lots of swell kids, played football. I guess I'm just one of those guys who had the run of the school and never bothered to study.

No, I'm not bragging. I'm just telling you why high school was never like college.

A lot of people graduate from high school every year. A good percentage go to college and the rest go out and get a job. Four years later, the college student graduates. Does that mean he's going to get a better job than the fellow who went from high school directly to a job?

No. It doesn't mean a thing unless the guy in college really studied and hit the books. What I'm trying to bring out is that a person who goes to college and doesn't study is no better off than a guy who goes out and gets a job immediately after high school graduation.

So college for me is the "big jump." I fooled around in high school, and if I don't get right down and study now, I might as well quit school and start that $75.00 a week job.

No, I don't have anything against a $75.00 a week job. It's just that twenty years from now, I'd probably still be there getting the same $75.00. This is it, so I guess it's time for me to bear down and study hard. I think this will be the "big jump."

DICTION REVIEW EXERCISE. Revise each of the following sentences according to what you have learned in Sections 31-33 ("Exactness," "Directness," "Appropriateness").

(1) Even though homemaking is an important occupation, only a small number of homemakers have thorough preparation for the task.

(2) By reading *Yachting* I am able to keep abreast with the tide of affairs in the sailing world.

(3) The sheriff suspicioned that the prisoners had hacksawed their way out of the jail.

(4) Coaches are paid for the type of teams they produce or for the number of winning games per season.

311

(5) The principal censored the boy's actions in a meanly manner.

(6) I thought I was doing the best thing when I signed up for the army.

(7) Her eyes were like limpid pools of clear, crystal water; her skin glowed as though it had been touched by a fairy's wand. She was a knockout.

(8) The pup was a nuisance. The little mongrel chased after other curs and followed the dumb brutes to their homes. Then we had to spend our evenings hunting for the hound.

(9) Reading every new novel that comes out may give a person a broader aspect of life.

(10) The knowledge we receive in our home economics classes is very useful and economical to us.

(11) Compared to Johnson, Coleman is a lily-fingered shortstop.

(12) He left our domicile a boy; he returned to our outstretched arms a man. His rugged, weather-beaten face had been tanned by the blazing sun of darkest Africa, lined by sorrows and sufferings that would forever remain a secret between him and his God.

(13) Child care is taught in the clinic, as well as other matters which the attendants desire.

(14) Them people in Washington don't seem to understand that you can't get no blood out of a turnip.

(15) My superior, the commanding general of this area, has just instructed me to activate the regiment. I shall implement his directive and communicate with him when his instructions have been carried out.

(16) Our language should be adjusted into whatever situation we find ourselves.

(17) A college student has to invest most of his time with studying if he is going to be a successful student.

(18) Though Jack is able to rationalize very well in the field of philosophy, he has a striking unableness in the field of mathematics.

(19) Steinmetz worked with the mysteries of nature, electricity, and science and for years was the most valuable man in the General Electric Company.

(20) Professor Catlin's life was poor in terms of remunerative

values, but more students in the college remember him than any other teacher.

(21) The author was very successful in infiltrating into the minds of his readers the terrible confusion of war.

(22) Mr. Morris' frequent forgetfulness of his wife's shopping instructions was the ban of his wife's existent.

(23) As we rounded the curve, I could see that a crash was eminent, and I covered my head with my hands.

(24) A better job of supervision and management can be done if the administrator knows and can foresee the problems that might arise in the future.

(25) The authorship of the novel has not been authenticized, but the existing evidence points to one Joshua Fiddings.

34. GLOSSARY OF USAGE = GLOS

"AWFULLY NICE" IS AN EXPRESSION THAN WHICH FEW
COULD BE SILLIER: BUT TO HAVE SUCCEEDED IN GOING
THROUGH LIFE WITHOUT SAYING IT A CERTAIN NUMBER
OF TIMES IS AS BAD AS TO HAVE NO REDEEMING VICE.
—H. W. FOWLER

This glossary discusses a number of words and expressions which often present problems in "good usage." The list is not complete; space permits a discussion of only the more persistent troublemakers. An unabridged dictionary will give information on words not appearing here.

The assignment of a label of usage to a particular expression does not mean that an irrevocable judgment has been made. Usage is sometimes vague and it is constantly changing.* Moreover, it is often a local or sectional matter; errors common in parts of the Middle West may be rare in the East, the South, or the Far West. Therefore many judgments in this glossary are tentative. The following descriptions or labels of usage have been used:

Colloquial means "often used in informal conversation, but generally avoided in formal writing." Colloquial English has several levels of its own; for example, a "low colloquial" expression like "being as how" would be considered "illiterate" by some educated people.

Commercial jargon means "the specialized language of business and the market place." Such language is unsuitable for most expository writing.

Illiterate means "substandard, ignorant."

Informal means "the language of familiar, everyday affairs."

* See "Standards of Modern English" in the Introduction, pp. 4-9.

Jargon means "the special language of a particular occupation or group." Jargon is not appropriate for most general writing.

Journalese means "language suitable only to the commercial press, with its special problems of space and readability."

Legalism means "a technical expression used chiefly in legal documents."

Provincial means "regularly used in a particular region, but not elsewhere."

Slang means "language comprising certain widely current terms having a forced, fantastic, or grotesque meaning." Slang is generally unsuitable for formal and informal writing.

A, An. *A* is used before words beginning with a consonant sound even though the sound is spelled with a vowel (as in *universe*); *an* before words beginning with a vowel sound or with a silent *h*. Some speakers use *an* before words beginning with a pronounced *h*, as *an historian*, but *a* is preferred before such words.

> a dog, a wagon, a habit, a union; an apple, an Indian, an hour, an uproar

Above. *Above* is used chiefly as a preposition ("above the trees") or adverb ("birds flew above"). The use of *above* as an adjective or noun, often found in legal and business writing, is acceptable in standard English, though some writers (and readers) object to it as commercial jargon.

> AS ADJECTIVE: We refer you to the *above* agreement.
>
> AS NOUN: The *above* is not recorded in our office files.

Accept, Except. These verbs are sometimes confused because of their similarity in sound. *Accept* means "to receive." *Except* (as verb) means "to exclude."

> He *accepted* the gift with pleasure.
>
> We *excepted* George from the list of candidates.

Ad. A shortening of *advertisement* which is inappropriate in formal writing. Other clipped forms include *auto, exam, math, phone, photo.*

Affect, Effect. These words are sometimes confused because of their resemblance in sound. As verbs, *affect* means "to influence," and *effect* means "to bring about." As a noun, *effect* means "result."

His fame does not *affect* his personality.

We *effected* a truce with our enemies.

Her studying had a good *effect* on her grades.

Aggravate. In formal English *aggravate* means "to intensify" or "to make worse." Colloquially, it is often used as a substitute for "annoy" or "provoke."

FORMAL   The hot sun *aggravated* his suffering.

COLLOQUIAL His teasing *aggravated* her.

Aid. *Aid* means "help" and should not be confused with *aide,* "a military assistant."

Ain't. A vulgate form, originally a contraction of "are not," but now used indiscriminately for "am not," "is not," "has not," "have not."

Alibi. In formal English, *alibi* has the technical legal meaning "a plea of having been elsewhere than at the alleged place where an act was committed." Colloquially, *alibi* means "an excuse."

All the farther, All the faster, etc. Unidiomatic when used as a substitute for *as far as, as fast as,* etc. Sometimes used in familiar conversation but not appropriate in writing.

FORMAL   Lane Avenue is *as far as* this bus goes.

COLLOQUIAL Lane Avenue is *all the farther* this bus goes.

Allusion, Illusion. *Allusion* means "an indirect reference." *Illusion* means "a misleading image" or "a false impression."

The speaker made an *allusion* to the President.

The heat waves from the road produced the *illusion* of a pool of water.

Already, All ready. The adverb *already* means "previously." The adjective phrase "all ready" means "completely prepared."

When he reached the station, his train had *already* gone.

By eight o'clock we were *all ready* to start hiking.

All right. *All right* is the only correct spelling. *Alright,* though occasionally used by writers of advertising and fiction, has not been generally accepted. *All right* in the sense of "satisfactory" or "very well" is a colloquialism which is becoming standard.

Alot. Should be rendered as two words: *a lot.*

Also. Not to be used, without good reason, as a substitute for *and*.

> We packed a tent, our guns, *and* (not *also*) our fishing tackle.

Altogether, All together. The adverb *altogether* means "wholly, completely." The adjective phrase "all together" means "in a group."

> I am *altogether* pleased with my new piano.
> We were *all together* for the family reunion.

Alumnus, Alumna. An *alumnus* (plural *alumni*) is a male graduate. An *alumna* (plural *alumnae*) is a female graduate.

Among, Between. *Among* implies more than two persons or things; *between* implies only two. To express a reciprocal relationship, or the relationship of one thing to several other things, however, *between* is commonly used for more than two.

> She divided the toys *among* the three children.
> Jerry could choose *between* pie and cake for dessert.
> An agreement was reached *between* the four companies.
> The surveyors drove a stake at a point *between* three trees.

Amount, Number. *Amount* refers to quantity or mass. *Number* refers to countable objects.

> Irrigation requires a large *amount* of water.
> The farmer raised a small *number* of beef cattle.

And etc. Etc. (Latin *et cetera*) means "and so forth." The redundant *and etc.* means literally "and and so forth."

And/or. A legalism which should be used with caution.

Angle. Overused in the sense of "point of view" or "aspect." In formal writing *angle* often seems inappropriate: "Newton had a new *angle* on the laws of physics."

Any. *Any* is provincial for *at all* when it modifies a verb.

> PROVINCIAL   It hasn't rained *any* today.

Anyplace. Colloquial for *anywhere*.

Anyways, Anywheres. Vulgate forms of *anyway* and *anywhere*.

Apt, Likely. In formal writing *apt* usually refers to a natural ability or habitual tendency. *Likely* refers to a probability. In informal English, *apt* is often used as a synonym for *likely*.

FORMAL	Grandma is *apt* to lose her glasses.
FORMAL	The hockey game is *likely* to be exciting.
INFORMAL	The hockey game is *apt* to be exciting.

As. In introducing clauses, *as* is somewhat less precise than *since* or *because.*

LOOSE	*As* we were late, we rode to the theater in a taxi.
MORE PRECISE	*Because* we were late, we rode to the theater in a taxi.

As a method of. Overused and wordy when followed by a gerund.

WORDY	Swimming is useful *as a method of* developing coordination.
REVISED	Swimming is useful *for developing* coordination.

As . . . as, so . . . as. In negative comparisons formal English prefers *so . . . as* to *as . . . as.* This distinction is not usually observed in informal English.

FORMAL	He is *as* tall *as* I am.
FORMAL	He is not *so* tall *as* I am.
INFORMAL	He is not *as* tall *as* I am.

As for my part. A confusion of the two idioms *as for me* and *for my part.*

Asset. *Asset* has a specific meaning in law and accounting but may be used informally to mean "value," "merit," or "qualification."

At about, At around. An unnecessary doubling of prepositions. Deadwood may be avoided by using *at, about,* or *around,* whichever is the most exact.

EXACT	He arrived *at* (or *about*) one o'clock.
INEXACT	He arrived *at about* one o'clock.

Auto. *See* Ad.

Badly. Used informally in the sense of "very much" or "greatly" with the verbs *need* and *want.*

FORMAL	I *very much* need a new coat.
INFORMAL	I need a new coat *badly.*

Balance. Colloquial when used to mean "the rest," "remainder" (except when referring to a "bank balance").

> FORMAL   I stayed at home for the *rest* of the evening.
>
> COLLOQUIAL I stayed at home for the *balance* of the evening.

Being that, Being as how. Illogical substitutes for the appropriate subordinating conjunctions *as, because, since.*

Beside, Besides. *Beside* is a preposition meaning "by the side of." *Besides,* generally used as an adverb, means "moreover," "in addition to."

> He sat down *beside* her.
>
> Who, *besides* you, is going to the auction?

Between, Among. *See* Among.

Blame on, Blame it on. In formal English the verb *blame* is followed by the preposition *for.*

> FORMAL   Don't *blame* me *for* it.
>
> INFORMAL   Don't *blame it on* me.

Bursted, Bust, Busted. The principal parts of the verb are *burst, burst, burst. Bursted* is an old form of the past and past participle which is no longer considered good usage. *Bust* and *busted* are slang.

But that, But what. In formal usage *that* is preferable to *but what.*

> FORMAL   I don't doubt *that* you are right.
>
> INFORMAL   I don't doubt *but what* you are right.

Can, May. In formal English *can* means "to be able"; *may* means "to have permission." Colloquially, *can* is commonly used to imply both ability and permission.

> FORMAL   She *can* bake delicious pies.
>
> FORMAL   *May* I go to the church supper with you?
>
> COLLOQUIAL *Can* I go to the church supper with you?

Can't hardly. A double negative; not considered acceptable usage.

Can't help but. A double negative. Though sometimes found in formal and informal writing, this expression is strongly objected to by many writers.

> FORMAL   I *can't help* disliking him.
>
> COLLOQUIAL   I *can't help but* dislike him.

Can't seem to. Formal usage prefers "seem unable to."

> FORMAL　　　He *seems unable to* pass his history courses.
>
> INFORMAL　　He *can't seem to* pass his history courses.

Claim. In formal usage *claim* means "to demand as one's right." In informal English *claim* is commonly used as a synonym for *say* or *maintain.*

> FORMAL　　　She *claimed* the fortune found in the old well.
>
> INFORMAL　　He *claims* that he is a good horseman.

Complected. Colloquial for *complexioned.*

Considerable. Informal when used as an adjective to indicate *amount;* colloquial when used as a noun.

> INFORMAL　　They lost *considerable* property in the flood.
>
> COLLOQUIAL　They lost *considerable* in the flood.

Contact. There is some prejudice, which seems to be disappearing, against the verb *contact* meaning "to meet or talk with." The word is borrowed from commercial jargon. In formal and informal writing a more specific word, such as *meet* or *interview,* is preferable.

Continual, Continuous. *Continual* means "frequently repeated." *Continuous* means "without interruption."

> He was distracted by *continual* telephone calls.
>
> We heard the *continuous* sound of the waves.

Could of. Vulgate form of *could have.*

Couple. *Couple* in the sense of "two or three' is colloquial, but in any case it should be followed by the preposition *of.*

Credible, Creditable, Credulous. These adjectives are sometimes confused. *Credible* means "believable." *Creditable* means "praiseworthy." *Credulous* means "inclined to believe on slight evidence."

> His story seemed *credible* to the jury.
>
> She gave a *creditable* piano recital.
>
> The *credulous* child thought the moon was made of cheese.

Criticizer. Illiterate substitute for *critic.*

Cute. Overused and trite as a vague word of approval.

Data, Phenomena. These nouns are the plural forms of *datum,* "a fact on which an inference is based," and *phenomenon,* "an observable fact or event." In informal usage *data* is frequently treated as a collective noun with a singular verb.

FORMAL   *This datum is* (or *these data are*) valuable.

INFORMAL   *This data is* valuable.

Deal. A commercial or colloquial substitute for *bargain* or *transaction.*

Definite, Definitely. Often misspelled "definate, definately," these words suggest fixed limits and are colloquial as vague intensifiers ("He is definitely handsome").

Different than. *See* "Exactness," Section 31g.

Don't. A contraction for *do not,* not for *does not.*

He *doesn't* (not *don't*) want his dinner.

Doubt but what. *See* But that.

Due to. Since *due* is in origin an adjective, some writers object to the use of *due to* as a preposition introducing an adverbial phrase. It is interesting to note that *owing to,* which developed from a participle to a preposition in the same way, is accepted without question. The prepositional use of *due to* is increasingly widespread, and it is appropriate except in the most formal writing.

due AS AN ADJECTIVE   His failure was *due to* laziness.

FORMAL   The festival was postponed *because of* (or *owing to*) rain.

INFORMAL   The festival was postponed *due to* rain.

Each and every. Wordy jargon.

Each other, One another. Although some writers prefer *each other* when referring to two persons or things, and *one another* when referring to more than two, the distinction is not widely observed. The two expressions are interchangeable.

Educational. Overused and inaccurate as a synonym for *instructive, informative,* etc.

Effect, Affect. *See* Affect, Effect.

Emigrate, Immigrate. *Emigrate* means to move from a country. *Immigrate* means to move into a country.

Erik *emigrated* from Sweden.

Erik *immigrated* to America.

Enthuse. Colloquial for "become enthusiastic."

FORMAL   We *were enthusiastic* about our vacation.

COLLOQUIAL   We *were enthused* about our vacation.

Environment. *Environment* (often misspelled and mispronounced *enviorment*) is jargon when used to mean *neighborhood, surroundings, atmosphere.*

Equally as good. The *as* is unnecessary. *Equally good* is more precise.

Etc. Italics are correct but not necessary. Always preceded by a comma.

Everyplace. Colloquial for *everywhere.*

Everyone. Should be written as two words except when used as a synonym for *everybody.*

Every so often. This expression and *every bit as, every once in a while, every which way* are colloquial.

Everywheres. A vulgate form of *everywhere.*

Exam. *See* Ad.

Except, Accept. *See* Accept, Except.

Except for the fact that. Wordy and colloquial substitute for *except that.*

Expect. In colloquial English "expect" is sometimes used to mean "suppose."

FORMAL   I *suppose* I should mow the lawn.

COLLOQUIAL   I *expect* I should mow the lawn.

Extra. There is some prejudice against the overuse of *extra* as an adverb meaning "unusually."

FORMAL   Monday was an *unusually* warm day

COLLOQUIAL   Monday was an *extra* warm day.

Farther, Further. In formal English some writers use *farther* when referring to distance and *further* when referring to degree or quantity. In informal English this distinction is not widely kept.

FORMAL　　　We walked two miles *farther*.

INFORMAL　　We walked two miles *further*.

Faze. Colloquial for *disconcert, bother,* or *daunt.*

FORMAL　　　Ridicule did not *bother* him.

COLLOQUIAL　Ridicule did not *faze* him.

Feel of, Smell of, Taste of. The *of* is unnecessary in these expressions.

The tailor *felt* (not *felt of*) the cloth.

Fellow. Colloquial when used to mean "person."

Fewer, Less. *Fewer* refers to number. In formal English *less* refers only to degree or quantity. In informal English *less* is sometimes used to refer to number.

FORMAL　　　*Fewer* than half the students could solve the problem.

FORMAL　　　He is *less* friendly than he used to be.

INFORMAL　　*Less* than half the students could solve the problem.

Fiancé, Fiancée. These words, borrowed from the French, are sometimes confused. *Fiancé* (plural *fiancés*) refers to the betrothed man. *Fiancée* (plural *fiancées*) refers to the betrothed woman. In informal writing the accent marks are often dropped.

Fiction book. Illiterate for *novel.*

Fine. As an adjective to express approval ("a *fine* person") *fine* is vague and overused. As an adverb meaning "well" ("works *fine*") *fine* is colloquial.

First-rate. A generally accepted adjective meaning "of the first order." Colloquial as an adverb meaning "very well."

ADJECTIVE USE　He is a *first-rate* swimmer.

FORMAL　　　He swims *very well*.

COLLOQUIAL　He swims *first-rate*.

Fix. Colloquial when used as a noun meaning "predicament"; informal as a verb meaning "repair."

FORMAL　　　John is in a *predicament*.

COLLOQUIAL　John is in a *fix*.

FORMAL　　　We *repaired* the leaking faucet.

INFORMAL　　We *fixed* the leaking faucet.

Former, Latter. *Former* refers to the first named of two; *latter* refers to the last named of two. *First* and *last* are used to refer to one of a group of more than two.

Function. Suggests elaborateness or formality when used to describe a social occasion. Pretentious or ironic when used loosely for *activity*.

Funny. Colloquial when used to mean "strange," "queer," or "odd."

Further, Farther. *See* Farther, Further.

Gentleman, Lady. *Man* and *woman* are preferable to the more pretentious *gentleman* and *lady* unless the speaker is intentionally making a distinction between refined and ill-bred persons. "Ladies and Gentlemen" is a conventional expression used in addressing an audience.

Get. The verb *get* is used in many colloquial and slang expressions which are inappropriate in formal writing. Among these are "get going," "get to go," "get at it," "get wise to," "get away with."

Goes on to say. Wordy and colloquial for *adds* or *continues.*

Good. An adjective which is often used colloquially as an adverb in such sentences as "The motor runs *good.*" (Formal English would use the adverb *well* to modify the verb *runs.*)

Good and. Colloquial in such expressions as "good and hot," "good and ready."

Guess. Formal usage prefers "suppose" or "think" to the overworked *guess.*

Had of. A vulgate form.

I wish I *had* (not *had of*) seen the eclipse.

Had ought, Hadn't ought. Vulgate for *ought* and *ought not.*

He *ought* (not *had ought*) to treat his wife better.

Hanged, Hung. The principal parts of *hang* when referring to death by hanging are *hang, hanged, hanged.* When *hang* is used to mean "suspend," the principal parts are *hang, hung, hung.* In informal English the distinction is not rigidly kept, *hang, hung, hung* being used in all senses.

FORMAL   The outlaw was *hanged* from a cottonwood tree.
INFORMAL   The outlaw was *hung* from a cottonwood tree.

Have got. Formal usage prefers *have.*

> FORMAL   I *have* a headache.
> COLLOQUIAL *I've got* a headache.

Healthful, Healthy. *Healthful* means "giving health." *Healthy* means "having health."

Himself, Myself, Yourself. *See* Myself, Yourself, Himself.

Home. Formal usage prefers *at home.*

> FORMAL   Our neighbors are not *at home.*
> INFORMAL   Our neighbors are not *home.*

Humans. Most careful writers prefer *people* or *human beings.*

Idea. Often vague for *belief, conjecture, intention, plan, theory,* and should be replaced whenever possible by a more specific noun.

If, Whether. Formal English prefers *whether* to *if* after such verbs as *say, ask, know, doubt, wonder, understand.*

> FORMAL   He did not say *whether* he would return.
> INFORMAL   He did not say *if* he would return.

Illusion, Allusion. *See* Allusion, Illusion.

Immigrate, Emigrate. *See* Emigrate, Immigrate.

Imply, Infer. *Imply* means "to hint" or "to suggest." *Infer* means "to draw a conclusion."

> He *implied* that I was ungrateful.
> I *inferred* from his remark that he did not like me.

In, Into. In formal usage *in* denotes location; *into* denotes direction. In colloquial English *in* is often used for *into.*

> FORMAL   We were studying *in* the library.
> FORMAL   I fell *into* the pool.
> COLLOQUIAL I fell *in* the pool.

In back of. Colloquial for *behind, back of, at the back of.*

Individual, Party, Person. *Individual* refers to a person particularly. *Person* refers to a human being in general. *Party* refers to a group of people, except in legal language.

Jefferson defended the rights of the *individual*.

She is a *person* (not *an individual*) of strong character.

You are the *person* (not *party*) I am looking for.

Indulge. *Indulge* means "to be tolerant toward" or "to gratify one's desire"; it is not a synonym for *to take part in*.

    ACCURATE   The old man *indulged* (*tolerated*) the noisy parrot.

    INACCURATE   The ladies *indulged in* (*took part in*) a quarrel.

Infer, Imply. *See* Imply, Infer.

Ingenious, Ingenuous. *Ingenious* means "clever." *Ingenuous* means "frank" or "naïve."

    Inventors are usually *ingenious* people.

    He was too *ingenuous* to suspect that he was being tricked.

In my estimation. Like *in my opinion, in my judgment,* this phrase is often unnecessary, or is pretentious for *I think, I feel, I believe.*

In regards to. A confusion of the British idiom *as regards* with the American idiom *in regard to*.

Inside of. The *of* is unnecessary when *inside* is used as a preposition. *Inside of* is colloquial for *within* when used in reference to time.

    FORMAL   We stayed *inside* (not *inside of*) the house.

    FORMAL   He will arrive *within* an hour.

    COLLOQUIAL He will arrive *inside of* an hour.

Into, In. *See* In, Into.

Irregardless. A double negative which grows from the confusion of *irrespective* and *regardless*.

Is when, Is where. Noun clauses introduced by *when* or *where* are avoided by careful writers. *See* "Logic," Section 28a.

    LOOSE   A first down *is when* the football is advanced ten yards in four plays or fewer.

    PRECISE   A first down *is made when* the football is advanced ten yards in four plays or fewer.

It being. Awkward and colloquial substitute for a clause introduced by *since*.

Its, It's. The possessive pronoun has no apostrophe. *It's* is a contraction of *it is*.

Just. Colloquial for *very, quite*.

FORMAL	The customer was *very* indignant.
COLLOQUIAL	I was *just* furious.

Kind of, Sort of. Colloquial when used adverbially to mean "somewhat" or "rather."

FORMAL	She is *rather* pleased.
COLLOQUIAL	She is *kind of* pleased.

Kind of a, Sort of a. The *a* is omitted in formal usage.

FORMAL	The child wanted some *kind of* toy.
COLLOQUIAL	The child wanted some *kind of a* toy.

Lady, Gentleman. *See* Gentleman, Lady.

Latter, Former. *See* Former, Latter.

Lay, Lie. In colloquial usage, these verbs are often confused. *See* Section 6d.

Lead. *Lead* is not the past tense of *to lead; led* is the correct form.

Learn, Teach. *Learn* means "to gain knowledge." *Teach* means "to impart knowledge."

We *learn* from experience.
Experience *teaches* us many things.

Leave, Let. *Leave* means "to depart." *Let* means "to permit."

I must *leave* now.
Will you *let* (not *leave*) me go with you?

Less, Fewer. *See* Fewer, Less.

Lie, Lay. *See* Lay, Lie.

Like, As, As if. *Like* is a preposition; *as* and *as if* are conjunctions. In informal English *like* is often used as a conjunction to introduce clauses. Formal English prefers *as* or *as if* in such constructions.

FORMAL	He looks *as if* (or *as though*) he might be tired.
INFORMAL	He looks *like* he might be tired.

Likely, Apt. *See* Apt, Likely.

Literature. Commercial jargon when used to mean *advertising matter*.

Locate. Colloquial when used to mean "settle."

> FORMAL   The immigrant *settled* in Iowa.
> COLLOQUIAL   The immigrant *located* in Iowa.

Loose, Lose. *Loose* means "to free." *Lose* means "to be deprived of."

> He *loosed* the dog from its leash.
> Did you *lose* (not *loose*) your money?

Lots, Lots of. Colloquial for "much" or "a great deal."

> FORMAL   We had a *great deal* of time for recreation.
> COLLOQUIAL   We had *a lot of* (or *lots of*) time for recreation.

Mad. Colloquial when used to mean "angry."

Manner. Often unnecessary in phrases like "in a precise manner," where a single adverb ("precisely") or a "with" phrase ("with precision") would do.

Marvelous. Overused as a vague word of approval.

Math. *See* Ad.

May, Can. *See* Can, May.

May of. Vulgate for *may have*.

Might of. Vulgate for *might have*.

Minus. Journalese for *lacking* or *without*. *See* Plus.

Most. Colloquial when used in sense of *almost*.

> FORMAL   *Almost* everybody in the hall cheered the speaker.
> COLLOQUIAL   *Most* everybody in the hall cheered the speaker.

Mr. In American usage *Mr.* is followed by a period and is never written out except humorously or ironically.

Muchly. Illiterate for *much*.

Must of. Vulgate for *must have*.

Myself, Yourself, Himself. In formal English these intensive pronouns are inappropriate as substitutes for the personal pronouns *I, you, him*.

| FORMAL | Jack and *I* trimmed the hedge. |
| COLLOQUIAL | Jack and *myself* trimmed the hedge. |

Never-the-less. Should be written as a single word: *nevertheless.*

Nice. Overused as a vague word of approval.

No account, No good. Colloquial for *worthless, useless.*

Noplace. Colloquial for *nowhere.*

Nothing else but. Colloquial for *nothing but.*

| FORMAL | There was *nothing but* pity in her voice. |
| COLLOQUIAL | There was *nothing else but* pity in her voice. |

Nowhere near. Informal and colloquial for *not nearly.*

Nowheres. A vulgate form of *nowhere.*

Number. A collective noun which takes a singular or plural verb depending on whether it means items taken collectively or individually.

A number of students *are* absent.
The number of absentees *is* great.

O.K. Colloquial for *all right* or *correct.*

Off of. The *of* is unnecessary.

He jumped *off* (not *off of*) the wagon.

One and the same. Trite and tautological for *the same.*

One another, Each other. *See* Each other, One another.

On the average of. Trite and tautological for *about* or *almost.*

Ought to of. Vulgate for *ought to have.*

Out loud. Informal and colloquial for *aloud.*

Outside of. Colloquial for *except, besides.*

| FORMAL | Nobody was there *except* me. |
| COLLOQUIAL | Nobody was there *outside of* me. |

Over with. Colloquial for *over, ended.*

| FORMAL | I am glad the cold weather is *over.* |
| COLLOQUIAL | I am glad the cold weather is *over with.* |

Party, Person, Individual. *See* Individual, Party, Person.

Per. Used mainly in commercial expressions, such as "forty hours per week," "thirty cents per yard," or in phrases of Latin origin, such as *per capita, per diem.* In ordinary writing, *per* is less appropriate than *a* or *an:* "twice a day," "forty cents a dozen."

Per cent. This abbreviation, meaning "by the hundred," is not followed by a period and may be written as one word. In formal English, *per cent* usually follows a numeral ("50 per cent") and is not used as a synonym for *portion* or *part.*

> FORMAL   A small *part* of the class was absent.
> INFORMAL   A small *per cent* of the class was absent.

Percentage. Informal for *number, part, portion.*

> FORMAL   The bay is rough a large *part* of the time.
> INFORMAL   The bay is rough a large *percentage* of the time.

Person, Party, Individual. *See* Individual, Party, Person.

Phenomena, Data. *See* Data, Phenomena.

Philosophy. A vague term when used to describe *mental attitude, values, knowledge,* etc.

Phone. *See* Ad.

Photo. *See* Ad.

Plan on. Unidiomatic for *plan to.*

Plenty. Colloquial when used as an adverb meaning "very" or "amply."

> FORMAL   He is a *very* big man.
> COLLOQUIAL   He is a *plenty* big man.

Plus. Journalese for *in addition to.* *See* Minus.

Poorly. Colloquial or provincial for *unwell, in poor health.*

> FORMAL   Mother is in *poor health* this winter.
> COLLOQUIAL   Mother is *poorly* this winter.

Practical, Practicable. *Practical* means "useful, not theoretical." *Practicable* means "capable of being put into practice, feasible."

> Franklin's *practical* mind made him a good statesman.
> His political schemes were unusually *practicable.*

Practically. Colloquial for *almost*.

> FORMAL   The wrestlers were *almost* exhausted.
> COLLOQUIAL   The wrestlers were *practically* exhausted.

Principal, Principle. As an adjective *principal* means "chief, main"; as a noun it means "leader, chief officer." The noun *principle* means "fundamental truth" or "basic law or doctrine."

> He owns the *principal* store in the village.
> Mr. Alvin is the school's *principal*.
> She defended the *principle* of democracy.

Prior to. Usually pretentious for *before*.

Proposition. *Proposition* means "proposal." Colloquial when used to mean "venture, plan, affair."

> FORMAL   The community carnival was a successful *venture*.
> COLLOQUIAL   The community carnival was a successful *proposition*.

Proven. A past participle of the verb *prove,* used less often than *proved*. Both *proven* and *proved* are acceptable.

Put across, Put over, Put in. *Put across* and *put over* are colloquialisms meaning "to accomplish something against opposition." *Put in* is informal for *spend*.

> FORMAL   The club was successful in its membership drive.
> COLLOQUIAL   The club *put across* its membership drive.
> FORMAL   He *spent* a busy day at his office.
> INFORMAL   He *put in* a busy day at his office.

Quite a few, Quite a little, Quite a bit. Colloquial for *many, more than a little, a considerable amount*.

Raise, Rise. *Raise, raised, raised* is a transitive verb.

> I *raise* flowers. I *raised* flowers. I *have raised* flowers.

Rise, rose, risen is an intransitive verb.

> I *rise* at daybreak. I *rose* at daybreak.
> I *have risen* at daybreak.

Rarely ever. Unidiomatic for *rarely, rarely if ever, rarely or never, hardly ever*.

Real. Colloquial for *really* or *very*.

> FORMAL   The sky was *very* cloudy.
>
> COLLOQUIAL   The sky was *real* cloudy.

Reason is because. A noun or noun clause should be used instead of "because" in this expression.

> FORMAL   The reason for his absence *is* his illness (that he is ill).
>
> ILLOGICAL   The *reason* for his absence *is because* he is ill.

Religion. *Religion* is not a synonym for *sect, cult, denomination,* or *faith.*

> INACCURATE   He belongs to the Presbyterian *religion.*
>
> ACCURATE   He belongs to the Presbyterian *denomination.*

Remember of. The *of* is unnecessary.

> I *remember* (not *remember of*) seeing you before.

Reverend. The title *Reverend* is properly preceded by *the* and followed by *Mr.,* or followed by the first name or initials of the person referred to.

> The Reverend Mr. Wells (not Reverend Wells)
> Reverend John Wells, The Reverend John Wells
> Reverend J. W. Wells, The Reverend J. W. Wells

Right, Right along, Right away. *Right* is colloquial when used to mean "very" or "directly."

> FORMAL   Being *very* tired, we went *directly* home.
>
> COLLOQUIAL   Being *right* tired, we went *right* home.

Right along and *right away* are colloquial for *continuously* and *immediately.*

Rise, Raise. *See* Raise, Rise.

Run. Colloquial for *manage, operate.*

> FORMAL   He *manages* a department store.
>
> COLLOQUIAL   He *runs* a department store.

Said. The adjective *said* ("the *said* paragraph," "the *said* person") is a legal term and inappropriate in formal writing.

Seeing as how, Seeing that. Low colloquial for *since* or *because.*

Seldom ever, Seldom or ever. Unidiomatic for *seldom, seldom if ever, seldom or never, hardly ever.*

Set, Sit. *See* Section 6d.

Shall, Will, Should, Would. American usage tends to use *will* and *would* in all persons except when a condition or obligation is expressed. *Should* is used for all persons in conditions and obligations.

> If he *should* come, call me immediately.
> We *should* visit our new neighbors.

Would is used for all persons to express a wish or customary action.

> *Would* that he had listened to my plea!
> I *would* ride on the same bus every morning.

Shape. Colloquial for *condition.*

> FORMAL   Wrestlers must keep themselves in good *condition.*
> COLLOQUIAL   Wrestlers must keep themselves in good *shape.*

Should of. Vulgate for *should have.*

Show up. Colloquial for *appear, expose.*

> FORMAL   He did not *appear* at the office.
> COLLOQUIAL   He did not *show up* at the office.

Sit, Set. *See* Set, Sit.

Size up. Colloquial for *estimate, judge.*

> FORMAL   We *estimated* our financial needs.
> COLLOQUIAL   We *sized up* our financial needs.

Smell of. *See* Feel of.

So. In clauses of purpose, *so* instead of *so that* is colloquial.

> FORMAL   We camped by a spring *so that* we would have fresh water.
> COLLOQUIAL   We camped by a spring *so* we would have fresh water.

So is colloquial or informal when used to introduce a main clause in place of a subordinating conjunction introducing the subordinate clause.

> FORMAL   *Because* the rain began to fall, the swimmers left the beach.

COLLOQUIAL   Rain began to fall, *so* the swimmers left the beach.

The "feminine" so, meaning "very," is colloquial and overused.

FORMAL   She is *very* happy.
COLLOQUIAL   She is *so* happy.

Some. Colloquial when used as an adverb meaning "somewhat" or "a little."

FORMAL   He seems *somewhat* gayer.
COLLOQUIAL   He seems *some* gayer.

Some is slang when used as an intensive: "He is *some* actor!"

Someplace. Colloquial for *somewhere.*

Somewheres. Vulgate for *somewhere.*

Sort of, Kind of. *See* Kind of, Sort of.

Sort of a, Kind of a. *See* Kind of a, Sort of a.

Stop. Colloquial or informal when used as a substitute for *stay.*

FORMAL   I *stayed* overnight at a hotel.
INFORMAL   I *stopped* overnight at a hotel.

Such. As an intensive, *such* is colloquial.

FORMAL   He told a *very* interesting story.
COLLOQUIAL   He told *such* an interesting story.

No such a is vulgate for *no such.*

FORMAL   There is *no such* place.
COLLOQUIAL   There is *no such a* place.

Suspicion. Vulgate when used as a verb.

Take and. Vulgate in such expressions as "I'll *take and* swim across the lake."

Taste of. *See* Feel of.

Teach, Learn. *See* Learn, Teach.

That. Colloquial when used as an adverb.

FORMAL   Nobody can be *so* exhausted after such a short swim.

COLLOQUIAL   Nobody can be *that* exhausted after such a short swim.

There being. *See* It being.

Thing. Whenever it is possible, *thing* should be replaced with a more specific word.

This here, That there. Vulgate for *this, that.*

Through. Formal usage prefers "finished."

FORMAL   I have *finished* working.

INFORMAL   I am *through* working.

Thusly. A pretentious or illiterate form of *thus.*

Transpire. *Transpire* means "to become known." The use of *transpire* in the sense of "to come to pass; happen, occur" is disapproved by some writers, though this meaning is fairly common in informal writing.

Try and. Colloquial for *try to.*

FORMAL   *Try to* hold your head erect.

COLLOQUIAL   *Try and* hold your head erect.

Unique. The adjective *unique* cannot logically be compared, since it means "single in kind or excellence." In colloquial English, however, it is sometimes used in the sense of "rare" or "odd" and is compared.

FORMAL   His deeds are *unique* in history.

COLLOQUIAL   His deeds are *more unique* in history than people suspect.

Very. In formal English *very* is usually followed by *much, well,* or *greatly* when it modifies a past participle.

FORMAL   We were *very much* embarrassed.

INFORMAL   We were *very* embarrassed.

Wait on. Colloquial or provincial in the sense of *wait for. Wait on* means "to serve, attend."

FORMAL   I *waited for* a bus.

COLLOQUIAL   I *waited on* a bus.

Want in, Want out, Want off, etc. Colloquial for *want to come in, want to go out, want to get off,* etc.

Want to. Colloquial for *ought, should.*

> FORMAL   You *should* be alert when crossing the street.
>
> COLLOQUIAL   You *want to* be alert when crossing the street.

Way, Ways. *Way* is colloquial when used to mean "away" ("*way* across the mountains"). *Ways* is used colloquially for *way* in such expressions as "a little *ways* up the hill."

Weird. Overused slang for *unusual, queer.*

Where. Vulgate when used for *that.*

> FORMAL   I read in the mayor's report *that* many local crimes are unsolved.
>
> VULGATE   I read in the mayor's report *where* many local crimes are unsolved.

Where at. A redundancy.

> ACCURATE   *Where* is my pipe?
>
> REDUNDANT   *Where* is my pipe *at?*

Whether, If. *See* If, Whether.

Wonderful. Overused as a vague word of approval.

Would of. Vulgate for *would have.*

Yourself, Myself, Himself. *See* Myself, Yourself, Himself.

Spelling $=$ *SP*

SPELLING IS NO LONGER COMMONLY REGARDED AS A
PROPER FIELD FOR INDIVIDUALITY OR EXPERIMENTA-
TION.

—STUART ROBERTSON

L ANGUAGE EXISTED first as speech, and the alphabet is basically a device to represent speech on paper. When letters of
the alphabet have definite values and are used consistently, as in
Polish or Spanish, the spelling of a word is an accurate index to its
pronunciation, and vice versa. Not so with English. The alphabet
does not represent English sounds consistently. The letter *a* may
stand for the sound of the vowel in *may, can, care,* or *car; c* for the
initial consonant of *carry* or *city; th* for the diphthong in *both* or in
bother. Different combinations of letters are often sounded alike,
as in *rec(ei)ve, l(ea)ve,* or *p(ee)ve.* In many words, moreover,
some letters appear to perform no function at all, as in *i(s)land,
de(b)t, of(t)en, recei(p)t.* Finally, the relationship between the
spelling and the pronunciation of some words seems downright
capricious, as in *through, enough, colonel, right.*

Though the fact hardly comforts a poor speller, much of the inconsistency of English spelling can be explained historically. English
spelling has been a poor index of pronunciation since the Norman
Conquest, when French scribes gave written English a French spelling. Subsequent tampering with English spelling has made it even
more complex. Early classical scholars with a flair for etymology
added the unvoiced *b* to early English *det* and *dout* to show what
they thought was the relationship of these words to Latin *debitum*

and *dubitum*. Dutch printers working in England were responsible for changing early English *gost* to *ghost*. Even more complicating was the fact that the spelling of many words changed less rapidly than their pronunciation. The *gh* in *right* and *through,* and in similar words, was once pronounced, much like the German *ch* in *nicht. Colonel* was once pronounced *col-o-nel.* The final *e* in words like *wife* and *time* was long ago dropped from actual speech, but it still remains as a proper spelling form.

The English tendency to borrow words freely from Latin and French has given us groups like the native English *sight,* the French *site,* and the Latin *cite.* Our word *regal,* with its hard *g,* comes from the Norman French. Our word *regent,* with the *g* sounded as a *j,* comes from Parisian French. Words like *machine, burlesque,* and *suite* come directly from the French, without changes in spelling or in pronunciation. *Envelope,* on the other hand, maintains its French spelling but is given an English pronunciation. From Spanish comes the proper noun *Don Quixote;* its Spanish pronunciation (dȯn kĕ·hō/tä) is still frequently heard, but the English adjective *quixotic* is pronounced kwĭks·ot/ĭk.

THE NECESSITY OF SPELLING CORRECTLY

The complex history of the English language may help to explain why our spelling is illogical, but it does not justify misspelling. Society tends to equate bad spelling with incompetent writing. That particularly American institution—the spelling bee—has for generations put a higher premium on the correct spelling of *phthisis* than on a clearly constructed sentence. To illustrate, we might experiment with our own attitude. Which of the two selections below seems better?

(1) Parants should teech childern the importence of puntuallity.
(2) The condition of unpunctuality which exists in the character of a great many members of the younger generation should be eliminated by every means that lies at the disposal of parents who are responsible for them.

On first reading, (1) seems inferior to (2). Actually (1) is the better sentence—more direct and succinct. But the misspellings make it difficult for us to take it seriously. We have been conditioned to treat misspelling as one of the greatest sins a writer can commit. So have our readers.

PREFERRED AND SECONDARY SPELLINGS

35a. Secondary and British spelling forms should be avoided by American writers.

Many words have a secondary spelling, generally British. Though the secondary spelling is not incorrect, most American writers avoid it. The following list of preferred and secondary spelling forms is partial; a good dictionary will supply additional examples:

(1) American *e*	British *ae, oe*
anemia	anaemia
anesthetic	anaesthetic
encyclopedia	encyclopaedia
medieval	mediaeval
(2) American *im-, in-*	British *em-, en-*
incase	encase
	But
inquiry	inquiry
insure	insure
(3) American *-ize*	British *-ise*
apologize	apologise
(4) American *-or*	British *-our*
armor	armour
clamor	clamour
flavor	flavour
humor	humour
labor	labour
odor	odour
vigor	vigour
(5) American *-er*	British *-re*
center	centre
fiber	fibre
somber	sombre
theater	theatre

(6) American -o	British -ou
mold	mould
plow	plough
smolder	smoulder

(7) American -ction	British -xion
connection	connexion
inflection	inflexion

(8) American -l	British -ll
leveled	levelled
quarreled	quarrelled
traveled	travelled

(9) American -e omitted	British -e
acknowledgment	acknowledgement
judgment	judgement

IMPROVING SPELLING

For a chronic misspeller of college age, a cure must be effected at once. None of his readers will continue to ignore his misspellings. The first step, which is the hardest, is the most necessary: he must recognize the fact that correct spelling is essential and that it is useless for him to dodge the issue any longer. He can then profit from the practical measures suggested below.

35b. Careful proofreading will eliminate many misspellings.

In a first draft, a writer's mind is forming words into sentences faster than he can write them down. He is concentrating not on the words he is actually writing but on the words to come. Foolish mistakes occur that can be corrected easily in five or ten minutes of final proofreading.

The failure to proofread accounts for the fact that the words most often misspelled are not, for example, *baccalaureate* and *connoisseur,* but *too, its, lose, receive,* and *occurred.* Not trusting ourselves to spell hard words correctly, we consult a dictionary and take pains to get the correct spelling on paper. But most of us *think* we can spell a familiar word. Either we never bother to check a spelling, or we assume that a word pictured correctly in our minds must automatically spell itself correctly on the paper in front of us. One or both of these reasons account for the careless omission of the final *o* in *too,* the confusion of the possessive *its* with the contraction *it's,* and the spelling *loose* when *lose* is meant. The difficulty with *receive* and *occurred* would disappear if we gave a few moments to memorizing the correct spelling.

On pages 349 to 354 is a list of 350 words often misspelled. Almost every one of them is a common word; to misspell any of them in a finished paper is sheer carelessness.

35c. Careful pronunciation will eliminate the cause of some misspellings.

As an aid to correct spelling, precise pronunciation should be used cautiously. It is foolish to force a pronunciation into accord with a spelling which is illogical to begin with. Yet many try to do so in the belief that the final syllables of words like *adviser, beggar,* and *doctor* should be pronounced exactly as they are spelled. Actually the correct pronunciation of these final syllables is the same—the unstressed *ur.* On the other hand, the frequent misspelling of some English words, particularly those listed below, is undoubtedly the result of faulty pronunciation:

accidentALly		note the **AL**
accUrate		note the **U**
canDidate		note the first **D**
incidentALly		note the **AL**
mathEmatics		note the **E**
probABly		note the **AB**
quanTity		note the first **T**
represenTAtive		note the **TA**
sophOmore		note the second **O**
suRprise		note the first **R**
aTHLetics	*not*	athEletics
disasTRous	*not*	disastErous
heighT	*not*	heightH
grIE-vous	*not*	grE-vI-ous
ir-reL-e-vant	*not*	ir-reV-e-lant
mis-chIE-vous	*not*	mis-chE-vI-ous

35d. A confusion between similar words is often the cause of misspelling.*

English abounds in words whose spelling or sound is similar to those of other words: for example, *rain, rein, reign.* The most troublesome of such words are listed below:

ascent: climbing, a way sloping up
assent: agreement, to agree

all ready: everyone is ready
already: by this time

all together: as a group
altogether: entirely, completely

altar: a structure used in worship
alter: to change

breath: air taken into the lungs
breathe: to exhale and inhale

capital: chief; leading or governing city; wealth, resources
capitol: a building which houses the state or national lawmakers

cite: to use as an example, to quote
site: location

clothes: wearing apparel
cloths: two or more pieces of cloth

complement: that which completes
compliment: praise, flattering remark; to praise

corps: a military group or unit
corpse: a dead body

council: an assembly of lawmakers
counsel: advice; one who advises; to give advice

dairy: a factory or farm engaged in milk production
diary: a daily record of experiences or observations

descent: a way sloping down
dissent: disagreement; to disagree

* Such a confusion may be in spelling or meaning. See Section 31b.

dining: eating
dinning: making a continuing noise

dying: ceasing to live
dyeing: process of coloring fabrics

formally: in a formal manner
formerly: before

forth: forward in place or space, onward in time
fourth: the ordinal equivalent of the number 4

loose: free from bonds
lose: to suffer a loss

personal: pertaining to a particular person; individual
personnel: body of persons employed in same work or service

principal: chief, most important; a school official
principle: a belief, rule of conduct or thought

respectfully: with respect
respectively: in order, in turn

stationery: writing paper
stationary: not moving

their: possessive form of *they*
they're: contraction of *they are*
there: adverb of place

whose: possessive form of *who*
who's: contraction of *who is*

your: possessive form of *you*
you're: contraction of *you are*

35e. Knowledge of spelling rules is an aid to correct spelling.

Ei AND *Ie*

(1) ie *and* ei *should be carefully distinguished.* This jingle is easy to learn and useful:

> Write *i* before *e*
> Except after *c*
> Or when sounded like *a*
> As in *eighty* and *sleigh.*

343

i BEFORE *e*	*ei* AFTER *c*	*ei* WHEN SOUNDED LIKE *a*
thief	receive	weigh
believe	deceive	freight
wield	ceiling	vein

SOME EXCEPTIONS

leisure
financier
weird

DROPPING FINAL -*E*

(2) *Final* e *is dropped before a suffix beginning with a vowel but not before a suffix beginning with a consonant.*

(a) Suffix beginning with a vowel: final *e* dropped:

please + ure	= *pleasure*
ride + ing	= *riding*
locate + ion	= *location*
guide + ance	= *guidance*

EXCEPTIONS:

In some words final *e* is retained to prevent confusion with other words.

dyeing (to distinguish it from *dying*)

Final *e* is retained to keep *c* or *g* soft before *a* or *o*.

notice + able	= *noticeable*
change + able	= *changeable*
singe + ing	= *singeing*

BUT

practice + able	= *practicable* (*c* has sound of *k*)

(b) Suffix beginning with a consonant: final *e* retained:

sure + ly	= *surely*
arrange + ment	= *arrangement*
like + ness	= *likeness*
entire + ty	= *entirety*
hate + ful	= *hateful*

344

EXCEPTIONS:

Some words taking the suffix *-ful* or *-ly* drop final *e:*

awe + ful	= *awful*
due + ly	= *duly*
true + ly	= *truly*

Some words taking the suffix *-ment* drop final *e:*

judge + ment	= *judgment*
acknowledge + ment	= *acknowledgment*

FINAL -*Y*

(3) *Final* y *is usually changed to* i *except before a suffix beginning with* i.

defy + ance	= *defiance*
forty + eth	= *fortieth*
ninety + eth	= *ninetieth*
rectify + er	= *rectifier*

BUT

cry + ing	= *crying* (suffix begins with *i*)

DOUBLING A FINAL CONSONANT

(4) *A final single consonant is doubled before a suffix beginning with a vowel when* (a) *a single vowel precedes the consonant, and* (b) *the consonant ends an accented syllable or a one-syllable word. Unless both these conditions exist, the final consonant is not doubled.*

stop + ing	= *stopping* (*o* is a single vowel before consonant *p* which ends word of one syllable.)
admit + ed	= *admitted* (*i* is single vowel before consonant *t* which ends an accented syllable.)
stoop + ing	= *stooping* (*p* ends a word of one syllable but is preceded by double vowel *oo*.)
benefit + ed	= *benefited* (*t* is preceded by a single vowel *i* but does not end the accented syllable.)

EXERCISE 1. Spell each word correctly and explain what spelling rule applies:

argue + ment	=	?	change + able	=	?
beg + ar	=	?	change + ing	=	?
bury + ed	=	?	awe + ful	=	?
conceive + able	=	?	precede + ence	=	?
eighty + eth	=	?	shine + ing	=	?
associate + ion	=	?	busy + ness	=	?
hop + ing	=	?	defer + ed	=	?
droop + ing	=	?	peace + able	=	?

PLURALS

(5) *Nouns ending with a sound which can smoothly unite with -s form their plurals by adding -s. (Verbs ending in a sound which can smoothly unite with -s form their third person singular by adding -s.)*

SINGULAR	PLURAL
picture	pictures
radio	radios
flower	flowers
chair	chairs
ache	aches
fan	fans

SOME EXCEPTIONS

buffalo	buffaloes
Negro	Negroes
zero	zeroes

(6) *Nouns ending in a sound which cannot be followed smoothly by -s form their plurals by adding -es. (Verbs ending in a sound with which -s cannot unite smoothly form their third person singular by adding -es.)*

SINGULAR	PLURAL
porch	porches
bush	bushes
pass	passes
tax	taxes

(7) *Nouns ending in y preceded by a consonant form their plurals by changing y to i and adding -es.*

346

SINGULAR	PLURAL
army	armies
nursery	nurseries
sky	skies
mercy	mercies
body	bodies

EXCEPTIONS

The plural of proper nouns ending in *y* is formed by adding *-s*. ("There are three Marys in my history class.")

(8) *Nouns ending in* y *preceded by* a, e, o, *or* u *form their plurals by adding* -s *only.*

SINGULAR	PLURAL
day	days
key	keys
boy	boys
guy	guys

(9) *The spelling of plural nouns borrowed from French, Greek, and Latin frequently retains the plural of the language the words were borrowed from.*

SINGULAR	PLURAL
alumna (feminine)	alumnae
alumnus (masculine)	alumni
analysis	analyses
basis	bases
datum	data
crisis	crises
hypothesis	hypotheses
phenomenon	phenomena

The tendency now, however, is to give many such words an anglicized plural. The result is that many words have two plural forms, one foreign, the other anglicized. Either is correct.

SINGULAR	PLURAL (*foreign*)	PLURAL (*anglicized*)
appendix	appendices	appendixes
beau	beaux	beaus

SINGULAR	PLURAL (*foreign*)	PLURAL (*anglicized*)
focus	foci	focuses
index	indices	indexes
memorandum	memoranda	memorandums
radius	radii	radiuses
stadium	stadia	stadiums

EXERCISE 2. Spell the plural of each word correctly and explain what spelling rule applies.

(1)	frame	(11)	echo
(2)	rose	(12)	stratum
(3)	dash	(13)	church
(4)	maze	(14)	lady
(5)	table	(15)	mass
(6)	branch	(16)	Charles
(7)	bass	(17)	no
(8)	cameo	(18)	potato
(9)	fly	(19)	play
(10)	box	(20)	pain

COMPOUNDS

Whether a compound should be written as two distinct words, as two words joined by a hyphen, or as a single word is, with some standard exceptions, a matter almost impossible to fix at any given time—at least with any degree of permanence or realism. Not only does the spelling often change as time passes, but practice varies at any one time among quite reputable writers. Even the best dictionaries often disagree. It seems safe to say only that as two words begin to appear frequently in combination, they tend, first, to join themselves with a hyphen and then, ultimately, make themselves into one word, as *sales man* became *sales-man* became *salesman*. For the spelling of a compound at any particular moment, the writer should take the advice of a good dictionary. (For the general use of the hyphen, see Section 47; 47b, 47c, 47d, and 47e give what rules are possible about the spelling of compounds.)

SPELLING BY DRILL

Spelling is primarily a habit. Once we learn to spell a word, we do not think about it. Our fingers know how to write or type it correctly, and our thought is about the word, not its spelling. The ability to spell a word correctly aloud is merely an additional skill, reinforcing the ability to write it correctly. But this ability is not any more necessary to spelling correctly on paper than being able to explain his putting stance is necessary to a champion golfer.

What a chronic misspeller must do, then, is to develop the habit of spelling a word correctly. His problem is one of *relearning*. He has already learned a habit, but the wrong one. He writes *grammer, recieve, truely* instead of *grammar, receive, truly*. Now he must unlearn the wrong and learn the right. Merely *noticing* how a word is spelled correctly will not help him; he must train his fingers to write the word correctly until they do so almost without his thinking about it.

First, he should look carefully at the word and say it to himself. If it has more than one syllable, he should look carefully at each syllable.

Second, he should look at the individual letters, dividing the word into syllables as he says the letters.

Third, he should try to visualize the correct spelling before he writes the word. If his visualization is not clear, he should begin again with the *first* step.

Fourth, he should write the word without looking at his book or list.

Fifth, he should look at his book or list and see whether he wrote the word correctly. If he did, he should cover the word and write it again. If he writes it correctly the second time, he should repeat the procedure. If he writes the word correctly the third time, he has probably learned it and will not have to think about it again.

Sixth, if he spells the word incorrectly any one of the three times, he should look very carefully at the letters he missed. He should then start over again and keep on until he has spelled it correctly three times as indicated in step five.

SPELLING LISTS

The following lists contain most of the words whose spelling is consistently troublesome.

Group 1

1 accidentally
2 accommodate
3 achieved
4 accompanied
5 address

349

6 aggravate
7 anxiety
8 barren
9 believe
10 ceiling
11 confident
12 course
13 disappear
14 disappoint
15 dissipate
16 efficiency
17 emphasize
18 exaggerate
19 exceed
20 fiery
21 finally
22 financial
23 forehead
24 foreign
25 forfeit
26 grief
27 handkerchief
28 hurriedly
29 hypocrisy
30 imminent
31 incidentally
32 innocence
33 intentionally
34 interest
35 legitimate
36 likely
37 manual
38 mattress
39 misspell
40 niece
41 parallel
42 psychiatrist
43 psychology
44 occasion
45 organization
46 piece
47 receive

48 religious
49 severely
50 villain

Group 2

1 arctic
2 auxiliary
3 business
4 candidate
5 characteristic
6 chauffeur
7 colonel
8 column
9 cylinder
10 environment
11 especially
12 exhaust
13 exhilaration
14 February
15 foremost
16 ghost
17 government
18 grievous
19 hygiene
20 intercede
21 leisure
22 library
23 lightning
24 literature
25 mathematics
26 medicine
27 mortgage
28 muscle
29 notoriety
30 optimistic
31 pamphlet
32 parliament
33 physically
34 physician
35 prairie
36 prejudice
37 pronunciation

38 recede
39 recognize
40 reign
41 rhetoric
42 rhythm
43 schedule
44 sentinel
45 soliloquy
46 sophomore
47 studying
48 surprise
49 twelfth
50 Wednesday

Group 3

1 apparent
2 appearance
3 attendance
4 beggar
5 brilliant
6 calendar
7 carriage
8 conqueror
9 contemptible
10 coolly
11 descent
12 desirable
13 dictionary
14 disastrous
15 eligible
16 equivalent
17 existence
18 familiar
19 grammar
20 guidance
21 hindrance
22 hoping
23 imaginary
24 indispensable
25 incredible
26 indigestible
27 inevitable

28 influential
29 irresistible
30 liable
31 marriage
32 momentous
33 naturally
34 nickel
35 noticeable
36 nucleus
37 obedience
38 outrageous
39 pageant
40 permissible
41 perseverance
42 persistent
43 possible
44 pleasant
45 prevalent
46 resistance
47 similar
48 strenuous
49 vengeance
50 vigilance

Group 4

1 allot
2 allotted
3 barbarian
4 barbarous
5 beneficial
6 benefited
7 changeable
8 changing
9 commit
10 committed
11 committee
12 comparative
13 comparatively
14 comparison
15 compel
16 compelled
17 compulsion

18 competent
19 competition
20 conceivable
21 conceive
22 conception
23 conscience
24 conscientious
25 conscious
26 courteous
27 courtesy
28 deceit
29 deceive
30 deception
31 decide
32 decision
33 defer
34 deference
35 deferred
36 describe
37 description
38 device
39 devise
40 discuss
41 discussion
42 dissatisfied
43 dissatisfy
44 equip
45 equipment
46 equipped
47 excel
48 excellent
49 explain
50 explanation

Group 5

1 hesitancy
2 hesitate
3 instance
4 instant
5 intellectual
6 intelligence

7 intelligent
8 intelligible
9 maintain
10 maintenance
11 miniature
12 minute
13 ninetieth
14 ninety
15 ninth
16 obligation
17 oblige
18 obliged
19 occur
20 occurrence
21 occurred
22 omission
23 omit
24 omitted
25 procedure
26 proceed
27 picnic
28 picnicking
29 possess
30 possession
31 precede
32 precedence
33 preceding
34 prefer
35 preference
36 preferred
37 realize
38 really
39 refer
40 reference
41 referred
42 repeat
43 repetition
44 transfer
45 transferred
46 tried
47 tries
48 try

49 writing
50 written

Group 6

 1 obstacle
 2 operate
 3 opinion
 4 persuade
 5 presence
 6 politician
 7 practically
 8 restaurant
 9 region
10 reservoir
11 ridiculous
12 sacrifice
13 sacrilegious
14 safety
15 salary
16 scarcely
17 secretary
18 separate
19 similar
20 supersede
21 tendency
22 temperament
23 temperature
24 tournament
25 truly
26 tragedy
27 unanimous
28 unusual
29 usage
30 valuable
31 yoke
32 yolk
33 quantity
34 tyranny
35 propeller
36 professor
37 recommend
38 representative

39 suppress
40 syllable
41 suffrage
42 symmetry
43 wholly
44 pastime
45 piece
46 relieve
47 science
48 shriek
49 seize
50 siege

Group 7

 1 accept
 2 across
 3 aisle
 4 all right
 5 amateur
 6 annual
 7 appropriate
 8 argument
 9 arrangement
10 association
11 awkward
12 convenient
13 definite
14 desperate
15 eighth
16 eliminate
17 bachelor
18 biscuit
19 cafeteria
20 career
21 cemetery
22 completely
23 cruelty
24 curiosity
25 diphtheria
26 discipline
27 disease
28 distribute

29 dormitories
30 drudgery
31 ecstasy
32 eminent
33 enemy
34 except
35 exercise
36 extraordinary
37 fascinate
38 fraternity
39 furniture

40 grandeur
41 height
42 hypocrisy
43 imitation
44 interest
45 livelihood
46 loneliness
47 magazine
48 material
49 messenger
50 mischievous

Punctuation = P

PUNCTUATION IS FAR FROM BEING A MERE MECHANICAL
DEVICE. IT IS MECHANICAL AS A MATTER OF COURSE,
LIKE WORD-SPACING OR THE USE OF INITIAL CAPITALS;
BUT PUNCTUATION IS MUCH MORE THAN THAT. IT IS AN
INTEGRAL PART OF WRITTEN COMPOSITION.

—GEORGE SUMMEY, JR.

WHEN SPEAKING, we use pauses and gestures to get emphasis, and we use changes in tempo and inflection to mark the beginning and ending of units of thought. We punctuate writing for the same purpose, but are restricted to devices that can be shown on the printed, typed, or handwritten page.

The first of these devices is *spacing:* that is, closing up or enlarging the space between letters or words. For example, we do not

runwordstogetherthisway

Instead, we identify a word *as a word* by setting it off from its neighbors. Spacing is therefore the most basic of all punctuating devices.

In addition to the obvious function just mentioned, space has other uses. Writers of advertising copy use space in clever ways to focus a reader's eye on the name of a product, a trademark, or a slogan. Moreover, many modern writers manipulate the spacing between words and sentences to get certain rhetorical effects. John Dos Passos describes the activity on an assembly-line as

> . . . the Taylorized speedup everywhere, reach under, adjust washer, screw down bolt, shove in cotterpin, reachunder adjust washer, screwdownbolt reachunderadjustscrewdownreachunderadjust. . . .
>
> —"The Big Money," *U.S.A.*

Standard practice, which can seldom be so extreme as this, is limited generally to:

(1) setting off and identifying words,
(2) keeping paragraphs distinct from one another,
(3) listing items in a series by setting them off in space just as we are doing here.

But we can see at once that *spacing* is seldom the only punctuation needed.

> yes madam jones was heard to say to the owl like old dowager without a doubt the taming of the shrew by shakespeare would be a most appropriate new years present for your husband

To make this passage immediately intelligible, we need to add two other kinds of punctuation: (1) *changes in the size and design of letters* (capitals and italics); and (2) *marks or "points"* (periods, commas, quotation marks, apostrophes, and other special signs).

> "Yes, Madam," Jones was heard to say to the owl-like old dowager, "without a doubt, *The Taming of the Shrew* by Shakespeare would be a most appropriate New Year's present for your husband."

Now the reader knows at once that we are reproducing the words of a speaker named Jones; that Jones is probably not a female himself but is addressing someone who is; that Jones is speaking not to an owl but to a lady who looks like one; that *without a doubt* is a statement of Jones and not that of the person who overheard the remark; that Shakespeare did not tame a shrew but wrote a play about one; that *new* is not an ordinary adjective but a part of a proper noun; and finally that *years* is not a plural noun but a singular possessive.

More generally, this example shows us that punctuation performs four functions:

(1) It shows the beginning and ending of a sentence; this function is "end punctuation," and capitals, periods, question marks, and exclamation points constitute it.

(2) It separates words and groups of words so that their relationship to the rest of the sentence is immediately clarified; this function is "internal punctuation," and commas, semicolons, colons, dashes, and parentheses constitute it.

(3) It indicates a change in speakers; this function is "punctuating direct quotations," and quotation marks and brackets designate it.

(4) It identifies proper nouns and words having a special character and usage; this function is "punctuating words," and capitals, italics, quotation marks, apostrophes, and hyphens designate it.

In the "owl-like dowager" selection given above, the use of each punctuating device is rather arbitrarily fixed. Probably no other way of signaling the reader would satisfy the dictates of general practice. In this instance, as in many others, punctuating properly means observing customary usage—in short, punctuating as our readers expect us to punctuate.

But the value attached to many punctuating devices is not always so rigidly defined. The functions of some devices overlap and shade into one another. The statement ·

> He closed his eyes and jumped. Then he felt the waters close over him.

might just as "correctly" be punctuated

> He closed his eyes and jumped; then he felt the waters close over him.

or even

> He closed his eyes and jumped—then he felt the waters close over him.

Each of these statements makes a slightly different impression on the reader. The first emphasizes the equal importance of the two actions. The second emphasizes their close and immediate relationship. The third emphasizes the element of suspense between the two actions. Yet this interpretation is really the result of our personal tastes and our understanding of the writer's "intention." There is no absolute standard, no authoritative convention to which we can refer for a "correct" answer. Sometimes the choice of commas rather than dashes, of semicolons rather than colons, is a stylistic or personal matter.

How then, in this confusion of arbitrary usage and personal taste, do we learn to punctuate?

First, by understanding that punctuation is an *aid to* and *not a substitution for* clear and orderly sentence structure. The proper beginning of a study of punctuation is careful attention to sentence structure. Even the most elaborate punctuation will not save a sentence that is badly written in the first place. Until we can distinguish phrases from clauses, subjects from predicates, and compound from complex sentences, our punctuation may be more confusing than clarifying. *Second,* by observing conventional practice in punctuation matters. Most sentences are constructed in conventional patterns; there is a community of agreement about punctuating them. This agreement is reflected in the rules of punctuation which follow.

36. END PUNCTUATION

The chief function of periods, question marks, and exclamation points is to signal the end of a sentence. The question of which to use is determined by the character of the sentence itself. Plain assertions or commands are terminated with periods; interrogative statements with question marks; strongly emotional assertions or ejaculations with exclamation points. Usually, the character of a sentence is obvious, and its proper punctuation easily determined. Occasionally, however, a writer has to determine for himself just what he *intends* the character of his sentence to be. These sentences illustrate the difference in the writer's intention:

> He struck out with the bases loaded.
> He struck out with the bases loaded?
> He struck out with the bases loaded!

In addition to their chief function, the period and the question mark have a few special uses, illustrated in Sections 36b, 36c, and 36e below.

THE PERIOD

36a. A period is used to signal the end of an assertion or command.

> ASSERTION   He mowed the hay with easy strokes.
> COMMAND   Mow the hay with easy strokes.

36b. A period is used after most abbreviations.

> Dr.   Mr.   Mrs.   R.N.   C.P.A.   Sen.   B.A.

Recent practice eliminates the period after many abbreviations, particularly those of organizations or government agencies (NEA, AFL,

RFC, TVA). For standard practice in the punctuation of a given abbreviation, consult a good dictionary.

36c. A series of three periods [. . .] is used to indicate an ellipsis.

An ellipsis is an intentional omission of words. The sign of an ellipsis appears most frequently in quoted material. The writer quoting the material thinks it unnecessary to reproduce all the words of the original author. For example, the first selection below is taken without any omissions from *Foundations of Speech,* ed. C. M. Wise, *et al.* (New York, 1942), p. 271. The second selection shows the use of ellipsis by a writer quoting the original material. Note that when the ellipsis comes at the end of a sentence, a fourth period is used.

(1) Every well-written composition has a dominant unity, a single, main impression which the author wishes to establish, or a purpose which he wishes to serve, and to which everything else is subordinate

(2) Every well-written composition has a dominant unity . . . which the author wishes to establish, or a purpose which he wishes to serve. . . .

36x. The period fault.

The *period fault* or *sentence fragment* results from an assumption by a writer that a group of words is a sentence, whereas actually it is not. Of the two terms, *sentence fragment* is the more realistic; incomplete sentences generally result from an ignorance of sentence structure, not of punctuation. (*See* "Confused Structure," Section 2a.)

THE QUESTION MARK

36d. A question mark is used after a direct question.

Direct questions are easily recognizable. They often begin with one of the interrogative pronouns or adverbs (*who, when, what,* etc.). They generally make use of inverted word order (*verb* before *subject* instead of *subject* before *verb*). The inversion may occur at either the beginning or the ending of the sentence.

(1) Did you study *Ivanhoe* in high school?

(2) You want to make a good impression, don't you?

36e. A question mark is used within parentheses (?) to indicate a writer's doubt or uncertainty about the correctness of a preceding statement.

This is not a device to save writers from checking on their facts but a method of showing that the correct fact is not known.

John Pomfret, an English poet, was born in 1667 (?) and died in 1702.

For general purposes, the qualifying term *about* is more suitable:

John Pomfret, an English poet, was born about 1667 and died in 1702.

36y. Faulty use of the question mark.

The question mark is not used after indirect questions. If a writer is uncertain about the difference between *direct* and *indirect* questions, he should compare the indirect questions below with the direct questions under 36d.

(1) They asked me whether I had studied *Ivanhoe* in high school.

(2) He asked me whether I wished to make a good impression.

Business-letter practice permits the use of a period instead of a question mark after a direct question phrased as a request. The writer's intention determines his choice of mark.

Will you be sure to let us know if this arrangement does not satisfy you.

BUT

May we hear from you by the end of next week?

THE EXCLAMATION POINT

36f. The exclamation point is a mark of emphasis used after a highly emotional or forceful statement.

(1) What! It can't be true! I've never heard of such a thing!

(2) Attention!

(3) Why, he implies that Shakespeare was a student of Milton's!

36z. Faulty use of the exclamation point.

The exclamation point is a mark of special emphasis and should be used sparingly. A writer who overuses it raises his statements to the level of a shout or scream and deafens his readers. For this reason, the sentences below are ineffective.

> War is hell! Think of what it does to young men to have their futures interrupted and sometimes cut off completely! Think of what it does to their families! Think of what it does to the nation!

EXERCISE 1. Supply the appropriate punctuation in each of the following sentences. If a choice of marks is possible, indicate why you chose the one you did.

(1) He asked whether Jim had come home

(2) What do you mean by saying that I lied to Professor Brown

(3) Mr T J Roberts, who formerly worked for the G R McBane Co, is now with the U S Army

(4) The chairman asked the audience to give careful attention to the speaker

(5) The speaker said, "May I have your careful attention please"

(6) The sergeant yelled, "Attention"

(7) Prof J R Greenbriar, B A, M A, P h D, lives at 20 N 4th Street, Columbus, O

(8) "Has Jim come home yet" he asked

(9) "Get out of my way" the driver shouted

(10) "Oh, why do you torment me so" she cried

(11) He wondered if the severe frost would kill the roses

(12) He wonders if the severe frost will kill the roses

(13) Is Jas the abbreviation for James or Jason

(14) The newspaper reported that after the 1st of February Lieut and Mrs J G Todd would live at 467 E 69th St N W

(15) Just as the roller coaster hit the top he frightened us by standing up in his seat and yelling "Here we go "

(16) When Rush asked if he could leave before the class was over, Mr Nathan looked at him for a moment and then said fiercely but quietly, "You will remain here until the bell rings do you understand "

(17) Mr Monroe, who was an analyst for the R F C for many years, is a C P A

(18) [Assume that in quoting the following passage you wish to omit the phrase "At any time," the sentence beginning "This is the cause," and the clause "its surface is actually a poor reflector." Show how you would indicate to a reader that you were omitting material that appeared in the original.]

We see the Moon by means of sunlight falling upon it which is re-flected back by its surface. At any time one half of the surface is in sunlight and the other half in darkness. Near New Moon the sun-light is mostly falling on the hemisphere that is turned towards us. This is the cause of the varying phases of the Moon. Though the Moon appears very bright, its surface is actually a poor reflector; less than ten per cent of the sunlight that falls on it is reflected back, the remainder being absorbed and going to heat the surface.

—H. SPENCER JONES, *Life on Other Worlds*

37-42. INTERNAL PUNCTUATION

Internal punctuation, or punctuation within the sentence, involves five marks (commas, dashes, parentheses, semicolons, colons), the use of which is closely associated with the structure and meaning of the sentence. Indeed, such punctuation reveals that structure. As an example of the very skillful use of internal punctuation, consider the following:

> People who do not understand pigeons—and pigeons can be understood only when you understand that there is nothing to understand about them—should not go around describing pigeons or the effects of pigeons. Pigeons come closer to a zero of impingement than any other birds. Hens embarrass me the way my old Aunt Hattie used to when I was twelve and she still insisted that I wasn't big enough to bathe myself; owls disturb me; if I am with an eagle I always pretend that I am not with an eagle; and so on down to swallows at twilight who scare the hell out of me.
>
> —JAMES THURBER, *There's an Owl in My Room**

In this passage, the parenthetical thought beginning "and pigeons can be" gains emphasis by being set off with dashes. Commas might have been used, but they would have weakened the humorous force of the aside. Parentheses would have given the statement more formality than the writer wished. The brevity and simple structure of the second sentence, coming as it does between two long and involved sentences, give it emphasis. The fact that it is a statement about just one kind of bird, and that the third sentence contains statements about four kinds of birds, indicates that the third is intended as a contrast to the second; if the four statements in the third sentence had been punctuated as four separate sentences, then each

* First published in *The New Yorker*.

of the four would have been parallel with, rather than in contrast to, the single statement about the pigeon.

The precision and subtlety of this illustration may seem rather exceptional. But that is not the point. For us, the real importance of the passage is that it illustrates that internal punctuation is basically a rhetorical, not a mechanical, matter: in other words, that it is impossible to talk about the punctuation of a sentence without talking about the meaning of that sentence. We will find this statement to be true, though less obviously so, of even simple and conventional sentences. And it is in this light that the "rules"—which are simply generalizations of conventional practice—must be interpreted.

EXERCISE 2. Analyze the internal punctuation in the following passages just as your editors analyzed the selection from Thurber above:

(1) There is no record in human history of a happy philosopher: they exist only in romantic legend. Many of them have committed suicide; many others have turned their children out of doors and beaten their wives. And no wonder. If you want to find out how a philosopher feels when he is engaged in the practice of his profession, go to the nearest zoo and watch a chimpanzee at the wearying and hopeless job of chasing fleas. Both suffer damnably, and neither can win.

—H. L. MENCKEN

(2) The modern miser has changed much from the miser of legend and anecdote; but only because he has grown yet more insane. The old miser had some touch of the human artist about him in so far that he collected gold—a substance that can really be admired for itself, like ivory or old oak. An old man who picked up yellow pieces had something of the simple ardour, something of the mystical materialism, of a child who picks out yellow flowers. Gold is but one kind of coloured clay, but coloured clay can be very beautiful. The modern idolater of riches is content with far less genuine things. The glitter of guineas is like the glitter of buttercups, the chink of pelf is like the chime of bells, compared with the dreary papers and dead calculations which make the hobby of the modern miser.

—GILBERT CHESTERTON

(3) The chances and changes, the personal history of any absolute genius, draw us to watch his adventure with curiosity and inquiry, lead us on to win more of his secret and borrow more of his experi-

ence (I mean, needless to say, when we are at all critically minded);
but there is something in the clear safe arrival of the poetic nature,
in a given case, at the point of its free and happy exercise, that pro-
vokes, if not the cold impulse to challenge or cross-question it, at
least the need of understanding so far as possible how, in a world in
which difficulty and disaster are frequent, the most wavering and
flickering of all fine flames has escaped extinction.

—HENRY JAMES

(4) Fifty years ago, when I was a boy of fifteen and helping to
inhabit a Missourian village on the banks of the Mississippi, I had a
friend whose society was very dear to me because I was forbidden by
my mother to partake of it. He was a gay and impudent and satirical
and delightful young black man—a slave—who daily preached sermons from the top of his master's woodpile, with me for sole audience. He imitated the pulpit style of the several clergymen of the
village, and did it well and with fine passion and energy. To me he
was a wonder. I believed he was the greatest orator in the United
States and would some day be heard from. But it did not happen;
in the distribution of rewards he was overlooked. It is the way, in
this world.

—MARK TWAIN

(5) In those days Sir Austin Feverel was thought a royal man,
and was in a fair way to be beloved. He was frank and warm with
his friends; generous to the poor, and above all, delicate with them,
who have the keenest instinct for a gentleman, and venerated him
accordingly. When his disaster befell him, and his home was suddenly desolate, it was as though his tree of life had shrunk under a
blight. He shut himself up as he did his Dining-hall; relinquished
Parliament, and bade a mute adieu to Ambition. People were astonished at the utter change wrought in so apparently proud and
self-reliant a man: but old folks, that knew the family, said they
expected it some day or other. It was in the blood, they said: Sir
Caradoc, his father, was a strange hand, and so was his father, Sir
Algernon, before him: they were all sure to turn out a little wrong
some day or other. And the old folks tapped their foreheads mean-
ingly.

—GEORGE MEREDITH

37. SEPARATING MAIN CLAUSES

37a. Main clauses joined with a co-ordinating conjunction (*and, but, or, nor, for, yet* and *so*) are usually separated with a comma.*

(1) The patrol planes were delayed by a heavy rain, and they barely had enough fuel to get back to the carrier.

(2) The patrol planes were delayed by a heavy rain, but they succeeded in making safe landings on the carrier deck.

(3) The patrol planes could land near the enemy lines, or they could risk night landings on the carrier deck.

(4) The return of the patrol planes must have been delayed, for they made night landings on the carrier deck.

EXCEPTIONS:

(1) In short compound sentences, the comma is usually omitted.

I caught the morning train but my neighbor missed it.

(2) A semicolon is often used to separate main clauses joined by a co-ordinating conjunction, especially when commas have already been used to separate subordinate elements.

Babe Ruth, the greatest of home run hitters, was the most colorful figure in baseball; but many people think Ty Cobb was a better player.

The life of every man is a diary in which he means to write one story, and writes another; and his humblest hour is when he compares the volume as it is with what he vowed to make it.

—SIR JAMES BARRIE

* In formal English *yet* is sometimes used to mean *but*. Informal English often uses *so* as a co-ordinating conjunction.

I first gave it a dose of castor-oil, and then I christened it; so now the poor child is ready for either world.

—SIDNEY SMITH

(3) A semicolon is often used in place of a comma when a stronger pause is desired.

We haven't all had the good fortune to be ladies; we haven't all been generals, or poets, or statesmen; but when the toast works down to the babies, we stand on common ground.

—MARK TWAIN

37b. Main clauses not joined with a co-ordinating conjunction are separated with a semicolon.

Children begin by loving their parents; as they grow older they judge them; sometimes they forgive them.

—OSCAR WILDE

To educate a man is to educate an individual; to educate a woman is to educate a family.

Bermuda consists of nineteen square miles of land; the islanders import most of their food.

EXCEPTION: A comma may be used to separate very short main clauses not joined by co-ordinating conjunctions.

I stopped, I aimed, I fired.

37c. Main clauses joined with a conjunctive adverb are separated with a semicolon.

Americans spend millions of dollars for road-building; however, our roads are rapidly deteriorating.

Conjunctive adverbs are different from *subordinating conjunctions*. This list, though incomplete, will be helpful:

CONJUNCTIVE ADVERBS	SUBORDINATING CONJUNCTIONS
however	when
nevertheless	although
moreover	though
therefore	since
consequently	if
hence	because

368

CONJUNCTIVE ADVERBS	SUBORDINATING CONJUNCTIONS
indeed	so that
likewise	as
furthermore	after
namely	in order that
still	while
then	unless

37d. Two main clauses, the second of which amplifies or explains the first, are separated with a colon.*

His reasons are as two grains of wheat hid in a bushel of chaff: you shall search all day ere you find them, and when you do they are not worth the search.

—WILLIAM SHAKESPEARE

A gentleman of our day is one who has money enough to do what every fool would do if he could afford it: that is, consume without producing.

—G. B. SHAW

Over the piano was printed a notice: Please do not shoot the pianist. He is doing his best.

—OSCAR WILDE

37x. Comma splice (or comma fault).

The use of a comma to join main clauses not connected by a coordinating conjunction is called the comma fault or the comma splice. (*See* Section 2b.)

EXERCISE 3. Separate the main clauses in the following sentences:

(1) Thompson had made reasonably good grades in introductory French courses however, he almost failed French 34.

(2) The *Record* supported Earle but the *Times* was neutral.

(3) Conway Motors pays a low dividend rate still it seems entirely safe and has never passed a dividend.

(4) During the period around 1950 the T-formation became more and more popular in college circles but some eastern colleges of the conference, notably Winnemac and Southeastern, clung to the old formation.

(5) Very few of the office staff had been able to come in on time

---

* Some writers prefer to use a dash instead of a colon, particularly when they wish to give an emotional emphasis to the amplifying statement. (*See also* 42b.)

the morning of the big snow and the manager decided not to go ahead with the interviews planned.

(6) The telegram brought him the news he had been hoping for Kenneth had obtained a large contract with the Armstrong Company.

(7) There were a good many disadvantages in attempting to build on the river lots moreover the price asked seemed much too great.

(8) Then Knox came to realize what his lawyer had meant by his guarded hints his partner had been defrauding the company for years.

(9) Sugar stock prices declined alarmingly when the news reached Wall Street nevertheless the syndicate persisted in its extensive buying operations.

(10) The difference between men and women is a simple one men know that purple and black are not the same as navy blue.

(11) When Ziegler had died very suddenly the summer before, the company had been unable to piece together all the transactions he had conducted and consequently orders were issued, affecting all executives, that every transaction, in or out of the city, had to be explained in duplicate memoranda.

(12) The proposed new bridge would have cost nearly a million dollars furthermore extensive changes would be needed in the streets around Oak Square.

(13) The majority of the judges clearly favored the Blue Persian for the grand prize but a few still held out for the best Siamese.

(14) Finally Carter went by train and Kane drove to the meeting.

(15) The invasion of the adjacent small countries, which was carried out with speed and efficiency, stirred some more responsible leaders to action but unfortunately at that time their efforts, viewed with resentment by some and suspicion by others, came too late to prevent the fall of the country.

(16) Mr. Endicott was able to arrange much more favorable rates for the conference at the Nichols Hotel hence the committee voted unanimously to meet there.

(17) One of Will Rogers's chief assets was a boyish grin seldom is such a grin seen except on an Oklahoman.

(18) The cat attempted to catch a goldfish but in his eagerness he

370

fell into the bowl and drowned, learning thereby that all that glitters is not gold.

(19) The value of the lesson to the cat is, however, doubtful cats are rarely interested in precious metals.

(20) Gray, the author of "Elegy Written in a Country Church-Yard," composed a poem commemorating the cat's death however he gave us no indication of the fate of the goldfish.

EXERCISE 4. The following sentences are accompanied by directions calling for various changes in wording. Make the changes directed and any changes in punctuation entailed by the change in wording.

1. Change *however* to *although*.

At that time Simmons had seen no cause for alarm; however, he recalled later that the pressure gauge was rising.

2. Change *and* to *also*.

Mr. Edwards' insurance did not approach covering the loss, and the owners of the adjacent property were filing damage claims.

3. Change *when* to *then*.

The crowd waited impatiently until 9:30, when they began to become very restless and hiss and boo at the delay.

4. Change *who* to *they*.

Carlsen was sure that these were the men who had been sitting in the restaurant at the table next to his.

5. Change *otherwise* to *or*.

Guests' valuables must be kept in the hotel safe; otherwise the management will assume no responsibility whatever for them.

6. Change *but* to *still*.

There were a number of trees along the hillside, but the winds last year loosened the roots by blowing the soil away.

7. Omit *because*.

Because the figures on the left side of the canvas made that side seem bulky, the artist added a cluster of clouds on the right.

8. Change *therefore* to *consequently*.

The ferry operated with no other power than the current of the river; therefore it had a very low overhead.

9. Change *but* to *however*.

The psychiatrists announced that television and comics were certainly having an effect upon children, but they were not sure what the effect was or whether it was good or bad.

10. Omit *and.*

The herd disappeared into the foliage along the creek bank, and the cowboys very soon found themselves scratched and their clothes torn by the low branches of mesquite.

38. SEPARATING SUBORDINATE ELEMENTS

38a. Introductory clauses and phrases.

Long introductory clauses and prepositional phrases are separated from a main clause by a comma.

(1) When I saw the grizzly bear coming toward me, I raised the gun to my shoulder and took aim.

(2) As soon as he finished his dessert, he left.

(3) After his long exile to France during the Commonwealth, Charles II returned to England in 1660.

(4) In his indifference to criticism from those who could not hurt his political chances, he revealed his callousness and vicious self-interest.

(5) If you wish to avoid foreign collision, you had better abandon the ocean.   —HENRY CLAY

Short introductory clauses or prepositional phrases need not be separated from a main clause by a comma.

(1) When he arrived she was taking the cat out of the piano.

(2) After his defeat he retired from public life.

Introductory verbal modifiers, regardless of their length, are usually separated from the rest of the sentence by a comma.

(1) Having been a teacher for fifty years, he felt perfectly relaxed among young people.

(2) Exhausted, the swimmer fell back into the pool.

(3) To be quite honest about it, that dog has been known to climb trees.

NOTE: Verbal modifiers should not be confused with verbals used as subjects:

373

Having been a teacher for fifty years made him perfectly relaxed among young people.

38b. Clauses or phrases following the main clause.

If a clause or phrase following the main clause is closely related to the main clause, it is usually not set off with a comma.

(1) She loves me because I tolerate her petty moodiness.
(2) The defendant objected to paying income tax while the money was being used for war purposes.
(3) My daughter is seldom in one place long because she married a circus performer who takes her with him from town to town.
(4) He has visited all the small towns in Pennsylvania.

However some clauses and phrases following the main clause *are* set off with a comma. Usually these explain or amplify the main clause, or offer a contrast to it.

(1) I know she loves me, because she tolerates my petty moodiness.
(2) My neighbor objects to paying income tax, although he seems to approve of the war's being fought with the money.
(3) Henrietta married a circus performer, which is the reason she travels from town to town.
(4) He has visited *all* the small towns, in Pennsylvania, in Ohio, in practically every state in the union.
(5) It is a common rule with primitive people not to waken a sleeper, because his soul is away and might not have time to get back.   —JAMES FRAZER

38c. Nonrestrictive elements.

The final clauses and phrases in Section 38b which were not set off with a comma are called restrictive modifiers because they are necessary to the basic meaning of the main clause. Those which were set off with a comma are called nonrestrictive modifiers. A nonrestrictive element in a sentence is a word or group of words which does not limit the word it modifies. Being parenthetical, it is an addition to, rather than an integral part of, the main idea of the sentence.

   (1) RESTRICTIVE   A man *who is honest* will succeed.
   (2) NONRESTRICTIVE   Jacob North, *who is honest, will succeed.*

In (1) the clause *who is honest* is the reader's only means of knowing what kind of man will succeed. The clause is *restrictive* and not set off with commas. In (2), however, the clause *who is honest* is only an additional comment on a man already identified as Jacob North. The clause is *nonrestrictive* and set off with commas.

We have identified the nonrestrictives in the example below by italicizing them. Note that although the nonrestrictives contribute an essential part of the humor, they may be eliminated without destroying the basic meaning of the main clauses.

> One day not long ago, *idling through the pages of a sophisticated 35-cent monthly while waiting for the barber to give me my sophisticated 65-cent monthly haircut,* I was suddenly oppressed by the characteristic shortness of breath, *mingled with giddiness and general trepidation,* that results whenever one gets too near an advertisement for Tabu. This exotic scent, *in case you have been fortunate enough to forget it,* is widely publicized as "the 'Forbidden' Perfume," which means, *when all the meringue is sluiced away,* that it is forbidden to anyone who doesn't have $18.50 for an ounce of it.
>
>   —S. J. PERELMAN, *Keep It Crisp.*

Punctuation of such sentence elements should express clearly the author's intention. For instance, the following sentences vary greatly in meaning merely because one uses commas where the other does not.

   (1) Oklahomans, who have oilwells in their backyards, can afford
       the hotel's high prices.
   (2) Oklahomans who have oilwells in their backyards can afford
       the hotel's high prices.

The first sentence applies to all Oklahomans; the second only to the lucky few. A mistake in the use of commas here would affect seriously the accuracy of the statement.

NOTE: Observe that *two* commas enclose the nonrestrictive modifier unless it begins or ends the sentence.

NOT   The old mare, half-blind and lame was hardly able to stand in the traces.

BUT   The old mare, half-blind and lame, was hardly able to stand in the traces.

OR   Half-blind and lame, the old mare was hardly able to stand in the traces.

38d. A comma is used wherever it is necessary to prevent mis-reading, even in violation of other standards of usage.

(1) Long before, she had left everything to her brother.

(2) Pilots who like to see sunbathers, fly low over apartment houses.

(3) Inside the house, cats are sometimes a nuisance.

The omission of a comma after *before* in sentence (1) would be momentarily confusing; we get off to a false start by reading *Long-before-she-had-left* without interruption. If there were no comma in sentence (2) we might think we were reading about flying sunbathers. A similar difficulty arises in sentence (3) if *house* is not separated from *cats*. Often it is best to rewrite such sentences so that the confusion is avoided.

38e. Commas are used to separate direct quotations from un-quoted material. (See Section 43g-1.)

EXERCISE 5. Supply commas where necessary:

(1) We could see the garden walk from our bedroom window.

(2) After he had completed his formal education and had worked in his father's office for two years he went abroad.

(3) Having completed his formal education he went abroad for two years.

(4) Can you imagine killing a chicken with an automobile?

(5) The private began laying out his bedroll over the sergeant's objection.

(6) After completing his education he went abroad for two years.

(7) He went abroad for two years after completing his formal education.

(8) Forced to make an emergency landing the pilot let the plane lose altitude at a rapid rate.

(9) When all the returns had come in and had been tallied it was found that Wright was ahead by 154 votes.

(10) To view the incident in the most charitable light perhaps we may say that Simmons was unaware of the implications of his comments.

(11) That night when he was taking advantage of a period of peace and quiet to reconsider the plan seemed more hopeless than it had before.

(12) Since Goldman had won his last three games in September the manager picked him to oppose the Seals in the play-offs.

(13) After the flour had been tested and inspected thoroughly by the inspector the workmen on the floor were ready to put it in the sacks.

(14) Because he was eager to display his medical knowledge the young doctor interrupted his patient.

(15) Rocket ships will avoid landings on the moon's equator which has a noonday temperature of 220 degrees Fahrenheit.

EXERCISE 6. Remembering the rules for punctuating subordinate elements, indicate whether the following sentences are punctuated correctly. If they are not, indicate why.

(1) After plans had been made and supplies accumulated for the proposed invasion, the high command dropped the idea.

(2) When investigations were made he remembered that as he was eating the food seemed to have an odd taste.

(3) When the car had been raised far enough to remove the tire Harris noticed that the jack was beginning to slip.

(4) To explain the matter in more detail, Ingalls was unable at that time to say exactly what the letter did mean.

(5) While he was painting the planks under him seemed firm enough to support him and his assistant too.

(6) When he started to play the piece seemed more difficult than it had during rehearsal sessions.

(7) Since the publishers had not expected any great sales for the book, the first printing was exhausted in about ten days.

(8) While Wood was reading the same news was being broadcast on the radio program his wife was listening to upstairs.

(9) Having turned state's evidence during the trial, Crawford was given a lighter sentence than others in the trial.

(10) To finish the report before final grades were given in the course Dorsey would have to work day and night for two days.

(11) When a driller starts, setting his machine at exactly the right angle is his main problem.

(12) After Mrs. Elliott told her guests to feel free to smoke the cigarets were passed around.

(13) Fawcett having been found guilty the judge called him a menace to society and gave him the maximum term.

(14) Irritated by the sarcastic tone in which he was greeted Harvey was about to answer bitterly, but decided to hold his tongue.

(15) As the northern route was uncertain at best in midwinter the Allies had to hold Port Stanley at all costs.

39. SETTING OFF PARENTHETICAL ELEMENTS

Aside from nonrestrictive modifiers (*See* Section 38c) there are several sentence elements such as appositives, nouns of direct address, inserted remarks, and transitional words and phrases which are parenthetical to the basic meaning of a sentence. Usually these are set off with commas.

39a. Appositives.

An *appositive* is a substantive (a word or group of words used as a noun) placed beside another substantive and used to denote the same person or thing.

(1) The professor, *an elderly and gentle man,* led the student from the class by the ear.

(2) Daisy Mae, *our old Irish setter,* has never missed or won a fight.

(3) "Hello, Mitty. We're having the devil's own time with McMillan, *the millionaire banker and close personal friend of Roosevelt."*   —JAMES THURBER, *The Secret Life of Walter Mitty*

When appositives are restrictive the comma is omitted.

The poet Bryant was a leader in New York literary circles. (*Bryant* is essential to the meaning of the sentence.)

Among the holiday visitors were Doris, Wilma, and my Aunt Martha. But notice:

Among the holiday visitors were Ted Stevens, Gertrude Williams, and my aunt, Martha Johnson. (The speaker has only one aunt. Had he more than one he might have said "and Martha Johnson, my aunt.")

Compound appositives are set off by dashes to prevent confusion. A sentence like the following would cause one to wonder what sort of creatures Bill, Dave, and Blacky are:

Three men, Bill, Dave, and Blacky, were sitting in the office with their feet on the desk.

But dashes tell us that not six people but three were meant:

Three men—Bill, Dave, and Blacky—were sitting in the office with their feet on the desk.

39b. Words and expressions which do not severely interrupt the structure of the sentence may be set off with commas.

WORDS IN DIRECT ADDRESS	Yes, Louise, you should file your fingernails.
MILD INTERJECTIONS	Oh, I never get *A's*—always *C's* and more *C's!*
TRANSITIONS, PARENTHETICAL EXPLANATIONS, AND AFTER-THOUGHTS	Horses, *unlike tractors,* must be fed in the winter.
	You may, *if you wish,* leave your teeth in the bathroom.
	Christians, *on the other hand,* are opposed to violence.
	Come when you can, *the sooner the better.*
	"The grave's a fine and private place. But none, *I think,* do there embrace."
	—ANDREW MARVELL, "To His Coy Mistress"

NOTE: There is an increasing tendency to leave very slight pauses unpunctuated.

FORMAL	Thinking is, *nevertheless,* not required for a college degree.
INFORMAL	Thinking is *nevertheless* not required for a college degree.

39c. Parenthetical expressions that interrupt abruptly are set off by dashes or parentheses.

The choice here is largely one of personal taste, though most writers use dashes to set off interrupters which they wish to emphasize, and parentheses to set off statements which are unemphatic.

| EMPHATIC PARENTHETICAL STATEMENT | The power of the *Trib-une*—one million peo-ple read it daily—is enormous. |
| UNEMPHATIC PARENTHETICAL STATEMENT | The power of the *Trib-une* (one million peo-ple read it daily) is enormous. |

39d. Two commas are used to enclose nonrestrictive or paren-thetical elements unless they begin or end a sentence.
(*See* Section 38c, Note.)

NOT   She insisted, however that he bring her home before mid-night.

BUT   She insisted, however, that he bring her home before mid-night.

OR   She insisted that he bring her home before midnight, how-ever.

EXERCISE 7. Supply the appropriate punctuation in the sentences below. If a choice of marks is possible, explain why you chose the one you did.

(1) No one not even his wife knows what Roy paid for his collec-tion of jazz records.

(2) Jay Elliott a stocky youth with black hair is an excellent stu-dent.

(3) The result of his attempt to climb up the roof was as you can guess very unfortunate.

(4) Robert Powell an aggressive union leader is a self-educated man.

(5) The aggressive union leader Robert Powell is a self-educated man.

(6) We submit Mr. Chairman that the effects of the new policy are already detrimental to the institution.

(7) These people for reasons unexplained until later were all try-ing to get possession of the Maltese Falcon the black statuette of a bird.

(8) August which is always a hot and humid month in Washington is likely to be even worse this year.

(9) Most of the time the man doing the actual steering on commercial ships is not an officer he is only an A. B.

(10) The *Solway* an expensive new ship was the first of the Marston Line to be taken over by the government.

(11) This peculiar property of small quantities of mercury expanding and contracting with temperature changes is the reason that it is used in thermometers.

(12) Men who do not wish to join the group insurance plan should turn in blank cards; the others who are evidently satisfied with it should fill in every detail.

(13) Motorists intending to enter the city on 182 were advised to detour on old Route 76 which crossed Heather Creek two miles north.

(14) Under the circumstances Professor Sears we may be able to grant you a year's leave of absence.

(15) He was playing or rather attempting to play "Home in Tennessee" on his brother's old clarinet.

EXERCISE 8. Remembering that *nonrestrictive* elements are set off from other parts of the sentence with commas and that *restrictive* elements are not, indicate which of the following sentences are correctly punctuated.

(1) Children being treated at the clinic were carefully examined for signs of diphtheria.

(2) Most of the crew, being dissatisfied with conditions on the ship refused to sign for a second cruise.

(3) Girls, working near the drills and presses, received very strict orders against wearing loose-fitting clothing.

(4) Carter could not, under the circumstances even hint that he had already read the telegram on her desk.

(5) The designs and patterns which had been most popular in the cities, did not sell at all well in the rural districts.

(6) Binghampton, the largest city in the area involved, was hard hit by the floods.

(7) On Christmas which came on Friday that year, there was a record-breaking snow.

(8) Animals, which hibernate during the winter, are usually good fur-bearers.

(9) Radium, which is the world's most valuable commodity, has been found in the Urals in fair quantities by Soviet prospectors.

(10) Trenton the capital of the state, was the nearest place at which one could obtain comfortable hotel accommodations.

(11) No one back in America, on the other hand, had any reliable way of knowing that the news was not correct.

(12) Our policy is, as you know to submit bids even though we know that there is little chance of their being accepted.

(13) Train Number 22 having been delayed by the wreck at High Falls, arrived in Spokane two hours late.

(14) The proprietor of the Green Dragon, having been convicted of negligence, was sentenced to a workhouse term.

(15) His right arm which had been crushed in the train wreck was amputated at the city hospital.

40. SEPARATING ITEMS IN A SERIES

40a. Three or more words, phrases, or clauses forming a co-ordinate series are separated by commas.

(1) He talked fluently, wittily, penetratingly.

(2) He is honest, he is courageous, but he is wrong.

(3) There is not a more mean, stupid, dastardly, pitiful, selfish, spiteful, envious, ungrateful animal than the Public. It is the greatest of cowards, for it is afraid of itself.

—WILLIAM HAZLITT

Informal practice permits the omission of the comma before the *and*, unless it is required for clarity.

I'll have roast beef, potatoes and salad.

A comma before the last item in a series, however, is sometimes necessary.

Our resort is equipped with comfortable cabins, a large lake with boating facilities and a nine-hole golf course. (A lake with a nine-hole golf course!)

I am interested in a modern, furnished apartment with two bedrooms, kitchenette, living room, bathroom with shower, and garage.

Adjectives in a series are co-ordinate and are separated by commas if each may be thought of as modifying the noun separately.

(1) You are a *greedy, thoughtless, insensitive* prig.

Commas are not used if each adjective in the series modifies the whole concept which follows it.

(2) The boys are planning an *exciting holiday canoe* trip.

384

In Sentence (1) each adjective has a kind of independence from the others; they could be rearranged in the sentence without seriously affecting the sense of what is being said—*thoughtless, insensitive, greedy* prig; *insensitive, greedy, thoughtless* prig. Moreover, the conjunction *and* could be inserted in place of the first two commas and the basic meaning would remain—*greedy* and *thoughtless* and *insensitive* prig. But in Sentence (2) the adjectives have an interdependent relationship. Their order cannot be changed, none of them can be deleted, nor can *and* be substituted, without making hash of the original meaning—*canoe holiday exciting* trip; *holiday exciting canoe* trip; *exciting* and *holiday* and *canoe* trip. The adjectives in Sentence (2) may be thought of as making a *restrictive* phrase, as distinct from the *nonrestrictive* quality of the adjectives in Sentence (1), and therefore are not separated from one another by commas.

It must be said, however, that actual usage in punctuating coordinate adjectives varies a great deal. Though few writers would punctuate Sentences (1) and (2) above other than we have, many of them would be unable to choose between the punctuation of Sentences (3) and (4) below.

(3) He presented the ambassador with a *dirty, yellowed, gnarled* hand to shake.

(4) He presented the ambassador with a *dirty yellowed gnarled* hand to shake.

Some writers feel that the meaning differs slightly in each case: that Sentence (4) suggests a more unified image than Sentence (3). That is, they feel that in Sentence (4) the three adjectives partake of one another's qualities—*dirty-yellowed-gnarled* rather than *dirty and yellowed and gnarled*.

40b. Items in dates, addresses, and geographical names are set off by commas.

DATES   I was born on July 17, 1931, the day the municipal hospital burned down.

BUT   I was born in July 1931.

The military services and some other organizations now observe the practice of putting the day of the month before the name of the month, as 17 July 1931, 6 August 1950. If a writer follows this practice, he should remember *not* to put a comma after the day of the month.

ADDRESSES He gave 39 West 46th Street, Olean, New York, as his forwarding address.

GEOGRAPHICAL NAMES He pretended to make the grand tour in three months, but he spent a whole month at Bremen, Germany, and the rest of the time in Tunbridge Wells, Kent, a small village in England.

40c. When the items of a series contain commas, semicolons are used to separate the items.

The following people were present: John Smith, the doctor; Paul Brown, the dentist; and Elmer Wilson, the psychiatrist.

The bureaucracy consists of functionaries; the aristocracy, of idols; the democracy, of idolaters.

—G. B. SHAW

EXERCISE 10. Supply the appropriate punctuation marks in the sentences below:

(1) Among those I invited were the following: James Walley an author Harold Wilson a painter and Percival Derby a sculptor.

(2) The heading of the letter contained the following information: January 23 1950 266 East Longview Road Susanburg Alabama.

(3) The barn has an aluminum roof a concrete floor and steel window sash.

(4) He was terribly hungry; all he had eaten that day was a little potato salad cake with ice cream and bread and butter.

(5) I purchased some nails a small power saw with an electric motor and a flashlight.

(6) Taking the trip to Denver paying his income tax and saving a little left him with almost no ready cash for the rest of the month.

(7) The ship touched at Cape Town South Africa before going past Madagascar through the Indian Ocean and the Red Sea and through the Suez Canal.

(8) Her painting was dominated by three blue objects overhanging

386

what appeared to be a yawning forbidding perhaps bottom-
less chasm.

(9) The house has new copper piping Eckles plumbing fixtures
new redwood storm windows with copper screens and electrical outlets in many convenient places.

(10) According to this new authoritative American history text by
Professor Withers, Benedict Arnold at that time was a brave
efficient loyal officer.

(11) The men at the convention demonstrated their adherence to
the good old American way by snatching a hat from an aged
beggar woman shattering the peace by driving an old French
boxcar through the street filled with screaming noisy drunks
and by passing a resolution against movies in which actors
whom they termed subversive appeared.

(12) The Ellington chief of police reports that the town has no
North Ninth Street that there is no similar address on South
Ninth and that no one named Edmund Carpenter is known
there.

(13) This city in southern Yugoslavia has a mixed population of
Mohammedan Albanians Roman Catholic Italians and Orthodox Catholic Slavs.

(14) The adventurous playful Persian kitten had climbed up on the
table and knocked down a very expensive Dellani vase.

(15) Frantically twisting the wheel feeding as much gasoline as
possible despairingly hoping that the shoulder was firm Craven
swung the car sharply to the right.

41. SUPERFLUOUS COMMAS

Too many marks confuse a reader as much as too few; they clutter up a sentence and make communication difficult. The "comma-rash" is especially prevalent among untrained writers. The reader of the following sentence, for example, is constantly jarred by unnecessary punctuation:

> The people of this company, have, always, been aware, of the need, for products of better quality, and lower price.

Not one of the commas is necessary.

41a. A single or final adjective is not separated from its noun.

NOT   He was a discourteous, greedy, deceitful, boy.

BUT   He was a discourteous, greedy, deceitful boy.

41b. A subject is not separated from its verb unless there are intervening words requiring punctuation.

NOT   The worth of real estate, is determined by the demand for it.

BUT   The worth of real estate is determined by the demand for it.

OR   The worth of real estate, tangible property, is determined by the demand for it. (The commas set off an appositive.)

41c. A verb is not separated from its complement unless there are intervening words requiring punctuation.

NOT   After the meeting, Bob was, of the opinion that fraternities should be ruled off the campus.

BUT   After the meeting, Bob was of the opinion that fraternities should be ruled off the campus.

NOT   The boys always made Peanut, the butt of their pranks.

BUT   The boys always made Peanut the butt of their pranks.

OR   The boys always made Peanut, an undersized and immature smart aleck, the butt of their pranks.

41d. Two words or phrases joined by a co-ordinating conjunction are not separated.

NOT   He is very honest, and patient.

BUT   He is very honest and patient.

NOT   I decided to work during the summer, and relax in the fall.

BUT   I decided to work during the summer and relax in the fall.

41e. An introductory word, phrase, or short clause is not usually separated from the main body of the sentence.

NOT   On Wednesday, the ice in the river began to break up.

BUT   On Wednesday the ice in the river began to break up.

Occasionally, however, a comma must be inserted to prevent misreading. *See* Section 38d.

NOT   Notwithstanding *Drums at Dusk* is a worthy successor to *Black Thunder*.

BUT   Notwithstanding, *Drums at Dusk* is a worthy successor to *Black Thunder*.

41f. A restrictive modifier is not separated from the main body of the sentence. (*See* Section 38c.)

NOT   The girl, who slapped my face, also kicked my shins.

BUT   The girl who slapped my face also kicked my shins.

NOT   The band, in the park, played the same tired old marches we had heard, for fifteen years.

BUT   The band in the park played the same tired old marches we had heard for fifteen years.

41g. Indirect quotations and single words or short phrases in direct quotations are not set off with commas. (*See* Section 43g-l.)

CORRECT   After drinking ten bottles of pop Henry insisted he could drink ten more.

CORRECT   Claude said he was "weary of it all" and that he had "absorbed" his "fill of monotony."

EXERCISE 9. Eliminate any superfluous commas in the sentences below:

(1) Violins, viols, and harps, supply the melody during the second part of the sonata, and many critics, dubious about this procedure, are likely to object.

(2) What Tillotson did in meeting the same attack, was to advance his bishop to the queen's knight's file; he drew his game with Laforgue, the French champion, who was considered a stronger player.

(3) The *Dictionary of National Biography,* which is usually correct, agrees with Mendell in stating, that she was born in 1709.

(4) The wild, savage, nature of the terrain discouraged early explorers from going far into the LaFayle mountains, and the other ranges to the west.

(5) Men from McMaster's, Joyce's, and Kendrick's details were busy on the beach unloading parts of planes, and bringing ashore other supplies.

(6) Whatever Ewell bid, his wife was sure to look puzzled, and to re-examine her hand anxiously.

(7) Across the river, was a protected cove in which there were anchored, two yawls, two knockabouts, and some dinghys.

(8) The troops on Manet and New Hope Islands, were being supplied from Port Osburne, which was about seventy miles away, to the north across the bay.

(9) When this edition was printed, Secretary Harris had not yet fired Addison, and announced that Fraley would succeed him.

(10) Inspecting the meat and making sure that it comes up to specifications is the next step, according to the procedure of all major packers.

(11) Armstrong, holding the king, queen, and jack, unwisely tried to confuse his opponents, and conceal his strength by leading a low card.

(12) Two different British armies, the Americans, and several Free French companies, were united in the fighting in Tunisia, and in mop-up operations to the south.

(13) The meeting began late, because Blackburn did not know where the Regency Hotel was, or when he was to meet Caldwell there.

(14) Allenby's Ford, and his friend's old Chevrolet were parked

390

side by side in the lot in front of the new, cream-colored, Buick, which their supervisor had just bought.

(15) The pilot, having received the come-in signal, the plane circled about the field, in preparation for the landing.

(16) Infantile paralysis, and cancer, and some heart troubles still resist the efforts of research men, but hope runs high, that our century will see great advances in conquering these ailments.

(17) At that time, countries allied with Nazi Germany included, Finland, Hungary, and Rumania.

(18) A little calico kitten marked with black, yellow, and white, had been mewing on the back porch for over an hour, until she had relented, and had brought it in to feed it.

(19) The reports in both the *Sentinel* and the *State,* had distorted, what the secretary of the Chamber of Commerce had said about new industries in the city.

(20) The captain of the ship feared an unannounced inspection, and ordered the mates to be careful about the lifeboats, and the davit stanchions on which they hung.

(21) The punter, seeing that it was too late to kick, elected to run the ball, and to everyone's surprise, the Wildcats gained fifteen yards, and made their first down after all.

(22) In granting the decree, the judge was morally certain, that there had been collusion between husband and wife, but he did not press the matter.

(23) The sturdy, old, oak timbers of the little bridge withstood the force of the flood, until every one had been rescued from the island.

(24) The policy offered by the Midwest General Insurance Company, offers the same guarantees, and insures against wind damage also.

(25) Melton, Shoemaker, and Parmelee, made up the rest of the regular staff that year, and Terry was justified in being confident, that his pitching would hold up.

(26) Robbins decided that he could take the night job, and still take courses in chemistry, math, and English, in the mornings.

(27) The ice near the southern bank was too thin, soft, and cracked, to support the child's weight, when he tried skating all the way across the river.

42. DIRECTING ATTENTION TO
FINAL APPOSITIVES OR SUMMARIES

42a. Short final appositives or summaries are usually set off by dashes.*

(1) He had only one pleasure—eating.

(2) These are the two culprits—Joe Green and Miller Berg.

(3) Each person is born to one possession which overvalues all his others—his last breath.   —MARK TWAIN

(4) So I leave it with all of you: Which came out of the opened door—the lady or the tiger?   —FRANK STOCKTON

42b. Long or formal appositives or summaries are usually set off by colons. (See Section 37d.)

(1) Out of these things, and many more, is woven the warp and woof of my childhood memory: the dappled sunlight on the great lawns of Chowderhead, our summer estate at Newport, the bitter-sweet fragrance of stranded eels at low tide, the alcoholic breath of a clubman wafted on the breeze from Bailey's Beach.

      —S. J. PERELMAN, *Keep It Crisp*

(2) Men hang out signs indicative of their respective trades: shoemakers hang out a gigantic shoe; jewelers, a monster watch; and the dentist hangs out a gold tooth; but up in the mountains of New Hampshire, God Almighty has hung out a sign to show that there He makes men.

      —DANIEL WEBSTER

* A few writers prefer the comma to the dash:

The human species, according to the best theory I can form of it, is composed of two distinct races, the men who borrow, and the men who lend.

      —CHARLES LAMB

The use of the dash, however, would appear to make the writer's intention more immediately clear.

(3) I had three chairs in my house: one for solitude, two for friendship, three for society.

—HENRY DAVID THOREAU

(4) Humanity has but three great enemies: fever, famine and war; of these by far the greatest, by far the most terrible, is fever.

—SIR WILLIAM OSLER

(5) The great secret, Eliza, is not having bad manners or good manners or any other particular sort of manners, but having the same manner for all human souls: in short, behaving as if you were in Heaven, where there are no third-class carriages, and one soul is as good as another.

—G. B. SHAW

EXERCISE 11. Supply the appropriate punctuation marks in the sentences below. If a choice of marks is possible, explain why you chose the one you did.

(1) He had absolutely no virtues at all he would lie, cheat, or steal at the slightest opportunity.

(2) Of all the things I dislike, this is first studying.

(3) He came out of the war an old man his health impaired, his nerves shot.

(4) He is a fine teacher good-humored, clever, incisive.

(5) There isn't any point in losing your temper you look foolish and you frighten nobody.

(6) Why are you looking so downcast bad news?

(7) These are the marks that give the most difficulty commas, semicolons, and colons.

(8) There is only one teacher who can get any work out of him Mr. Benson.

(9) Do you know how fast he was going when he hit the curve near Atkinson's eighty miles an hour!

(10) He was not without honor in his own country people there referred to him as an elder statesman.

(11) His whole life seems wrapped up in one activity baseball.

(12) Professor Wahlstrom told Harry that only one thing would give him a passing grade in the course a miracle.

EXERCISE 12. Supply the correct internal punctuation in each of the sentences below. If a choice of marks is possible, indicate the reasons for your choices. Eliminate any superfluous punctuation.

(1) You may write the examination, in pencil if you wish.

(2) Outside the dog scratched on the door.

(3) No I have never seen him but I have talked to him, by telephone many times.

(4) Jud went hiking Marty saw a movie and Lou stayed home to nurse his cold.

(5) The names of the students and their fraternities are as follows John Miller Chi Psi Patrick O'Brien Sigma Nu Peter Cudworth Delta Tau Delta and Ramsden McCosky Phi Gamma Delta.

(6) Wendell was last seen walking perilously close to the edge of the dam that was thirty-six hours ago.

(7) You can insult him if you wish however I suggest you do so at a distance.

(8) His attitude is childish he expects his instructors to give him a magical shortcut to education.

(9) Bob Mark our plumber who can bend iron pipe in his bare hands recited Shakespeare as he fixed our leaky faucet.

(10) King Charles walked and talked a half hour after his head was cut off.

(11) No hotel restaurant dining room or kitchen shall be used, as a sleeping or dressing room by an employee.

(12) This is merely the cost it does not include any mark up.

(13) The comma splice is the least of my worries I think I have it under control now.

(14) To a football player I am one myself a student rally is an embarrassing event.

(15) The short story was only a pot boiler estimated life one month.

(16) The shipping department reported a lag period of ten weeks in its work and more and more orders were coming in.

(17) Dormitory regulations stated that each girl had to be in by eleven o'clock otherwise her privileges were restricted for the next week.

(18) The regulations say that this grant is available only to persons with a senior standing under the circumstances your request must be refused.

(19) There was a good deal of sympathy for the rebels in the eastern sections of the provinces and many volunteers joined their hastily formed armies.

(20) Having played in the backfield for two years with the Eagles Garner was surprised to find himself considered as a lineman.

(21) Answering the series of questions asked him by the defense attorney Robbins said angrily he was sure of the identification.

(22) From underneath the beams seemed to have been weakened a good deal when the charred wood was scraped away.

(23) As the miners continued panning and sluicing the claim seemed to become richer and richer.

(24) Cigarets which had cork tips became unexpectedly popular at that time among many smokers.

(25) The crew of the *Eldorado* to be sure deserves as much praise as any other crew that took part in the battle.

(26) The governor refused to everyone's surprise and bewilderment to sign the bill after the senate passed it.

(27) The element uranium which is now very important in atomic processes is found in parts of the Belgian Congo.

(28) Professor Loganberry has a bachelor's degree from Amherst a master's from Chicago and a Ph.D. from Michigan.

(29) The Indians held their lead despite injuries to key pitchers and infielders the suspension of their leading hitter and a long series of tiring doubleheaders.

(30) Henry Welch, a brisk, efficient, salesman was put in charge, of the new area, and company officials were quite optimistic.

43. PUNCTUATION OF QUOTED MATERIAL

The chief purpose of quotation marks and brackets is to indicate a change in speakers, usually from the writer himself to someone he is quoting.

> I had gone to the bathroom for a shower, the time he [Elliot Vereker] invited me to his lady's house, when he stalked into the room. "Get out of that tub, you common housebreaker," he said, "or I shall summon the police!" I laughed, of course, and went on bathing. I was rubbing myself with a towel when the police arrived—he had sent for them!
>
> —JAMES THURBER, "Something to Say" *

The quotation marks serve to separate the remarks of Vereker from the descriptive narrative of Thurber, who is telling the story. The brackets permit us, the authors of this handbook, to tell you directly that the antecedent of "he" is Elliot Vereker. In short, punctuation devices in this passage show that there are three different speakers: Vereker, Thurber, ourselves.

Double quotation marks enclose a direct quotation; single quotation marks enclose a quotation within a quotation. In addition, quotation marks are used to set off titles *not* published separately, and occasionally to identify words being used in special ways.

43a. Double quotation marks are used to enclose a direct quotation whether from a written or spoken source.

> DIRECT   He said, "Don't dive from that rock."
> INDIRECT   He said not to dive from that rock.

43b. Single quotation marks are used to enclose a quotation within a quotation.

* First published in *The New Yorker*.

She turned and said, "Remember Grandfather's advice, 'When other people run, you walk.' "

Note that a sentence within single quotation marks is not end-punctuated when it ends the complete quotation. The omission is sensible; the conjunction of several punctuation marks (.'.") would be awkward.

43c. If the quoted material consists of several paragraphs, quotation marks are placed at the beginning of each paragraph and at the end of the final paragraph.

"She [Dorothy Thompson] isn't fussy about clothes. She usually wears suits of excellent quality and cut, although she brightens them up with red hats and high-heeled shoes. She likes a lot of blouses, too, and appears to have an uncommonly varied collection of fur coats.

"Sometimes she is too busy to buy things for herself, and then her two secretaries are expected to shop for her. But there are periods—possibly when affairs pall—which find her in Bergdorf-Goodman's, buying energetically and extravagantly. The sprees are usually succeeded by spells of household economy, general retrenchment, and penitent visits to less extravagant shops.

"She is probably closer to her fellow women at those times than at any other. And yet, her appearance on the radio program 'Information, Please' is remembered for another example of kinship; she fell down on a question about the signers of an old treaty, but tore into the question about bits of verse dealing with a kiss and got four out of five. It seemed unexpected, somehow, in a lady with six honorary college degrees."

—CHARLES FISHER, "Dorothy Thompson,
Cosmic Force," in *The Columnists*

Ordinarily, however, long quotations are not enclosed in quotation marks but are single-spaced and indented.

> To maintain his standing Carroll was obligated to accept Benton's challenge. Jackson accompanied him to the field. The affair that followed provided Tennessee with a standing jest for many years. Benton fired, and, in a fit of panic, doubled up at the waist so that the most conspicuous part of his person exposed was that covered by the seat of his trousers. Into this target

Lieutenant-Colonel Carroll plumped a bullet which
did far more injury to the spirit than to the flesh.
—MARQUIS JAMES, *The Life of Andrew Jackson*

43d. Titles published as part of a larger work are set off in quotation marks. (See "Italics," Section 44a.)

The distinction between the use of quotation marks and italics to
set off titles is observed by careful writers.

(1) "Preparing the Manuscript" is a chapter in *Report Writing,* a
text for engineers.

(2) "The Easy Chair" is a section of informal literary review appearing in *Harper's.*

(3) "Wintergreen for President" is a song from the play *Of Thee I
Sing.*

43e. Words used in special senses or for special purposes are sometimes set off by quotation marks.

(1) He referred to me as a "briarhopper."

(2) Is this what you call "functional" architecture?

The use of quotation marks for such purposes is often unnecessary.
In the examples above, the quotation marks might be omitted without affecting the intention of the sentence. (*See* 43x (2) below.)

43x. Faulty use of quotation marks.

(1) The use of quotation marks instead of italics to set off titles
of books, magazines, and newspapers is sometimes found in very informal writing and in newspaper usage. In most writing this practice
has no real advantage: a writer saves no time, for italics are as easy
to make as quotation marks. Moreover, the distinction between
italics and quotation marks serves as a useful and accurate short-
hand in bibliographical notations. (See "Library Paper," Section
48.)

(2) The use of quotation marks to set off slang and words used in
special senses is often unnecessary. (See 43e, above.) In the sentence

He told me that my writing was full of "deadwood"; that it read like
the work of a "stuffed-shirt."

the quotation marks should be omitted if they are intended as an apology for the use of slang. But if they are meant as the sign of a direct quotation, they should be retained.

(3) Quotation marks should not be used with indirect quotations. (*See* Section 42g.)

BRACKETS

43f. Brackets are used to set off editorial remarks in quoted material.

Editors often find it necessary to insert explanatory comment in statements they are quoting. If these explanations are enclosed in brackets, the reader knows at once that it is the editor who is speaking, not the original author.

> John Dryden, a famous English poet, said, "Those who accuse him [Shakespeare] to have wanted knowledge, give him the greater commendation; he was naturally learned."
>
> The favorite phrase of their [English] law is "a custom whereof the memory of man runneth not back to the contrary."
>
> —RALPH WALDO EMERSON

In bibliographical notation, brackets are used to enclose the names of writers reputed to be the author of the work in question. For an illustration of this practice, see line 5 on page 404.

To indicate that a grammatical or spelling mistake or peculiarity is the work of the original author, or perhaps a misprint, the editor uses the word *sic* ("thus it is") in brackets.

> The high school paper reported, "The students spoke most respectively [*sic*] of Mrs. Higginbottom."

OTHER PUNCTUATION MARKS WITH QUOTATIONS

43g. The comma and the period are always placed within quotation marks.

> "There is no use in working," he complained, "when it only makes me more sleepy than usual."

This rule may sometimes seem illogical, but it nonetheless describes general practice.

> According to Shakespeare, the poet writes in a "fine frenzy."

43h. The colon and the semicolon are always placed outside the quotation marks.

> According to Shakespeare, the poet writes in a "fine frenzy"; by "fine frenzy" he meant a combination of energy, enthusiasm, imagination, plus a certain madness.

43i. The dash, question mark, and exclamation point are placed within the quotation marks when they apply only to the quotation; outside the quotation marks when they apply to the whole statement.

> (1) He said, "Will I see you tomorrow?"
>
> (2) Didn't he say, "I'll see you tomorrow"?
>
> (3) "You may have the car tonight"—then he caught himself abruptly and said, "No, you can't have it; I need it myself."

Note that a mark which applies to both the quotation and the sentence is not used twice.

> Has he ever asked, "May I come in?"

43j. The punctuation of the explanatory words (HE SAID, or their equivalent) that precede a quotation depends on the length and formality of the quotation.

NO PUNCTUATION	He yelled "Stop!" and grabbed the wheel.
PUNCTUATION WITH A COMMA	The old man said very quietly, "Under no circumstances will I tell you where my money is hidden."
PUNCTUATION WITH A COLON	The speaker rose to his feet and began:
	"The party in power has betrayed us. It has not only failed to keep its election promises but has sold out to the moneyed powers."

43k. **When a sentence begins with a quotation, a comma is used to separate it from the explanatory words** (HE SAID, **or their equivalent**) **that follow unless a question mark or exclamation point takes the place of the comma.**

(1) "The man is dead," he said with finality.

(2) "Is the man dead?" he asked.

(3) "Oh, no!" he screamed hysterically. "My brother can't be dead!"

43l. **When a quotation is divided by explanatory words** (HE SAID, **or their equivalent**) **the first part of the quotation is followed by a comma. The punctuation which follows the explanatory words is determined by the rules for punctuating clauses and phrases.**

(1) "I am not unaware," he said, "of the dangers of iceboat racing."

(2) "I have always worked hard," he declared. "I was peddling newspapers when I was eight years old."

(3) "John has great capacities," the foreman said; "he has energy, brains, and personality."

EXERCISE 13. Supply the appropriate punctuation in each of the sentences below:

(1) He declared that if I proofread my themes my grades would probably be C's instead of E's.

(2) Have you read the chapter on Common Women in Philip Wylie's Generation of Vipers? he asked.

(3) He said, I was walking slowly down the street when John stopped me and said, Do you know your house is burning down?

(4) Fix the picture in your mind, sir, Charles was always saying. Here's Jackson, a fine figure of a man, the first of the heavies to get up on his toes, faster than Louis and every bit the puncher. And here in front of him is solid Frank, a great rock of a man who's taken everything the black man had to offer and had him on the verge of a kayo in the early rounds. They're locked for a moment in a furious clinch. Jackson, who's made a remarkable recovery, a miraculous recovery, sir, breaks away and nails old Frank with a right that travels just this far—Charles demonstrated, reaching over the bar and rapping me sharply on the side of the jaw—just that far.

—BUDD SHULBERG, *The Harder They Fall*

(5) He said, When you asked me, Where did you get that crew-cut? I thought you were poking fun at me.

(6) Andrews never agrees with me, Professor Tapley commented; he subscribes entirely to the McCartney theory of inflation.

(7) The notice said curtly, We regret to inform you that your services are no longer needed by the Elliott-Robbins company.

(8) Are you entirely sure of the identification of this man as your brother? the chief of police said.

(9) McAndrews had also written in his test paper the sentence: It is doubtful if General Forrest ever said, Git thar fustest with the mostest.

(10) The chairman asked, Do we need a formal vote on Martin's suggestion? If so, does any one care to put it in the form of a motion?

(11) The Passing of Arthur is one of the last poems in Tennyson's series *The Idylls of the King*.

(12) The Cubs are much improved this year, said the new manager, and I am sure we will give the other teams quite a battle.

(13) The mayor said, I have every confidence in Commissioner Sellers and have no intention of asking for his resignation.

(14) The historian said, President Hoover's exact words about the prohibition amendment were, This is an experiment noble in motive.

(15) Lasswell contributed a chapter, Dynamic Socialism, to the collection called *Political Thought of Our Times*.

(16) Whatever happens to you and wherever you go, Esmond told his friend, remember that you are always welcome at our house.

(17) His secretary asked Howells, Wasn't that number Klondike 3-1981, not Klondike 2-1981?

(18) The song Who's Afraid of the Big Bad Wolf was taken from a Disney movie *Three Little Pigs*.

(19) We find the defendant guilty as charged, the foreman of the jury said clearly, but we recommend clemency.

(20) The F.B.I. asked, Have you any reason to suspect the loyalty of this man?

44-47. WORD PUNCTUATION

The purpose of italics, capitals, apostrophes, and hyphens is to identify words which have a special use or a particular grammatical function in a sentence.

> Our two-week reading program, assigned in Wednesday's class, is Shakespeare's *King Lear*.

Here the italics (underlining) set off the two words *King Lear* as a single title. The capitals identify *Wednesday, Shakespeare, King,* and *Lear* as proper names. The apostrophes indicate that *Shakespeare* and *Wednesday* are singular possessives and not plurals. The hyphen between *two* and *week* makes the two words function as a single adjective before *reading.* Such conventional practice helps us communicate more quickly.

44. ITALICS

Strictly speaking, italics are type faces that slope upward toward the right. In typed or handwritten manuscript, however, they are designated by underlining.

> on the printed page: *italics*
> on typewritten copy: italics
> in handwritten copy: *italics*

Three centuries ago printers italicized words much as they pleased. They set off important words and phrases in italics and sometimes used italics in place of quotation marks:

> The *Gravity* and *Piety* of their looks, are of great Service to these *American* Christians: It makes strangers that come amongst them,

give Credit to their Words. And it is a Proverb with those that know them, *Whosoever believes a* New-England Saint, *shall be sure to be Cheated: And he that knows how to deal with their Traders, may Deal with the Devil and fear no Craft.*
—[NED WARD], *A Trip to New England,* 1699

Now, however, the use of italics is carefully distinguished from that of capitals and quotation marks.

44a. Titles of books, newspapers, magazines, and all publications issued separately are italicized.

"Issued separately" means published alone as a single work and not as an article or story in a magazine, nor as a chapter or section of a book. (For the proper punctuation of such titles, see "Quotation Marks," Section 43d.)

the *Reader's Digest*   the New York *World-Telegram*
Desire under the Elms   *Webster's New Collegiate Dictionary*
The Winning of Barbara Worth

Special care must be taken not to add *The* to titles unless it belongs there properly.

NOT   *The Saturday Evening Post*
BUT   the *Saturday Evening Post*
NOT   the *Red Badge of Courage*
BUT   *The Red Badge of Courage*

44b. Names of ships, aircraft, and works of art are italicized.
the *Titanic*   H.M.S. *Queen Mary*   the *Spirit of St. Louis*
the *Sistine Madonna*

44c. Letters, words, and numbers used as words are italicized.
(1) Your *r's* look very much like your *n's.*
(2) Eliminate the *ain't's* and *git's* from your speech.
(3) I can't tell your *7's* from your *1's.*

44d. Foreign words and phrases not yet Anglicized (i.e., not yet accepted into the English language) are italicized.
(1) The Communists made a *coup d'état* in Roumania.

(2) He made a great deal of money very quickly and is now a member of the *nouveau riche.*

Occasionally, as above, a writer finds that a foreign word or phrase expresses his meaning more aptly or concisely than an English one. If he is sure that his readers understand the expression, he may use it, setting it off in his sentences by italicizing it. But the constant use of such words is pedantry. Most foreign words whose meaning cannot be duplicated precisely in native English have been Anglicized and therefore need not be italicized. The following words, for example, are no longer aliens and do not require italics:

> bourgeois   milieu   menu   liqueur

To determine whether a word has been Anglicized, the writer should consult a good dictionary. See "Dictionary," Section 29. *Webster's New Collegiate* identifies words requiring italics by the sign ||; the *American College Dictionary* labels such words as *French, Spanish,* and so on. The following is a partial list of words which require italics:

> *ibid.   raison d'être   sang-froid   op. cit.   sine qua non*
> *i.e. (id est)*

44e. A word in a direct quotation is italicized to show that the speaker wishes to give it a special stress.

(1) "It was a *perfect* day," she said.

(2) "You are *so* right," she remarked.

A writer frequently italicizes a word to show that he is using it in a special context or wishes to give it special emphasis.

> I heard him say once that in a democracy (a *democracy,* mind you) a division of opinion cannot be permitted to exist.

The use of italics for such purposes is not always justifiable. See "Unnecessary Italics," Section 44x.

44x. Unnecessary italics.

Italicizing words to emphasize their importance is one of the marks of a schoolgirl style. A writer who resorts to such mechanical devices is usually not writing very well in the first place. The examples below suggest that the writer is pretending to be more profound than his vocabulary permits.

(1) Any good education must be *liberal*.

(2) America is a *true* democracy, in every sense of the word.

(3) This book has what I call *real* depth of meaning.

EXERCISE 14. Italicize as necessary in the sentences below:

(1) The Cocktail Party, a play by T. S. Eliot, was a tremendous success on Broadway.

(2) The letters w and a in the neon sign are broken.

(3) During the war he served on the U.S.S. Missouri.

(4) The pronunciation of the verb envelop is different from that of the noun envelope.

(5) The airplane the Spirit of St. Louis is now in the Smithsonian Institute, Washington, D. C.

(6) Your novel The Children of the West has surprised us by its sales.

(7) The American Literary Review, the critical periodical published at Denby University, has entirely dropped such scholarly tags as op. cit., loc. cit., passim, etc.

(8) There was no justification, according to the statistics in the World Almanac and those in the Department of Agriculture Yearbook, for Senator Cope's comments on wheat imports.

(9) The word italics now suggests the country of Italy only to a few students of philology interested in word origins.

(10) It is characteristic of midwestern speech not to pronounce the g in the ing ending.

45. CAPITALS

Modern writers capitalize less frequently than did older writers, and informal writing permits less capitalization than formal writing. Two hundred years ago, a famous author wrote:

> Being ruined by the Inconstancy and Unkindness of a Lover, I hope a true and plain Relation of my Misfortune may be of Use and Warning to Credulous Maids, never to put much Trust in deceitful Men.
>
> —JONATHAN SWIFT, "The Story of the Injured Lady"

A modern writer would eliminate all capitals but the initial *B* and the pronoun *I*.*

45a. The first word of a sentence and the first word of a line of poetry are capitalized.

(1) Education is concerned not with knowledge but the meaning of knowledge.

(2) True ease in writing comes from art, not chance,
As those move easiest who have learned to dance.

—ALEXANDER POPE, *Essay on Criticism*

---

* The practice of capitalizing nouns persisted long after Swift. The Nineteenth Century poet Byron wrote

> Near this spot are deposited the remains of one who possessed Beauty without Vanity, Strength without Insolence, Courage without Ferocity, and all the Virtues of Man without his Vices. This Praise, which would be meaningless Flattery if inscribed over human ashes, is but a just tribute to the Memory of Boatswain, a Dog.

Some modern humorous or satiric writers sometimes capitalize nouns as a way of personifying abstractions and pointing up irony:

> "Well," she said hesitatingly, "the idea is to reduce all employees to a Curve."
>
> —STEPHEN LEACOCK, *Frenzied Fiction*

407

Some modern poets ignore this latter convention, perhaps in the belief that an initial capital letter gives a word an unwanted emphasis.

> a man who had fallen among thieves
> lay by the roadside on his back
> dressed in fifteenthrate ideas
> wearing a round jeer for a hat
>   —e.e. cummings, "a man who had fallen among thieves"

45b. The pronoun I and the interjection O are capitalized.

Unless it is the first word of a sentence, *oh* is not capitalized.

45c. Proper nouns, their derivatives and abbreviations, and common nouns used as proper nouns are capitalized.

(1) *Specific persons, races, nationalities:*

William	Bob	George A. Smith	Negro
Oriental	American	Mongolian	Cuban
Canadian	English		

(2) *Specific places:*

Dallas	Jamestown	California	Lake Erie
Newfoundland	Iran	Jerusalem	

(3) *Specific organizations, historical events and documents:*

Daughters of the American Revolution	the French Revolution
the Locarno Pact W.C.T.U.	

(4) *Days of the week, months, holidays:*

Thursday	April	Christmas	Sunday	**Thanksgiving**

(5) *Religious terms with sacred significance:*

the Virgin	God	Heavenly Father	the Saviour

(6) *Titles of books, magazines, newspapers, journals, articles, poems:* the first word and all others except unimportant prepositions and articles are capitalized. (See also "Italics" and "Quotation Marks.")

Gone with the Wind   *The Country Wife*   *Pippa Passes*
Paradise Lost   *Much Ado about Nothing*
Journal of Higher Education   *Atlantic Monthly*

(7) *Titles, when they precede a proper noun:* Such titles are an essential part of the name and are regularly capitalized.

Professor Wilson   Mr. Gottschalk
Dr. James Spence   Judge Paul Perry
President Eisenhower   Secretary Hawkins

When titles *follow* a name, they are not capitalized unless they indicate high distinction:

Robert F. Jones, president of the National Bank
J. R. Derby, professor of English

BUT

Dwight Eisenhower, President of the United States
Robert Jackson, Associate Justice, United States Supreme Court

"High distinction" is, however, becoming more and more broadly interpreted. Some people write

Robert F. Jones, President of the National Bank
J. R. Derby, Professor of English

This practice is at variance with the trend toward less capitalization, but is perhaps explained by (1) a writer's desire to seem polite, and (2) copying the style of capitalization used in the inside address of formal letters, as

Robert F. Jones
President of the National Bank
West Third Avenue
Kokoma Hills, Georgia

(8) *Common nouns used as an essential part of a proper noun:* These are distinct from "titles," being generic names (street, river, avenue, lake, county, ocean, college, etc.).

Vine Street   Fifth Avenue   Pacific Ocean   Lake Huron
General Motors Corporation   New York Central Railroad
Hamilton College   Mississippi River

409

When the generic term is used in the plural, it is not usually capitalized.

> Vine and Mulberry streets   Hamilton and Lake counties
> the Atlantic and Pacific oceans

Informal practice sometimes omits the capital in the generic term of proper nouns.

> Fifth avenue   Vine street   Mississippi river
> Franklin county   New York Central railroad

Newspaper style permits

> Vine-st   Fifth-av   James-rd   Montrose-blvd

However, this practice is merely a device to save ink and newsprint.

45x. Unnecessary capitals.

Most inexperienced writers use too many capitals. A good general rule is not to capitalize unless a specific convention warrants it.

(1) North, east, south, west *are capitalized only when they come at the beginning of a sentence or refer to specific geographical locations:*

> Birds fly south in the winter
> BUT
> She lives in the western part of the Old South.

(2) *Names of the seasons are not capitalized:*

> fall   autumn   winter   midwinter
> spring   summer

(3) *A noun indicating relationship is not capitalized when it is used without a proper noun and is preceded by a possessive:*

> I wrote to my father.
> BUT
> I wrote Father.

> My uncle has ten children.
> BUT
> My Uncle Ben has ten children.

410

(4) *Common nouns and adjectives used in place of proper nouns and adjectives are ordinarily not capitalized.*

I went to high school in Cleveland.

BUT

I went to John Adams High School in Cleveland.

I left for Chicago by railroad.

BUT

I left for Chicago by the New York Central Railroad.

I am a university graduate.

BUT

I am a Columbia University graduate.

I took a psychology course in my senior year.

BUT

I took Psychology 653 in my senior year.

Proper nouns and adjectives, such as English, French, Spanish, are always capitalized.

I took a French course in night school.

AND

I took French 63 in college.

EXERCISE 15. Capitalize as necessary in the following sentences. Remove unnecessary capitals.

(1) thousands of university students look forward to the christmas holidays; so do their professors.

(2) on a columbia album of records called *i can hear it now* you can hear the actual voices of franklin roosevelt, lou gehrig, arthur godfrey, neville chamberlain, and many other prominent people.

(3) william simpson spent the summer writing a book of poetry which he intends to call *a saddle for pegasus.*

(4) much of the southern area of texas is devoted to the raising of hereford cattle.

(5) the chairmanship of the security council of the u.n. changes each month.

(6) After leaving the Suburbs of detroit, we turned North toward

Mackinac island for our Summer vacation with my uncle Jim and aunt Sarah.

(7) The reverend James Oakley, the Minister of the Third Reformed church, was hurt slightly in the accident at Elm avenue and fourth street.

(8) The Doctor told Nurse Praley that she should wait perhaps fifteen minutes before taking Mrs. Connors down to the Delivery room.

(9) That Winter the Department offered mathematics I, a course in Mathematics designed for students with poor High School preparation.

(10) Dr. Samuels, the Chemist who has just left whityby college to teach here at this University, has done research work on the inert gaseous elements like Neon, Freon, and Argon.

46. APOSTROPHE

46a. An apostrophe is used to show the possessive case of nouns and indefinite pronouns.

(1) *If the word (either singular or plural) does not end in* s, *the apostrophe and* s *are added.*

the woman's book	the women's books
the child's book	the children's books
the man's book	the men's books
someone's book	anybody's book
another's book	

(2) *If the singular ends in* s, *the apostrophe and* s *are added unless the second* s *makes pronunciation difficult; in such cases, only the apostrophe is added:*

Lois's book   James's book

BUT

Moses' leadership   Sophocles' dramas

(The addition of a second *s* would change the pronunciation of *Moses* to *Moseses* and *Sophocles* to *Sophocleses*.)

(3) *If the plural ends in* s, *only the apostrophe is added:*

the girls' books   the boys' books
the Smiths' books (referring to at least two persons named Smith)

(4) *In compounds, the possessive form is taken by the last word only:*

father-in-law's book (*singular possessive*)
mothers-in-law's books (*plural possessive*)
someone else's book

(5) *In nouns of joint possession, the possessive form is taken by the last noun only; in nouns of individual possession, by both nouns.*

> John and Paul's book (*joint possession*)
> John's and Paul's books (*individual possession*)

The following list demonstrates standard spelling forms:

SINGULAR	PLURAL
child	children
man	men
lady	ladies
father-in-law	fathers-in-law
passer-by	passers-by

POSSESSIVE SINGULAR	POSSESSIVE PLURAL
child's	children's
man's	men's

POSSESSIVE SINGULAR	POSSESSIVE PLURAL
lady's	ladies'
father-in-law's	fathers-in-law's
passer-by's	passers-by's

46b. An apostrophe is used to indicate the omission of a letter or number.

> doesn't   can't   won't   o'clock
> the blizzard of '89

In reproducing speech, writers frequently use an apostrophe to show that a word is given a loose or colloquial pronunciation.

> "An' one o' the boys is goin' t' be sick," he said.

A too-frequent use of the apostrophe for such purposes, however, clutters up a page and annoys the reader.

46c. An apostrophe and s are used to form the plurals of letters, numbers, and words used as words. (Such words are also italicized.)

(1) Cross your *t*'s and dot your *i*'s.
(2) Count to 10,000 by *2*'s.
(3) Tighten your sentence structure by eliminating unnecessary *and*'s.

46x. Faulty use of the apostrophe.

The personal pronouns *his, hers, its, ours, yours, theirs,* and the pronoun *whose* are possessives as they stand and do not require the apostrophe. Because the apostrophe is the sign of the possessive in most words, the tendency to use it with the personal pronouns must be guarded against.

THE POSSESSIVES	*and*	THE CONTRACTIONS	
its		it's	(it is)
your		you're	(you are)
their		they're	(they are)
whose		who's	(who is)

EXERCISE 16. Insert apostrophes as necessary in the sentences below:

(1) Its true that Robert Thomas car was found shortly after it was stolen, but its fenders were smashed and its tires were missing.

(2) The presidents secretary has ordered a three-weeks supply of carbon paper.

(3) Womens fashions change every year—to everyones satisfaction but their husbands.

(4) After working with this company for a years time, you are given a two weeks vacation with pay.

(5) This book is Hans, whose collection of dime novels numbers over a thousand items.

(6) On the wall is a picture of Jesus Last Supper.

(7) Tex McCready, Associated Studios leading western actor, was a childrens and juveniles favorite during the 30s; his income wasnt far from a hundred thousand dollars a year.

(8) Dr. Daniels wouldnt have spent his whole years leave trying to establish the Ellins Brothers theory if he hadnt been convinced of its validity.

(9) Its too bad that the city of Newbridge cant keep its streets in the condition of those of the wealthier suburbs like Glen Ridge.

(10) The Stevenses arent at home this month; theyre visiting their relatives in Florida and wont be back until Christmas.

47. HYPHEN

The hyphen has two distinct uses: (1) to indicate compound words, and (2) to divide a word between the end of one line and the beginning of the next. Proper use of the hyphen for (2), commonly called "syllabication," is arbitrarily fixed. See "Syllabication," Section 11. The proper use of the hyphen for compounding words, on the other hand, is continually changing as the language grows and words become associated in new combinations.

47a. A hyphen is used to compound words not yet accepted as one word.

The spelling of compound words which express a single idea is in a state of continual transition. Originally spelled as two separate words, then as hyphenated words, they finally are combined into a single word.

> base ball *became* base-ball *became* baseball
> post man *became* post-man *became* postman

The proper spelling of a compound at the moment a writer wishes to use it cannot always be arbitrarily determined. Even the best and most recent dictionaries tend to be too conservative in the matter; they hyphenate many compounds which in actual practice are written as one word. In the absence of more authoritative reference, however, the dictionary must suffice.

47b. A hyphen is used to join two or more words serving as a single adjective before a noun.

Such an adjective following the noun, however, is not hyphenated.

> a well-known speaker   BUT   The speaker was well known.
> a well-bred child   BUT   The child is well bred.

a grayish-green coat	BUT	The coat was grayish green.
a never-to-be-forgotten moment	BUT	The moment was never to be forgotten.

The hyphen is generally omitted when the first word is an adverb ending in *ly*.

a slow-curving ball	BUT	a slowly curving ball
a quick-moving runner	BUT	a quickly moving runner

47c. A hyphen is used to avoid an ambiguous or awkward union of letters.

NOT	reenter	BUT	re-enter
NOT	preeminence	BUT	pre-eminence
NOT	readdress	BUT	re-address
NOT	preelection	BUT	pre-election

In printed copy, the dieresis mark (..) is often used in place of the hyphen.

reënter	reäddress
preëminence	preëlection

In words having great currency, the hyphen (or dieresis) is sometimes omitted.

coeducational   coöperation   zoölogy

47d. A hyphen is used to compound numbers from twenty-one through ninety-nine, and to separate the numerator from the denominator in written fractions.

twenty-nine   fifty-five   two-thirds   four-fifths

47e. A hyphen is used with the prefixes SELF, ALL, EX, and the suffix ELECT.

self-important   all-Conference   ex-mayor
governor-elect

The prefix *ex-* and the suffix *-elect* are not capitalized, even when used in titles that are essential parts of a name.

ex-Mayor Kelley   Governor-elect Jones   ex-President Hoover

417

EXERCISE 17. Insert hyphens as needed:

(1) Change this ten dollar bill into ten dollar bills.

(2) The ¾ inch cable is anchored to a 500 ton concrete pier.

(3) The editor in chief owns a well designed house.

(4) The tousle headed child poured a whole bottle of ink on our new nine by twelve rug.

(5) The secretary elect likes to think of himself as a self made man.

(6) Mr. Collins's assistant, a competent although self effacing man named Downes, is in charge of the reinventory of the Woods estate assets.

(7) A three way contract permitted the exmayor to operate a fly by night cigar store chain while engaged in his regular employment.

(8) There were suggestions that the enlisted men's tight fitting dark blue uniforms be modified.

(9) Harold was able to get a part time job with the antihedonism program of the Third Avenue church.

(10) My father in law participated in the hundred meter relay, over thirty division; his team went as far as the semifinals.

EXERCISE 18. Supply the necessary italics, capitals, apostrophes, and hyphens in the sentences below:

(1) The book review section of the new york times is the bible of liberal american readers.

(2) its tail wagging, the little beagle saw its dinner disappear down the throat of the snarling cheshire cat.

(3) george lyman kittredge professor of english at harvard university for many years, was a world renowned scholar.

(4) it isnt the cough that carries you off its the coffin they carry you off in.

(5) its a well known fact that baseball players, old timers as well as fresh faced rookies, are the most remarkably successful penny pinchers in professional sport.

EXERCISE 19. Correct the punctuation in the following sentences.

(1) Garland's Novel, called Main-travelled Roads, one of the Realistic novels of the latter part of the Nineteenth century,

focussed attention on the sordidness of the average farmer's existence.

(2) The Desk Sergeant, T. A. Wheeler, ordered detective Carpenter and patrolman Winters to make a thorough Investigation into the explosion in the cellar of the *Cranmore Country Club.*

(3) The Kintners achieved an *odd* effect by planting American Beauty Roses against a background of Ramblers along the fence.

(4) Nickels' next two books, seven hundred page Romantic novels, were'nt reviewed favorably, but they turned out to be popular as clubwomens' choices.

(5) Ex Mayor Williams *request* that the Council *improve* conditions in the childrens' playgrounds has'nt received *any* action as yet.

(6) Those in the crowd who's ancestors had come from Norway cheered when the Norwegian flag's were unfurled at the King's and Queen's reception in New York.

(7) The half dead seaman from the Serapis' first request wasnt about himself; instead he asked what'd happened to his brothers boat.

(8) That dog of Mr. Jones' keeps it's tail between it's legs most of the time.

(9) The sailor on the bow's appearance was *statuesque.*

(10) *WSGD's* chief television actor that year was Martin Sims, a handsome blond haired singer who hadnt had previous network experience.

(11) Mrs. Barry'es many colored calico kitten was awarded it's first blue ribbon as the *Cleveland Cat Club's* best of show.

(12) Morris fourteen year old sister, to his familys suppressed delight, was beginning to ridicule his and his friends choice of neckties.

(13) The four cylinder sixty horsepower car wasnt able to pull Jones custom built limousine out of the ditch.

(14) The Dividends from the supposedly-worthless Flatrock mining company stock were a *real* help to Mrs. Fredericks after the sudden death of her Husband.

(15) According to the arrangement made by the committee of the Dean's, the Spring Semester would have started that year on Lincoln's birthday, officially a Holiday in the State.

PUNCTUATION REVIEW EXERCISE. Supply all the necessary punctuation in each of the sentences below:

(1) Dobbs hand contained only two sevens and two fives and he wasnt confident when he called Bowers ten chip raise

(2) Is not a patron my lord one who looks with unconcern on a man struggling for life in the water and when he has reached ground encumbers him with help

—SAMUEL JOHNSON

(3) I like any woman who enjoys a bath insist upon a soap that smells pleasant.

(4) His favorite writers are Sinclair Lewis Willa Cather T. S. Eliot and Eugene O'Neill.

(5) His favorite writers are contemporary ones Sinclair Lewis Willa Cather T. S. Eliot and Eugene O'Neill.

(6) His favorite writers Sinclair Lewis Willa Cather T. S. Eliot and Eugene O'Neill are contemporary ones.

(7) His favorite writers Sinclair Lewis and Willa Cather novelists T. S. Eliot poet and Eugene O'Neill playwright are contemporary ones.

(8) The first to recover his senses after the explosion he rushed to call an ambulance.

(9) The speaker of the evening began his address Ladies and gentlemen we meet here this evening. . . .

(10) Harper's Magazine and the Atlantic Monthly which observe high standards of usage are widely read.

(11) I am sorry replied Robert I did not mean to be rude.

(12) His faults are these an uncontrollable temper inexperience in dealing with people and their problems and indifference to his work.

(13) His faults are an uncontrollable temper inexperience and indifference to his work.

(14) The tree having been hopelessly damaged we decided to cut it down.

(15) He then introduced Thomas Bryce Ph. D. as the speaker of the evening.

(16) Although seventy per cent of our english vocabulary comes from the Latin and Greek most of the words in our everyday speech are short vigorous Anglo-Saxon words.

(17) John wanted a Ford Jean a Chrysler Bob a Buick Henry a custom made English car.

(18) Arizona where the sun shines every day is healthful as a matter of fact any place where the sun shines every day is healthful.

(19) If siege is spelled ie why is seize spelled ei asked Tommy. Because replied his sister seize is one of the exceptions to the rule.

(20) The republicans in the senate attacked the secretary of state their object being to embarrass the presidents advisers.

(21) The town is not progressive most of the energetic ambitious young people leave it as soon as they finish high school.

(22) Designed as a basic text for sophomores in a university Fundamentals of Physics by John Carr of Duke university provides a sound background for advanced study.

(23) Mr. Adams who enjoys good conversation dislikes Mrs. Knight whose talk is merely gossip.

(24) He is a man who enjoys good conversation and he dislikes women whose talk is merely gossip.

(25) All of our clothes which were left outside were stolen.

(26) The speaker was faced with a difficult task he had to persuade a skeptical antagonistic audience to a new point of view.

(27) Imagine what would happen in this crowded auditorium said the speaker if someone should shout fire.

(28) Effective writing has one prerequisite which is inescapable the writer must have something to say.

(29) The mutiny having been quelled and the mutineers being all in irons the passengers began to breathe easily.

(30) Mother decided that she a friend and I would go to the beach for a short vacation.

(31) I believe that Parrington Hall University of Washington Seattle 5 Washington is his correct address.

(32) The statement that was issued early in the morning was later confirmed by the same announcer.

(33) The members are willing to support any candidate but Mr. Scott who now holds the office.

(34) My son John seems too tall for submarine duty however my

421

only nephew Philip Ames has been accepted and he is even taller than John.

(35) In his advice to freshmen Dean Carlson made the statement that the trouble with students who stay up half the night studying is that usually theyre either too exhausted the next day to go to class or too sleepy to be much good if they do go

(36) The storm having passed our party climbed into two waiting cars and drove on.

(37) The audience had been assembled for an hour and was growing more and more restless but still the speaker did not appear.

(38) Outside the house looked rather dilapidated within it was very cozy and comfortable.

(39) The first thing we notice is that our thought moves with such incredible rapidity that it is almost impossible to arrest any specimen of it long enough to have a look at it.

(40) We have found that most students in the dormitory do their work satisfactorily very few fail to pass their tests.

(41) If the weight of a medium-sized man were to stand for that of the sun then the weights of most other stars would lie between those of a large man and a ten-year-old boy.

(42) This tree is remarkable for its airy widespread tropical appearance which suggests a region of palms rather than of cool resiny pine trees.

(43) Larry Brown my former roommate had gone home for the holidays Leo Lamb whose home I had often visited was ill and every other student whom I had known seemed to be busy whenever I called.

(44) Dick and Andy changed their clothes put on heavy shoes and brought spades and rakes from the basement then they prepared the soil for planting corn.

(45) For want of airplanes MacArthur was forced to a bitter decision make the enemy pay for what it gets.

(46) I do not think that Harry will be on time for this concert for he is almost always late when we meet downtown.

(47) We started out with every desirable condition for our hunting trip the weather was cool our dogs were well trained and our huntsmen were excellent.

(48) Please Alice don't stare at people like that they will think you

are very rude her mother said to little Alice who thought watching people was great fun.

(49) Many people do not know where their daily milk supply comes from whether cotton grows on a tree a bush or a vine or from what products their cereals plastics and linens are made.

(50) It is not a simple task to plan daily meals which are nutritionally valuable attractive as well as palatable reasonable in their demands on time and energy and respectful of the food budget.

(51) I found this the hardest question in the whole test What is the difference between wit and humor?

(52) This phrase from The Great Lover one of the poems in our textbook puzzles most students The inenarrable godhead of delight.

(53) It isn't the way the words are strung together that makes Lincoln's Gettysburg speech immortal it is the feelings that were in the man who made it.

(54) It is more than likely that the student who has imagination and who is able to synthesize facts will some day be the employer of the student who does little except repeat what he reads or what he is told.

(55) The boll-weevil the cotton growers' greatest enemy had devastated the cotton crop heavy rains had ruined the wheat which needs dry weather when the grain is forming.

REVIEW EXERCISE. Supply all the necessary punctuation in the passages below:

(1) the best books are not read even by those who are called good readers what does our concord culture amount to there is in this town with a very few exceptions no taste for the best or for very good books even in english literature whose words all can read and spell even the college bred and so called liberally educated men here and elsewhere have really little or no acquaintance with the english classics and as for the recorded wisdom of mankind the ancient classics and bibles which are accessible to all who will know of them there are the feeblest efforts anywhere made to become acquainted with them i know a woodchopper of middle age who takes a french paper not for the news he says for he is above that

but to keep himself in practice he being a canadian by birth and when i ask him what he considers the best thing he can do in this world he says besides this to keep up and add to his english this is about as much as the college bred generally do or aspire to do and they take an english paper for the purpose one who has just come from reading perhaps one of the best english books will find how many with whom he can converse about it or suppose he comes from reading a greek or latin classic in the original whose praises are familiar even to the so called illiterate he will find nobody at all to speak to but must keep silence about it

—HENRY DAVID THOREAU, "Reading"

(2) everybody knows that einstein has done something astonishing but very few people know exactly what he has done it is generally recognized that he has revolutionized our conception of the physical world but his new conceptions are wrapped up in mathematical technicalities it is true that there are innumerable popular accounts of the theory of relativity but they generally cease to be intelligible just at the point where they begin to say something important the authors are hardly to be blamed for this many of the new ideas can be expressed in non mathematical language but they are none the less difficult on that account what is demanded is a change in our imaginative picture of the world a picture which has been handed down from the remote perhaps pre human ancestors and has been learned by each one of us in early childhood a change in our imagination is always difficult especially when we are no longer young the same sort of change was demanded by copernicus when he taught that the earth is not stationary and the heavens do not revolve around it once a day to us now there is no difficulty in this idea because we learned it before our mental habits had become fixed einsteins ideas similarly will seem easy to a generation which has grown up with them but for our generation a certain effort of imaginative reconstruction is unavoidable

—BERTRAND RUSSELL, *The A B C of Relativity*

SECTION 48

The Library Paper

KNOWLEDGE IS OF TWO KINDS: WE KNOW A SUBJECT
OURSELVES, OR WE KNOW WHERE WE CAN FIND INFOR-
MATION UPON IT.

—SAMUEL JOHNSON

THE LIBRARY paper is an exercise. In learning how to write
it, the student must go through procedures intended to establish habits. Such discipline is a means to an end, not an end in
itself. The end desired is a respect for accuracy and authenticity,
sciousness of the difference between what one has ac-
rough reading and research, and what one contributes
1 the form of fact, opinion, or synthesis.

THE USE OF THE LIBRARY

uninitiated a large library seems a mysterious place, and
s a rather forbidding lot. Neither impression is correct.
ems mysterious is really very logical and orderly, and what
1 unnecessary firmness in librarians is generally an admin-
essential. The enormous task of acquiring, arranging, and
out books and periodicals requires a system which must be
held to if disorder is not to result. A library is organized and
d so that all its material may be made most useful to the
number of people. All the regulations of a good library are
meant to serve this purpose.

A library has three principal kinds of holdings: (1) a general
collection of books; (2) a collection of reference works; (3) a col-

lection of periodicals (newspapers and magazines), bulletins, and pamphlets.

General collection of books

This is the classification which includes most of the books in a library—all those which are available for general circulation. In small libraries these books are usually placed on open shelves and are available to all who have library privileges. In large libraries, however, these books are kept in stacks, access to which is denied to all except librarians, graduate students, faculty, and persons holding special permits. A person wishing to borrow books from such libraries must first present a call slip, bearing the call number of the book he wants, the name of its author and its title. This information he must obtain from the *card catalog.*

Card catalog. This catalog is an alphabetical index of all the books in the library. For most books there are at least three cards, the first called the *author card,* the second the *title card,* the third the *subject card.* (Title cards are not used when the title begins with words as common as "History of. . . .") Here is a specimen *author card,* filed according to the surname of the author.

820.903

        Wilson, John Harold, 1900–
           The court wits of the Restoration, an introduction. Princeton, Princeton Univ. Press, 1948.

           vi, 264 p. ports. 23 cm.
           Bibliography : p. ₍218₎–222.

           1. English literature—Early modern (to 1700)—Hist. & crit. 2. English wit and humor—Hist. & crit.   I. Title.

        PR437.W54   820.903   48—4835*
        Library of Congress   ₍49q7₎

---

(1) "820.903" gives us the *call number* of the book.

(2) "Wilson, John Harold, 1900—" gives us the name of the au-

thor, the date of his birth, and tells us that he was still living
at the time this card was printed.

(3) "The court wits . . . 1948" gives us the full title of the book,
the place of publication, the name of the publisher, and the
date of publication. (Note that library practice in capitalizing
differs from general practice.)

(4) "vi, 264 p. ports. 23 cm." tells us that the book contains 6
introductory pages numbered in Roman numerals and 264
pages numbered in Arabic numerals; that portraits appear in
the book; and that the book is 23 centimeters high. (An inch
is 2.54 centimeters.)

(5) "Bibliography: p. [218]-222." tells us that the book contains
a bibliography which begins on page 218 and ends on page
222. The brackets around *218* tell us that the page is not
actually numbered but appears between numbered pages 217
and 219.

(6) "1. English Literature . . . I. Title." tells us that the book is
also listed in the card catalog under two subject headings—
(1) English Literature, and (2) English Wit and Humor
—and under one title heading, "Court wits of the Restora-
tion. . . ." We note that the subject heading "English Literature" has the subdivision "Early modern (to 1700)" and that
this latter heading has the subdivision "Hist. & crit.," the
heading under which the first subject card may be found. The
second subject card will be found under a division of "English
wit and humor" called "Hist. & crit." The Arabic numerals are
used to indicate subject headings; the Roman numeral ("I.
Title.") is used to indicate a title heading.

(7) "PR437.W54" is the Library of Congress call number.

(8) "820.903" is the Dewey system call number of the card.

(9) "48-4835*" is the order number used by librarians when they
wish to order the card.

(10) "Library of Congress" tells us that a copy of the book is
housed in, and has been catalogued by, the Library of Congress.

(11) "[49q⁷]" is a printer's key to the card.

A *title card* is simply a copy of the author card, with the title
typed just above the author's name. The *title card* is filed in the card
catalog according to the first important word in the title.

A *subject card* is also a copy of the author card with the subject typed just above the author's name; it is filed in the catalog accordingly. The cards filed under a subject provide a list of references on that subject. Consequently, a student making a preliminary bibliography on a subject should consult *subject cards* first of all.

Call numbers. American libraries generally follow one of two systems in classifying books: (1) the Dewey decimal system, or (2) the Library of Congress system. The *call number* of any book is determined by which of the two systems is followed.

The Dewey system, used by more libraries than any other, divides books by numbers into ten classes:

000-099	General Works
100-199	Philosophy
200-299	Religion
300-399	Social Sciences
400-499	Philology
500-599	Pure Science
600-699	Useful Arts
700-799	Fine Arts
800-899	Literature
900-999	History

Each of these divisions is further divided into ten parts, as:

800	General Literature
810	American Literature
820	English Literature
830	German Literature
840	French Literature
850	Italian Literature
860	Spanish Literature
870	Latin Literature
880	Greek Literature
890	Minor Literatures

Each of these divisions is further divided, as:

821	English poetry
822	English drama
823	English fiction
824	English essays

825   English oratory
826   English letters
827   English satire
828   English miscellany
829   Anglo-Saxon

Further subdivisions are made by using decimals.

The Library of Congress classification system—used by large libraries—divides books by letters into the following classes:

A   General Works
B   Philosophy—Religion
C   History—Auxiliary Sciences
D   Foreign History and Topography
E-F   American History
G   Geography—Anthropology
H   Social Sciences
J   Political Science
K   Law
L   Education
M   Music
N   Fine Arts
P   Language & Literature
Q   Science
R   Medicine
S   Agriculture
T   Technology
U   Military Science
V   Naval Science
Z   Bibliography—Library science

Each of these sections is further divided by letters and numbers which show the specific call number of a book.

Reference books

These books will generally be found in the main reading room of a library. They are usually placed on open shelves and available to anyone who wishes to consult them. They may not, however, be removed from the reading room. A student who cannot find the reference book he wants should consult the reference librarian.

Among the most useful reference books are the following:

429

1. GENERAL ENCYCLOPEDIAS

Columbia Encyclopedia. 2nd ed. Ed. by William Bridgwater and Elizabeth J. Sherwood. New York: Columbia University Press, 1950.

Encyclopedia Americana. New York: Americana Corporation, 1948. 30 vols.

Encyclopaedia Britannica. 14th ed. New York: Encyclopaedia Britannica, Inc., Dec., 1929. 24 vols.

New International Encyclopedia. 2nd ed. New York: Dodd, Mead and Company, 1914-16. 24 vols. Plate revision, 1922. Supplements, 1925, 1930.

2. DICTIONARIES, WORD BOOKS

Dictionary of American English on Historical Principles. Ed. by Sir W. A. Craigie and J. R. Hulbert. Chicago: The University of Chicago Press, 1936-44. 4 vols.

Fowler, Henry W. *Dictionary of Modern English Usage.* New York: Oxford University Press, 1944.

New Standard Dictionary. New York: Funk and Wagnalls Company, 1938.

Oxford English Dictionary. Ed. by A. H. Murray *et al.* Oxford: The Clarendon Press, 1888-1933. 10 vols. and supplement. Reissue, corrected, 1933. 12 vols. and supplement. The original issue is known as *New English Dictionary.*

Perrin, Porter G. *An Index to English.* rev. ed. Chicago: Scott, Foresman and Company, 1950.

Webster's Dictionary of Synonyms. Springfield, Massachusetts: G. & C. Merriam Company, 1942.

Webster's New International Dictionary. 2nd ed. Springfield, Massachusetts: G. & C. Merriam Company, 1934.

3. YEAR BOOKS

Britannica Book of the Year, 1938 to date. Chicago: Encyclopaedia Britannica, Inc., 1938—.

Facts on File. A weekly digest of world events. New York: Person's Index, Inc., 1940—.

New International Year Book, 1907 to date. New York: Dodd, Mead and Company, 1908-31; Funk and Wagnalls Company, 1932—.

Stateman's Year Book, 1864 to date. London: Macmillan and Co., 1864—.

World Almanac and Book of Facts, 1886 to date. New York: The New York World-Telegram, 1886—.

4. ATLASES

Commercial Atlas. Chicago: Rand, McNally and Company. Issued annually.

Cosmopolitan World Atlas. Chicago: Rand, McNally and Company, 1949.

Encyclopaedia Britannica World Atlas. New York: Encyclopaedia Britannica, Inc. Frequently revised.

Webster's Geographical Dictionary. Springfield, Massachusetts: G. and C. Merriam Company, 1949.

5. GENERAL BIOGRAPHY

Biography Index. New York: H. W. Wilson Company, 1946—.

Cattell, Jacques. *Directory of American Scholars.* Lancaster: The Science Press, 1951.

Cattell, Jacques. *American Men of Science.* 8th ed. Lancaster: The Science Press, 1949.

Current Biography: Who's News and Why. New York: H. W. Wilson Company. Published monthly with half-year and annual cumulations.

Dictionary of American Biography. Ed. by Allen Johnson and D. Malone. New York: Charles Scribner's Sons, 1928-37. 20 vols. and index. Supplement, 1944.

Dictionary of Canadian Biography. 2nd ed. Ed. by W. S. Wallace. Toronto: The Macmillan Company of Canada, 1945. 2 vols.

Dictionary of National Biography. Ed. by Leslie Stephen and Sidney Lee. London: Smith, Elder and Company; Oxford University Press, 1885-1937. 63 vols., supplements.

International Who's Who, 1936 to date. London: Europa Publications, 1936—.

Webster's Biographical Dictionary. Springfield, Massachusetts: G. & C. Merriam Company, 1943.

Who's Who, 1848 to date. London: A. & C. Black, 1849—.

Who's Who in America, 1899-1900 to date. Chicago: A. N. Marquis Company, 1899—.

6. BOOKS OF QUOTATIONS

Bartlett, John. *Familiar Quotations.* 12th ed. Ed. by Christopher Morley and Louella Everett. Boston: Little, Brown and Company, 1948.

Mencken, H. L. *A New Dictionary of Quotations on Historical Principles from Ancient and Modern Sources.* New York: Alfred A. Knopf, 1942.

Stevenson, Burton. *The Home Book of Quotations.* New York: Dodd, Mead and Company, 1934.

7. CLASSICAL LITERATURE, MYTHOLOGY

Cary, M. *et al. The Oxford Classical Dictionary.* Oxford: Clarendon Press, 1949.

Frazer, Sir James G. *The Golden Bough.* 3rd ed. London: Macmillan and Company, 1911-15. 12 vols. Supplement, 1936.

Hamilton, Edith. *Mythology.* Boston: Little, Brown and Company, 1942.

Harvey, Sir Paul. *Oxford Companion to Classical Literature.* 2nd ed. New York: Oxford University Press, 1925.

Sandys, John E. *Companion to Latin Studies.* 3rd ed. Cambridge: Cambridge University Press, 1925.

Whibley, Leonard. *Companion to Greek Studies.* 4th ed. Cambridge: Cambridge University Press, 1931.

8. MODERN LITERATURE

Cambridge Bibliography of English Literature. Ed. by F. W. Bateson. New York: Macmillan Company, 1941. 4 vols.

Literary History of the United States. Ed. R. E. Spiller, *et al.* New York: The Macmillan Company, 1949. 3 vols. Vol. 3 is bibliography. Reissued, 1953, first two volumes in one.

Cambridge History of English Literature. Ed. by A. W. Ward and A. R. Waller. Cambridge: Cambridge University Press, 1907-16. 14 vols. Index issued, 1927. Reissued, without bibliographies, 1933. 15 vols.

Hart, J. D. *Oxford Companion to American Literature.* 2nd ed. New York: Oxford University Press, 1948.

Harvey, Sir Paul. *Oxford Companion to English Literature*. 3rd
ed. Oxford: The Clarendon Press, 1946.

Kunitz, S. J., and Howard Haycraft. *American Authors,* 1600-
1900. New York: H. W. Wilson Company, 1938.

Kunitz, S. J., and Howard Haycraft. *British Authors of the Nineteenth Century*. New York: H. W. Wilson Company, 1936.

Kunitz, S. J., and Howard Haycraft. *Twentieth Century Authors*.
New York: H. W. Wilson Company, 1942.

Millett, Fred B. *Contemporary American Authors*. New York:
Harcourt, Brace and Company, 1944.

Millett, Fred B., John M. Manly, and Edith Rickert. *Contemporary British Literature*. 3rd ed. New York: Harcourt, Brace
and Company, 1935.

Parrington, V. L. *Main Currents in American Thought*. New
York: Harcourt, Brace and Company, 1927-30. Reissued,
1939, 1 vol.

9. HISTORY

Cambridge Ancient History. Ed. by J. B. Bury *et al*. Cambridge:
Cambridge University Press, 1923-39. 12 vols.

Cambridge Medieval History. Ed. by H. M. Gwatkin *et al*. Cambridge: Cambridge University Press, 1911-36. 8 vols.

Cambridge Modern History. Ed. by A. W. Ward *et al*. Cambridge: Cambridge University Press, 1902-26. 13 vols. and
atlas.

Dictionary of American History. Ed. by J. T. Adams. New York:
Charles Scribner's Sons, 1940. 5 vols. Vol. 6 (index), 1941.

Keller, Helen R. *The Dictionary of Dates*. New York: The Macmillan Company, 1934. 2 vols.

Langer, William L. *An Encyclopedia of World History*. Revised
ed. Boston: Houghton-Mifflin Company, 1948.

Schlesinger, Arthur M., and D. R. Fox, ed. *A History of American Life*. New York: The Macmillan Company, 1927-48. 13
vols.

10. MUSIC, PAINTING

Bryan, Michael. *Bryan's Dictionary of Painters and Engravers*.
Revised edition. London: George Bell and Sons, 1903-05. 5
vols.

Grove's Dictionary of Music and Musicians. Ed. by H. C. Colles. 3rd ed. London and New York: Macmillan, 1927-28. 5 vols. Supplement, 1940.

Reinach, Solomon. *Apollo: An Illustrated Manual of the History of Art throughout the Ages.* Tr. by F. Simmonds. Revised ed. New York: Charles Scribner's Sons, 1935.

Thompson, Oscar. *International Cyclopedia of Music and Musicians.* 3rd ed. New York: Dodd, Mead and Company, 1944.

11. PHILOSOPHY, RELIGION

Catholic Encyclopedia. New York: Catholic Encyclopedia Press, 1907-14. 16 vols. Supplement, 1922. Revised ed., 1936—.

Encyclopedia of Religion and Ethics. Ed. by James Hastings. New York: Charles Scribner's Sons, 1908-27. 12 vols. and index. Reissued, 1928. 7 vols.

Ferm, Vergilius. *Encyclopedia of Religion.* New York: Philosophical Library, 1945.

Jewish Encyclopedia. New York: Funk and Wagnalls Company, 1901-06. 12 vols. Reissued, 1925.

New Schaff-Herzog Encyclopedia of Religious Knowledge. Ed. by S. M. Jackson. New York: Funk and Wagnalls Company, 1908-12. 12 vols. and index.

12. SCIENCE, TECHNOLOGY

Hutchinson's Technical and Scientific Encyclopedia. Ed. by C. F. Tweney and I. P. Shirshov. New York: The Macmillan Company, 1936. 4 vols.

Van Nostrand's Chemical Annual, 1907 to date. New York: D. Van Nostrand Company, 1907—.

Van Nostrand's Scientific Encyclopedia. 2nd ed. New York: D. Van Nostrand Company, 1947.

Weld, Le Roy D. *Glossary of Physics.* New York: McGraw-Hill Book Company, 1937.

13. SOCIAL SCIENCES

Cyclopedia of Education. Ed. by Paul Monroe. New York: The Macmillan Company, 1925. 3 vols.

Encyclopedia of the Social Sciences. Ed. by E. R. A. Seligman and Alvin Johnson. New York: The Macmillan Company, 1930-35. 15 vols.

Fairchild, Henry P. *Dictionary of Sociology.* New York: Philosophical Library, 1944.

Munn, G. G. *Encyclopedia of Banking and Finance.* New York: Bankers Publishing Company, 1935. 2 vols. Reissued, 1 vol., 1937.

Warren, H. C. *Dictionary of Psychology.* Boston: Houghton Mifflin Company, 1934.

Periodicals, bulletins, pamphlets

A *periodical* is a publication that appears at regular (periodic) intervals. *Bulletins* and *pamphlets* may or may not be periodicals depending on whether they are issued as parts of a series of publications or as separate, single publications. They are usually kept in the stacks with the main collection of books. Recent issues of magazines and newspapers are usually kept in the open shelves of the reading room. Older issues are bound in volumes and shelved in the stacks.

Most libraries have a special index to periodicals. Sometimes this index is nothing more than a drawer in its proper alphabetical order in the main card catalog. Larger libraries, however, usually have a separate set of drawers marked *periodical catalog.* This catalog is the key to the whereabouts and call numbers of all the periodicals held by a library.

The periodical catalog, however, merely shows what periodicals are available. For an index to the material appearing in periodicals, a person must consult other guides and indexes. These latter are usually shelved in the reference room.

1. GENERAL INDEXES

Poole's Index to Periodical Literature, 1802-81, supplements through January 1, 1907. This is a subject index only; no author entries are given.

Reader's Guide to Periodical Literature, 1900 to date. This is published monthly; each year the accumulated issues are bound in volumes. The *Reader's Guide* gives entries under author, title, and subject.

International Index to Periodicals, 1907 to date. This index deals with more scholarly publications than the *Reader's Guide.* Although most of the periodicals it indexes are American, it also covers many foreign publications.

2. SPECIAL INDEXES. These indexes list articles published in periodicals devoted to special fields. A few also index books.

Agricultural Index, 1916 to date. This is a subject index, appearing nine times a year and cumulated annually.

The Art Index, 1929 to date. This is both an author and subject index.

Dramatic Index, 1909 to date. This index appears annually and indexes articles which relate to the drama, playwrights, plays, actors and actresses.

The Education Index, 1929 to date. This is both an author and subject index.

Engineering Index, 1884 to date. This is an author and subject index.

Experimental Station Record, 1889 to date. This is an index to and a digest of articles and other literature on agriculture.

Industrial Arts Index, 1913 to date. This is an author and subject index, published monthly with annual cumulations.

Index to Legal Periodicals, 1908 to date. This is an author and subject index, issued quarterly.

Quarterly Cumulative Index Medicus, 1927 to date. This is a continuation of the *Index Medicus,* 1899-1926. It indexes books as well as periodicals.

New York Times Index, 1913 to date. This is a monthly index of all the news stories appearing in the pages of the *New York Times.*

Public Affairs Information Service, 1915 to date. This is issued weekly, with bimonthly and yearly cumulations. It indexes literature relating to economics, politics, and sociology.

3. INDEXES TO BULLETINS AND PAMPHLETS

Boyd, Anne M. *United States Government Publications.* 2nd ed. New York: H. W. Wilson Company, 1941.

Vertical File Service Catalog: An Annotated Subject Catalog of Pamphlets, 1932-34. New York: H. W. Wilson Company, 1935. Supplements, 1935 to date.

United States Government Publications: Monthly Catalog, 1895 to date. Washington: Government Printing Office, 1895 to date.

EXERCISE 1. Draw a diagram of the reference room of your library, indicating the position of the following reference books and indexes:

(1) *Encyclopaedia Britannica*

(2) *Encyclopedia Americana*

(3) *Encyclopedia of Social Sciences*

(4) *Encyclopedia of Religion and Ethics*

(5) *Jewish Encyclopedia*

(6) *Dictionary of American History* (DAH)

(7) *Dictionary of National Biography* (DNB)

(8) *Dictionary of American Biography* (DAB)

(9) *Current Biography*

(10) *Twentieth Century Authors*

(11) *British Authors of Nineteenth Century*

(12) *American Authors, 1600-1900*

(13) *Who's Who*

(14) *Facts on File*

(15) *World Almanac*

(16) *New English Dictionary* (NED) sometimes referred to as *Oxford English Dictionary* (OED)

(17) *General Card Catalog*

(18) *Reader's Guide to Periodical Literature*

(19) *International Index*

(20) *New York Times Index*

(21) *Agricultural Index*

(22) *Education Index*

(23) *Industrial Arts Index*

(24) *Art Index*

(25) *Drama Index*

EXERCISE 2. Each of the following questions may be answered correctly by consulting one of the standard reference guides listed in Exercise 1:

(1) What occasions did the ancient Hebrews celebrate by dancing?

(2) Among which tribe of American Indians is the highest development of shamanism found?

(3) What was the minimum equipment of a typical "forty-niner"?

(4) When and how did the expression *lime-juicer* originate?

(5) How many articles on moving pictures in adult education are listed in the *Education Index* for 1941-1944?

(6) Where can you find listed a scholarly article on Greek geometry, written in 1942?

(7) Where can you find listed a 1945 article on the possibility of blending aralac (a synthetic fabric) with cotton?

(8) Where can you find listed articles on American stained glass, printed in 1940?

(9) What was the first invention of Peter Cooper, American inventor, manufacturer, and philanthropist (d. 1883)?

(10) What was the occupation of Frances Kyte, an Englishman (b. 1710)?

EXERCISE 3. Each of the following questions may be answered correctly by consulting one of the standard reference guides listed in Exercise 1:

(1) What is the Indo-Chinese version of the Old Testament story of the origin of the human race?

(2) Describe the color pattern of the bird called the Kentucky warbler.

(3) What special meaning of the word *peeler* developed in Ireland and England in the nineteenth century?

(4) Whom did President Eisenhower name in December 1952 as Navy Secretary in his new Cabinet?

(5) On what day in 1945 did the *New York Times* report the sinking of Carabobo Island?

(6) How many articles on Musicology are listed in the *Education Index* for 1935-1938?

(7) Where can one find listed an article on the magnetic properties of crystals, published in an English periodical in 1937?

(8) Where can one find listed a 1948 article on labeling plastic products?

(9) What was the connection of John Ledyard, an American explorer, with the British explorer Captain Cook?

(10) For what anonymous work was Marmaduke Tunstall, British naturalist (b. 1743), noted?

CHOOSING AND LIMITING A SUBJECT

Interest and curiosity are good guides to a choice of subject, but unless a student has nothing to do but write a library paper, a sense of proportion will help him preserve his health and sanity. Common sense will tell him that the following topics are of a kind impossible for him to cope with:

(1) A History of Medicine
(2) Modern Warfare
(3) The Great American Sport: Baseball
(4) The American Indian

He will therefore limit himself to a particular aspect of such general subjects—for example,

(1) How Harvey Discovered the Circulation of the Blood
(2) The Use of the Mortar in Hilly Terrain
(3) What Happened in the Black Sox Scandal
(4) The Organization of the Iroquois Confederacy

EXERCISE 4. Write a short research paper which answers one of the following questions. Use your own ingenuity to determine what the question means and the best way of going about answering it.

(1) Was John Altgeld right in pardoning the Haymarket rioters?
(2) Was Margaret O'Neill Eaton unjustly maligned?
(3) What part did Theodore Roosevelt really play in the Spanish-American war?
(4) Did Alfred really defeat the Danes?
(5) How competent a general was Benedict Arnold?
(6) Was Billy the Kid really a desperado?
(7) Why was Joan of Arc burned at the stake?
(8) Why did General Grant write his memoirs?
(9) What caused the Reichstag fire?
(10) How extensively did the early Algonquins engage in agriculture?
(11) Was John Fitch cheated?
(12) What differences are there between the poetic and historical accounts of Roland?

(13) What was Theodore Roosevelt's attitude toward spelling?

(14) Who was Martin Marprelate and what happened to him?

(15) Was Samuel Tilden a victim of crooked politics?

(16) Where did the American Indians come from?

(17) How was Lincoln's "Gettysburg Address" received by his contemporaries?

(18) Can a pitcher really curve a baseball?

(19) What happened in the Scopes trial?

(20) Why did Robert G. Ingersoll turn atheist?

(21) What are the present theories on the migratory instincts of birds?

(22) Was "Shoeless Joe" Jackson an unfortunate victim of circumstances?

(23) Who won the Battle of Hampton Roads?

(24) Was Stanton involved in Lincoln's death?

(25) What happened to the settlers on Roanoke Island?

(26) What was the Teapot Dome scandal?

(27) What geographical knowledge did the man of 300 A.D. have?

(28) Is the climate really growing warmer?

(29) Was Lincoln really a good lawyer?

(30) What are the plausible explanations for the statues on Easter Island?

(31) Is the human race really growing taller?

(32) Does the legend that Pocahontas saved John Smith's life square with the probable facts in the case?

(33) Why did Thoreau go to jail?

(34) Did Anne Boleyn deserve to have her head chopped off?

(35) Did Fulton really invent the steamboat?

(36) Did the Norsemen make voyages to America before Columbus?

(37) Were Sacco and Vanzetti convicted by circumstantial evidence?

(38) Who won the Battle of the Coral Sea?

(39) Did Edgar Allan Poe die intoxicated or insane?

(40) What are the reasons for the disappearance of the dinosaur?

BIBLIOGRAPHY

Actual research begins with the making of a preliminary bibliography, a list of source materials compiled from such works as the following:

(1) Subject cards in the main card catalog.

(2) Bibliographies at the end of pertinent articles in the various encyclopedias.

(3) *Reader's Guide to Periodical Literature.*

(4) The special periodical indexes which are applicable (*Engineering Index, Education Index,* etc.).

(5) *New York Times Index.*

If the research writer cannot find enough satisfactory references by following these steps, he must seek special aid. His instructor or the reference librarian will probably provide some help. The writer can also consult one of the following books, all of which provide detailed information on the use of reference books.

(1) Brown, Z. *The Library Key.* 7th ed. New York: H. W. Wilson Company, 1949.

(2) Hirshberg, H. S. *Subject Guide to Reference Books.* Chicago: American Library Association, 1942.

(3) Hutchens, Margaret, A. S. Johnson, M. S. Williams. *Guide to the Use of Libraries.* 5th ed. New York: H. W. Wilson Company, 1936.

(4) Mudge, I. G. *Guide to Reference Books.* 6th ed. Chicago: American Library Association, 1936. Supplements, 1939, 1941, 1944, 1947.

(5) Shores, Louis. *Basic Reference Books.* 2nd ed. Chicago: American Library Association, 1939.

If the number of books on the research writer's list is so great that he cannot possibly consult them all, he may be able to get information on their applicability to his subject by consulting one of the following:

(1) *Book Review Digest.* New York: H. W. Wilson Company, 1906 to date.

(2) *Technical Book Review Index*. Pittsburgh: Carnegie Library, 1917-1929. Continued by Special Libraries Association, New York, 1935 to date.

BIBLIOGRAPHY CARDS

While engaged in actual research, an experienced writer keeps his working bibliography on 3″ x 5″ cards, one card for each book, magazine article, or newspaper story. This practice is a convenience to the writer. He can carry his pack of cards easily in his pocket or purse; and he can work with individual cards more conveniently than he can with a long list on one or two pages.

The form of a bibliographical entry is not arbitrarily fixed: different instructors will have different requirements. But all of them agree in requiring complete and accurate information. The system followed here is suggestive only:

(1) *For a book with one author*	Allen, Hugh. The Story of the Airship. Akron, Ohio: Goodyear Tire and Rubber Company, 1942.
(2) *For a book with two or more authors*	Gaum, Carl G., Harold F. Graves, Lyne S. S. Hoffran. Report Writing. 3rd ed. New York: Prentice-Hall, Inc., 1950.
(3) *For an edited book*	Crane, R. S., ed. A Collection of English Poems. New York and London: Harper & Brothers, 1932.
(4) *For a book with an author and editor*	Swift, Jonathan. Gulliver's Travels. Ed. by Arthur E. Case. New York: The Ronald Press Company, 1938.
(5) *For a book of two or more volumes*	Morison, S. E., and H. S. Commager. The Growth of the American Republic. 3rd ed. New York: The Oxford University Press, 1942. 2 vols.
(6) *For an article in an encyclopedia*	"Airship." Encyclopaedia Britannica. (14th ed., 1949), I, 469 ff.

(7) *For a maga-* *zine article,* *author given*	Adelt, Leonhard. "Last Trip of The Hindenburg." Reader's Digest, XXXI (November, 1937), 69-72.
(8) *For a maga-* *zine article,* *no author* *given*	"Commander Rosendahl Pleads for U. S. Airship." Science Newsletter, XXXI (May 7, 1938), 301.
(9) *For a news-* *paper article*	"Solons in $34-billion Spending Agreement." Ohio State Journal, August 25, 1950, p. 3.
(10) *For a bulletin*	U. S. Government. Manual of Style. Revised ed. Washington: Government Printing Office, 1945.
(11) *For an un-* *published* *thesis or* *dissertation*	Rider, Maurice L. Advanced Composition for Students in Engineering at The Ohio State University, Evaluation and Proposals. Unpublished Doctoral Dissertation. Columbus, Ohio: The Ohio State University, 1950.

EXERCISE 5. Prepare a short bibliography (on cards) on one of
the following topics:

(1) Color Television

(2) Socialized Medicine

(3) The Erie Canal

(4) Subsidization of College Athletes

(5) The Generalship of U. S. Grant

(6) Prison Reform

(7) The Assassination of Lincoln

(8) The Early Career of Benito Mussolini

(9) The Rocket Ship and Interplanetary Travel

(10) The Shakespeare-Bacon Controversy

EXERCISE 6. Prepare a short working bibliography of one of the
following. Hand in a brief biographical sketch with your bibliography.

Charles Steinmetz   Isadora Duncan

Samuel Insull   Andrew Carnegie

Rudolph Valentino   Frank Lloyd Wright

Langston Hughes	David W. Griffith
James (Jim) Thorpe	George Herman Ruth
Sarah Bernhardt	Henry George
Charles Chaplin	Eugene Debs
George M. Cohan	Douglas Fairbanks, Sr.
Luther Burbank	Kathleen Norris
James Thurber	Thorstein Veblen

PRELIMINARY ORGANIZATION

A writer's choice of his research subject shows that he has been thinking about the subject and has decided, roughly at least, on a plan of attack. As he begins his reading in his source material, his plan will become more and more definite and eventually crystallize into an outline. This outline, which will be constantly revised as research progresses, may be no more than a set of directions for the writer himself to follow. The writer of the specimen research paper on pp. 453 to 477, for example, began with the following outline:

I. Describe preparations for landing of *Hindenburg* at Lakehurst.

II. Show what a relatively unimportant affair it was meant to be.

III. Insert remarks of radio announcer.

IV. Describe the crash.
   A. The number killed
   B. Those who escaped

V. Describe the effect of the crash on the country at large.
   A. See newspaper accounts.
   B. Look for pictures of the crash in pictorial magazines.

VI. Find out the cause of the crash.

VII. See whether the crash had any significance for future airship travel.

With a directive outline such as this, the writer was prepared to go about his research in an organized way.

NOTE-TAKING

Reading notes are best taken on 4″ x 6″ cards. They are more easily carried than a notebook and more easily referred to than full sheets of paper. In taking his notes, a careful research writer observes the same principles he did in writing out his bibliography cards; his notes are accurate and complete. Nothing is more wearisome and time-wasting than second and third trips to the library to get information that could have been obtained on the first trip.

(1) *A sample note card paraphrasing information.*

Hindenburg measurements and construction details

803 ft long. 36 longitudinal girders. 15 wire-braced traverse frames. Four 1,100 h.p. Mercedes-Benz diesel engines. Max. speed 84 mph. Accommodations for 50 passengers. 8,750-mile range.

"Airship," Ency. Brit., I, 471

---

(2) *A sample note card on which is entered a direct quotation. Care should be taken to indicate on the card what material is quoted. Otherwise a writer may forget which are his own words and use a borrowed statement as his own.*

Report of Herbert Laughlin, passenger

"There was very little confusion among the passengers, no screaming.... Nobody knew what was happening.... Everybody just curious."

N.Y. Times, May 7, '37, p 18

If extensive information is desired, one note card may not suffice. In such instances, the writer should carefully identify each card.

Safety of airship travel ①

"Once the masting technique had been worked out, the Graf Zeppelin and the Hindenburg, in the years 1930-36, made a record of regularity which no other vehicle of transportation has approached. They took off at times over the ocean for Europe when all other aircraft in the area was grounded, when the fog hid the entire top half of the ship, and

(continued)

Safety of airship travel, cont'd ②

the ship disappeared into the fog within a few seconds after the "Up Ship" signal was given. What few delays appeared on the record were due to waiting for connecting airplanes to arrive with the latest European mail for the Americas."

Allen, *The Story of the Airship*, p. 38.

FOOTNOTES

Footnotes have three main uses:

(1) To give information or commentary which, though related to the subject being discussed, would interrupt the flow of narrative or argument. Some writers use this kind of note skillfully

(for example, Van Wyck Brooks in *The Flowering of New England*), but there is much prejudice against it.

(2) To give additional evidence or illustration in support of an assertion. For example, if the writer argues that Theodore Roosevelt was essentially a conservative, his note will cite one or more other writers who also think so. This is known as the *See also* footnote, and is the vehicle for much pedantry and pretense. Readers rarely check on the "other writers."

(3) To give the source of a fact or quotation.

The third is the most important for the student. It is perhaps overemphasized in college work because it is needed as training in accuracy, authenticity, and honesty. Once the student has acquired discipline in these matters, many teachers will encourage him to avoid footnotes as much as possible. Fortunately, the tendency now is away from excessive footnoting, even in formal scholarship. If the specimen library paper printed in this section seems overloaded with notes, it is simply because the editors wish to demonstrate as many of the forms of footnoting as possible.

The rules for footnoting are complex. Most of them were evolved to meet the needs of formal, professional scholarship, the intention of which is to add to the fund of established knowledge. Though the student is chiefly concerned with adding to *his own* knowledge, he is expected to adopt the habits of the professional scholar. It is easier for him to do so now than formerly because many of the conflicts and divergences of the different systems of footnoting have been resolved by the Modern Language Association, whose pamphlet on the subject, *The MLA Style Sheet,* is a very useful guide to the student and teacher. It is available at the Association's offices for ten cents.*

Footnote form. Unless the teacher instructs the student otherwise, footnotes should be placed at the bottom of the page on which the reference occurs and numbered consecutively throughout the paper. In typewritten manuscript, notes should be single-spaced with double space between notes (see Specimen Paper, pp. 453 to 477). A footnote is indicated by placing a raised figure at the end of the

* Address: Treasurer, Modern Language Association, 100 Washington Square East, New York 3, N. Y.

statement to be documented. This raised figure is then repeated at the beginning of the footnote itself:

[1] Hugh Allen, The Story of the Airship (Akron, Ohio. 1942), p. 34.

The following list illustrates the form recommended by the Modern Language Association (*note that the description of an item in a footnote is different from that of an item in a bibliography or list of references*):

(1) *For a book with one author, first edition*

[1] Lionel Trilling, The Liberal Imagination (New York, 1950). p. 129.

(2) *For a book with one author, later edition*

[2] Gail Plummer, Syllabus for Effective Speech, Rev ed. (New York, 1952), p. 154.

(3) *For a book with two or more authors*

[3] C. G. Gaum, H F. Graves, and L. S S Hoffman, Report Writing, 3rd ed. (New York, 1950). p 71.

(4) *For an edited book*

[4] R. S. Crane, ed., A Collection of English Poems (New York, 1932), p. 156.

(5) *For a book with an author and an editor*

[5] William Shakespeare, "The Tragedy of King Lear," The Complete Works of William Shakespeare, ed. G L Kittredge (Boston, 1936), pp. 1203-1205.

(6) *For a book of two or more volumes*

[6] S. E. Morison and H. S. Commager, The Growth of the American Republic, 3rd ed. (New York, 1942), I, 347.

(7) *For a book article by one of several contributors*

[7] Cleanth Brooks, "A Plea to the Protestant Churches," in Who Owns America?, ed. by Herbert Agar (Cambridge, Mass , 1936), p 105.

(8) *For an article in an encyclopedia*

[8] "Airship," Encyclopaedia Britannica (14th ed., 1949). I, 470.

(9) *For a magazine article, author given*

[9]J. R. Aswell, "Flying Saucers New in Name Only," Reader's Digest, LXI (July, 1952), 7-9.

(10) *For a magazine article, no author given*

[10]"What Are These Things They Call Flying Saucers," Popular Science, CXLIX (August, 1951), 74-75.

(11) *For a newspaper article, author given*

[11] G. Milton Kelly, "Unfit Canadian Wheat Milled into U.S. Flour," The Seattle Daily Times, LXXVI (January 29, 1953), 1.

(12) *For a newspaper article, no author given*

[12]"Flying Saucers: Fact or Fancy," Columbus Citizen, LIV (August 10, 1952), 11.

(13) *For a bulletin*

[13]U.S. Government, Manual of Style (Rev ed., 1945), p 48.

(14) *For an unpublished thesis or dissertation*

[14]Maurice L. Rider, Advanced Composition for Students in Engineering at The Ohio State University, Evaluation and Proposals (Unpublished Ohio State University Doctoral Dissertation. 1950). pp 17-21

Abbreviations. Abbreviations used in documentation fall into two classes: (1) abbreviations of English words, most of which are clear to general readers and thus to be preferred; (2) abbreviations of Latin words, the use of which is frequently a sign of affectation.

anon.	anonymous
art., arts.	article(s)
ca.	*circa* (about)
cf.	*confer* (compare)
ch., chs.	chapter(s)
col., cols.	column(s)
diss.	dissertation
ed., eds., edn.	editor(s), edition
e.g.	*exempli gratia* (for example)
esp.	especially
et al.	*et alii* (and others)
f., ff.	the following page(s)

ibid.	*ibidem* (in the same place)
i.e.	*id est* (that is)
introd.	introduction
loc. cit.	*loco citato* (in the place cited)
MS, MSS	manuscript(s)
N.B.	*nota bene* (take notice, mark well)
n.d.	no date given
n.p.	no place given
numb.	numbered
op. cit.	*opere citato* (in the work cited)
p., pp.	page(s)
rev.	revised
trns.	translator, translated, translation
v.	*vide* (see)
vol., vols.	volume(s)

Of all these, only *ibid., loc. cit.,* and *op. cit.* are troublesome. *Ibid.* is used to refer to the title cited in the note immediately preceding:

[1] Hugh Allen, The Story of the Airship (Akron, Ohio, 1942), p. 34.

[2] Ibid., p. 38.

If the second note refers to exactly the same page as the first, only the entry *ibid.* is needed; otherwise the different page number must be given. The need for the term *ibid.*, however, is rapidly disappearing. Modern practice permits the use of an abbreviated title or the author's name in a second or succeeding note:

[2] Airship, p. 34

[2] Allen, p. 34

Similarly with *loc. cit.* and *op. cit.* It is easier and clearer generally to use the abbreviated title or the author's name. Technically *loc. cit.* means "in the same passage referred to in a recent note" and is never followed by a page number:

[1] Hugh Allen, The Story of the Airship (Akron, Ohio, 1942), p 34

[2] loc. cit.

or more clearly:

[2] Allen, p. 34.

The term *op. cit.* is properly used in citing a passage on a different page of a work recently noted. But, as the *MLA Style Sheet* points out, in such cases the author's name alone may suffice or his name and a short title be clearer:

[1]Hugh Allen, The Story of the Airship (Akron, Ohio, 1942), p 34.

[2]Allen, op. cit., p. 56.

or more simply:

[2]Allen, p. 56.

SPECIMEN LIBRARY PAPERS

SPECIMEN LIBRARY PAPER "A" AND CRITICAL COMMENT

Specimen A is not a perfect model, not an "A" paper. Though it has real merits, it violates several principles in the mechanics and presentation of research, some of which will be obvious. Other violations involve the author's treatment of source material. The student may ask why a paper not absolutely correct in all details was put before him. The answer is that the best way of discussing the problems of handling research materials is to show how an author actually failed to meet them successfully in his own paper. In matters such as this one may profit more by other people's failures than by their excellences.

The title page

This is an excellent title page; the necessary information is presented in a simple, well-balanced format. Note that the information (sometimes called the "endorsement") answers six basic questions about the library paper:

(1) *What* is it about?   (the title)
(2) *By whom* is it?   (the author)
(3) *For whom* is it?   (the instructor assigning it)
(4) *For what* is it?   (the course it was assigned in)
(5) *Where* was it written?   (the college or university)
(6) *When* was it written?   (the date)

It is of course not necessary that these items be arranged precisely as they are here; the instructor may give other directions. This title page simply presents an example of good standard practice.

LAST OF THE ZEPPELINS:

THE HINDENBURG

By

Susan Ann Sheldon

For

Professor Mark Roberts

English 401

THE OHIO STATE UNIVERSITY   October 7, 1950

Pages 1-3

The next three pages are meant to give the reader a quick summary of the whole library paper. You should note that all this prefatory material falls into three divisions: (1) *the title,* which is a very general statement; (2) *the statement of purpose,* which explains briefly what the paper attempts to do; and (3) *the outline,* which is a rather full statement of the contents of the paper.

(1) *The title.* The appearance of the title on this page is a necessity, and its position on the page is correct. But, as a moment's glance through the outline will show, the title is not appropriate. Nowhere in her outline or in her paper does Miss Sheldon identify the term *Zeppelin,* and she has no right to assume that her reader knows what it means. More seriously, the title is inaccurate. The *Hindenburg,* as Miss Sheldon's research must have informed her, was not the "last" Zeppelin. Both the American *Los Angeles* and the German *Graf Zeppelin I* were in existence before, during, and after the *Hindenburg's* crash. Further, the *Graf Zeppelin II,* sister ship of the *Hindenburg,* was completed after 1937 and not dismantled until after 1940. We can appreciate Miss Sheldon's desire for an eye-catching, dramatic title. But accuracy is more important. A better title would be, simply, "The Crash of the *Hindenburg.*"

(2) *The statement of purpose.* This statement serves to prepare the reader for the outline that follows, giving him an idea of what to expect. Note that Miss Sheldon's statement of purpose is an accurate one; she does what she says she is going to do.

(3) *The sentence outline.* The sentence outline serves a double purpose: as a kind of table of contents, and as a summary, or abstract, of the paper. In a longer paper, a regular table of contents giving page references, or perhaps a formal summary, would be necessary. In a paper as short as this, the sentence outline alone can well serve this double purpose.

Note that this outline is not a *directive* outline; it is meant primarily as a guide to the reader, not to the writer. The major headings (those indicated by Roman numerals) are the topic sentences, sometimes rephrased, of the paragraphs appearing in the library paper itself. The sub-divisions are statements which either support or follow from the topic sentence.

The outline has some weaknesses. "II. B.," for example, seems less significant than its position in the outline would indicate. And "IV. C." seems inconsistent with its main topic. "V. A." seems similarly inconsistent. Moreover, "VIII. A." and "B." are co-ordinate, not subordinate, to the topic "VIII."; they suggest a poorly developed paragraph. It will be interesting to see what relation they have to the paragraphs they describe.

THE LAST OF THE ZEPPELINS: <u>THE HINDENBURG</u>

<u>Statement of purpose</u>

      The purpose of this paper is to describe the crash of the dirigible <u>Hindenburg</u> at Lakehurst, N. J., and to comment briefly on the implications of that crash to the future of airship travel.

<u>Sentence outline</u>

I. It was expected that the landing of the <u>Hindenburg</u> at Lakehurst, N. J., on May 6, 1937, would be of minor interest only.

    A. The <u>Hindenburg</u> had been observing a regular schedule of flights between Frankfort and Lakehurst since the previous year.

    B. This particular flight was significant only because it inaugurated a new series of flights for 1937 and because Captain Ernst A. Lehmann, the airship authority, was aboard.

    C. The remarks of radio commentator Herbert Morrison would not go over the air directly but would be played for radio audiences later by electrical transcription.

II. The <u>Hindenburg</u> appeared over Lakehurst on schedule, shortly after 7:00 p.m.

    A. A fairly large crowd had gathered to see the landing of the world's largest dirigible.

    B. Morrison began to describe the landing in a calm voice.

III. The <u>Hindenburg</u> burst into flames at 7:25 p.m.

    A. The quarter-end of the ship suddenly took fire.

    B. As its front section nosed upward, the dirigible broke in two.

    C. The forward end of the ship then caught fire and the whole ship settled to the ground.

- 2 -

    D. The fire was over in exactly 32 seconds and only
        a smoking wreckage remained.

IV. In spite of the severity of the fire and the crash,
    some of the <u>Hindenburg's</u> crew and passengers escaped.

    A. Three members of the crew walked away from the
        wreckage, completely unharmed.

    B. An elderly woman passenger calmly walked to safety
        down what remained of the regular hatchway.

    C. One passenger escaped burning only to have another
        passenger jump on his back, injuring him severely.

    D. The cabin boy escaped burning when one of the
        dirigible's water tanks let go and drenched him.

V. However, of the 97 persons aboard, 35 perished; of
    these, 13 were passengers.

    A. Captain Pruss, the commander of the ship, was
        severely burned.

    B. Captain Lehmann, the airship expert, was brought
        out alive but died later in a hospital.

    C. John Pannes, a passenger who could have escaped,
        refused to leave until he had found Mrs. Pannes
        and thus perished with her.

    D. One man, burned black, walked away from the
        wreckage and then dropped dead.

VI. The disaster was front-page news for weeks.

    A. <u>Time</u> magazine called it "the worst and most
        completely witnessed disaster in aviation history."

    B. Dorothy Thompson, the columnist, thought the
        <u>Hindenburg</u> crash was symbolic of the passing of
        international peace.

VII. Investigation to determine why the hydrogen in the
    <u>Hindenburg</u> caught fire did not result in conclusive
    proof.

- 3 -

    A. The official board of investigators decided **that** leaking gas was ignited by a spark, but they were unable to determine what caused the **spark.**

    B. There was some talk that the spark had been intentionally caused by sabotage.

        1. On his death bed, Captain Lehmann attributed the spark to "an infernal machine."

        2. Commander Rosendahl, U. S. N., thought perhaps an incendiary bullet might have been fired into the <u>Hindenburg</u> as she was preparing to land.

VIII. Airship experts insisted that the crash was due not to a structural failure in the ship but to the use of hydrogen.

    A. They suggested that the accident would not have happened had the United States supplied Germany with helium gas.

    B. They pointed out that this was the first loss **of** life in a commercial dirigible and not to be taken as indicative of the danger of airship travel.

IX. The mass of people, however, looked upon the crash **as** the end of the long and tragic story of dirigible travel.

    A. Widely publicized accidents had put dirigible travel in disrepute.

    B. Relations between Germany -- the home of the dirigible -- and the United States were becoming more and more strained.

Page 4

Note the clean, well-balanced format of this page (and the succeeding ones). The title is neatly centered at the top of the page, in capitals; a solid line separates the text proper from the footnotes. Placing the footnotes at the bottom of the page is only one of several ways of handling them. Miss Sheldon might have placed all her footnotes together on a separate page (or pages) at the end of her paper. She might have inserted each one in the text itself, directly after the reference to it, as

All that was of real importance was that this particular flight inaugurated a new series for 1937.[2] It was true of course that

[2] New York *Times*, May 3, 1937, p. 21.

the great German airship expert, Ernst Lehmann, was aboard—

The method she did use was recommended by the instructor, whose directions in such matters should be followed.

Miss Sheldon begins her paper by pointing out how unimportant this particular landing of the *Hindenburg* was meant to be. In so doing she takes only one liberty with her source material. She does not really know that Morrison thought the job ahead of him would be routine. She knew that he seemed calm when he began to describe the landing, and she assumed that his calmness meant a casual attitude.

Note the documentation of three statements in the first paragraph. References 1 and 2 are not really necessary. The information in the statements appears in several different publications, not merely in the ones Miss Sheldon gives in her footnotes. Actually, the information is the result of her general reading in preparation for the paper and would have been adequately acknowledged by her listing of "References Consulted" at the end of her paper. Reference 3, on the other hand, is a necessary one; it documents information found in only one source, *Time* magazine.

The footnotes themselves follow an established form. They are separated from the text of the paper with a heavy black line, and the information they give is complete and precise. In the absence of a final bibliography or list of "References Consulted," the form of the entry would be different. Footnote 1 would then appear as

[1] Commander C. E. Rosendahl. What About the Airship? New York: Charles Scribner's Sons, 1938, p. 1.

And the titles and dates in footnotes 2 and 3 would be separated by periods, not commas.

LAST OF THE ZEPPELINS: THE HINDENBURG

It was shortly after seven o'clock on the evening
of May 6, 1937. For radio commentator Herbert Morrison,
assigned to Lakehurst, New Jersey, to cover the landing
of the dirigible Hindenburg, the job ahead appeared to be
routine. Since the summer of the previous year, the
great dirigible had been observing a regular schedule of
flights between Frankfort, Germany, and Lakehurst, N. J.[1]
All that was of real importance was that this particular
flight inaugurated a new series for 1937.[2] It was true
of course that the great German airship expert, Ernst
Lehmann, was aboard -- a celebrity to be welcomed -- but
this was hardly of sensational interest. In fact, Morrison
was not even going to broadcast directly; his voice would
be transcribed and played back for radio audiences at some
more convenient time.[3]

A fairly large crowd was at hand, made up mostly
of vacationers come to gape at the world's largest

---

[1] Commander C. E. Rosendahl, What about the Airship?
(New York, 1938), p. 1.

[2] "Hindenburg Is Off for U.S. Tomorrow," New York
Times, LXXXVI (May 3, 1937), 21 (col. 7).

[3] "Oh, the Humanity!" Time, XXIX (May 17, 1937), 37.
- 4 -

Page 5

Reference 4 illustrates one of the special uses of footnotes—that of adding information which, had it been inserted in the text of the paper, would have interrupted the flow of the narrative. Note that the new information which appears in the footnote is also documented in the footnote.

Reference 5 raises a question. If Miss Sheldon had spoken of the time as exactly 7:20, documentation would be required. But she generalizes about the time by writing "A few minutes before 7:20" and thereby eliminates any real need for specific documentation. Her general list of "References Consulted" would have been sufficient acknowledgment.

On the other hand, it is clear from even a cursory look at Miss Sheldon's paper that she has used Commander Rosendahl's *What About the Airship?* as her chief source of information. There are nine references to it in her paper. Miss Sheldon might have indicated her reliance on Rosendahl more precisely and yet more simply by the use of an "omnibus" footnote, as

[1]Unless otherwise indicated, information on the details of the landing and burning of the Hindenburg are drawn from Commander C. E Rosendahl *What about the Airship?* (New York, 1938), pp. 1-30.

Miss Sheldon's handling of the remarks of Morrison is excellent. She indents and single-spaces them, a procedure that identifies them immediately as direct quotations. Her bracketing of the word *comes* shows that the word is her own insertion; she could not make out exactly what word Morrison did use, so she guessed at it and told the reader she was guessing. The use of the three periods [. . .] indicates that she is omitting some words, either because she thought them not necessary to her purpose or because she could not make them out. Her capitalizing of all the letters in "It burst into flames!" is her attempt to show the force with which Morrison made the statement.

We have discovered by this time that part "II. B." of Miss Sheldon's outline, "Morrison began to describe the landing in a calm voice," is really far more significant than we first assumed. Actually, Miss Sheldon built her first three pages around Morrison's remarks, and the weakness of her outline is that it does not indicate this fact clearly enough.

- 5 -

airship.[4] Navy ground crewmen, a few photographers and
reporters were scurrying about, getting their equipment
in proper places. Customs officials were getting ready
to pass the Hindenburg's 36 passengers through the
necessary red tape. A few mintues before 7:20 a shout
went up from the crowd: the great silver ship broke through
the clouds and began to reduce speed in preparation for
landing.[5] Morrison turned to his microphone and in calm,
professional tones began to describe the landing.

> ...it [comes] majestically
> toward us like some great feather.
> . . .It's practically standing still
> now. They have dropped ropes out
> of the nose of the ship. The rain
> has slacked up a little bit. The
> back motors of the ship are just
> holding it just enough to keep it
> from -- IT BURST INTO FLAMES!
> Get this Charley. Get this
> Charley. It's [crashing] and it's

-----

[4] The Hindenburg, 803 feet long, was the largest
airship ever built, with a capacity of 7,070,000 cubic
feet of gas. The largest American dirigibles, the Akron
and the Macon, each had a capacity of 6,500,000 cubic
feet. See Hugh Allen, The Story of the Airship (Goodyear
Tire and Rubber Company, Akron, Ohio, 1938),p. 25. Also
the article "Airship," Encyclopaedia Britannica (1949 .
ed.) I, 471.

[5] What about the Airship?, p. 2.

Page 6

Miss Sheldon's use of the bracketed *sic,* meaning "thus it is," after *plane* shows that she wants her readers to understand that the error is Morrison's, not hers. Reference 6 is necessary; it gives the source of Morrison's remarks. The footnote itself is interesting: in referring to a recording, Miss Sheldon had no model to guide her. She had to use her own judgment. Note that she describes the recording quite precisely.

Reference 7 is unnecessary. In a formal report the exact time the fire started would be important. In a journalistic account such as this, it is hardly of great moment. Reference 8, on the other hand, is quite essential and quite correct. It documents a direct quotation.

Note the form of the citation of Rosendahl's book in footnotes 7 and 8. The author has referred to this book previously (footnote 1, p. 4). She need not repeat all this information in subsequent references to the book; the abridgement she uses here is correct. She might have used the form "Rosendahl, p. 2." had she not planned to make a subsequent reference to another book in which Rosendahl had a hand.

- 6 -

    smashing. It's crashing. Terrible.
Oh my. Get out of the way please. It's
burning, bursting into flames and it's
falling on the mooring mast and all
the folks. . . .This is terrible.
This is one of the worst catastrophes
in the world. Oh it's. . . Four or
five hundred feet into the sky. It
is a terrific crash ladies and
gentlemen. It's smoke and it's flames
now and the plane [sic] is crashing
to the ground not quite to the mooring
mast. Oh the humanity.[6]

At 7:25[7], just four minutes after the first landing

rope had touched the ground, the middle section of the

dirigible burst into flames, resembling, according to one

spectator, "a mushroom-shaped flower bursting into bloom."[8]

In a matter of seconds the whole quarter-end of the ship

was in flames. The forward part, still buoyant, nosed

upward 45 degrees; the dirigible broke in two. Fire then

shot forward, igniting one gas partition after another.

The whole ship settled on the ground. The Hindenburg was

---

   [6] Morrison's description of the crash is now part
of the Columbia Recording Corporation's Album I Can Hear
it Now...., ed. by Edward R. Murrow and Fred W. Friendly,
set #MM800. Except for the indicated omissions, Morrison's
remarks are exactly transcribed here.

   [7] This is the time Rosendahl gives (What about the
Airship?, p. 6). The New York Times (May 7, 1937, p. 1.)
gives the time as exactly 7:23.

   [8] What about the Airship?, p. 6.

Page 7

Reference 9 illustrates one way of documenting information which an author summarizes from several paragraphs of his original source material; rather than document each sentence which describes some part of the crash, Miss Sheldon completes the description and then gives a single reference. Footnote 9 seems rather lengthy, but the book's varied authorship needed comment. Reference 10 needs documentation, coming as it does after such a precise statement. Therefore footnote 10 needs the explanatory sentence that appears with it. Reference 11 and its footnote are also in good order.

The statement documented by footnote 11 illustrates a danger that beginning research writers must beware of—unconscious plagiarism. In her note-taking Miss Sheldon had prepared a card as follows:

> *Effect of the Hindenburg's burning*
>
> "The heat was so great that thermometers rose at the Naval Aerological School 500 yards away."
>
> *Time,* 17 May '37, p. 36

Her paraphrase of this quotation for her paper is too close; she simply adds the word *momentarily* and substitutes *intense* for *great*. She has borrowed *Time's* sentence structure and vocabulary without acknowledging the loan properly. She would have been wiser to say:

      Momentarily, "the heat was so great that thermometers rose
      in the Navy Aerological School 500 yards away." 11

The organization of the paragraph which begins on this page is not completely satisfactory. Miss Sheldon does not tell us how many people escaped; she merely lists some of the more sensational escapes. Moreover, the statement of the man who escaped the fire only to be severely injured by another passenger hardly follows from her topic "there were many survivors, some of them completely uninjured."

- 7 -

a twisted skeleton of girders and smoking wreckage.[9] The
fire had lasted exactly 32 seconds.[10]

For a moment spectators and ground crewmen either
stood in dumb wonder or fled for cover. The heat was
momentarily so intense that thermometers rose in the Navy
Aerological School 500 yards away.[11] Then ground crewmen
rushed to the wreckage to save what lives they could,
despairing of finding anyone alive. But strangely enough,
there were many survivors, some of them completely
uninjured. Three members of the Hindenburg's crew walked
out of the smoking wreckage, unharmed. An elderly woman
passenger calmly walked down what remained of the regular
hatchway to safety. A male passenger, who had jumped to
safety a moment before the ship crashed, was getting to his
feet when another passenger jumped squarely on his back,
injuring him severely. The fourteen-year-old cabin boy

---

[9] C. E. Rosendahl, "The Last Flight," the final
chapter in Zeppelin: the Story of Lighter-than-Air Craft
(London and New York, 1937), p. 357. Previous chapters
were written by Ernst Lehmann, who perished in the
Hindenburg crash, in collaboration with Leonhard Adelt,
a surviving passenger. Zeppelin was translated into
English by Jay Dratler.

[10] Time (May 17, 1937), 37. One of the reporters
carried a stop watch and timed the fire exactly.

[11] Ibid., 36.

Page 8

Reference 12 is not necessary. The story of the cabin-boy's miraculous escape appeared in almost all the news accounts of the disaster. At first glance, reference 13 also appears unnecessary. It takes but a moment to see, however, that Miss Sheldon's real purpose in 13 is to give her an opportunity to bring in Rosendahl's comment. Strictly speaking, she should have placed her 13 after ". . . death in the cabin," for that is the statement it explains. The statement of O'Laughlin in footnote 13 hardly justifies its presence. Rosendahl simply said it was unfortunate that passengers had gathered on the starboard side; he did not imply that they knew what was happening to them.

Reference 14 is puzzling. It implies that Adelt's article was the only one of Miss Sheldon's sources that gave the information. But this implication is simply not true. The incident was mentioned in most of the news accounts of the disaster. Reference 15 is also unnecessary. The heroic death of John Pannes was described in many news accounts.

The paragraph which begins on this page contains one sentence which belongs more properly in the previous paragraph. The topic sentence of the former suggests that the paragraph will recite a list of fatalities. But the first instance given is that of Captain Pruss, who was rescued alive.

- 8 -

jumped through a hatch in the bottom of the ship; just
as the flames of the wreckage began to choke him, one of
the dirigible's water tanks directly above him let go and
drenched him. He emerged wringing wet but totally
unharmed.[12]

Many of the others were not so lucky. Some passengers
were burned to death in the cabin; others were killed when
they jumped.[13] The commander of the ship, Captain Max Pruss,
though severely burned, was rescued. Ernst Lehmann, the
airship expert, broke his back in jumping,[14] and though
brought out alive, died later in a hospital. John Pannes,
who could have jumped to safety, turned his back to the
escape window to search for his wife. He found her and
perished with her.[15] One man, burned black, walked away
from the wreckage, said "I'm all right," and then fell to

---

[12] What about the Airship?, pp. 8-9.

[13] Rosendahl, Zeppelin, p. 358, thinks more passengers would have been saved had not they been gathered on the
starboard side of the main cabin. The wind was blowing in
that direction and driving the flames directly onto the
passengers. But the passengers, according to Herbert
O'Laughlin, who was one of those who escaped, "never knew
what happened" until it was all over (New York Times,
May 7, 1938, p. 18).

[14] Leonhard Adelt, "Last Trip of the Hindenburg,"
Reader's Digest, XXXI (November, 1937), 72.

[15] What about the Airship?, p. 11.

Page 9

Reference 16 is necessary. *Time* was the only publication Miss Sheldon saw that carried this particular piece of information, and documentation was mandatory. Reference 17 is also necessary; the statement gives precise figures. Reference 18 documents, correctly, a direct quotation. Reference 19, on the other hand, is superfluous. Note that the reference is not used to document the statement—for which Miss Sheldon herself is the best authority—but to permit Miss Sheldon to make an additional— and unnecessary—comment. As a pictorial magazine, *Life* would be expected to devote many pages of pictures to such a sensational crash.

Reference 20 illustrates poor research technique. If Miss Sheldon wanted to include a statement of Dorothy Thompson in her paper, she should have gone directly to Miss Thompson's article. She has used a secondary source (*Time*) when a primary source (Miss Thompson's own article) was available in several newspapers. Reference 21 is technically correct, but the statement it documents does not follow logically from the topic sentence of the paragraph. Miss Sheldon has again sacrificed the unity of her paper in order to bring in a rather sensational bit of information.

- 9 -

the ground dead.[16] Of the 97 persons aboard, 35 perished

immediately or died of their wounds; of these, 13 were

passengers.[17]

So ended what _Time_ magazine called "the worst and

the most completely witnessed disaster in the history of

commercial aviation."[18] For weeks the public press

carried eye-witness stories and pictures of the crash.[19]

Columnists commented on the significance of the accident.

Dorothy Thompson spoke of the _Hindenburg_ as one of the symbols

of international peace: of its passing as the passing of an

era.[20] For the German Chancellor Adolf Hitler, the news

was a tremendous shock. When informed of the disaster, he

paced his room all night, unable to sleep.[21]

Investigation to determine the cause of the burning

centered chiefly on the combustible characteristics of

---

[16] Time (May 17, 1937), 37.

[17] What about the Airship?, p. 10. Ordinarily the
crew totalled a few over 40, but unfortunately this trip
was a training cruise and the _Hindenburg_ carried about 20
extra men.

[18] _Time_ (May 17, 1937), 37.

[19] _Life_ (May 17, 1937), for example, devoted 5 pages
to pictures of the crash.

[20] _Time_ (May 17, 1937), 42.

[21] _Ibid._, p. 40.

Page 10

Reference 22 illustrates competent research technique. Almost all of the publications Miss Sheldon consulted contain some information on the investigation of the *Hindenburg* disaster. But Rosendahl's account was the fullest and the most expert. He had ideal qualifications to speak as an authority: he was a recognized expert in airship construction; he saw the crash of the *Hindenburg*; and he was technical adviser to the board which investigated the crash.

The statement documented by reference 23, on the other hand, does not show clearly what Miss Sheldon thinks it does. The words of Lehmann, "I don't understand it, etc." are not evidence in support of sabotage. They are simply the pathetic remarks of a man who was dying of injuries suffered in a crash, the cause of which he did not understand. The statement supported by reference 24, though vague and inconclusive, is more satisfactory. Rosendahl's statement, reference 25, is correctly documented, but inaccurate. Miss Sheldon has over-simplified Rosendahl's comments on the causes of the disaster; he spoke of an incendiary bullet as only one of many possible causes.

- 10 -

hydrogen, the gas with which the <u>Hindenburg</u> had been
inflated. A board of investigators finally decided, incon-
clusively, that one of the gas partitions sprang a leak,
that a spark ignited the gas, and that the extremely
combustible nature of hydrogen did the rest.[22] The investigators could only guess at what caused the spark. There was
talk for a while of sabotage. Captain Lehmann, as he was
carried off the field, repeated again and again "I don't
understand it, I don't understand it."[23] Just before he
died, he told Commander Rosendahl of the U. S. Navy that "it
must have been an infernal machine."[24] Rosendahl himself
thought that perhaps an incendiary bullet might have been
fired into the dirigible just before it landed.[25]

But the cause of the spark was never really determined. Airship experts attributed the disaster to the use
of hydrogen and not to a structural failure in the ship
itself. Some of them suggested that the real guilt rested
with the United States, which was too suspicious of

---

[22] <u>What about the Airship?</u>, p. 23.

[23] <u>Time</u> (May 17, 1937), 40.

[24] <u>What about the Airship?</u>, p. 28.

[25] <u>Ibid.</u>, p. 24.

Page 11

The paragraph which ends on this page does not focus clearly on any single point. It is a series of topic sentences no single one of which Miss Sheldon develops properly. Each of the final two sentences, for example, is tantalizingly brief. The reader would like supporting information for each statement.

Reference 26 is in good order. A number of airship experts made statements similar to Campbell's, and Miss Sheldon might have used any one of them. But Campbell's article, published a full year after the crash, represents a generalization of the attitudes of airship experts toward the *Hindenburg* crash. Miss Sheldon was wise to use such an article.

Reference 27 represents a very unscholarly use of source material. Miss Sheldon takes Teale's words and gives them an interpretation directly the reverse of what he intended. Teale's whole article is a refutation of the notion that the story of the dirigible is closed. Miss Sheldon, inadvertently or not, has misused her source.

Reference 28 illustrates how material which would be intrusive if placed in the text can be used in a footnote.

- 11 -

Germany's motives to relax its monopolistic control of
helium and had thereby forced Germany to use a dangerous
gas in the Hindenburg. They were also quick to point out
that this accident represented the first loss of life in
a commercial dirigible and should not therefore be taken
as proof of the danger of airship travel.[26]

But most people the world over accepted the crash
of the Hindenburg as bringing to a close the long and
tragic story of the dirigible.[27] In spite of the fact that
tens of thousands of people had traveled safely in airships,[28]
the commercial dirigible was in disrepute. Previous
airship disasters had been too widely publicized -- that of
the Shenandoah in 1925, the Akron in 1933, the Macon in 1935,

---

[26] G. N. Campbell, "They Won't Stay Down,
Collier's, CI (May 28, 1938), 13.

[27] Edwin Teale, "Can the Zepplin Come Back?"
Popular Science, CXXXII, No. 4 (April, 1938), 29.

[28] Campbell, p. 13. See Allen, p. 38, who
commented ". . .the Graf Zeppelin and the Hindenburg,
in the years 1930-36, made a record of regularity
which no other vehicle of transportation has approached."
See also "Airship," Ency. Brit., I, 471.
The Graf Zeppelin, at the time of its decommission in 1937,
had made 590 trips, had crossed the ocean 144 times, and
had carried 13,110 passengers over a total of 1,000,000
miles, all without a serious mishap.

Page 12

Anyone reading Miss Sheldon's paper is aware of her hurry to conclude it. It is true that her major concern was a description of the crash; she was not expected to deal with the significance of the crash in detail. But her final two paragraphs cover too much ground too rapidly.

- 12 -

to mention only the American ones.[29] That fact, coupled
with the ever-widening break between Germany -- the home
of the dirigible -- and the United States, was more than
the proponents of airship travel could overcome. The
Zeppelin was doomed, its place shortly to be taken over
completely by giant, ocean-spanning airplanes.

---

[29] "Airship," Ency. Brit., I, p. 73

Page 13

Note first the heading, *References Consulted.* This is a more accurate heading than *Bibliography* or *Selective Bibliography.* The first would imply that Miss Sheldon's list of books and articles was exhaustive; the second that she was listing only those sources she thought most important. The heading *References Consulted,* on the other hand, indicates that the listing is neither full nor critical. It shows that Miss Sheldon has purposely limited herself to listing the source material she used in actually writing her paper.

Note that the items are arranged in alphabetical order and that each item is described more completely in the final bibliography than in the footnotes.

- 13 -

REFERENCES CONSULTED

Adelt, Leonhard. "Last Trip of the Hindenburg." Readers's
    Digest, XXXI (November, 1937), 69-72.

"Airship," Encyclopaedia Britannica, I (14th edition,
    1949), 469-476.

Allen, Hugh. The Story of the Airship. Akron, Ohio:
    Goodyear Tire and Rubber Company, 1942.

Campbell, G. N. "They Won't Stay Down." Collier's, CI
    (May 28, 1938), 12-13.

Lehmann, Captain Ernst A. Zeppelin: The Story of Lighter-
    than-Air Craft. With collaboration of Leonhard
    Adelt, translated by Jay Dratler, preface and
    final chapter by Comdr. C. E. Rosendahl, U. S. N.
    London and New York: Longmans, Green and Co., 1937.

Life, II, No. 20 (May 17, 1937), 25-30.

New York Times, LXXXVI (May 3-10, 1937).

"Oh, the Humanity!" Time, XXIX (May 17, 1937), 35-42.

Rosendahl, Comdr. C. E. What about the Airship? London
    and New York: Charles Scribner's Sons, 1938.

Teale, Edwin. "Can the Zeppelin Come Back?" Popular
    Science, CXXXII, No. 4 (April, 1938), 29-31.

Time, May 17, 1937.

SPECIMEN LIBRARY PAPERS "B" AND "C"

Like Specimen Paper A, the following brief papers are designe to illustrate student research. Study the papers with these question in mind:

(1) Does the topic strike you as one worthy of even brief researc

(2) Or—if question (1) strikes you as needlessly stuffy—does t subject matter of the paper interest you?

(3) Does the writer do what he sets out to do?

(4) Does the writer display a clear knowledge of manuscript ar bibliography form?

(5) How does each paper compare with Specimen Paper A, bo as a composition and as an exercise in research technique?

SPECIMEN LIBRARY PAPER B

THE NIGHT LIFE OF THE GRUNION

The All Year Club, the Los Angeles Chamber of Commerce, and
the other purveyors of publicity concerning the wonders of Southern California are well acquainted with the grunion. But if a
newcomer to California were invited to go on a fishing trip in the
middle of the night with only a gunny sack and a flashlight for
fishing tackle he might, and not unnaturally, suspect that he was
about to be the victim of a practical joke. If he did accept the
invitation and spent several hours walking around on the beach, it
is quite possible that he would return with an empty sack and serious
doubts as to the integrity of his host. However, the sight of
hundreds of other persons gathered on the dark beach and carrying
the same equipment would lead him to believe that if the story
were not true, at least it was well believed.

Do small, silvery fish actually come up on the beach and dance
on their tails in the moonlight? If one is of a persistent nature
and continues to visit the beaches at the times of the predicted
runs, he will sooner or later witness the amazing phenomenon of the
fish that leaves the ocean and comes ashore to lay its eggs.

The grunion (Leuresthes tenuis) is a small fish of seven inches
or less in length, with a grayish-green back and silver sides and
belly. It is a member of the silver-side family (Atherindae) and
inhabits the waters off Central California to central Baja California.[1]
With the exception of Hubbsiella sardina, a closely related species
occurring in the upper Gulf of California, it is the only fish in the

- - - - -

[1] Phil M. Roedel, "Common Marine Fishes of California," California
Division of Fish and Game, Fish Bulletin 68, 1948, p. 43.

- 2 -

world to exhibit such unusual spawning habits.[2] In fact the grunion,
not a particularly abundant species, would probably be unknown to
the general public if its nocturnal appearances on the beaches did
not provide such exciting sport The grunion is exceptionally good
eating, but its uncommon spawning habits rather than its epicurean
qualities cause its pursuers to be so numerous.[3]

The law protects the grunion to the extent of prohibiting
its take for two of the six months of its spawning season and requires that it be caught with the hands rather than with strainers,
dip nets, or holes dug into the beach.[4]

A run commences at high tide or shortly after, with a few lone
fish, usually males, riding the waves up on the beach and lying
there until the next wave washes them to sea. Spawning commences
about twenty minutes later. Hundreds to thousands of fish may
appear on the beach at one time in the course of the run. The female swims up on the beach with a wave as far as she can go and is
followed by one to eight males. As the wave recedes, she stands
on her tail with a wriggling motion and literally digs herself into
the sand to a depth equal to half her length. In this position she
exudes her eggs while the males, lying horizontally upon the sand,
arch around her and discharge their milt.[5]

- - - - -

[2] Boyd W. Walker, "A Guide to the Grunion," California Fish and
Game, XXXVIII (1952), 410.
[3] J. Charles Davis, 2nd, California Salt Water Fishing, (New York,
1949), p. 174.
[4] California Administrative Code, "Title 14, Division 1," (1952),
Sec. 5 (h) (6)
[5] Walker, California Fish and Game, p. 410.

- 3

The males then begin to wriggle toward the water, and the female,
spent and tired, digs herself out of the sand and returns to sea
on the next wave. The process of digging in and laying takes about
thirty seconds, although individual fish may be on the beach for
several minutes.[6]

More astonishing than the actual laying of the eggs is the
delicate adjustment of the grunions' habits to the tidal cycle.
The eggs require two weeks to ripen within the female. The same
time is required for the eggs to hatch after they are laid. Two
series of very high tides occur each month coinciding with the
full and new moons. Each day there are two high tides, one higher
than the other, and in the spring and summer months these higher
tides are at night. The grunion spawn every two weeks on three
consecutive nights The spawning takes place only at night and
commences on the highest tide of the series. On any one night
spawning begins only after the turn of the tide.[7] Thus by de-
positing the eggs on the receding tide and on the descending
series, the grunion minimize the chance of the immature eggs being
washed to sea. Two weeks after the eggs are laid, the next series
of high tides occurs. The eggs are freed from the sand; the baby
grunion are hatched and are washed into the sea The grunion have
a further safeguard: the eggs will not hatch until they are actually
washed from the sand, and they remain alive for at least a month
after their deposit.[8] If some factor should prevent the release

- - - - - -

[6]Frances N. Clark, "Grunion in Southern California," California
Fish and Game, XXIV (1938), 50.
[7]Clark, California Fish and Game, p. 50
[8]Clark, California Fish and Game, p 51

- 4 -

of the eggs as scheduled, the next series of high tides will
hatch them.

The why, when, and where of the grunions' appearance on the
beach has been determined by scientific observation, but the reason
for its preference of the sand rather than the sea as an incubator
can only be guessed at.

List of References

California Administrative Code, "Title 14, Division 1."
(February 23, 1952), Section 5 (h) (6)

Clark, Frances N., "Grunion in Southern California ' California Fish and Game, XXIV (1938), 49-54.

Davis, J. Charles, 2nd   California Salt Water Fishing, New
York, 1949.

Roedel, Phil M., "Common Marine Fishes of California,"
California Division of Fish and Game, Fish Bulletin 68,
1948.

Walker, Boyd W. "A Guide to the Grunion," California Fish
and Game, XXXVII (1952), 409-20.

SPECIMEN LIBRARY PAPER C

FLYING SAUCERS: THE SITUATION IN AUGUST, 1952

Flying Saucers are new in name only. They had been seen at
least as far back as 1877, when the Royal Meteorological Society of
Great Britain received a strange report from the captain of the sailing ship Lady of the Lake.[1] While homeward bound for England from
tropic ports, crewmen of the vessel had called Captain Frederick Banner's
attention to an amazing sight in the sunset-stained sky. They had seen
something like a most curious shaped cloud -- circular, light gray,
and luminous.[2] However, the object did not behave like a cloud, for
it moved against the wind instead of with it. What was this object?
No one knew, and the matter was soon forgotten. Nothing more was heard
about such a phenomenon again for almost seventy years.[3]

Then one day during the summer of 1943, the radar watch of a
Navy Task Force off the Aleutian Islands picked up circular objects
flying above them. In the next forty-five minutes the battle force
expended more than one thousand rounds of 14-inch and 8-inch ammunition.
Confused lookouts reported that the flares and shells from their own
battle stations belonged to the "invisible" Japanese; radar operators
called in corrections for what seemed to be near-misses. In time, however, it was clear that no one was returning fire. Eventually a bewildered Task Force decided that it had been "slugging it out" with
phantoms, and so left another weird experience unsolved.[4]

- - - - -

[1] J. R. Aswell, "Flying Saucers New in Name Only," Reader's Digest,
XLI (July, 1952), 7-9.

[2] R. L. Unger, "Flying Saucers Are Old Stuff," Popular Science, CLX
(May, 1952), 145-148.

[3] Ibid., 146.

[4] Time, LX (August 11, 1952), 58.

- 2

Late in July, 1952. Washington itself seemed to be under attack
by flying saucers This time jet-fighters were called in to hunt
down the phantoms [5] No saucers were shot down, but two jets reported
they had found radar targets Later it appeared that they had been
drawing a bead on each other [6] Again the United States seemed to be
fighting phantoms [7] But flying saucers did not long drop out of sight;
they continued to be seen throughout the world: Korea, Canada, South
America Europe, and various parts of the United States. [8] From all
over this country frightened phone calls and irate demands for information rang through the Pentagon.

In order to give some relief to its frantic intelligence section,
the Air Force announced that a temperature inversion which caused a
high riding layer of warm air to act as an electronic ceiling and
made the radar pulse bounce back was responsible for flying saucers. [9]
In a Pentagon conference General Samford said that

> such things as meteors, missiles, ice
> formations, birds and honest mis-
> interpretations of natural phenomenon
> accounted for all but 20 per cent of
> the flying saucers. [10]

And Major General Ramey said that after six years of study the Air
Force was convinced that there are no such things as flying saucers. [11]
A well-known professor of meteorology backed up the Air Force by saying
that it is totally absurd to consider that flying saucers really exist. [12]

- - - - -

[5] "Blips on the Scopes," _Time_, LX (August 4, 1952), 38.
[6] _Time_, LX (August 11, 1952), 58
[7] "Flying Saucers: Fact or Fancy," _Columbus Citizen_, LIV (August 10, 1952), 11.
[8] _Ibid._, 11
[9] _Time_, LX (August 11, 1952), 58.
[10] _Ibid._, 58.
[11] _Ibid._, 58.
[12] "What are These Things They Call Flying Saucers," _Popular Science_, CXLIX (August, 1951), 74-75.

- 3 -

The Air Force had given explanations for the recent invasions of the phantoms; but what was responsible for the phantoms in 1877 and 1843? When this question was posed to Dr. Maurice A. Birt, top United States' aerodynamicist, he stated:

> Flying Saucers and unexplainable lights
> in the sky at night are evidence of visitations
> from some other planet. These objects may not
> be manned, but they may be radio controlled;
> rigged up by some world's notion of television
> to record what we are doing. Judging by re-
> ports since 1877, they have been watching a
> long time [13]

Dr. Birt's theory is backed by many other scientists.

There are, then, two "scientific" but conflicting theories regarding flying saucers: first, flying saucers do not exist; second, flying saucers do exist. Which theory will be proved correct, no one! (at this point) can say. But it is interesting to note one peculiar and perhaps inconsistent statement of the Air Force -- which has been insisting that flying saucers are figments of the imagination:

> We will distribute 200 special cameras
> to competent observers and have ordered
> some powerful new telescopes that will
> scan the sky continuously from horizon to
> horizon. [14]

Are those the words of a complete unbeliever?

- - - -

[13] R. L. Unger, op. cit., 148

[14] Time, LX (August 11, 1952), 58.

List of References

Aswell, J. R.   "Flying Saucers New in Name Only." Reader's Digest, LXI (July, 1952), 7-9.

"Blips on the Scopes." Time, LX (August 4. 1952), 40.

"Flying Saucers: Fact or Fancy." Columbus Citizen, LIV (August 10, 1952), 11.

"Something in the Air." Time, LX (August 11, 1952), 58.

Unger, R L.   "Flying Saucers Are Old Stuff " Popular Science, CLX (May, 1952), 145-147

"What Are These Things They Call Flying Saucers." Popular Science, CXLIX (August, 1951), 74-75.

Business and Social Correspondence

MEND YOUR SPEECH A LITTLE,
LEST YOU MAY MAR YOUR FORTUNES.
—WILLIAM SHAKESPEARE

BUSINESS LETTERS

BUSINESS LETTERS follow standards of mechanical form which emphasize clarity, neatness, and symmetry. They are usually typewritten on letter paper 8½ by 11 inches in size; the letter is folded twice across to fit a long envelope; or folded once across and twice in the other direction to fit a small envelope.

Although the style used in business letters varies greatly in its degree of formality, the tendency in most modern business firms is to avoid the clichés that once made business English seem quite different from ordinary English (*Yrs. of 4th inst., Your esteemed favor, I beg to inform,* etc.). Now, the successful writer of business letters, like the successful writer in any field, uses a language which is appropriate to his reader. He is direct and exact. He knows that he will be judged by his letter, and he is therefore particularly careful with his punctuation, grammar, and spelling.

489

PARTS OF THE BUSINESS LETTER

The six parts of a business letter are as follows:

(1) The Heading
(2) The Inside Address
(3) The Salutation
(4) The Body of the Letter
(5) The Complimentary Close
(6) The Signature

(1) *The Heading.* Included in the heading are the writer's full address and the date of the letter. The heading is (1) blocked with open punctuation, or (2) indented with open punctuation, or (3) indented with closed punctuation. Though all of the three methods are correct, (1) is practiced most frequently.

Blocked, with open punctuation	617 Lake Street Tucson, Arizona April 7, 1954
Indented, with open punctuation	617 Lake Street Tucson, Arizon April 7, 1954
Indented, with closed punctuation	617 Lake Street, Tucson, Arizona, April 7, 1954.

If the paper has a letterhead, giving the address, the writer types the date directly under the letterhead or flush with the right-hand margin.

(2) *The Inside Address.* The inside address gives the name and full address of the person written to. Personal titles, as Mr., Mrs., Messrs., Dr., may be used before the name of the person addressed. The form *Mr. James C. Smith* or *Mr. James Smith,* or *Mr. J. C. Smith* is used; never the form *Mr. Smith* or *Mr. Jas. Smith.* Either the blocked or the indented form may be used, depending on which is in accord with the form used in the heading. But whatever his choice, the writer should be consistent throughout the letter. The first line of the inside address is typed flush with the left-hand margin.

Blocked, with open punctuation

```
Mr. J. C. Smith
School of Veterinary Medicine
Michigan State College
East Lansing, Michigan
```

Indented, with open punctuation

```
Mr. J. C. Smith
  School of Veterinary Medicine
    Michigan State College
      East Lansing, Michigan
```

Indented, with closed punctuation

```
Mr. J. C. Smith,
  School of Veterinary Medicine,
    Michigan State College,
      East Lansing, Michigan.
```

(3) *The Salutation. Dear Sir: Dear Mr. Howe:* or *Gentlemen:* is the usual business salutation. If a woman is being addressed, the forms *Dear Madam:, Dear Miss (or Mrs.) Walker:,* or *Mesdames:* are used. *My dear Sir: (or Madam:), My dear Mr. (or Mrs.) Kane:, Sir:,* or *Madam:* are more formal salutations. The writer may safely depend upon *Dear Sir:* when in doubt about the sex or rank of his addressee.

The salutation is written flush with the left-hand margin and is followed by a colon. The comma after the salutation appears only in business letters of the most informal kind.

(4) *The Body of the Letter.* Most business letters are single-spaced with double spaces between paragraphs; only very short letters are double-spaced throughout. Paragraph indentations should be equal. General practice indents the first sentence of each paragraph five spaces from the left-hand margin. However, if the block form is used, the writer may make the first sentence of each paragraph flush with the left-hand margin. Indentation is not logically necessary, for the spacing between paragraphs sets them off sufficiently.

The effective business letter observes the principles of good writing; it has unity and clarity. The writer avoids cumbersome clichés and unconventional abbreviations, and expresses facts and opinions in simple, direct English. Above all, the careful writer remembers the importance of *proofreading* and (if necessary) of revising. Has he made any careless mistakes in grammar or spelling? Any omissions of essential information? Has he said exactly what he means to say? Will the form and neatness of the letter make a good impression?

(5) *The Complimentary Close.* It is customary to close a business letter with one of several courteous phrases. The most common of these are *Yours truly, Very truly yours,* and *Yours very truly.* More formal, and used only in appropriate circumstances, are *Respectfully yours* and *Yours respectfully.* Informal business letters, such as those addressed to friends or acquaintances, often close with *Sincerely yours, Yours sincerely, Cordially yours, Faithfully yours,* or simply *Yours.*

The first word of the complimentary phrase is capitalized, and the entire phrase is followed by a comma. The complimentary close is written two spaces below the body of the letter and begins near the center of the page.

(6) *The Signature.* The signature is written with pen and ink. Since signatures are often illegible, the writer's name is usually typewritten below the autograph. Professional titles and academic degrees are not used with a signature. A married woman signs her own name rather than her married name: *Mary Jane Hale,* not *Mrs. John D. Hale.* The following kind of signature is also appropriate:

Mary Jane Hale
(Mrs. John D.)

SPECIMEN LETTER

The following letter of application shows the form of a typical business letter. For the envelope, the address follows the pattern of the inside address. The return address appears in block form in the upper left-hand corner.

100 Corbin Street
Mackton, Indiana
May 27, 1954

Mr. J. R. Darwin
The Calvinsville _Courier_
212 Holmes Street
Calvinsville, Indiana

Dear Mr. Darwin:

Please consider me an applicant for the position which
you have recently advertised, that of news reporter for
the _Courier_.

In June I will graduate from the Journalism School of
Holton College. You will find enclosed a transcript of
my academic record.

I am twenty-two years old and unmarried. Last summer I
worked for the Hillton _Times_, which is owned and published
by Mr. R. I. Dana. While employed by the _Times_, I worked
at a variety of jobs, including reporting, copy reading,
and feature writing. I feel that this experience has
helped to qualify me for a position with your newspaper.

Further information about my academic record can be obtained from Professor D. O. Homer, Head of the Journalism
School, Holton College. Mr. Dana will gladly write you
about my practical work with his newspaper.

If I qualify for the position with the _Courier_, and if you
will let me know when it will be convenient for you to see
me, I will be glad to come to Calvinsville for an interview.

Very truly yours,

Roger Preston

Roger Preston

PERSONAL LETTERS

The form of a personal letter is similar to that of a business letter. It is simply more relaxed. Personal letters often omit the inside address, and follow the salutation with a comma instead of a colon. A great variety of phrases may be used for the complimentary close, the choice being determined by the intimacy of the correspondents. The effect of a personal letter depends largely on the personality of the writer and his ability to write interestingly. A simple, cordial, informal style is a part of that ability.

Following is a specimen personal letter, a "bread and butter" note:

207 Lilac Road
Martin, Wisconsin
August 24, 1950

Dear Mr. and Mrs. Bell,

    Since my arrival home on Tuesday I have thought many times of my pleasant stay with you last weekend. It was certainly considerate of you to take me in, because I know my sudden appearance with your son Dick must have caused you some inconveniences.

    Here at home I found everyone well and very busy. In one way, I arrived at a bad time. Mother was canning tomatoes — bushels of them — and immediately put me to work in the assembly line. However, that job is nearly finished, and in another day or two I'll have plenty of time to do some of the things I want to do before school starts.

                   Cordially yours,
                   Jim Rust

Formal social notes follow established patterns in form and style. They are usually not typed, but are engraved or handwritten. They are written from the point of view of the impersonal third person. Abbreviations are not used, except for *Mr., Mrs., Dr.* and *R.S.V.P.* (*please reply*). Numbers, except street numbers, are written out. Here is a specimen invitation:

> Mr. and Mrs. John Peele request the pleasure of Mr. and Mrs. Henry Tyler's company at dinner on Thursday, May the eleventh, at eight o'clock.
>
> 931 King Road
> May the fourth

Acceptances and regrets repeat the invitation's details, including the date and hour:

> *Mr. and Mrs. Henry Tyler accept with pleasure the kind invitation of Mr. and Mrs. John Peele to dinner on Thursday, May the eleventh, at eight o'clock.*
>
> *323 Oakhurst Drive*
> *May the fifth*

> *Mr. and Mrs. Henry Tyler regret that another engagement prevents their acceptance of Mr. and Mrs. John Peele's kind invitation to dinner on Thursday, May the eleventh, at eight o'clock.*
>
> *323 Oakhurst Drive*
> *May the fifth*

Informal invitations are written in a simple, friendly style. There are, of course, various degrees of informality, as the following examples illustrate:

Dear Mrs Trent,

    My husband and I are giving an informal dinner at home on Thursday, May the eleventh, at seven o'clock We shall be pleased if you can come

        Sincerely yours,
        Helen Carson
        (Mrs J. S)

101 Kay Street
May fourth

---

        101 Kay Street
        May 4, 1950

Dear Jane,

    George and I are having a few friends in for dinner on Thursday evening, May 11, at seven. We hope you can come.

        Sincerely,
        Helen

SECTION 50

An Index to Grammatical Terms

THIS INDEX gives definitions of common grammatical terms. These terms are defined briefly; you may need to refer to specific sections of the handbook now and then for a fuller discussion.

Absolute. An expression that is grammatically independent of the rest of the sentence An absolute phrase, usually consisting of a noun followed by a participle, is often called the *nominative absolute.*

> *The hour being late,* we hurried home.
> *The job finished,* we put away our tools.

Adjective. A word used to describe or limit the meaning of a noun or pronoun. *Descriptive adjectives* name some quality of an object: *white* house, *small* child, *leaking* faucet. *Limiting adjectives* restrict the meaning of a noun to a particular object or indicate quantity or number. The kinds of limiting adjectives are as follows:

POSSESSIVE:	*my* suit, *their* yard.
DEMONSTRATIVE:	*this* carriage, *those* people.
INTERROGATIVE:	*whose* cat? *which* boy?
ARTICLES:	*a* picture, *an* egg, *the* book.
NUMERICAL:	*one* day, *second* inning.

(See also Section 3, "Adjectives and Adverbs.")

Adjective Clause. A subordinate, or dependent, clause used like an adjective.

> The man *who lives here* is an Irishman. (The adjective clause modifies the noun *man.*)

Dogs *that chase cars* seldom grow old. (The adjective clause modifies the noun *dogs.*)

Adverb. A word used to describe or limit the meaning of a verb, an adjective, or another adverb. Classified by meaning, adverbs may indicate:

PLACE: Put the cat *outside.* (*Outside* modifies the verb *put.*)

TIME: He was *never* healthy. (*Never* modifies the adjective *healthy.*)

MANNER: She was *secretly* envious. (*Secretly* modifies the adjective *envious.*)

DEGREE: I was *quite* easily angered. (*Quite* modifies the adverb *easily.*)

(See also Section 3, "Adjectives and Adverbs.")

Adverb Clause. A subordinate, or dependent, clause used like an adverb.

When you leave, please close the door. (The adverb clause, indicating time, modifies the verb *close.*)

The sheep grazed *where the grass was greenest.* (The adverb clause, indicating place, modifies the verb *grazed.* Adverb clauses also indicate manner, purpose, cause, result, condition, concession, and comparison.)

Adverbial Objective. A noun used adverbially.

We walked *home.* I ran a *mile.*

Agreement. Correspondence in person and number between a subject and verb; in person, number, and gender between a pronoun and its antecedent; and in number between a demonstrative adjective and its noun.

(See also Section 5, "Agreement.")

Antecedent. A word or group of words a pronoun stands for.

She is a *woman who* seldom complains. (*Woman* is the antecedent of the pronoun *who.*)

Uncle Henry came for a brief visit, but *he* stayed all winter. (*Uncle Henry* is the antecedent of the pronoun *he.*)

Appositive. A substantive (a word or group of words used as a noun) placed beside another substantive and denoting the same person or thing.

> *John,* my younger *brother,* is visiting in *Albany,* the state *capital.* (*Brother* is in apposition with *John,* and *capital* is in apposition with *Albany.*)

Most appositives are *nonrestrictives* (*i.e.,* not essential to the basic meaning of the sentence) and so are set off with commas. *Restrictive* appositives limit the meaning of the sentence and are not set off with commas.

NONRESTRICTIVE   Tom Edison, *the inventor,* often worked sixteen hours a day.

RESTRICTIVE   The *inventor* Edison often worked sixteen hours a day.

Article. The articles *a, an,* and *the* are used as adjectives. The definite article is *the.* The indefinite articles are *a* and *an.*

Auxiliary. A "helping verb," used to make the form of another verb. The common auxiliaries are *be* (and its various forms), *have, shall, will, should, would, may, can, might, could, must, ought,* and *do.*

> I *am* studying.   He *may* return.   You *must* leave.

Case. The inflectional form of nouns and pronouns to show their relation to other words in the sentence. In English the three cases are nominative (*boy, I*), possessive (*boy's, my*), and objective (*boy, me*).
(See also Section 4, "Case.")

Clause. A grammatical unit containing a subject and verb. Clauses are of two kinds: *main* or *independent,* and *subordinate* or *dependent. A main clause* makes an independent assertion.

> When the moon shone, *the dog barked.*

A *subordinate clause* is used as a noun, adjective, or adverb and is dependent on some other element in the sentence.

501

That he would survive was doubtful. (The subordinate clause is the subject of the verb *was*.)
(See also Section 1, "Sentence Sense.")

Collective Noun. The Merriam-Webster *New Collegiate* defines the term as "a noun naming a collection or aggregate of individuals by a singular form (as *assembly, army, jury*). It takes a singular verb when the group is thought of as a unit, and a plural when the component individuals are in mind; as, the majority *decides;* the majority *were* slaves."

Common and Proper Nouns. A *common noun* names the general class to which a person, place, or thing belongs, as *man, country, state, river, ocean, dog, pencil, beauty*. A *proper noun*, on the other hand, distinguishes an individual person, place, or thing, as *Wallace, Europe, Massachusetts, Amazon, Atlantic, Rover, Parker, Beethoven's Fifth*.

Comparison. A term used to describe the changes in the forms of adjectives or adverbs to show degrees of quality or quantity. The three degrees are positive, comparative, and superlative.

Positive	Comparative	Superlative
loud	louder	loudest
bad	worse	worst
slowly	more slowly	most slowly

(See also Section 3, "Adjectives and Adverbs.")

Complement. A term used to describe the word or words which complete the meaning of a verb. A complement may be a *direct object*, as

The sexton rang the *bell*.
An *indirect object*, as
Give *me* the dollar.
A *predicate noun* (as *subjective complement*), as
Harry is a *baker*.
A *predicate noun* (as *objective complement*), as
We made him our *secretary*.
A *predicate adjective* (as *subjective complement*), as
The man was *silent*.

A *predicate adjective* (as *objective complement*), as

Tom painted the fence *white*. (The adjective *white*, modifying the direct object *fence*, is also called the *objective complement*.)

An *infinitive*

We had George *cook* pancakes.

Conjugation. A term used to describe the changes in the inflectional forms of a verb to show tense, voice, mood, person, and number. (For the conjugation of the verb *choose*, see Section 6, "Tense and Mood.")

Conjunction. A word used to connect words, phrases, and clauses. Conjunctions are of two kinds: *co-ordinating* and *subordinating*. *Co-ordinating conjunctions* (*and, but, or, nor, for,* etc.) join words, phrases, or clauses of equal grammatical rank. *Subordinating conjunctions* (*after, as, because, if, when,* etc.) join subordinate clauses with main clauses.

(See also Correlative conjunctions, Section 16c, "Parallelism.")

Conjunctive Adverb. An adverb used to join main clauses in a sentence. Common conjunctive adverbs are *also, besides, consequently, furthermore, however, likewise, moreover, nevertheless, then, thus.*

Co-ordinate. Having equal rank, as two main clauses in a compound sentence.

Copula. *See* Linking Verb.

Correlative Conjunctions. Conjunctions used in pairs to join sentence elements of equal rank. Common correlatives are *either . . . or, neither, . . . nor, not only . . . but also.*

Declension. *See* Inflection *and* Case.

Direct Address. A noun or pronoun used parenthetically to point out the person addressed, sometimes called *nominative of address* or *vocative.*

George, where are you going?

I suppose, *gentlemen,* that you enjoyed the lecture.

Direct and Indirect Quotations. A direct quotation is an exact quotation of a speaker's words (sometimes called direct discourse). In indirect discourse the speaker's thought is summarized without direct quotation.

> DIRECT: He said, "I must leave on the morning train."
> INDIRECT: He said that he had to leave on the morning train.

Elliptical Expression. An ellipsis is an omission of words necessary to the grammatical completeness of an expression but assumed in the context. The omitted words in elliptical expressions can be supplied by the reader or hearer.

> He is older than I (am).
> Our house is small, his (house is) large.

Expletive. The word *it* or *there* used to introduce a sentence in which the subject follows the verb.

> *It* is doubtful that he will arrive today. (The clause *that he will arrive today* is the subject of the verb *is*.)
> *There* are two ways of solving the problem. (The clause *two ways of solving the problem* is the subject of *are*.)

Finite Verb. A verb form that makes an assertion about its subject. Verbals (infinitives, participles, gerunds) are not finite forms.

Gender. The classification of nouns and pronouns as masculine (*man, he*), feminine (*woman, she*), and neuter (*desk, it*). Some English nouns have special forms to indicate gender: *salesman, saleswoman; hero, heroine.*

Genitive Case. The possessive case. (See Section 4, "Case.")

Gerund. A verbal used as a noun. Gerunds, which end in *-ing*, have the functions of nouns, such as subject or object of a verb.

> *Fishing* is an interesting sport.
> He enjoyed *hiking*.

Idiom. An expression established by usage and peculiar to a particular language. Idioms are often unusual in grammatical construction or make little sense if taken literally. Examples of

504

English idioms are "by and large," "catch a cold," "have a try at," "look up an old friend."

Independent Element. An expression that has no grammatical relation to other parts of the sentence. (*See* Absolute.)

Indirect Discourse. *See* Direct and Indirect Quotations.

Infinitive. A verbal usually preceded by *to* and used as a noun, adjective, or adverb.

NOUN: *To swim* is relaxing. (Subject.)

We didn't dare (to) *leave*. (Object.)

(*To* is usually omitted in infinitives after *dare, hear, make, see,* and some other verbs.)

ADJECTIVE: I have nothing *to say*. (*To say* modifies the noun *nothing*.)

There is no time *to waste*.

ADVERB: We were ready *to begin*. (*To begin* modifies the adjective *ready*.)

He came *to inspect* the house. (*To inspect* modifies the verb *came*.)

Inflection. Variation in the form of words to show changes in meaning or to indicate case (*he, him*), gender (*aviator, aviatrix*), number (*man, men*), tense (*walk, walked*), etc. *Declension* is the inflection of nouns and pronouns; *conjugation* the inflection of verbs; and *comparison* the inflection of adjectives and adverbs.

Interjection. A word used to express emotion. An interjection is grammatically independent of other words in the sentence.

Oh, you startled me.

Ouch! You are stepping on my foot.

Irregular Verb. *See* Strong Verb.

Linking Verb. A verb which shows the relation between the subject of a sentence and an adjective or a noun in the nominative case. The chief linking verbs are *be, become, appear, seem,* and the verbs pertaining to the senses (*look, smell, taste, sound, feel*).

He *seems* timid. The cake *tastes* sweet. He *is* a thief.

505

Modification. Describing or limiting the meaning of a word or group of words. Adjectives and adjective phrases or clauses modify nouns; adverbs and adverb phrases or clauses modify verbs, adjectives, or adverbs.

(See also Section 3, "Adjectives and Adverbs.")

Mood. The form of the verb used to show how the action is viewed by the writer or speaker. English has three moods: *indicative, imperative,* and *subjunctive.*

The *indicative mood* states a fact or asks a question.

The wheat *is* ripe. *Is* breakfast ready?

The *imperative mood* expresses a command or request.

Report to the office at once. Please *give* me your attention.

The *subjunctive mood* expresses doubt, supposition, concession, probability, a condition contrary to fact, a regret, or wish.

The grass looks as if it *were* dying.

I wish that he *were* more congenial.

(See also Section 6, "Tense and Mood.")

Nonrestrictive Modifier. A modifying phrase or clause which is not essential to pointing out or identifying the person or thing modified. Nonrestrictive modifiers are set off with commas.

Mr. Smith, *who was watching from the window,* saw the boys stealing the apples.

Television, *which is growing in popularity,* has great educational value.

Noun. A word used to name a person, place, or thing.

A *common noun* names any one of a class of persons, places or things: *man, table, valley, carrot.*

A *proper noun* names a specific person, place, or thing: *Stephen, Kansas, Canada, Labor Day, Last Supper.*

A *collective noun* names a group by using a singular form: *committee, herd, jury.*

A *concrete noun* names something that can be perceived by the senses: *house, lake, flower.*

An *abstract noun* names an idea or quality: *hope, tragedy, kindness.*

Noun Clause. A subordinate clause used like a noun.

> *What I saw* was humiliating. (Subject.)
> I shall accept *whatever he offers.* (Object of the verb.)
> We will be ready for *whatever happens.* (Object of the preposition *for.*)

Number. The form of a noun, pronoun, verb, or demonstrative adjective to indicate one (*singular*) or more than one (*plural*).

Object. A word, phrase, or clause that is affected by the action of a transitive verb; also the substantive that follows a preposition. A *direct object* receives directly the action of a transitive verb.

> I followed *him.*
> You may keep *whatever you find.*

An *indirect object* receives indirectly the action of a transitive verb.

> Give *me* the money. (*Money* is the direct object of *give; me* is the indirect object.)

The *object of a preposition* is a substantive which follows the preposition.

> We sat on the *porch.* (*Porch* is the object of *on.*)
> The horse galloped across the *meadow.* (*Meadow* is the object of *across.*)

Parenthetical Expression. An inserted expression which interrupts the thought of a sentence. Parenthetical items are set off by commas, dashes, or parentheses.

> His failure, *I suppose,* was his own fault.
> I shall arrive—*this will surprise you*—on Monday.
> The old seaman (*actually he was only forty*) loved children.

Parse. To analyze the function of a word or group of words in a sentence.

Participle. A verbal used as an adjective. Though a participle cannot make an assertion, it is derived from a verb and can take an object and be modified by an adverb. As an adjective, a participle can modify a noun or pronoun. The present participle ends in

-ing: *running, seeing, trying*. The past participle ends in *d, ed, t, n, en,* or changes the form of the vowel: *walked, lost, seen, rung*.

Parts of Speech. The classification of words on the basis of their function in the sentence. The eight parts of speech are: *noun, pronoun, adjective, verb, adverb, preposition, conjunction,* and *interjection*. Each of these is discussed in this section.

Person. The form of a pronoun and verb used to indicate the speaker (first person—*I am*); the person spoken to (second person—*you are*); or the person spoken about (third person—*he is*).

Phrase. A group of related words lacking both subject and predicate and used as a noun, adjective, adverb, or verb. On the basis of their form, phrases are classified as *prepositional, participial, gerund, infinitive,* and *verb* phrases.

PREPOSITIONAL:	We walked *across the street*. (Adverb)
PARTICIPIAL:	The man *entering the room* is my father. (Adjective)
GERUND:	*Washing windows* is tiresome work. (Noun)
INFINITIVE:	*To see the sunset* was a pleasure. (Noun)
VERB:	He *has been educated* in Europe. (Verb)

Predicate. The part of a sentence that makes a statement about the subject. The predicate consists of the verb and its complements and modifiers.

Preposition. A word used to relate a noun or pronoun to some other word in the sentence. A preposition and its object form a prepositional phrase.

The sheep are *in* the meadow.
He dodged *through* the traffic.

Principal Clause. A main or independent clause. *See* Clause.

Principal Parts. The three forms of a verb from which the various tenses are derived.

Present Infinitive	Past Tense	Past Participle
join	joined	joined
go	went	gone

(See also Section 6, "Tense and Mood.")

508

Progressive. The form of the verb used to describe an action occurring, but not completed, at the time referred to.

> I *am studying*. (Present progressive.)
> I *was studying*. (Past progressive.)

Pronoun. A word used in place of a noun. The noun for which a pronoun stands is called its *antecedent*. (For a discussion of the relation of pronouns and antecedents, see Section 5b, "Agreement.") Pronouns are classified as follows:

PERSONAL:	*I, you, he, she, it*, etc. (See the declension in Section 3, "Case.")
RELATIVE:	*who, which, that.* I am the man *who* lives here. We saw a barn *which* was burning.
INTERROGATIVE:	*who, which, what.* *Who* are you? *Which* is your book?
DEMONSTRATIVE:	*this, that, these, those.*
INDEFINITE:	*one, any, each, anyone, somebody, all*, etc.
RECIPROCAL:	*each other, one another.*
INTENSIVE:	*myself, yourself, himself*, etc. I *myself* was afraid. You *yourself* must decide.
REFLEXIVE:	*myself, yourself, himself*, etc. I burned *myself*. You are deceiving *yourself*.

Regular Verb. *See* Weak Verb.

Relative Clause. A clause introduced by a relative pronoun.

Restrictive Modifier. A modifying phrase or clause which is essential to pointing out or identifying the person or thing modified. Restrictive modifiers are not set off with punctuation marks.

> People *who live in glass houses* shouldn't throw stones.
> The horse *that won the race* is a bay mare.
> (*See also* Nonrestrictive.)

Sentence. A group of words expressing a unit of thought and normally containing a subject and predicate. Sentences are classified on the basis of their form as *simple, compound, complex,* or *compound-complex.*

A *simple sentence* has one main clause. Either the subject or the verb may be compound.

The sun rises.

The boys and girls are playing tag.

A *compound sentence* has two or more main clauses.

He went to the store, but I stayed at home.

A *complex sentence* has one main clause and one or more subordinate clauses.

The twins ran when they heard their father coming.

A *compound-complex* sentence has two or more main clauses and one or more subordinate clauses.

He seized the reins, and the horses reared because they were frightened.

Sentences are classified as *declarative, interrogative, imperative,* and *exclamatory*. A *declarative sentence* states or asserts something.

John smiled. The crowd cheered.

An *interrogative sentence* asks a question.

Where are you going? What is his name?

An *imperative sentence* expresses a request or command.

Please pass the bread. Watch your step.

An *exclamatory sentence* expresses strong emotion and is followed by an exclamation point.

What a temper he has! I will not go!

Strong Verb. A verb that forms its past and past participle by a vowel change.

begin, *began, begun;* spring, *sprang, sprung.*

Subject. The person or thing about which the predicate of a sentence or clause makes an assertion.

Substantive. A word or group of words used as a noun. Substantives include nouns, pronouns, infinitives, gerunds, and noun clauses.

Substantive Clause. A subordinate clause used as a noun. *See* Noun Clause.

Syntax. The relationship between words in a sentence.

Tense. The time or the state of the action expressed by a verb. (For a discussion of verb tenses see Section 6, "Tense and Mood.")

Verb. A word or phrase used to assert an action or state of being. A *transitive verb* is one that takes an object.

> Jack *mowed* the grass.
> An *intransitive verb* is one that does not require an object.
> The children *are laughing*.
> Some verbs may be either transitive or intransitive.
> The whistle *blew*. (Intransitive.)
> Tom *blew* the whistle. (Transitive.)
> (*See* Finite Verb.)

Verbal. A word derived from a verb, but unable to make an assertion. *See* Infinitive, Gerund, *and* Participle.

Vocative. *See* Direct Address.

Voice. The property of a verb which shows whether the subject acts (*active voice*) or is acted upon (*passive voice*).

> ACTIVE   Ed *is taking* a walk.
> PASSIVE   A walk *is being taken* by Ed.
> ACTIVE   Grace *bought* some flowers.
> PASSIVE   Some flowers *were bought* by Grace.

Weak Verb. Also called a regular verb. A verb that forms its past and past participle by adding -*d*, -*ed*, or -*t* to the infinitive: *move, moved, moved: kneel, knelt, knelt.*

Writing Summaries

Definition and history

Frequently a student needs to reduce lectures, articles, or long chapters of books to a short, manageable size for purposes of review and study. For this purpose it is valuable to be able to write a formal summary called a précis (pronounced *pray-see'*) or abstract. The word *précis* literally means "cut down" or "trimmed"; making a précis is very much like trimming a bush down to its trunk and main branches: whatever in the original passage is devoted to beauty of style, to illustration or to detailed explanation is eliminated, leaving the gist of the material unadorned. Unlike a restatement or paraphrase, which have their value in clarifying or simplifying difficult material, a précis is primarily a miniature embodiment of an author's thought and approach to his subject, sometimes using his own words and retaining his proportion and emphasis. The writer of a précis assumes the author's voice—it is never necessary to use such locutions as, "In this paragraph the author says . . ."—and he writes as though he were himself the author condensing his own statement.

Since the reign of Queen Anne (1700-1712), when diplomats began asking their undersecretaries to condense long documents as a necessary simplification of business, the writing of précis has had a formal tradition in England. Summaries are not only useful in distilling vast amounts of material, but also are a valuable discipline for learning to read accurately and to write with conciseness and directness. They require a careful analysis of the material to be condensed and acute discrimination between principal and subordinate ideas; hence they sharpen a student's own style, teaching him to avoid the prolixity which creeps into all careless writing.

Procedure

Before attempting to write a précis of a passage, read it carefully to discover the author's purpose and his point of view. As you read,

513

pick out his central ideas and arrange them in your mind as he arranges them. Be on the lookout for the author's own compact summaries, which may occur at the beginning or end of a passage or at points of transition.

After studying the passage, you are ready to organize your summary. Ordinarily a paragraph may be reduced to a sentence, although some very complex paragraphs may require more than one, and some groups of paragraphs, such as those illustrating a single point, may become a single sentence. Most paragraphs with unity and direction contain a topic sentence (See Section 13a) which should provide you with the subject of your summarizing sentence. (WARNING: *Don't lean too heavily on the topic sentence, forgetting necessary qualifications and explanations in the remainder of the paragraph.*) The predicate of the summarizing sentence will usually consist of a collection of assertions about the subject which you will find scattered throughout the paragraph. Ask yourself what the author is talking about and what he is asserting about the subject; then arrange subject and assertions into a compact sentence of summary.

Usually a simple or complex sentence (See Section 50) is better for summary of a paragraph than a compound sentence—unless the paragraph itself is poorly organized. A compound sentence implies that two or more ideas in the paragraph compete equally to dominate it. If this seems to you to be the case, check the paragraph again to be sure that the author did not imply some subordinating relationship, which you have missed, between the ideas. Parallel clauses and phrases (See Section 16) are very helpful in clarifying the amount of emphasis to be put on a series of subordinate ideas of equal strength. Brief but accurate transitions (See Section 23) are very important in keeping the author's thought coherent and his procedure clear. As a rule you should keep ideas in the order in which they occur in the original passage; but it is usually wiser to avoid the author's wording except for key terms and phrases; too close adherence to his wording is apt to swell your précis to needless length. Key terms and phrases, however, selected and repeated judiciously, are useful in binding the précis together. Discard figures of speech, digressions, anything which is not essential to the "trunk and main branches," reducing the material to not over one third of its original length.

EXAMPLE

We very rarely consider, however, the process by which we gained our convictions. If we did so, we could hardly fail to see that there was usually little ground for our confidence in them. Here and there, in this department of knowledge or that, some one of us might make a fair claim to have taken some trouble to get correct ideas of, let us say, the situation in Russia, the sources of our food supply, the origin of the Constitution, the revision of the tariff, the policy of the Holy Roman Apostolic Church, modern business organization, trade unions, birth control, socialism, the League of Nations, the excess-profits tax, preparedness, advertising in its social bearings; but only a very exceptional person would be entitled to opinions on all of even these few matters. And yet most of us have opinions on all these, and on many other questions of equal importance, of which we may know even less. We feel compelled, as self-respecting persons, to take sides when they come up for discussion. We even surprise ourselves by our omniscience. Without taking thought we see in a flash that it is most righteous and expedient to discourage birth control by legislative enactment, or that one who decries intervention in Mexico is clearly wrong, or that big advertising is essential to big business and that big business is the pride of the land. As godlike beings why should we not rejoice in our omniscience?

—JAMES HARVEY ROBINSON, *The Mind in the Making*

In reading the paragraph carefully we find that it hinges on the sentence in the middle beginning "And yet most of us have opinions on all these. . . ." This sentence suggests the pattern that the summary sentence should probably take. The central idea of the paragraph is that we do not ordinarily take pains in forming our convictions on important matters, *but* we nevertheless express our opinions as a matter of right and even take delight in our apparent omniscience. The main clause of the précis will express the second idea, retaining the author's ironic approach:

We are godlike beings who delight in our ability to form and express convictions on birth control, on intervention in Mexico or on the role of big business, without a moment's thought.

To include the author's qualification in the first part of the paragraph, we must precede the main clause with a subordinate clause:

> Although the few pains we take to understand such things as the situation in Russia, the sources of our food supply, the origin of the Constitution, the revision of the tariff, the policy of the Holy Roman Apostolic Church, modern business organization, trade unions, birth control, socialism, the League of Nations, the excess profits tax, preparedness, and advertising in its social bearings give us little reason to have confidence in our opinions on these matters, we are godlike beings who delight in our ability to form and express convictions on birth control, on intervention in Mexico or on the role of big business, without a moment's thought.

This reduction, however, is unsatisfactory as a précis, as it is almost half as long as the original. It can be further reduced by finding general terms to replace the specific examples.

> Although the few pains we take to understand such things as social, political, economic, religious and medical issues give us little reason to have confidence in our convictions on these matters, we are god-like beings who delight in our ability to form and express such convictions without a moment's thought.

This précis, less than one third the original length, would be acceptable for most purposes. But occasionally even a shorter summary is desirable:

> Although we have little reason to trust our convictions on the important issues of life, we delight in forming and expressing such opinions without a moment's thought.

We should not make the mistake of supposing that the last sentence expresses everything expressed in Robinson's paragraph, in which the concreteness and the vigor of short sentences are perhaps even more valuable than its central thought. But a summary is concerned *only* with the central thought, and that is preserved even in the shortest statement above.

> EXERCISE 1. Write a two-sentence précis of the paragraph beginning "Speech and language have contrasting advantages . . ." on page 144.

> EXERCISE 2. Write a one-sentence précis of the same paragraph.

EXERCISE 3. Try to write a one-sentence précis of the following paragraph. Does the effort tell you anything about the weakness of the paragraph itself?

Among one of the many interesting aspects of dietary training is the living together of the students. This allows each to get acquainted with people from all over the States and to exchange ideas and viewpoints from different sections of the country. By living in such a home, many girls grow into more mature individuals. It provides a good chance for girls who have always lived at home to become more independent. It also helps to establish feelings of self-sufficiency in those who have never before been on their own.

EXERCISE 4. Write the briefest précis you can of the following paragraph:

Great care and attention is given in the organisation of pageants and other popular feasts, and of these a Russian crowd is particularly appreciative, throwing itself wholeheartedly into the enjoyment of every detail. The "crowd sense," which is just another expression of the corporate instinct, is peculiarly strong in Russia, and it is often curiously reminiscent of an English crowd, particularly in its broad and jolly sense of humour. But Russians of any class have a much stronger artistic sense than we have. This was so before the revolution, and it comes out in the organisation of these festivals. They are all out to enjoy themselves, and anything particularly clever or pretty gets them at once. In Kiev, still as always a beautiful city on its lovely site, in the late summer of 1936, I saw a march past of all the wards in turn. They swung past with splendid vigour, squads of men or of women—one squad of women had in the middle of it a fine old man with a long beard who looked very pleased with his company. There were flowers and dancing everywhere; each ward was preceded by a dancing band of girl skirmishers in the picturesque Ukrainian costume, sometimes singing the charming Ukrainian folk songs. At one point various forms of recreation and amusement were represented: the fishermen carrying long fishing rods with coloured paper fish hooked to them, the chess players carrying enormous cardboard knights, bishops and castles. Interspersed between the detachments came curious and fanciful constructions, sometimes very ingenious; an effigy of Trotsky with long nose and black eyes and curls made an excellent Mephistopheles. It was a family feast of old and young, and we all exchanged our comments as each new surprise went past. With the usual courtesy to guests there was a chair set for me, and when I wanted to let a lady have it, I was genially told "that I had to submit to the will of the majority." At one time a torrent of rain came down, but the marchers swung past with all the more vigour and enjoyment. And so it was with the onlookers. After several hours of it, I asked a neighbouring policeman whether I couldn't go away: "No," he said very nicely, "you must stay and enjoy it." And enjoy it they certainly did, for in spite of more downpours of rain, from my room in my hotel I could hear them singing and dancing on the square outside till two in the morning. The one thing that fell below the level of all the rest was the exhausting reiteration of the portraits of Stalin and the other "big noises" of Communism. There must have been about forty of Stalin alone: one ten foot high, of the face alone. I noticed a sympathetic cheer when there came past a single portrait of Lenin.

—BERNARD PARES, *Russia: Its Past and Present*

Supplementary Exercises

THE NINE one-page papers which follow are specimens of freshman writing. Discuss them on the basis of the questions below:

General organization (Section 12)

1. Does the title fit the discussion?
2. Is the material of the paper separated into distinct sections?
3. Are these sections arranged in logical order? (Is there an orderly sequence of thought from one section to the next and from the beginning to the end of the paper?)
4. Is all the material relevant to the central purpose of the paper?
5. Is the beginning direct and pertinent?
6. Does the ending of the paper give an impression of finality and completeness?

Paragraphing (Section 13)

1. Does each paragraph have a clearly stated or implied purpose? (Sections 13a, 13b, "Paragraph Unity")
2. Is each paragraph coherent? (Does each sentence proceed logically and clearly from the previous one and to the next?) (Sections 13c, 13d, "Paragraph Coherence")
3. Is the idea of each paragraph developed sufficiently? (Section 13e, "Paragraph Development")

Sentence structure (Sections 14-27); **Logic** (Section 28)

1. Are less important ideas in the sentence clearly subordinated to the principal one? (Section 14a, 14b, "Subordination")
2. Does unnecessary detail obscure the main thought of any sentence? (Section 14d, "Subordination")
3. Are the parts of each sentence arranged in a natural and clear order? (Section 18, "Misplaced Parts," Section 19, "Dangling Constructions")

4. Do pronouns refer clearly to their antecedents? (Section 15, "Reference of Pronouns")

5. Is the grammatical point of view which is established in the opening sentences of the paper maintained consistently? Are the lapses justifiable? (Section 26, "Point of View")

6. Is the sentence pattern monotonous? Does the writer know how to vary short emphatic sentences with longer, more sophisticated ones? (Section 24, "Emphatic Elements," Section 27, "Variety")

7. Do the sentences hold up logically? (Section 28, "Logic")

Word choice (Sections 31-33)

1. Does the word choice seem precise? Does the writer seem able to find the word that expresses his meaning exactly? (Section 31, "Exactness")

2. Is the writer's use of words economical? Does he express his meaning quickly and cleanly? (Section 32, "Directness")

3. Does the writer use words in "good use"? Is his choice of words appropriate for the tone and subject matter of his paper? (Section 33, "Appropriateness")

Grammar (Sections 1-6)

1. Are there any clumsy incomplete sentences? (Section 2a, "Sentence Fragment")

2. Is there any confusion in the use of adjectives and adverbs? (Section 3, "Adjectives and Adverbs")

3. Is there any violation of agreement of subject and verb, of pronoun and antecedent? (Section 5, "Agreement")

SPECIMEN PAPER 7

THE CONSTRUCTION OF A MODEL AIRPLANE

The first thing to do is to obtain the proper model kit. If you have not had previous experience with these kits, the best model for you is the R.O.G. If you have built models before and know what you can do, you can choose from a large assortment ranging from radio-controlled models to microfilm floaters.

When you are ready to assemble the kit, you should clear a table of all but the necessary equipment. Take all parts from the box. You should read the instructions at least twice before starting to work on the model. Follow the instructions step by step. Always allow sufficient time for the glue to dry before adding another part. If the model is supposed to be light, go easy on the glue. If you are trying to make a strong and sturdy model, be quite free in the use of type B glue.

After you have completed the basic inner frame, you may find it difficult to apply the covering tissue properly. For curved surfaces, use small pieces of tissue so that you can avoid wrinkles in the surface. When you have finished covering the model, water should be sprinkled on the tissue quite liberally. This will give a tight fit.

The last and most interesting phase is the painting and decorating phase. This applies only to the heavier models. Ordinarily two clear base coats should be applied before the two coats of color paint. It is best to use sandpaper after each coat except on the outside one. In order to keep your paint brushes pliable, clean them thoroughly after each job. Use scotch tape as masking tape. Various decorations can be applied by using decals made and sold especially for the purpose.

SPECIMEN PAPER 8

MY FIRST JOB

One summer day, when I was eleven years old, I was sitting on the front porch in deep thought, dreaming about the paper route I hoped to acquire. Suddenly I was brought to my senses by a truck stopping in the driveway. He had arrived, the route man whom I had been waiting for anxiously. He had offered me the job a couple days before, and when I told him I needed my father's approval, he said he would speak to him in a couple days. He walked up on the porch, asked for my father, and I knew that in a few minutes I would know the result.

Inviting the route man in, and introducing him to my father, I waited anxiously while they talked. My father wanted to know how heavy the papers were, what sort of district I would have, whether I would have to cross a lot of busy intersections. Finally my father gave his approval, and I was thrilled that the route was mine.

Before departing, the route man gave me a few final instructions and wished me luck. It was Saturday and I wouldn't start my deliveries until Monday. It seemed as though that day was very far off. But before I knew it, Monday had arrived.

The first thought that entered my mind upon rising Monday was my newspapers. I dashed downstairs and there were the newspapers on the front porch. I carried them inside, counted them, and then went in to eat with great speed, for which my mother scolded me, although in an understanding way.

After eating breakfast, I bid farewell to my parents, loaded the newspapers on my wagon and very proudly started out on my first job, an experience that I will always remember.

SPECIMEN PAPER 9

THE BIG SNOW OF 1950

Let it snow, let it snow, let it snow. This was the theme song of Brookville residents last weekend. For the first time since 1935, Brookville had sixteen inches of snow. The big snow hit Friday afternoon and continued to fall for three days. Stores closed, transportation came to a standstill, garage owners had nervous breakdowns, citizens pleaded with hardware dealers to sell them snow shovels and tire chains.

No one, looking at stalled cars practically covered with snow, could help remarking that grandfather's mode of transportation was the best and safest after all. Grandfather could really depend on old Dobbin to get him from one place to the next. A slippery road only makes a sleigh more efficient than ever.

But today a heavy snow is a paralyzing thing. People can't get to work without walking, and walking means a trip of two to five miles, for people now live far from their place of employment. And stores can't open because clerks can't get to work. Food and milk supplies run short. The farmer can get the milk out of the cow but he can't get it to the dairy.

In Brookville most people stayed in their homes and listened all day to radio accounts of the storm. They shoveled their driveways and waited for one of the town's half-dozen snowplows to begin plowing their own particular street. When the driveways and streets were cleared, people got out their cars and got stuck in slippery spots. The man who depended on an automobile was one mass of solid frustration for three days.

SPECIMEN PAPER 10

PROBLEMS OF A COMMERCIAL FISHERMAN

The first thing that anyone who starts in commercial fishing needs is a boat. Just any boat will not do, it must be seaworthy and have a powerful motor. A new boat that fits this description costs in the neighborhood of seven thousand dollars. There are many boat builders around Lake Erie who build nothing but this kind of boat.

Next in importance to the commercial fisherman is his nets. The average trap net costs about one thousand dollars; a fisherman needs about sixteen. It would not be profitable to start commercial fishing with less than this amount. The fisherman works on the law of average. He places his nets here and there, hoping that he will get a good catch in a few of them at least.

After you have the boat and the nets, you have to know where the fish are feeding. This knowledge is really gained only through years of working around the lake on fish boats. The hardest part is learning where the fish are during the different seasons of the year.

The worst thing about commercial fishing is the weather in which you must work. In the spring the cold rains numb your hands, and in the winter the cold winds chill you to the bone. But you are forced to go out on the lake even in the roughest weather, for you must check your nets constantly. Your investment is too great to be neglected.

So you can see that commercial fishing is not a business for fly-by-night promoters and tenderfeet. Commercial fishing requires a large capital investment and a rugged constitution. Above all, it requires "know-how" -- an attitude compounded largely of a willingness to work, courage, and patience.

SPECIMEN PAPER 11

MY IDEA OF INTELLIGENT READING

Intelligent reading is a very important medium by which a person may educate himself and be well informed. Students, professional people, laborers, and people in all walks of life find intelligent reading to be a great asset. Intelligent reading is a way of getting an education, and if a person cannot afford a conventional kind of education he can always educate himself by intelligent reading.

But what is intelligent reading? It means the kind of reading that forces a person to think. Intelligent reading is not just reading for fun. People who want to educate themselves by reading should select their materials carefully. They should select something that interests them, about which they wish to know more.

When a person has selected the right material, he should make himself comfortable. This means a comfortable chair and a good reading light. If the book is his own, he should read with a pencil in his hand, marking in the margin of the page or underscoring the important parts. He should make sure that he understands where the writer is taking him. When he begins to tire, he should stop reading, for that is a sign that his mind is tired and unable to absorb any more information.

The habit of reading a little each day is a good one. It provides a pattern and a direction, and a person who gets himself into such a habit will be surprised at the end of a year how much he has learned, how different he is intellectually from what he was before. He will know a great many more words and he will also know much more language in general. For he has exposed himself to a liberal education, and the effects of that exposure are more telling on him than he thought possible.

SPECIMEN PAPER 12

WOMEN DRIVERS

The other day as I was driving along Green Street I happened to get behind a woman driver   I followed her for a few blocks and since the traffic was heavy that day I could not pass her. There I was stuck behind her with the worst yet to come. Then I noticed that her turn signal was on for a right turn and her arm was out for a left turn. I didn't know what she was going to do. As I approached the corner, I waited to see what her next move would be; she went straight ahead. I guess she was drying her nail polish and conducting calisthenics for her turn signal at the same time.

Another incident, rather accident, that I happened to observe was when an aunt of a friend of mind was trying to back out of a parking space. She was parked with the front bumper against the curb rather than in the legal way for this town with the side of the car to the curb. The car had a hydromatic transmission, and when the lady pulled down the gearshift lever for reverse she was looking backwards and didn't notice that the lever stopped at low instead of at reverse. She then tramped on the accelerator, and the car went bounding up over the curb, knocking over a parking meter and smashing into the side of the adjoining bank building. What a way to rob a bank!

Now I realize that these are only two incidents to illustrate my thesis, but they are so typical and there are so many others that I could give, that I think they will suffice. A woman behind the wheel of an automobile is not to be trusted, not merely because she doesn't have the proper awareness of the mechanical monster she is sitting in, but also because she won't pay attention to what she's doing.

SPECIMEN PAPER 13

TELEVISION

Television is a great threat to the future intelligence of the American public. In the last few years television has become one of the most time-consuming pastimes of many people. Those who have sets use most of the time they previously spent on hobbies, reading, and in friendly conversation watching television. The programs they watch are: wrestling show, cheap vaudeville acts, and many programs that represent the lowest form of entertainment

Television has put an end to many of the friendly visits that people once made to see one another. Even if one does go to visit a friend now, he must sit silent watching a twenty-year-old movie or some other program just as unenlightening. No more do people talk about politics, the state of the world, or the latest happenings around town. Instead they laugh together at some foolish comedian or wear themselves out watching one man twist another man's arms, or something just as meaningless.

One can read or at least look at the pictures in a magazine while he is listening to radio, but he cannot do so while watching television. Also to watch television is hard on the eyes. TV manufacturers may not admit this, but they are constantly experimenting to develop a tube which is not so hard on the eyes. This may have little effect on the present generation, but it may harm the eyes of our children and ultimately affect their ability to read. People who do not read can never make an intelligent, informed public.

The increasing popularity of television is discouraging reading and intellectual conversation, and it is affecting the coming generation greatly. If this trend continues and the quality of the programs does not improve, television -- a great step forward in science -- can do the American people more harm than good.

SPECIMEN PAPER 14

SUCCESS IN THE MODERN WORLD

Have you ever stopped to think about yourself? To think about what you, as an individual, are fitted for and will be able to do as your occupation in later life? Surely at one time or another everyone has and at that time charts his course in life. Every course of life has a destination, some higher than others, but still a definite goal to work and strive to reach. As you and I charted this course and the many steps along the way, doubtless one major step was education. Why is this? Why is education such a major step?

The major portion of our education is acquired in the period from childhood to manhood. Its' purpose is to help make a place for every individual in life. By this, I mean to reach the goal of the individual.

Let us take my own case, as a young child I wanted to be a policeman, then a fireman, then a truck driver. When I matured I set my goal, I decided I would like to work in the field of radio, however if I did not attain that goal I will not consider myself a failure. If I am successful in another field, I will be happy. Here I believe we come to the key word of human life, Success.

There are many kinds of success; business, financial, social and many others. A well rounded education paves the way for success, no matter what the type.

Many people ridicule modern education, however I believed that as the modern world is modernized, so much education be modernized. Quoting a contemporary businessman we find "Many of my former college mates are in fields of activity which did not exist twenty years ago." So as the world improves and progresses, education must do likewise.

In conclusions, I think it is safe to say that education is the key to success; and to be a success in the modern world the individual must possess a modern education.

SPECIMEN PAPER 15

MY OPINION OF POLITICAL CAMPAIGNS

Let us review some of the elements of the typical political campaign. A candidate for public office has been selected. His private life is discussed at great length in the newspapers. His parents were "humble" citizens of the land; his wife is the home-loving type; his children are all fine, intelligent young people. The candidate himself was a prominent attorney or teacher or merchant before his election some years before to a little-known public office. He carried out these duties with "promptness and dispatch" and his constituents insisted that he run for a higher office.

The opposing party is then attacked. Its failure to keep promises made in earlier campaigns is cited, and its lack of ability to handle our current problems is thoroughly reported on. The present incumbent of the office is mentioned, and his qualifications judged inadequate. The promise is then made that "when our candidate is elected, everything will be different."

Rarely do facts back up the statements of politicians. Voters have to ferret them out for themselves. All we have is a fine network of words -- words which, if listened to carefully, tell us almost nothing really valuable. Everything is all black or all white; both parties claim all virtue for themselves and consign all sin to the opposition.

It can be seen that I heartily dislike the present methods by which a party tries to win votes for its candidates. The thousands of dollars that are wasted to present practically nothing of value to the voter is almost criminal. The whole purpose of present campaigns seems designed to confuse the voters with irrelevancies, half-truths, and unimportant statistics. Let us give more attention to the qualifications of the candidate and put less emphasis on his party affiliations.

529

General Index

A, an, 315
Abbreviations:
  in footnotes, 449-451
  in formal usage, 88
  names of countries, months, etc., 88
  period after, 359
  street, volume, page, etc., 88
  titles, 87
  when permissible, 87
Above, 315
Absolute, defined, 499
Abstracts, writing of, 513-516
Accept, except, 315
Active voice:
  defined, 511
  used for emphasis, 220
Ad, 315
Adjective clause:
  defined, 24, 499
  diagramed, 77
Adjectives:
  classes of, 499
  comparison of, 37-38
  defined, 19, 499
  demonstrative, 53
  diagramed, 71-72
  distinguished from adverbs, 35-37
  with linking verbs and verbs of the
    senses, 36
Adverb clause:
  defined, 24, 500
  diagramed, 77
Adverbial objective, defined, 500
Adverbs:
  classes of, 500
  comparison of, 37-38
  defined, 20, 500
  diagramed, 71
  distinguished from adjectives, 35-37
  position of, 190-191

Affect, effect, 315
Aggravate, 316
Agreement, defined, 500
Agreement of demonstrative adjective,
  53
Agreement of pronoun and antecedent:
  antecedent joined by *or* or *nor,* 52
  collective nouns, 52
  person, man, one, etc., 51
Agreement of subject and verb:
  collective nouns, 49
  confusion of subject with predicate
    nouns, 49
  each, either, any, etc., 48
  intervening nouns, 47-48
  relative pronouns, 50
  subjects joined by *and,* 49
  subjects joined by *and, or,* or *nor,*
    49
  with verbs preceding the subject, 49
Ain't, 316
Alibi, 316
All ready, already, 316
All right, 316
All the farther, 316
All together, altogether, 317
Allusion, illusion, 316
Already, all ready, 316
Altogether, all together, 317
Alumnus, alumna, 317
Among, between, 317
Amount, number, 317
An, a, 315
And etc., 317
And sentences, 173
Angle, 317
Antecedent:
  agreement with pronoun, 51-52
  ambiguous reference to, 180-181

Antecedent—*Continued:*
  defined, 19, 500
  remote from pronoun, 180
  unexpressed, 181
Any, as provincialism, 317
Any, in comparisons, 188
Any, number of, 48
Anyplace, 317
Anyways, anywheres, 317
Apostrophe:
  misused with personal pronouns, 415
  to form plurals of letters, numbers, etc., 414
  to indicate omissions, 414
  to show possessive case, 413-414
Appositive:
  defined, 379, 501
  use of colon with, 392
  use of comma with, 379
  use of dash with, 392
Appropriateness (*see also* Diction), 302-311
Apt, likely, 317
Article, defined, 501
As, as connective, 176
As . . . as, so . . . as, 318
As, for *since* or *because,* 318
As if, like, 327
At about, at around, 318
Atlases, list of, 431
Auto, 315
Auxiliary, defined, 501
Awkwardness, 207-208, 296-297

Badly, 36, 318
Balance, 319
Be, case of pronoun after, 42
Because clause, 30
Begging the question, 244
Beginning a paper, 105-107
Beginning the sentence:
  with a co-ordinating conjunction, 229
  with an expletive, 228
  with a prepositional phrase, 228
  with a subordinate clause, 228
  with a verbal phrase, 228
Beside, besides, 319
Between, among, 317

Bibliography:
  cards, 442-443
  preparation of, 441-443
Biography, reference books of, 431
Blame on, blame it on, 319
Body, of business letter, 491-492
Brackets:
  to indicate grammatical or spelling error, 399
  to set off editorial remarks, 399
Bursted, bust, busted, 319
Business letters:
  addressing the envelope, 492
  body, 491
  complimentary close, 492
  heading, 490
  inside address, 490
  salutation, 491
  signature, 492
  specimen letter, 492-493
But, as connective, 176
But that, but what, 319

Can, may, 319
Can't hardly, 319
Can't help but, 319
Can't seem to, 320
Capitals:
  common nouns as part of proper noun, 409
  days of the week, months, holidays, 408
  first word of sentence or line of poetry, 407
  I and *O,* 407
  organizations, historical events, documents, 408
  proper nouns and their derivatives, 408-409
  religious terms, 408
  specific persons, places, races, nationalities, 408
  titles of books, etc., 408
  titles preceding proper noun, 409
  unnecessary, 410-411
Card catalogue:
  author, title, and *subject* cards, 426-428
  Dewey decimal system, 427-428

Card catalogue—*Continued:*
  Library of Congress system, 429
  use of, 426-427
Case:
  defined, 40, 501
  nominative, 41-42
  objective, 44-45
  possessive, 43-44
Cause and effect, 243-245
Causes, explanation of, in paragraph
    development, 147
Choppy sentences, 172
Claim, 320
Classical literature, reference books of,
    432
Clauses:
  adjective, 24, 499
  adverb, 24
  dangling elliptical, 199
  defined, 24, 503
  dependent, 24-25
  diagramed, 76-77
  independent, 25-26
  main, 25-26
  misused as sentences, 29-30
  noun, 25, 507
  recognition of, 24
  restrictive and nonrestrictive, 374-
    375
  subordinate, 24-25
Clichés, 305-306
Coherence in the paragraph:
  consistent point of view, 130-131
  logical order, 127-128
  parallel structure, 131
  repetition, 131-132
  transitional expressions, 133-134
Coherence in the sentence:
  dangling constructions, 196-199
  incomplete constructions, 202
  misplaced parts, 190-195
  mixed constructions, 204-205
  parallelism, 185-187
  point of view, 222-223
  reference of pronouns, 179-183
  transitions, 211-212
Collective nouns:
  defined, 502
  number of pronoun with, 52
  number of verb with, 50

Colloquial usage, 8-9, 314
Colon:
  position outside quotation marks,
    400
  to separate main clauses, 369
  to set off long appositives, 392
Combining forms, 275
Comma:
  after introductory clause or phrase,
    373, 400
  position inside quotation marks, 399
  superfluous, 388-389
  to prevent misreading, 376
  to separate dates, addresses, geo-
    graphical names, 385-386
  to separate items in series, 384-386
  to separate main clauses, 367-369
  to set off appositives, words in di-
    rect address, and mild interjec-
    tions, 379-381
  to set off nonrestrictive elements,
    374-375
Comma fault:
  defined, 31-32, 369
  elimination of, 31-32, 369
Comparative form, 37
Comparison:
  adjectives and adverbs, 37-38
  defined, 37, 502
Comparison or contrast, in paragraph
    development, 144-145
Comparisons, 188-189, 502
Comparisons, illogical, 309
Complement, defined, 502
  diagramed, 70
Complex sentence, defined, 26, 510
Complimentary close:
  of business letter, 492
  of personal letter, 494
Composition:
  beginning the paper, 105-107
  framing a thesis statement, 99
  limiting the subject, 96-97
  outlining, 98-104
  planning, 93-94
  revising, 109
  selecting a subject, 94-96
Compound-complex sentence, defined,
    26, 510
Compound sentence, defined, 26, 510

Compound words, hyphenated, 416
Conjugation:
    defined, 503
    of the verb *to choose,* 56-60
Conjunctions:
    co-ordinating, 21
    defined, 21, 503
    subordinating, 21
Conjunctive adverb, defined, 503
    list of, 368-369
    punctuation with, 368
Connectives, accurate use, 176-177
Connotation, 278-279
Considerable, 320
Consonants, final, in spelling, 345
Contact, 320
Continual, continuous, 320
Contractions, 415
Co-ordinate, defined, 503
Co-ordinating   conjunction,   defined,
    503
Copula, *see* Linking verb
Correlatives:
    defined, 503
    parallelism with, 187
Could of, 320
Couple, 320
Credible, creditable, credulous, 320
Cute, 320

Dangling constructions:
    elliptical clause, 199
    gerund, 197
    infinitive, 198
    participle, 196-197
Dash:
    position with quotation marks, 400
    to set off appositives or summaries,
        392
    to set off parenthetical expressions,
        380-381
Data, phenomena, 321
Deal, 321
Declension, *see* Inflection
Definitely, 321
Definition:
    in paragraph development, 142-144
    methods of, 136-139
Demonstrative pronoun, 509
Denotation, 278-279

Dependent   clause,   *see*   Subordinate
    clause
Development of the paragraph:
    by chronological order, 140
    by comparison or contrast, 144
    by definition, 142
    by elimination of alternatives, 148-
        149
    by examples or details, 145-146
    by explanation of causes, 147-148
    by explanation of effects, 107
    by logical order, 142
    by spatial order, 141
    establishing the topic sentence, 136-
        138
Diagraming:
    adjectives, 71-72
    adverbs, 71-72
    clauses, 76-77
    complements, 70-71
    direct object, 70
    gerunds, 72-73
    independent elements, 78-79
    indirect object, 70
    infinitives, 73
    modifiers, 71
    participles, 72
    phrases, 74
    predicate adjective, 71
    predicate noun, 71
    subject and verb, 69-70
    verbals, 72-73
    verbs, 69-70
Dialogue, quotation marks with, 396-
    397
Diction (*see also* Words):
    appropriateness, 302-311
    directness, 292-300
    exactness, 278-291
    "fine writing," 308
    glossary of usage, 314-336
    jargon, 307-308
    levels of usage, 314-315
    slang, 302-303, 315
    substandard English, 304-305
    trite expressions, 305-306
Dictionaries:
    abridged, desk, 251-252
    etymology, 255
    grammar, 257

534

Dictionaries—*Continued:*
  meaning of words, 256
  pronunciation, 254
  specialized, 430
  spelling, 253
  unabridged, 249-251, 430
  uses of, 253-258
  word labels, 258
Different than, 286
Direct address:
  defined, 503
  punctuation of, 380
Direct discourse, defined, 504
Direct object:
  defined, 502, 507
  diagramed, 70
Direct quotation, punctuation of, 376
  defined, 504
Directness:
  avoiding awkward repetition, 296-297
  avoiding circumlocutions, 294-295
  avoiding complex language, 298-300
  avoiding "deadwood," 293-294
  avoiding "omnibus" words, 289-291
  avoiding redundancy, 295-296
Don't, 321
Double negative, *can't hardly,* 319
Doubling a final consonant, 345
Doubt but what, 321
Due to, 321

Each other, one another, 321
Effect, affect, 315
Either, number of, 48
Either . . . or, parallel structure, 187
"Elegant variation," 284-285
Elimination of alternatives, in paragraph development, 148-149
Ellipsis:
  defined, 360, 506
  use of, 361
Elliptical clauses, in dangling constructions, 199
Emigrate, immigrate, 321
Emphasis in the sentence:
  by order of climax, 217
  by periodic structure, 215-216
  by position of words, 214

Emphasis in the sentence—*Continued:*
  by repetition, 218
  by use of active voice, 220
Encyclopedias, list of, 430
End punctuation:
  exclamation point, 361-362
  period, 359-360
  question mark, 360-361
English language, development of, 1-4
Enthuse, 322
Envelope of letter, 492
Equally as good, 322
Etc., 322
Etymology, 255
Every so often, 322
Everyplace, 322
Everywheres, 322
Exactness:
  connotation and denotation, 278-279
  "elegant variation," 284-285
  homonyms, 280
  idioms, 285-287
  "improprieties," 282
  "invented" words, 281
  "omnibus" words, 289-291
  synonyms, 279
Exam, see *Ad*
Examples, in paragraph development, 145-146
Except, accept, 315
Excessive detail, 174
Exclamation point:
  as a mark of emphasis, 361
  faulty use of, 362
  position with quotation marks, 400
Expect, 322
Explanation of causes, in paragraph development, 147-148
Explanation of effects, in paragraph development, 147-148
Explanatory words, punctuation of, 400-401
Expletive, defined, 504
Extra, 322

Fairness in argument, 241-242
False analogy, 244-245
Farther, further, 322
Faze, 323

Feel of, smell of, taste of, 323
Fellow, 323
Fewer, less, 323
Fiancé, fiancée, 323
Figures, plural of, 414
Final consonant, in spelling, 345
Final *e*, in spelling, 344-345
Final *y*, in spelling, 346
Fine, 323
"Fine writing," 308
Finite verb, defined, 504
First-rate, 323
Fix, 323
Footnotes, 446-451
Foreign words, italicized, 404-405
Formal usage, 7-9
Former, latter, 324
Fragment, misused as sentence, 28-30
Function, 324
Funny, 324
Further, farther, 322
Fused sentence, 32

Gender, defined, 504
Generalizations, supporting and quali-
    fying, 239-240
Genitive case, *see* Possessive case
Gentleman, lady, 324
Gerund:
    in dangling constructions, 197
    defined, 506
    diagramed, 72-73
Gerund phrase, 508
Get, 324
Glossary of usage, 314-336
Good, 324
Good and, 324
Grammar:
    adjectives and adverbs, 35-38
    agreement, 47-54
    case, 40-45
    clauses, 24-25
    diagraming, 69-79
    index of grammatical terms, 499-511
    information in dictionary, 257
    mood, 64-65
    parts of speech, 18-21
    phrases, 22-23
    sentence fragment, 29-30

Grammar—*Continued:*
    sentence sense, 16-27
    tense, 55-63
Guess, 324

Hackneyed expressions, 305-306
Had of, 324
Had ought, hadn't ought, 324
Hanged, hung, 324
Have got, 325
Heading, of business letter, 490
Healthful, healthy, 325
Himself, myself, yourself, 328
History, reference books of, 433
Home, 325
Homonyms, 280
Hung, hanged, 324
Hyphen:
    in compound words, 90, 348, 416
    to avoid awkward union of letters,
        417
    used in writing numbers, 417
    used with prefixes and suffixes, 417

Ibid., 450
Idioms, 285-287
    defined, 504
If, whether, 325
Illiterate usage, 314
Illogical comparison, 309
Illusion, allusion, 316
Immigrate, emigrate, 321
Imperative mood, defined, 64, 506
Imply, infer, 325
Improprieties, 282
In back of, 325
Incomplete comparisons, 188-189
Incomplete constructions, 202
Incomplete sentences, 28-30
Increasing vocabulary, 272-277
Indefinite pronoun, 509
Indention:
    in outlines, 101
    of addresses, 491
    of long quotations, 397
Independent clause, *see* Main clauses
Independent element:
    defined, 505
    diagramed, 78-79
Indicative mood, defined, 64-65, 506

Indirect discourse, *see* Direct discourse
Indirect object:
    defined, 502, 507
    diagramed, 70-71
Indirect quotation, defined, 504
Individual, party, person, 325
Indulge, 326
Infer, imply, 325
Infinitive:
    after verb, 60
    defined, 505
    diagramed, 73
    in dangling constructions, 198
    pronoun following, 42
    split, 193-194
Infinitive phrase, 508
Inflection, defined, 505
Informal usage, 7-9, 314
Ingenious, ingenuous, 326
In, into, 325
Inside of, 326
Intensive pronoun, 509
Interjections:
    defined, 21, 505
Internal punctuation:
    final appositives or summaries, 379
    function of, 364-366
    separating items in a series, 384-386
    separating main clauses, 367-369
    separating subordinate elements, 373-376
    setting off nonrestrictives, 374-376
    superfluous punctuation marks, 388-389
Interrogative pronoun, 509
Into, in, 325
Intransitive verb, defined, 511
Invented words, 281-282
Invitations, 498
Irregular verb, *see* Strong verb
Is when, is where, 326
It being, 326
Italics:
    for foreign words, 404-405
    function of, 403
    indicated by underlining, 403
    for letters, words, numbers used as words, 404
    for names of ships, aircraft, works of art, 404

Italics—*Continued:*
    for special stress, 405
    for titles of publications, 404
    unnecessary use of, 405
Its, it's, 327

Jargon, 307-308, 315
Journalese, 315
Just, 327

Kind, with a demonstrative adjective, 53
Kind of, sort of, 327
Kind of a, sort of a, 327

Lady, gentleman, 327
Latter, former, 324
Lay, lie, 327
Learn, teach, 327
Leave, let, 327
Legalism, 315
Less, fewer, 323
Let, leave, 327
Letters:
    business letters, 489-493
    parts of, 490
    personal letters, 494-495
    social notes, 496-498
    specimen letters, 493, 495, 496, 497, 498
Levels of usage, 5-9
    colloquial level, 8-9
    formal level, 7-8
    informal level, 7-8
    standard, substandard, 6
Library, use of, 425-436
Library paper:
    bibliography, 441-443
    catalogue cards, 427-429
    finding a subject, 439
    footnotes, 446-451
    note-taking, 444-446
    preliminary outline, 444
    specimen library paper and critical comment, 452-487
    title page, 452
Lie, lay, 327
Like, as conjunction, 177
Like, as, as if, 327
Likely, apt, 317

Linking verb, defined, 36, 505
Lists:
    glossary of usage, 314-336
    grammatical terms, 499-511
    idioms, 285-287
    principal parts, 61-64
    reference books, 430-441
    spelling list, 349-354
    theme titles, 95-96
    transitional expressions, 133-134
    vocabulary, 262-271
Literature, 328
Loc. cit., 450
Locate, 328
Logic in the sentence:
    definition of terms, 236-239
    fairness in argument, 241-242
    sound reasoning, 243-245
    supporting generalizations, 239-240
Loose, lose, 328
Lots, lots of, 328

Mad, 328
Main clauses:
    defined, 24, 501
    diagramed, 76-77
    separated by colon, 369
    separated by comma, 367
    separated by semicolon, 367-368
Manner, 328
Manuscript mechanics:
    abbreviations, 87-88
    endorsement, 83
    indenting, 82
    legibility, 81
    margins, 82
    paging, 82
    proofreading, 83
    revision, 83
    syllabication, 90
    title, 82
    writing of numbers, 85
Marvelous, 328
Math, see Ad
May of, 328
May, can, 319
Measurement of vocabulary, 262-271
Mechanics, 81-90
Might of, 328
Minus, 328

Misplaced parts, 190-195
Mixed constructions, 204
Mixed metaphors, 309
Modern literature, reference books of, 432-433
Modification, defined, 506
Modifiers:
    clear reference of, 192-193
    dangling, 196-199
    diagramed, 71-72
    nonrestrictive, 374-375
    position of, 190-195
    "squinting" construction, 193
Mood:
    defined, 55, 64, 506
    shift in, 224
    subjunctive, 65
Most, 328
Mr., 328
Music, reference books of, 433
Must of, 328
Myself, himself, yourself, 328
Mythology, reference books of, 432

Negative, double, can't hardly, 319
Neither, number of, 48
Neither . . . nor, parallel structure, 187
Nevertheless, 329
Nice, 329
No account, no good, 329
Nominative absolute, see Absolute
Nominative case:
    predicate complement, 42
    subject of a verb, 41
Nominative of address, see Direct address
None, number of, 48
Nonrestrictive element:
    defined, 374, 501, 506
    use of commas with, 374-375
Non-sequitur, 244
Noplace, 329
Not only . . . but also, parallel structure, 187
Note-taking:
    card system, 444-447
    paraphrased information, 445
    quoted information, 445
Nothing else but, 329

Noun clause:
  defined, 25, 507
  diagramed, 77
Nouns:
  abstract, 506
  agreement of, 49-50
  case of, 40-45
  collective, 49, 502, 506
  common, 502, 506
  concrete, 506
  defined, 18, 506
  proper, 502, 506
Nowhere near, 329
Nowheres, 329
Number, 329
Number:
  defined, 507
  each, either, etc., 48
  of collective nouns, 49-52
  of pronouns with antecedents, 50-51
  shift in, 223
  subjects joined by *and,* 49
  subjects joined by *or* or *nor,* 49
  of verbs agreeing with subjects, 49-50
Number, amount, 317
Numbers:
  at beginning of sentence, 85
  compound, hyphen with, 417
  in dates, 85
  in street numbers, decimals, etc., 85
  repeated in parentheses, 85
  when spelled out, 85

O.K., 329
Object:
  defined, 507
  diagramed, 70
  direct, 507
  indirect, 507
  of a preposition, 507
Objective case:
  with infinitive *to be,* 44-45
  with prepositions, 45
  with verbals, 44
  with verbs, 44
Objective complement, 502-503
Obscurity, 208
Obsolete words, 258
Off of, 329

Omissions, 201
"Omnibus" words, 289-291
One another, each other, 321
Only, position of, 190
Op. cit., 450
Ought to of, 329
Out loud, 329
Outlines:
  paragraph, 102-103
  sentence, 102, 454
  topic, 101-102
Outlining:
  arrangement of details, 100
  numbering and indenting, 101
  parallel structure, 103
  preliminary, 98-99
  single subhead avoided, 103
  thesis statement, 99, 454
  vague headings avoided, 104
Outside of, 329
Over with, 329
Overloaded sentences, 174-175

Painting, reference books of, 433
Paragraphs:
  coherence, 127-134
  defined, 114
  development, 136-150
  indention, 114
  logical order, 127-128
  tone, 150-153
  topic sentence, 117-119
  transitions, 133-134
  unity, 117-121
Parallelism:
  defined, 185
  faulty parallelism, 186
  for co-ordinate elements, 185-186
  in outlines, 103
  with correlatives, 187
Parentheses:
  to set off parenthetical expressions, 380-381
  used with question mark, 361
Parenthetical expression:
  defined, 507
  punctuation of, 380-381
Parse, defined, 507
Participial phrase, 508

General Index

Participle:
  in dangling constructions, 196-197
  defined, 507
  diagramed, 72
Parts of speech:
  adjectives, 19
  adverbs, 20
  classification of, 18-21
  conjunction, 21
  defined, 18, 508
  interjections, 21
  nouns, 18
  prepositions, 20
  pronouns, 19
  verbs, 19
Party, individual, person, 325
Passive voice:
  defined, 511
  unemphatic use of, 220
Per, 330
Per cent, 330
Period:
  after abbreviations, 359
  at end of sentence, 359
  position inside quotation marks, 399
  to indicate ellipsis, 359
Period fault, 360
Periodic sentence:
  defined, 215
  for emphasis, 215-216
Periodicals:
  general indexes, 435
  indexes to bulletins, pamphlets, 436
  special indexes, 436
Person:
  defined, 508
  shift in, 223
Person, party, individual, 325
Personal letters, 494-495
Personal pronouns:
  case of, 41-44
  declension, 41
Phenomena, data, 321
Philosophy, 330
Philosophy, reference books of, 434
Phone, see *Ad*
Photo, see *Ad*
Phrases:
  classified, 508
  dangling, 197-199

Phrases—*Continued:*
  defined, 22-23, 508
  diagramed, 74
  misplaced, 191
  recognition of, 22
  restrictive and nonrestrictive, 374-375
Plenty, 330
Plurals:
  of letters, numbers, etc., 414
  spelling of, 414
Plus, 330
Point of view:
  consistency in the paragraph, 130
  defined, 222
  shift in person or number, 223
  shift in subject or voice, 222
  shift in tense or mood, 224
Poorly, 330
Positive form, 37
Possessive case:
  apostrophe with, 413-414
  before a gerund, 43
  inanimate objects, 43
Practical, practicable, 330
Practically, 331
Précis, 513-516
Predicate, defined, 16, 508
Predicate adjective:
  defined, 19, 502-503
  diagramed, 71
Predicate noun (*see also* Complement):
  defined, 502
  diagramed, 71
Prefixes, 272-273
Prepositional phrases, 23, 508
Prepositions:
  defined, 20, 508
  hyphens with, 417
  idiomatic use of, 285-287
Primer style, 172-173
Principal, principle, 331
Principal clause, *see* Main clause
Principal parts:
  defined, 508
  list of, 61-64
Prior to, 331
Progressive verb, defined, 509
Pronouns:
  agreement with antecedent, 51-52

540

Pronouns—*Continued:*
agreement with verb, 48
case of, 40-45
classified, 509
defined, 19, 512
reference of, 179-184
Pronunciation:
as spelling aid, 341
use of dictionary, 254
Proper nouns, capitalization of, 408-411
Proposition, 331
Proven, 331
Provincialism, 304, 315
Punctuation:
apostrophe, 413-415
brackets, 399
capitals, 407-411
colon, 369, 392, 400
comma, 367, 373-376, 379-381, 384-386, 388-389
dash, 380-381, 392
end punctuation, 359-363
exclamation point, 361-362
of explanatory words *he said,* 400
functions of, 355-358
hyphen, 416-417
internal punctuation, 364-366
italics, 403-405
parentheses, 380-381
period, 359-360
question mark, 360-361
of quoted material, 396-401
semicolon, 367-368
spacing, 355
superfluous commas, 388-389
Put across, put over, put in, 331

Question mark:
after direct question, 360
faulty use of, 360
position with quotation marks, 400-401
within parentheses, 360
Questions, diagramed, 69
Quite a few, quite a little, quite a bit, 331
Quotation marks:
faulty use of, 398
for direct quotations, 396

Quotation marks—*Continued:*
for quotation of several paragraphs, 397
for slang, 398
for titles, 398
for words used in special senses, 398
quotation within quotation, 396-397
Quotations, reference books of, 432
Quoted material, 396-401

Raise, rear, 331
Raise, rise, 331
Rarely ever, 331
Real, 332
Reason is because, 332
Reciprocal pronoun, 509
Redundancy, 295-296
Reference books:
atlases, 431
classical literature, mythology, 432
dictionaries, word books, 430
general biography, 431-432
general encyclopedias, 430
guides to reference books, 441
history, 433
modern literature, 432-433
music, painting, 433-434
philosophy, religion, 434
science, technology, 434
social sciences, 434-435
volumes of quotations, 432
year books, 430-431
Reference of pronouns:
ambiguous, 179
indefinite use of *they, you, it,* 183
remote, 180
vague use of *that* or *which,* 181
Reflexive pronouns, 509
Regular verb, *see* Weak verb
Relative clause, defined, 509
Relative pronouns, verbs with, 50
Religion, 332
Religion, reference books of, 434
Remember of, 332
Repetition, awkward, 296-297
Repetition, for paragraph coherence, 133-134
Repetition, for sentence emphasis, 218
Research paper, *see* Library paper

Restrictive element:
defined, 374-375, 509
punctuation of, 374-375, 389
Reverend, 332
Revision of manuscript, 83
Right, right along, right away, 332
Rise, raise, 331
Run, 332

Said, 332
Salutation, of a letter, 491
Science, reference books of, 434
Seeing as how, 332
Seldom ever, seldom or ever, 333
Semicolon:
position outside quotation marks, 400
to separate items in series, 386
to separate main clauses, 367-368
Sentences:
awkwardness, 207-208
classified, 509
complex, 26, 510
compound, 26, 510
compound-complex, 26, 510
dangling constructions in, 196-199
declarative, 510
defined, 16, 509
emphasis in, 214-218
exclamatory, 510
fragments, 28-30
imperative, 510
interrogative, 510
logic in, 209, 236-245
logical and complete comparisons, 188-189
misplaced parts, 190-195
mixed constructions, 204
obscurity, 208
overloaded, 174-175
parallelism in, 185-187
point of view in, 222-224
reference of pronouns in, 179-184
run-together, 32
simple, 26, 510
spliced, 31
transitions in, 211-212
unity in, 165-170
variety in, 225-228

Series, punctuation of, 384-386
Set, sit, 333
Shall, should, 333
Shape, 333
Shift:
in person or number, 223
in subject or voice, 222
in tense or mood, 224
Should of, 333
Show up, 333
Signature, of a letter, 492
Simple sentence, defined, 25, 510
Sit, set, 333
Size up, 333
Slang, 302-303, 315, 398
So, 333
Social notes, 496-498
Social sciences, reference books of, 434
Some, 334
Someplace, 334
Somewheres, 334
Sort, with a demonstrative adjective, 53
Sort of, kind of, 327
Sort of a, kind of a, 327
Sound reasoning, 243-245
Spacing, for punctuation, 355
Specimen library paper and critical comment, 452-487
Spelling:
changing final *y* to *i,* 346-347
confusion of *ei* and *ie,* 343-344
confusion of similar words, 342-343
doubling final consonant, 345
drill as an aid, 348-349
dropping final *e,* 344-345
improvement by proofreading, 340-341
list of common misspellings, 349-354
plurals, 346-347
pronunciation as aid, 341
rules for, 343-348
secondary and British forms, 339-340
use of dictionary, 253
Split infinitive, 193-194
"Squinting" constructions, 193
Standard English, 9, 314-315
Stop, 334

Strong verb, defined, 510
Subject of sentence:
  defined, 16, 510
  diagramed, 69-70
  recognition of, 16
  shift in, 222
Subject of theme:
  choosing, 94-95
  limiting, 96-99
  list of, 95-96
Subjective complement, 502
Subjunctive mood:
  defined, 64-65, 506
  in conditional clauses, 65
  in formal idioms, 65
  in *that* clauses, 65
Subordinate clauses:
  defined, 501
  diagramed, 76-77
  kinds of, 24-25
  misused as sentence, 29-31
Subordinating conjunction, defined, 503
Subordination:
  accurate use of connectives, 176-177
  and sentences, 173
  inexact co-ordination, 168-169
  "primer style," 172-173
  upside-down construction, 171
Substandard English, 4, 9, 304-305
Substantive, defined, 510
Substantive clause, defined, 510
Such, 334
Suffixes, 273-274
Summaries, 513-516
Superfluous commas:
  after final adjective, 388
  after introductory word or phrase, 389
  between subject and verb, 388
  between verb and complement, 388
  between words joined by co-ordinating conjunction, 389
Superlative forms of adjectives and adverbs, 37-38, 502
Suspicion, 334
Syllabication, 90
Synonyms, 279
Syntax, defined, 510

Take and, 334
Tautology, 295-296
Teach, learn, 327
Technology, reference books of, 434
Tense:
  conjugation of *to choose,* 56-60
  defined, 55, 511
  of infinitives, 60
  principal parts, 61-64
  sequence of tenses, 60
  shift in, 224
  statements that are generally true, 60
Term paper, *see* Library paper
Than and *as,* case of pronoun after, 45
That, 334
That clauses, 65
That there, this here, 335
This, that, agreement with word modified, 53
Through, 335
Thusly, 335
Title page, 452
Titles:
  capitalization of, 409
  of publications, 404, 442-443
  use of quotation marks with, 398
Topic sentence, 117-119
Transitions:
  inexact use of, 211
  in the paragraph, 133-134
  list of, 133-134
  omitted, 212
Transitive verb, defined, 511
Transpire, 335
Triteness, 305-306
Try and, 335

Unique, 335
Unity in the paragraph, 117-121
Unity in the sentence:
  illogical comparisons, 188-189
  overloaded sentences, 174-175
Usage, *see* Levels of usage

Variety in the sentence:
  overuse of compound sentences, 226-227

Variety in the sentence—*Continued:*
    overuse of simple sentences, 225
    subject-noun beginnings, 228
Verbal phrases, 23, 508
Verbals:
    defined, 19, 511
    diagramed, 72-73
    distinguished from verbs, 19-20
Verbs:
    agreement with subject, 47-51
    classified, 511
    conjugation of *to choose,* 56-60
    defined, 19, 511
    diagramed, 69-70
    linking, 36
    mood, 64-65
    principal parts of, 61-64
    recognition of, 19-20
    sequence of tenses, 60
    subject of, 41
    tense of, 55
Very, 335
Vocabulary:
    active and passive, 261
    enlargement of, 272-277
    test of, 262-271
Vocative, *see* Direct address
Voice:
    defined, 511
    shift in, 222
    weak passive voice, 220
Vulgarisms, 304

Wait on, 335
Want in, want out, want off, 335
Want to, 336

Way, ways, 336
Weak passive voice, 220
Weak verb, defined, 511
Weird, 336
Where, 336
Where at, 336
Whether, if, 336
Which, 44
While, 177
Who and *whom,* 44-45
Will, would, 333
Wonderful, 336
Word books, list of, 430
Word labels, 258
Word order, 190-194
Word punctuation, 403-405
Wordiness:
    awkward repetition, 296-297
    circumlocutions, 294-295
    complex language, 298-300
    "dead wood," 293-294
    "omnibus" words, 289-291
    redundancy, 295-296
Words (*see also* Diction):
    appropriateness, 302-311
    connotation and denotation, 278-279
    dictionaries, 249-260
    directness, 292-300
    exactness, 278-291
    glossary of usage, 314-336
    idioms, 285-287
    vocabulary, 261-271
Would of, 336

Year books, list of, 430-431
Yourself, himself, myself, 328

GRAMMAR =GR 1-6	SENTENCE SENSE =SS	CONFUSED STRUCTURE =STR	ADJECTIVES & ADVERBS
	1a Sentences 1b Parts of speech 1c Phrases 1d Clauses 1	2a Fragment = Frag 2b Comma splice = CS or CF 2c Fused, run-together = FS 2	3a Modifying nouns, pron 3b Modifying verbs 3c Comparative, superla

MANUSCRIPT MECHANICS =MS 8-11	THE MANUSCRIPT =MS	NUMBERS =NOS
	8a Materials 8c Arrangement 8b Legibility 8d Proof-reading 8	9a Spell out 9c Street numbers, decimals, 9b Dates 9d With ( )'s 9e Beginning sentences

LARGER ELEMENTS 12,13	THE WHOLE COMPOSITION =PLAN
	12a Subject 12c Rough outline 12e Complete outline 12b Limiting subject 12d Thesis statement 12f Beginning

EFFECTIVE SENTENCES =EF 14-27	SUBORDINATION =SUB	REFERENCE OF PRONOUNS =RE
	14a False, unrelated 14d Excessive subordina- co-ordination tion, overloading 14b "Upside-down" 14e Connectives 14c "Primer" sentences 14	15a Ambiguous 15d Illogical 15b Remote 15e Indefinite 15c Vague "this," "it," "you "that," "which"
	MISPLACED PARTS =MIS PTS	DANGLING CONSTRUCTIONS =D
	18a "Almost," "only," etc. 18e Split infinitives 18b Modifying phrase 18f Subject, verb 18c Modifying clause awkwardly split 18d "Squinters" 18	19a Participles 19b Gerunds 19c Infinitives 19d Elliptical clauses
	TRANSITIONS =TRANS	EMPHASIS =EMP
	23a Inexact 23b Omitted 23	24a Position 24c Logical ord 24b Periodic 24d Repetition

LOGIC =LOG 28	DEFINITION =DEF 28a	GENERALIZATION =GEN

DICTION =D 31	EXACTNESS =EX	DIRECTNESS =DIR
	31a Words nearly 31e Grammatical change synonymous 31f Elegant variation 31b Words similar sound 31g Idiomatic use 31c Invented words 31h Specific word 31d Improprieties 31	32a Deadwood 32b Approximate words 32c Needless repetition 32d Awkward repetition 32e Needless complexity

SPELLING =SP 35	PREFERRED SPELLING 35a	CARELESS SPELLING

PUNCTUATION =P 36-47	END	SEPARATING MAIN CLAUSES
	36a Assertions 36x Period fault 36b Abbreviations (also 2c) 36c Ellipsis 36y Question fault 36d Question 36z Exclamation 36e Use of (?) fault 36f Emphatic statements 36	37a With co-ordinating conjunction 37b Without co-ordinating conjunction 37c With conjunctive adv 37d Second clause amplifies 37x Comma fault (also 2b)
	FINAL APPOSITIVES	PUNCTUATING QUOTATIONS
	42a Short appositives 42b Long, formal appositives 42	43a Double quotes 43h (:) (;) with " 43b Single quotes 43i (-) (?) with " 43c Quoting 43j he said, etc. 43d Titles 43k Quotation at 43e Special sense beginning 43x Faulty use 43l Quotation at e 43f Brackets of sentence 43g (.) (,) with "